Eric J.
Jenkins

Drawn to Design

Analyzing
Architecture
Through
Freehand
Drawing

Birkhäuser | Basel

To my parents, Elizabeth and George

This book is also available in an EPUB eBook edition.

Editor:
Andreas Müller, Berlin

Layout and typography:
Alexandra Zöller, Berlin

Layout concept:
Ulises Chamorro, Barcelona

Cover design:
Hannah Schönenberg

A CIP catalogue record for this book is available from the
Library of Congress, Washington, DC, USA.

Bibliographic information published by the German National Library
The German National Library lists this publication in the Deutsche
Nationalbibliografie; detailed bibliographic data are available on the
Internet at http://dnb.d-nb.de.

© 2013 Birkhäuser Verlag GmbH, Basel
P.O. Box 44, 4009 Basel, Switzerland
Part of De Gruyter

Printed on acid-free paper produced from chlorine-free pulp. TCF ∞

Printed in Germany

ISBN 978-3-0346-0798-8

9 8 7 6 5 4 3 2 1

www.birkhauser.com

Contents

PART I
SKETCHING, THINKING,
LEARNING

PART II
DESIGN ACTS

Probing the Details

Engaging the Context

PART III
HOLISTIC ACTS

APPENDIX

Preface

Drawing a building is a way of remembering it properly. To draw you have to look very hard and I think it is in the looking itself that the building is impressed upon the mind. Often I measure it and make a plan, putting the dimensions on the drawing, because I know from experience that only by doing that can I understand what I'm looking at.

Caroline Mauduit, *An Architect in Italy*[1]

The intention of this book is to help students develop an appreciation for observation and learning about the designed environment through freehand drawing. By observing I mean, as Caroline Mauduit endorses in her introduction to *An Architect in Italy*, that we consider the designed, and by extension, the natural environment carefully with a critical and inquisitive eye. Carefulness is vital in reaching below the surface and beyond what is literal. Unlike the casual glance or photograph, even the fastest, literal drawing is an inherently careful and active engagement. Drawing is a way of digesting the environment in order to come away with a greater understanding of how the environment might have been formed, what it contributes or does not contribute and what lessons might be embedded in it. While I do not offer definitive methods, I do offer an approach that might lead to a disciplined search when truly looking at buildings. In the fifteen years of teaching freehand analysis, I have come to believe that students need an introduction to a methodology that can inform and guide yet not constrain them. I have made mistakes and have constantly revised the courses and ways to introduce a methodological approach. Some years I seem to get it and then, when I try to duplicate it the following year, I stumble.

An essential aspect of this book is the use of freehand drawing. Freehand drawing is helpful because, when all is said and done, the hand is connected to our minds and intrinsically related to who we are. The hand and its preceding iterations such as ganglia, tentacles or other prehensile limbs shape what, how and of whom we think. The drawing hand is linked with the least intermediary processes or devices to the world itself. Freehand drawing is as close as we can get to the thing itself without building. Just as hand drawing is relatively unmitigated, the hand can never be machine-like, but at the same time it can be accurate enough in recording the world beyond pure impression. The slip of the finger, the varied weight of a line or the wiggle resulting from too much coffee allows the building to remain alive.

Drawing the designed and natural environment is a process of analysis essential to observing and, hopefully, understanding the world. There are cautionary tales as in the fairy tale *The Goose that Laid the Golden Egg*. When trying to understand a thing we should be careful not to kill it. A danger of abstracting and diagramming analytically is that it might destroy what we find exciting or stimulating. While a risk, diagramming or analyzing buildings remains a primary means of understanding their nature as both utilitarian device and vessel of experience. The nature of architecture is one in which, as Le Corbusier writes in *Towards an Architecture*, "walls rise against the sky in an order such that I am moved. I sense your intentions."[2] More than building, architecture embodies intentions while expressing our values and our dreams. Looking at buildings is a combination of a phenomenological experience and one of dimensions, properties and functions. The magic of architecture is that it embodies both the utilitarian and the experience of place.

I would be pleased if the book is only considered. I would even be happy if even after reading it is rejected yet helps someone look at buildings more carefully. Either way, a student looks, truly looks at the built environment and learns from it.

1   Mauduit, Caroline, *An Architect in Italy*. New York: C. N. Potter (1988): 10.

2   Le Corbusier, *Towards an Architecture*, trans. John Goodman. Los Angeles: Getty Research Institute (2007): 215.

Introduction

This book really began, although I did not know it, when I was a graduate architecture student. In fact, it was just as I neared the end of my formal professional education that I experienced a seminal moment that changed my life.

This moment helped me realize that I was not at all near "the end" of my education but only just beginning to comprehend architecture and urban design. It occurred while I was a graduate student during a summer travel program in the small cities, villages and historical sites of western and central Turkey. I arrived in Istanbul a day in advance of the program's official start to acquaint myself with the city before setting out on the journey through the Turkish countryside. I strolled through the ancient city with the Ayasofya (Hagia Sophia) and the Sultanahmet Camii (Blue Mosque) as my ultimate goal. The buildings and their precincts were, of course, spectacular and after walking around and through them, I sat in Sultanahmet Square, looked at the Blue Mosque in the distance, opened the first page of my new sketchbook and began to draw.

The resultant sketch was fairly conventional in that what I drew corresponded to what I was seeing or at least represented it quite literally much like a photographic image. And like a photograph, it illustrated an event in time from one vantage point. Fortunately, for my self-esteem, it was not an awful sketch. In fact, I was quite relieved that the first attempt in the virginal sketchbook was at least adequate.

The next morning, my fellow students and I met our professor, William Bechhoefer, who distributed the syllabus for his course, *An Architectural Journal*. Bechhoefer asked us to use our sketchbooks in three ways: 1) to study specific conditions in Turkish architecture that might inform our own design process, 2) to scrutinize the designed and natural environment in Turkey, using specific drawing types and 3) to document those things that "strike you", using freehand diagrams, conventional architectural drawings (such as elevations and plans), texts and even, with some optimism, poetry. Fundamentally, the syllabus asked us to look at the built and natural environment as architects with a degree of inquiry. Rather than illustrate, we were to investigate.

ARCH 678, Selected Topics in Architecture: Turkish Journal
Summer, 1988: Prof. William Bechhoefer

Required Reading: Christopher Alexander
The Timeless Way of Building

Materials: 8-1/2 x 11 or 9 x 12 sketchbook(s)
your choice of media: pen/pencil/water color

The requirement of the course is that you document through drawing and writing the architectural experiences of 6 weeks in Turkey. The intention of the notebook is for you to study the characteristic forms and patterns of Turkish architecture. The continuity of tradition from the monuments of the past to the vernacular of the present is the subject of your study. The identification of characteristic use patterns, architectural and urban forms, and climatic responses will give you a basis from which to approach contemporary design problems.

A wide variety of subjects from different periods should be chosen; some kinds of drawings are:

1) Elevation and section sketches of typical walls of old and new buildings. The drawings should go from the ground to rooftop. Typical construction details.
2) Plans and urban plans.
3) Entry sequences, threshholds, stairs.
4) Axon or perspective sketches of typical buildings and selected details (residential, commercial, institutional).
5) City/town/villagescapes.
6) Landscapes.
7) Diagrams and/or sketches of patterns -- i.e., watch how people use "places". Discover hierarchies of circulation and spatial relationships at the urban, village, and building scales.
8) Diagrams and/or sketches of climatic factors and responses. Air flow, architectural details, etc.
9) Important or beautiful things which strike you.

Taken as a whole, the notebook will investigate Turkish building from the scale of urban settlements to details of construction, in all periods of its history. Each sketch should be identified and may be annotated. Personal reflections (and poetry) are appropriate. As you can see from the way the assignment is made, your drawings are to be analytical as well as descriptive. In this way, you will identify concepts which can be applied in your design work, rather than the more superficial aspects of specific form. Your aim is the understanding of the formal and cultural principles by which Turkish architecture has been generated.

Grading Criteria: "Density" of presentation and perception.

The first sketch in Turkey

The same view as in the first sketch

Bechhoefer's course syllabus

With the syllabus in hand, we set out on the trip across Turkey. Two days later we arrived in Bursa, a small city south of Istanbul, and visited, among other sites, the Yeşil Madrasa (now the Türk Islam Eserleri Müzesi/Museum of Turkish and Islamic Art) in the Yeşil Külliye (Green Complex). Keeping Professor Bechhoefer's syllabus in mind, I walked through the madrasa and noticed, or perhaps I might say "felt", something intriguing about its courtyard. At first, it was not clear exactly what was captivating. Nevertheless, I started to sketch, recalling Bechhoefer's suggested inquiries and methods. As I recall and might be perceived in the sketch, I started with a series of familiar drawing types: a section of the courtyard showing the colonnade, which led to a section of pathway and vault that, in turn, lead to a larger section, then a vignette section-perspective and so on. Other than the decision to draw, I did not preconceive of what drawings and in what order I might sketch but switched drawing types to help investigate and quench my curiosity. As I sketched, I began to formulate that which was intriguing to me.

And then … a seminal moment. I discovered that something which was at first interesting was in fact an important albeit subtle architectural moment. What I had noticed unconsciously was that the courtyard's floor did not terminate at the colonnade but appeared to "slide" beneath its edge and into the vaulted path. At that moment, I realized that a courtyard could overlap with a surrounding path and vice versa. Rather than a "here/there" segregation in which a colonnade delimited two zones, "this" courtyard and "that" path, here I discovered an architecture of "both/and". Though I know my design critics had mentioned transparency and ambiguity, when I sketched this space, these concepts finally made sense. I started to understand a greater idea of architecture.

But there was an even greater revelation that struck me as I sat there, and has continued to haunt me since then: it was that I had discovered something through sketching. While this revelation may be unremarkable to many, it was a moment that affected my immediate travel experience. From that point on in the trip through Turkey I sketched aggressively and with inquiry with multiple views of section, axonometric, elevation, perspective, diagrams, details, etc. More than affecting that summer's travel experience, it has affected my life. The moment and ensuing experience was, for me, liberating. The experiential static charge built up over the previous few years in architecture school suddenly sparked a eureka moment. A conjunction of thinking and learning was revealed by a simple request to draw what "strikes you". I discovered that sketching could be a means of inquiry; it was only later that I would fully comprehend that what mattered was not so much "what" I discovered, but "how" I discovered it.

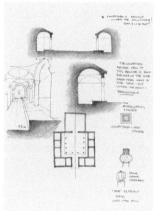

The Yeşil Madrasa courtyard and arcade

Sketchbook page of the Yeşil Madrasa

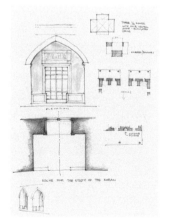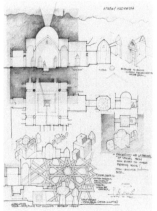

Subsequent Turkey sketchbook pages

Beyond my own sketching, the eureka moment began a continuing road of self-discovery and reflection on architectural education. Since then, I have endeavored in my teaching efforts to offer opportunities for learning through sketching, both in the United States and abroad, to help students develop a process of inquisitive sketching. One consequence has been the course *The Classroom in the City*, first developed at Virginia Tech's Washington-Alexandria Center and then expanded into a required undergraduate course at The Catholic University of America's School of Architecture and Planning in Washington, DC. The key idea of this course is that architecture students can come to understand and, in turn, inform their own spatial and material assemblages through sketching within the designed environment. In the process of sketching and diagramming, students engage in physical and psychological processes analogous to the design process. Moreover, it is hoped that students would develop a process or affinity for looking at buildings to see the unseen, to uncover hidden or at least obscured patterns and otherwise engage with the life-world that would inform their design process.

Students in the classroom of the city

While teaching, I started to explore what had happened to me as a graduate student: what preceded it and what impact this might have on me and others. This, in turn, led me to study physically what I had gone through (the physical skill that I had developed since childhood), the psychological underpinnings (why I had learned and how it related to drawing) and the phenomenological attitude (how I engaged with the world, my eureka moment and the subsequent change in perspective). The physical and thinking processes engaged while developing this awareness also seemed to parallel maturation in thinking and inquiry.

One clear example is that of a junior-level architecture student we will call "Alex". Alex's first sketch of the semester, completed on the weekend just before the first day of class, was a perspective of Washington DC's National Mall, showing the reflecting pool and Washington Monument. It was drawn while sitting on the Lincoln Memorial's steps. As to be expected, the sketch is fraught with good intentions: Alex, without prompting, picked up his sketchbook and ventured out to look at and sketch the city. As might also be expected, the sketch is somewhat naive and awkward. There is little line or tone control and the techniques of aerial and linear perspective are amateurish. Additionally, we can sense a degree of uncertainty in the line work as the lines are flimsy and frail to reveal the usual first-sketch insecurity.

Alex's first sketch of the semester

Most significant, however, is that the sketch is architectonically mute. Like my sketch of the Blue Mosque, Alex's sketch is a snapshot of a familiar scene. He has developed neither the graphic skills nor the sketch palette to uncover underlying systems of the view he admires. The patterning dimensions and assemblies remain unrevealed. The sketch records what is seen, but there is little inquiry or questioning. While the scene is striking and important to him, he has not yet explored beyond the view itself. This is not to say that a perspective sketch is unprocessed, unanalytical or non-transformative in nature, but for Alex, who is just starting his architectural education, the perspective sketch is an impression, a literal representation.

Within four weeks of taking the course, however, there is a noticeable maturation in exploration. This is best exemplified by his sketch of the Corcoran Gallery of Art in Washington, DC. The sketch is an analysis of the relationship of interior volumes to the exterior skin and to a spatial sequence. It gives some idea of how Alex has progressed from the purely picturesque, illustrative mode into a more analytical and critical mode.

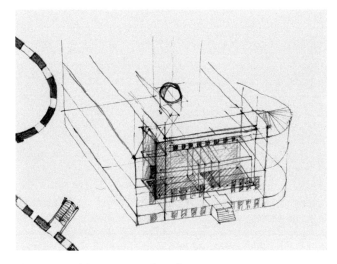

Alex's sketch of the Corcoran Gallery of Art

An obvious change is that Alex's sketch is more deliberate and confident. Following repeated and specific sketching exercises, he has begun to develop hand coordination and muscle memory and, as such, the sketch has become more disciplined, yet remains exploratory and flexible. Moreover, the sketch reveals a degree of inquiry. Alex is asking questions of architecture. As an analytical sketch it digests the spatial and material assemblies of this particular designed environment, which may, in turn, inform his own design thinking. What he sees now might translate into a conceptual representation and, eventually, back into the design environment.

While Alex and his sketches are explicit examples, fortunately most students go through this process during or just after their *Classroom in the City*. The course is designed for students with some experience in the design studio, as some *a priori* knowledge is necessary for the student to sketch analytically. Though the methodology continues to evolve, the pedagogical thread linking its continuing development is the opportunity for discovery and investigation through analytical sketching. The methodology – and its underlying pedagogy – link learning and cognitive development with observation and recording observations in freehand drawings to make a significant impact on semantic processing systems, or information concerned with discovering and modifying objects.

The translation of an architectural experience into an architectural process is a particularly important issue for architects. A part of this translation is understanding the role of material and dimension, those quantifiable aspects of architecture that frame an architectural experience. The experience of place, while one of quality, is ultimately one in which the architect or other designer writes directions for others to build. The madrasa in Turkey was more than likely built by a craftsman under directions of an architect. It can be imagined that the architect conceived, tested, resolved and otherwise designed the madrasa and then (or perhaps during construction) communicated those ideas in some form. The architect's decisions were communicated – either verbally or perhaps even graphically – to the craftsmen to position the columns, to keep the courtyard's floor continuous beyond the edge of the column line and then to step down a specific dimension were quantities that would lead to an experience by those who moved through and used the building.

An architect at the end of the design process can only write directions that she or he hopes will be followed and result in the anticipated outcome. To assess whether these directions are "good" or "bad" depends significantly on correlation, the correlation between direction and anticipated outcome, enhanced with an understanding of history, theory, human experience, nature of materials, dimension, scale and other qualities that might arise from quantities. All this will allow the architect to embed those directions (and hope that those directions are followed) with intentions in a way to result in a quality experience.

Drawing as a means to explore the world was not entirely new for me. According to my family, I had been doing similar things since I was a child. My mother saved two of my childhood drawings from when I was about seven or eight years old. Like many other children's depictions, these are worlds that I created and explored through drawing. The first drawing is a section through a house showing its rooms, stairs, furniture and fireplace. It also reveals secret subterranean chambers with piles of gold bullions and tunnels leading to a helicopter hangar with a movable roof. My next drawing is that same house but after a devastating deluge. Fortunately, Superman saves the day and lifts the house just as the water covers the ground and floods the tunnels. As he lifts the house, things are torn away and everything inside tumbles to one side. Fortunately, a tethered balloon lifts the car while the helicopter flies away without a second to spare!

While I cannot recall exactly what my strange little mind was thinking, it appears as if I was creating and exploring a world. I was speculating through drawing. Fortunately, my parents and most of my teachers encouraged this speculative exploration.

(From the author's files.)

Section through a house before the flood, followed by the house saved by Superman and a balloon

This book is conceived as a companion for architecture students and architects as they look at the world. In this looking, it is hoped that this book will help them articulate the seen and reveal the unseen that shape the designed environment. The reader may notice that the term "designed environment" is used as much as "architecture" or "urban design", as these disciplines often involve and overlap with interior architecture, furniture, lighting, electronic equipment, web design, writing and even advertising. Likewise, many students who complete their formal and even their practical architectural education move into related design fields, such as digital gaming and film production, and are informed by the principles outlined in schools, in practice – and in this book. Lastly, the environment that is considered here should not be limited to the "designed environment" but can include the natural environment. Looking carefully at a leaf or a natural system is just as vital as looking carefully at an urban space.

As a companion, the book is conceived to help students develop an eye for looking at the designed environment that leads to an individual analytical method. Through diagrams and analytical drawings, the architect looking at a building tries to understand the underlying systems or forces that make the building what it is.

Finally, the book tries to bridge formal analysis, in which the architectural artifact is analyzed as an autonomous object pulled from its physical and historical context, with the *in situ* experience. While formal analysis is necessary, an architect must also place analysis in the contextual and phenomenological framework in order to understand that architecture is more than the formal sum of it parts.

This book proposes specific reasons and methods for examining the designed environment through sketching. Rather than a definitive pedagogical method or answer, what is assembled here is a proposal based on my experience as a teacher, as a student and as an architect. More importantly, it is based on my conversations with other educators, architects and designers and my research in the fields of education, psychology and philosophy that have led me to this point and to writing this book.

A great influence on my teaching are the writings of Howard Gardner. A research psychologist, professor, writer and co-founder of Harvard University's *Project Zero*, Gardner has developed a theory of intelligence types that are examined in his book *Frames of Mind: The Theory of Multiple Intelligences*.[1] These types, which he has added to and modified since first devised, categorize the varied ways in which people conceive of the world. Intelligences do not simply mean that a person will learn this or that way or that there are specific learning styles with commensurate teaching methods. Rather they are ways to help us understand that there is no one way to conceive of the world. As Gardner writes: "Styles refer to the customary way in which an individual approaches a range of materials – for example, a playful or a planful style. Intelligence refers to

the computational power of a mental system: for example, a person whose linguistic intelligence is strong is able readily to compute information that involves language."[2] The concept of multiple intelligences requires that any educational method should accommodate multiple ways of investigating and observing the designed environment.

In his book *Five Minds of the Future*, Gardner speculates on the ways in which higher education and, specifically, professional programs might prepare effective thinkers and leaders for the 21st century. He proposes that to thrive and contribute on a global scale, professionals such as architects will need to nurture aptitudes that are *disciplined, synthesizing, creative, respectful and ethical*.[3] *Disciplined* in that the things be considered carefully and steadily with time and effort; *synthesizing* in that they process and blend information that arises unexpectedly and from unfamiliar sources; *creative* in that they propose alternative solutions to new problems; *respectful* in that they work with varied cultures and personalities; and *ethical* in that they consider and reflect upon the moral implications of our actions. All of these describe a designer who looks carefully at history, by processing it and transforming it. Architecture students can not only apply the lessons learned but by engaging in the intellectual inquiry itself can approach new and unforeseen, albeit informed, challenges. Much of this multiplicity can be anticipated by a multiplicity of thinking and representation in which the architect does not adopt isolated approaches, media or even design projects. By looking carefully at buildings, the designer may come to respect and learn from context and understand the role of designers in making and shaping the built environment.

A particularly important aspect of this book is the observation of buildings *in situ*. I have been asked by students, "Why can't we simply sketch from a photograph of a building or urban space?" For most students, educators and architects, these questions come as a surprise. Most *know* that sketching at a site is much more valuable than sketching from a photograph or slide. But why is it so? And if diagramming from a slide is ineffective, why do the same educators who disdain drawing from slides assign plan or façade analyses based on existing drawings to understand precedents in architecture?

Suffice it to say, there are many ways to look at a building. I am guilty, if that is the crime, of asking students to diagram plans and façade drawings, just as much as I expound the need to look at buildings, in the flesh. That said, the intention of this book is to explore the need to examine a building, space or designed object as an experience. The aim of any design object is experience. While architecture provides shelter and elevates our cultural, sacred, social and personal lives, it is ultimately about experience. As an experience, it is about moving through, walking into it, sitting in it, grasping it or looking around it. It is about the nature of the designed environment within its setting.

To link the lessons of formal analysis with the phenomenological is a particular intention of this book. Formal analysis is breaking the piece of art, architecture or other thing as an autonomous artifact separate from its social, cultural, economic and historical context in which it was formed and exists. The aim of formal analysis is to understand the artifact itself in order to digest the lessons of dimension, material, form and spatial sequence that are independent of ephemeral context. A door is just a door and, therefore, can be studied as such, without immediate concern for why it was chosen, the doorframe, who uses it and how it links to the spatial sequence. The value of formal analysis is that we can examine the thing in a discipline and with depth. That said, formal analysis of buildings may restrict thinking, especially if it embeds thinking that elevates formal organization strategies or, worse, adopts unprocessed formal elements unresponsive to needs beyond the formal type.

There is value in formal analysis. I employ many of its techniques in this book and in my courses and design studios. It is one essential method for examining architecture. But architecture is a contextual discipline. It does not stand alone but reflects and informs history, society, culture, physical context and tradition. It is part of a larger whole and contributes, one would hope, in some way to that whole. Therefore it is important that the designer be able to look at a thing both autonomously and contextually so that in the design process the designer might bridge the two and rather look at the artifact as "both/and" instead of "either/or". In order to develop a multifaceted design process, a designer must develop a multifaceted analytical approach that engages multiple contexts. Bill Buxton, a principal researcher at Microsoft Research and the author of *Sketching User Experiences: Getting the Design Right and the Right Design*, notes that "as technology becomes more and more pervasive, it is finding itself in increasingly diverse and specialized contexts. The technologies that we design do not, and never will, exist in a vacuum. In any meaningful sense, they only have meaning, or relevance, in a social and physical context. And increasingly, that social context is with respect to other devices as well as people."[4]

The approach adopted in this book and in my courses is one that attempts to bridge formal and phenomenological analysis of the designed environment. The analysis is primarily about looking at buildings as an experience that is shaped by formal material moves. This is a phenomenological approach that has as its basis the goal of becoming attuned to and conscious of the everyday. Essentially, the goal is to achieve what Christian Norberg-Schulz called "poetic awareness" in which an architect or architecture student is aware of that which makes architecture, urban design and other design more than a functional or utilitarian response to problems.[5] Often we are confronted with problem solving, but more than solving the problem we are asked perhaps to solve the problem poetically, to ask better questions that arise out of questioning.

The primary intention of this book is to foster an appreciation of the process of observation with the ultimate goals of attaining factual knowledge (what some call a "library" of images, ideas, solutions, etc.) and procedural knowledge (the ability to observe, develop a sense of looking) that leads, it is hoped, to a more informed, insightful and rounded design process.

The degree, use and deliberateness of factual and procedural knowledge are indefinite. For some designers, sketching is a means of assembling a catalog that is both literal and figurative. Some designers refer to and begin their own design solutions using the literal types, archetypes, elements or moves that they have observed. A particular window or a particular detail is literally transferred into their work. Others abstract the observed elements of their catalog in their work so that the idea of a particular window or a particular detail informs their work. Regardless of how literal or figurative this catalog reference system may be, it is difficult to say where in the literal/conceptual, conscious/unconscious spectrum the observer's past plays a role in a designer's work. Regardless of where the architect may fall in this spectrum, most architects would agree that the past does play an important role in their own work. Just as it is impossible to predict or stipulate how the observed past informs contemporary work, it is quite impossible to stipulate a way in which architects and designers learn about the designed environment. For some, drawing, drawing tools, sketchbook types or collage are individual means to observe the environment.

What is clear, however, is that regardless of method, the process requires carefulness and deliberateness. How can analysis investigate the underlying issues – the tectonic expression, the organization, etc. – yet in the dissection not "kill" the building? The major issue here is that sometimes the act of taking the thing apart kills it. Does a chef, in order to understand a good meal, destroy it or enjoy it? A musician hears music. Is this necessarily destroying it? Analysis and appreciation of the un-analyzable are not mutually exclusive. You can appreciate the unspoken quality and still dissect the formal characteristics.

Drawing can be intimidating and slow. There is often no immediate reward offered like that of a digital photograph. Once I asked a teacher of mine how long it took to sketch a particular building and he said "years". Even the accomplished and experienced architect will be frustrated by a mistake or ill-conceived diagram or perspective. The fundamental issue that helps anyone overcome this is practice.

Even those with the most advanced skills such as Olympic athletes, star dancers or chief surgeons must continually hone their talents. Though talent plays a role – especially in the most advanced athletes or elite in their fields – the simple answer of "practice" can elevate even the most awkward to some grace. For example, research in chess and spatial thinking examined the differences between the skills of master (professional), advanced (weekly or monthly) and novice (just starting) chess players. It was assumed that masters could see possible moves further into the future than the advanced and novice players. The research showed, however, that the primary difference between all levels was practice. More interesting was that the master and advanced player have a nearly equal ability to see potential moves, but the master who has practiced for thousands of hours (and has an interest to do so) is able to focus on those that are relevant to the situation and can review them more quickly. While aptitude and interest are key factors, even the most novice player can advance to near master level if time is dedicated to practice.

The book is divided into three parts. Part One is a review of the approach in terms of why it is important to observe, analyze and synthesize the design environment, the ways in which analysis and drawing are critical in developing architectural awareness and a review of research on diagramming and drawing. Part Two of the book is a collection of diagrams that students might use as models or as archetypes that can help them diagram buildings, urban spaces and other aspects of the designed environment. The critical step here is that analysis and synthesis must be learned. To simply ask a student to "diagram the building" is insufficient. Students must be shown what a diagram looks like, how it might have been developed and how to abstract that which is an experience. Diagramming, like outlining a book, dissecting a piece of music or taking apart a meal, is a skill that must be learned. Organized as *Actions of* and *Actions upon* plan, section and façade conventions and on urban and detail scales, these actions or acts can help both the novice and the experienced architect communicate, understand and ultimately question those actions. Part Three is a collection of sketchbook pages by architecture students and architects that combine multiple diagrams in order to understand a building, object, urban space or other place holistically. Like the many tools used to analyze and understand anything from the human body to car engines, the many diagrams combined in these sketchbook pages show how place is best understood through varied tools or lenses.

The book is meant to be a starting point. It is hoped that it can help develop an appreciation of observation and of really looking at and seeing the world. This in turn can only help the young architect learn and then add with a degree of responsibility to that environment. The methodology that is proposed should be seen as a framework that should be modified and adapted to the student's individual way of learning and thinking.

1   Gardner, Howard, *Frames of Mind: The Theory of Multiple Intelligences*. New York: Basic Books (1983).

2   Website: *Project Zero* http://www.howardgardner. com/FAQ/FREQUENTLY%20 ASKED%20QUESTIONS%20 Updated%20March%2009.pdf.

3   Gardner, Howard, *Five Minds of the Future*. Boston: Harvard Business School Press (2007): 30-35.

4   Buxton, William, *Sketching User Experiences: Getting the Design Right and the Right Design*. Amsterdam: Elsevier/ Morgan Kaufmann (2007): 32.

5   Norberg-Schulz, Christian, *The Concept Of Dwelling: On The Way To Figurative Architecture*. Milan: Electa (1985): 135.

SKETCHING, THINKING, LEARNING

PART I

SKETCHING, THINKING, LEARNING

Since I started teaching, I have been fortunate to hear stories of sketching experiences from former students who, after leaving the university, entered design practice or other allied fields. Often their stories revolve around job interviews, client meetings, travels or particular design problems in which sketching played a pivotal role. Two stories in particular illustrate why I am encouraged to keep helping students, to keep honing my courses and why I wrote this book about sketching and analysis.

One account is from Lindsey Dehenzel, who was in my sophomore-level introductory sketch analysis course and then in my junior-year semester in Barcelona. A typical undergraduate student, Lindsey explored architecture using multiple media: she used digital tools, hand-drafted drawings, collages and cardboard models with equal ease. Fortunately, she sketched daily, which helped her discover that sketching was not only calming and enjoyable but that it could help ask questions and help explore and discover things about the designed environment and herself. Immediately after that semester in Barcelona, Lindsey started her first summer internship. A few days after beginning the new job (days spent correcting drawings on a computer), the firm's two principals asked all the summer interns to sit in on a preliminary round-table design meeting with the associates and slightly more experienced intern architects. At one point during the meeting she picked up a pen and trace paper and started to analyze, diagram and draw multiple views of the site. The principals and others were quite impressed by her analytical insight and design abilities. Moreover, they were surprised that anyone in architecture schools today would be adept at sketching. As a result of her diverse abilities, she was offered more design responsibilities than her peers at the firm and even school friends who were interning at other firms. Unlike other young interns, she was able to sketch effectively, think aloud and communicate to many around the table with a pen and paper; she not only bridged the gap between the principals and the younger architects but was able to analyze and explore design ideas with agility.

A second anecdote is from Michael Licht, a former graduate student who, after a several years in architectural practice, decided to change careers and move into digital game design. As a student, Michael was what one might call a digitophile. Nearly everything he did was on a disc. While he did have a sketchbook somewhere on his studio desk or in his backpack, it was used very rarely and begrudgingly. Unlike Lindsey, Michael was a one-medium designer. So, when he sought out the best video game designers, he applied to LucasArts© with a portfolio filled with striking digital modeling and renderings of award-winning architectural projects that would surely impress someone at Skywalker Ranch. Unfortunately, Michael received a polite "thanks-but-no-thanks" reply. Undaunted, he applied again but this time filled the portfolio with his travel, analytical and design sketches. LucasArts© called Michael for an interview and, not long after, hired him as a game designer. Later, the lead designer who interviewed Michael mentioned that while LucasArts© received thousands of applications showing digital work, Michael's portfolio of sketches revealed Michael for what he was and what he could be: a person with talent, thoughtfulness and promise.

A common thread linking these and other stories is that sketching helped young architects and designers to question, investigate and explore manifold ideas and places as well as experience varied disciplines and fields. Of course, sketching alone may not be responsible for particularly insightful analyses and career success stories. Neither, for that matter, is sketching somehow unilaterally "better than" a digital or any other tool. Like any tool, sketching has its limits just as digital or other media. Rather, what I hope to show and for students to see is that instead of "this tool" or "that tool" a multiplicity of tools allow for extended design explorations.

I explore the one tool of sketching because I believe it can inform many tools. As a means toward multiplicity, sketching has helped me understand drawing as an interrelationship of Sketching, Thinking and Learning. The intention in this first part of the book is to explore these three interrelated characteristics in the context of anecdotal, observational and empirical research, to outline the theoretical and physical context in which sketching and analysis occur and, lastly, to explore how sketching is part of design learning. Hopefully, it can explain how and why sketching is an influential, in fact a vital tool in any design education.

Starting with Unremarkable Conclusions

At the end of "Ill-Structured Representations for Ill-Structured Problems", a synopsis of research on sketching and its role in the design process, psychologist Vinod Goel admits that his conclusions are "unremarkable".[1] He confesses a preaching to the choir, writing that "any designer can tell us that sketching is important for preliminary design".[2] And of course, Goel's conclusions come as no surprise. Many designers and educators simply *know* that statement to be true: it's a matter of fact. If it "goes without saying", however, it is astonishing to see the number that do talk or write about it with varied points of view, explanations and advice. Architects, industrial designers, film producers and other designers, including Zaha Hadid, Bill Buxton, Michael Graves, George Lucas, Jean Nouvel, Caroline Mauduit or Cesar Pelli, have spoken or written about drawing and how they think through or explain things in sketches, remember sketch-induced eureka moments or recall some connection between sketching and astute observations. Researchers and educators within architecture and design fields such as Rudolf Arnheim, Werner Oechslin, Norman Crowe, Paul Laseau and Edward Robbins validate commonly held beliefs with their own sketching anecdotes.[3] In the 1980s and 1990s, anecdotal evidence led to increased research into the role of sketching in architectural education including research by Ömer Akin, Donald Schön, Ellen

Yi-Luen Do, Mark D. Gross and Craig Zimring. Even beyond architectural and design fields, from the 1960s through today, researchers such as Jean Piaget, Vinod Goel, Herbert Simon, Jill Larkin and others have advanced our understanding of psychology and helped answer why, how and what it means to draw.

To help sort out the ideas, speculations and research, I examine sketch analysis and its relationship to design in three parts. Part 1 looks at sketching as a bodily skill in which the act of marking a surface is an extension of the hand and brain. Part 2 examines how analysis and diagrammatic sketching, as integral elements of our intellectual processes, help us examine the world and organize our thoughts. Part 3 examines sketching in its role as a learning tool so that we can adapt knowledge to new and unexpected situations. Though separated, these categories are less distinct in reality. When, for instance, does skill end and thinking or learning begin? How does learning a physical skill separate from learning a conceptual skill? When is declarative knowledge distinct from procedural knowledge? These and other overlaps will be apparent at times: the ambiguity of sketching, thinking and learning is what makes the topic significant and important to an inherently ambiguous design process.

1   Goel, Vinod, "Ill-Structured Representations for Ill-Structured Problems", *Proceedings of the Fourteenth Annual Conference of the Cognitive Science Society*. Hillsdale: Lawrence Erlbaum Associates (1992): 849.

2   *Ibid.*

3   The link between design thinking and drawing by architects, designers and filmmakers appears in books, journals and interviews, including Norman Crowe and Paul Laseau's *Visual Notes for Architecs and Designers*, Michael Graves' "The Necessity of Drawing: Tangible Speculation", Simon Unwin's *Analysing Architecture*, Sue Ferguson Gussow's *Architects Draw* and Marc Treib's *Drawing/ Thinking: Confronting an Electronic Age*. Fundamental research on the topic reveals an increased interest in the understanding of the interrelationship of drawing with physical and cognitive abilities and design including Ömer Akin's *Psychology of Architectural Design*, Gabriela Goldschmidt's "The Dialectics of Sketching", Douglas Graf's "Diagrams", the research of Ellen Yi-Luen Do and Mark D. Gross as well as Jill Larkin and Herbert Simon's seminal article "Why a Diagram is (Sometimes) Worth Ten Thousand Words". The bibliography includes references for additional research.

Tools of the Trade

Our tools are less innocuous than we would like to think. In fact, our tools help shape how we construct, how we investigate and, in a greater sense, how we think. It is essential, therefore, to select the right tool, learn to use that tool, know its limitations and, ultimately, understand why many tools fill a complete toolbox. Like any tool, choosing the right drawing media depends on an informed, individual user who faces varied tasks. Informed choice begins and continues with media experimentation.

Sketchbooks: Size, proportion, binding and paper color, weight and texture prompt an unending search for the perfect sketchbook. I prefer a square sketchbook with thicker "all-media" off-white, medium-tooth paper with sewn binding.

Wood graphite pencils produce varied line types at a low cost. While there are 20 hardness gradations from extremely soft (9B) to extremely hard (9H), the most common gradations are the middle range: B, HB, F, H and 2H. Though harder pencils produce lighter lines, all gradations can result in varied line weights depending on pressure and the paper. **Lead holders** offer the same line range as wood pencils but, if desired, a more precise line. A lead holder should not be confused with the click-to-advance mechanical pencil, which I avoid because of the uniformity: the same lead thickness appears with each click and thus there is little nuance. **Solid woodless pencils**, sheathed in a plastic or wax coating, offer the advantages of wood pencils but with possibility of broader strokes. Tactility plays a greater role in their preference: without the intervening wood there is a greater tactile connection to the lead itself. **Pastels and crayons** of clay, wax, charcoal or chalk are good for more broad-stroke, gestural drawing or diagramming. **Kneaded erasers**, unlike hard rubber erasers, "pick up" graphite in degrees rather than remove it completely, and **metal pencil sharpeners**, unlike plastic, tend to make a sharper point.

Fountain pens have loyal enthusiasts owing to line varieties produced from even the slightest pressure changes as well as choices in pen body types, weights and sizes, nib styles and ink colors. Though sometimes costly, even entry-level fountain pens can produce extensive line types and, with disposable ink cartridges, can last for years. **Felt-tip pens** come in a range of broad to thin and assorted shaped points at a low cost. The disadvantage, however, is less controlled ink flow and thus less response to pressure. **Rollerball pens**, like felt-tip pens, are inexpensive but produce a uniform, if precise, line width. **Brushes** with India or other bottled inks allow for broad-stroke gestural drawing that, in a sense, obliges broad design analysis.

Opposite page from left to right: Wood pencils, lead holder, solid graphite pencil, medium-soft General© 314, Conté© crayon, sharpener and kneaded eraser

From left to right: Pilot© Penmanship extra-fine fountain pen, Lamy© fine-point fountain pen, Pentel© Sign pen, Pilot© Fineliner, Pigma© Micron, Pilot© V5 Hi-Techpoint rollerball, #2 brush

Drawing the Lines

Draw a straight line by not drawing a straight line. To draw a straight line, it is helpful to think of riding a bicycle. When children first learn to ride a bicycle, their arms swing the handlebars back and forth as they compensate and adjust their balance. At first, the wheel turns wildly back and forth in order to move in a straight line without tipping over. Slowly after much practice, the back and forth motion diminishes and, seemingly, stops. Yet, when you think about it, the constant back and forth adjustments continue if imperceptibly. Imagine for a moment to lock your arms and the handlebar so that the wheel does not turn. You know that in a few seconds, the bike and yourself would be on the ground. Even professional bicyclists move their handlebars back and forth like a child. You just can't see it. Likewise, when drawing a line, it is helpful to maintain a straight line by wiggling or vibrating the line. Such a line is more of a high-pitched vibration akin to a vibrating mobile phone or an electric toothbrush. This has two results. First, by vibrating the line adjusts so that it can move straight. If

it veers too much in one direction, you can adjust it in the other direction. Secondly, a vibrating line gives the optical illusion that the line is straighter than it appears.

Move your pencil and hand, not your whole arm. When drawing, draw like you write. Rest your hand on the page and draw lines that are the extent of your hand's movement. When you want a longer line, pick up and plant your hand farther down the line and begin again.

Guidelines, massing lines, contour lines and surface lines. Develop your drawing by first only using guidelines. These guidelines are light lines that mark out the overall drawing. When the overall form is established, then add different line types and weights. Likewise, begin to develop a line vocabulary of different line types using varied pencils, pens or other media. Let the lines develop from light to dark, tapering, dashed, dotted, etc. Let the lines begin to help map, shape and form.

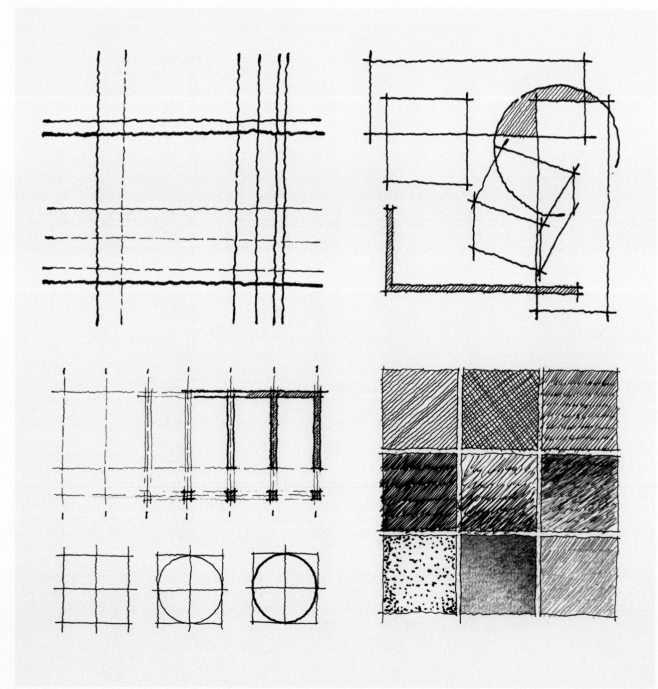

Start and stop the lines. Begin and end the line with a forward and backward stroke. This is done for two reasons. First, the strong beginning and end is an optical illusion in which the line appears more solid on the page. The line appears to have a definitiveness. Second, and slightly related, a definitive beginning and ending is a way to make a definitive mark, if only for this particular study, that the line begins here and ends there. There is no weakness or frailty. The line is strong and distinct – for at least that drawing. Subsequent drawings have their own beginnings and endings.

Cross corners. When two or more lines meet, cross them slightly. This is an optical illusion that makes the corners, and the drawing overall, for lack of a better word, more substantial. When the lines do not cross, your eyes will automatically connect them, with the result that the connections are weak and rounded. When they cross ever so slightly, the corners are emphasized and solidified.

Practice swimming by swimming. Sometimes there is a tendency to make a series of tentative and scratchy lines so that one day you can make one long line. This fallacy is similar to learning to swim by slowly moving one leg for a day, then another leg the next day, followed by a hand in the water the day after that and so on. The best way to learn a particular swimming stroke is to get into the water, with someone to help mind you, and do that stroke. Likewise, when drawing, it is best to draw in order to draw. Draw complete lines. At first it may be inelegant, but eventually (and usually quickly if practiced correctly), lines become beautiful and second nature.

Opposite page:
Top: Wiggly lines, guidelines with textures and tones
Bottom: Varied line weights and types to make a hierarchical tartan grid

Top: Varied line weights and tones used to diagram a façade
Bottom left: Drawing is like writing with a pencil
Bottom right: Varied line weights and types in analysis (drawing by Gregory Pray)

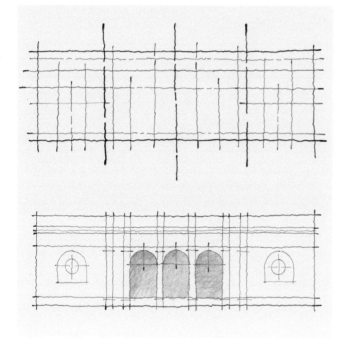

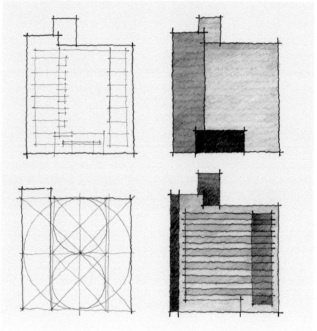

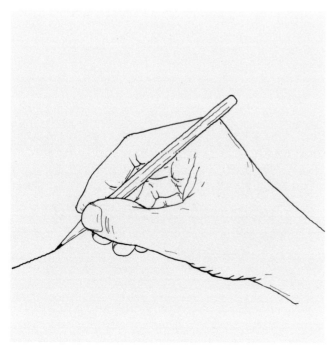

Building a Drawing

A building is an assemblage of elements layered one on another. Upon conceptual and physical foundations rest more complex frames that, in turn, support increasingly detailed elements and ideas. The building materializes as a whole so that, in the end, the overall and the detail interlink as a totality.

Likewise, when drawing at a site, it is helpful to start with the framework and then allow the drawing to grow into a complete entity. Developing out of a process, the drawing in turn reinforces the process of seeing layers and hierarchies and of seeing the comprehensive interrelationship of detail and whole.

For more practical reasons, beginning with the overall proportions and then adding increasingly detailed information helps ensure that the sketch fits on the page. Beginning a drawing in an upper corner and working at all levels simultaneously toward a lower corner may result in a drawing that, if finished, is off the page's edge. Additionally, a correctly proportioned façade is more likely to support

correctly proportioned bays, which in turn fit correctly proportioned windows. If the overall form is out of proportion, each subsequent element necessarily will also be out of proportion to make it fit.

Two ways to establish a framework and mapping the proportions are using either a length of a pencil or pacing out dimensions of a façade, an interior volume or an object. For the pencil technique, while holding a pencil between your forefinger and thumb, fully extend your arm so that the distance from your nose to the pencil remains constant. Look down your arm at your subject with your pencil in the foreground. Adjust your pencil's length as needed to match an element on the façade, such as a bay or floor height and let the pencil-to-thumb length be a standard unit of measurement.

Count the number of units for verticals and horizontals and then convert and transfer those units and their multiples to a unit on your page. Continue to adjust your pencil-to-thumb length for smaller elements as needed. You can also

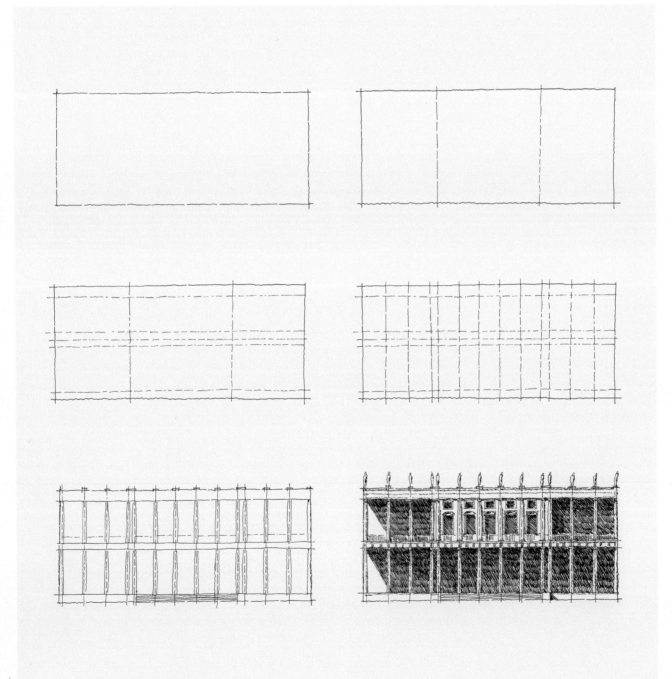

establish overall proportions by pacing off a room's width and length or a building's length. Make normal steps and count them out. Note the overall number and, most importantly, the number at significant moments, for example the column bays or changes in material. Transfer the number of steps to units on your page as in the pencil technique. For example, a courtyard may be 30 steps by 45 steps, with colonnades five steps on all sides. Those units, 35 x 45 with five on each side, can then be drawn to a scale so that the drawing fits on the page.

Draw the larger framework to its complete extent, using only guidelines while noting significant subdivisions. With these guidelines in place, begin to slowly but steadily overlay increasingly detailed information. Even if you do not complete all of the detail, you will have the overall idea of the building firmly established.

Opposite page:
Drawing of Palazzo Chiericati, Vicenza, Italy, scanned at six different stages from guidelines to finished drawing

Top: Using a pencil to find proportions
Bottom left: Underlying guidelines to draw the interior volumes (drawing by Fred Scharmen)
Bottom right: Pacing out a room's or square's proportions

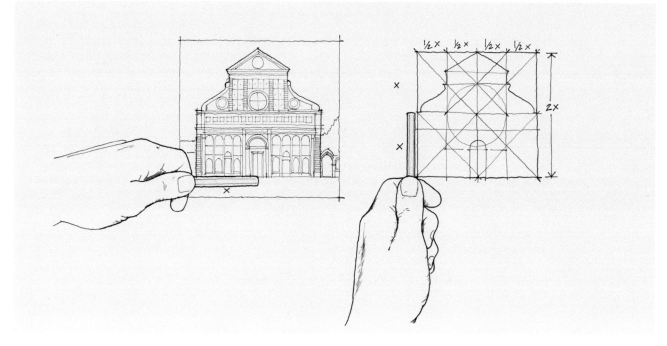

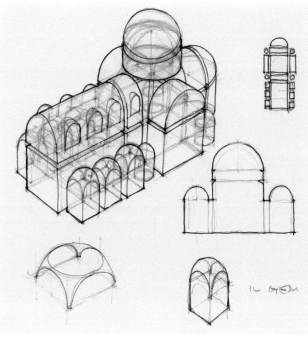

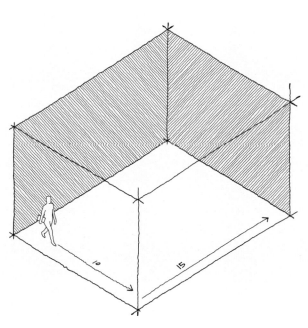

Sketching as a Bodily Skill

"Drawing for me is a fundamental act of an architectural thought process. Drawing is in part a mnemonic device, a visual diary. However, because of the intrinsic reciprocity between mind and act, drawing goes beyond simple information. It fixes in our inner experience what we have seen. As an essential part of the conception of architecture, as well as of painting and sculpture, it is also conjectural or speculative in nature and therefore exists at the heart of the creative process."

Michael Graves[4]

Sketching is rooted in the fundamental animal instinct to explore and manipulate the world with gangly extremities: From *amoebae* to *homo sapiens*, curious pseudopods, appendages and limbs reach out, grasp and manipulate the "world" to understand it, to move through it, to transform it (and often to eat it). While most animals manipulate the world to satisfy more immediate primal needs, humans grasp and maneuver to explore and speculate on the unknown. As our hands explore, our minds develop. This mutual development of hand and mind, of the physical and intellectual, propelled humankind forward to speculate and manipulate with unique agility. It is no accident that our hands, which are the most sophisticated among the primates, are paired with minds capable of sophisticated cognition. The hand-mind participated and continue to participate in mutual development. In his book, *The Hand: How Its Use Shapes the Brain, Language, and Human Culture*, neurologist Frank Wilson analyzes the human hand and its role in cognitive development. Wilson contends that we do a disservice to the hand and the mind (and the concept of humanity's uniqueness) if we bifurcate the hand from the mind. For him, the hand – its evolution, form and abilities – is essential to human identity. He asserts that this link and its influence on human development is so significant "that any theory of human intelligence which ignores the interdependence of the human hand and brain function, the historic origins of that relationship, or the impact of that history on developmental dynamics in modern humans, is grossly misleading and sterile".[5]

Similarly, a sketch, in which our hand and mind scratch, mark and otherwise explore through graphic and semiotic representations, is an essential part of who we are and what we hope to be. Training the hand and the eye to locate and perceive objects is an interlinked learning process between the mind and body that develop spatial knowledge: "the brain *teaches itself* to synthesize visual and tactile perceptions by *making* the hand and eye learn to work together."[6] Spatial knowledge, the ability to both mentally and graphically retrace and demarcate paths and spaces, to estimate dimension and to comprehend orientation and direction, is essential to developing three-dimensional thinking not only in varied professions but in daily life. Grasping and reaching are inextricably linked to our cognitive development in which we observe and react to both representations and physical experiences and to developing semantic processing systems concerned with "manipulating, identifying or transforming objects".[7]

Sketching is a type of drawing used to process information succinctly and, as such, it is in the same echelon as speaking, grasping and walking: it both affects and effects our thinking. Who we are, as human beings, has a great deal to do with the fact that we can speak complex languages, walk upright, grasp and use both delicate and coarse objects and communicate with visual representational systems. Likewise, it makes sense that any education, especially a design eduction, reinforces the hand-mind connection, the translation of the physical world through the conceptual graphic representation in direct use of the hand and eye and inculcates the fundamental nature of architecture as a material and volumetric process. In so doing, that education helps develop material and spatial knowledge informed by the "hand-mind complex", in which sketching or any direct manipulation and translation actively engages the physical and spatial world.[8]

Learning and then practicing sketching is part of the physical and experiential translation of the designed and natural world into a design language. The sketch is concerned with a deliberate examination of the procedural knowledge exercised in the physical act.

Learning (and Re-Learning) to Draw

For many young and older adults, and even for those enrolled in design programs or working in design fields, sketching can be challenging. Despite the challenge, it is comforting to remember that it is an innate ability. At an early age, nearly all children endeavor to speak, walk and draw. First footsteps are tentative and unbalanced and first words, to anyone but proud parents, seem like odd noises rather than something most would call speech. But with continued practice and encouragement children, if physically capable, walk and speak with little effort. Similarly, at an early age, nearly all children pick up a stick, pencil or crayon to mark surfaces. Those early sketches, usually quite inaccurate and awkward, slowly develop as our muscles and mind align intentions with consequence. Those early, mostly unconscious representations gradually reflect who we are, what we imagine, how we feel and what we experience.

Unfortunately, while most children continue to walk and speak with increased proficiency, many children simply stop drawing. Overtly talented children might continue to draw into their teens and adult life, however, at about age seven most children perceived by themselves or others to have below average or even moderate drawing abilities draw less frequently. By age twelve most stop drawing altogether. Besides observational and anecdotal speculations there is little research evidence to suggest exactly why this occurs.[9] Some speculate that increased dominance of linguistic and mathematical skills in daily discourse (generally we "talk to" or "write to" more than we "draw to" friends) is a factor, others suggest that increased standardized testing that emphasizes verbal and mathematic skills is a significant cause, a third group believes that the tenuous position of the arts in budgetary decisions plays a role, while others again blame disapproving teachers and peers.[10] For this discussion, two possible explanations have direct bearing on university-level design curricula and individual student learning.

First, psychologist Richard Jolley observes in his book *Children and Pictures: Drawing and Understanding* that many children are "disserviced by inappropriate or ineffective" curricula, especially concerning "how",

"where" and "when" sketching is taught and encouraged.[11] For example, a seemingly incongruous inhibiting factor to continued childhood drawing is isolating art-related activities from normal class periods and placing them in "art time". Scheduling drawing in a "non-normal" time and defining it as a "non-normal" activity has the unintended effect of relegating drawing to "an activity subordinate to other subjects that are considered more 'academic' and therefore more important".[12] This problem can and often does continue into university-level design programs. Some programs place sketching in specific courses (usually introductory levels) and thereafter discuss sketching primarily within the context of formal presentations or, if a student is fortunate enough, during travel programs. Sketching becomes separated from normal architectural discourse and is often presumed to be developed on its own. Unfortunately, sketching – especially analytical sketching as dealt with here – requires integration and practice throughout the design career.

A second issue is that educational programs from elementary school to Master's-level design programs face increased external and internal pressure to adopt standards, improve testing results, expand varied technologies and otherwise emphasize specialization and training within already stretched educational curricula.[13] This pressure comes from all sides: parents, students, faculty, upper echelon administrators, certification boards, professionals and even governmental agencies. Increasingly, curricula must incorporate more information, more courses and more technologies to remain relevant, advance theoretical positions, increase opportunities, obtain funds, achieve higher standards, develop a student's potential and even avoid derogatory labeling. Each supplement and each intention has its own validity and rationale – and it is increasingly difficult to dispute them. Nonetheless, more than marginalizing "traditional" methods and thinking, embellishments squeeze all facets of education (from digital to analog, from prosaic to profound) in an effort to provide what is deemed a proper education.[14]

Learning to Sketch Without Thinking

Regardless of the loss and its reasons, sketching as a bodily skill can be re-learned. Practice is the essential ingredient in the learning process. While this may seem quite obvious, it bears repeating since even the most gifted musicians, actors, athletes or others who engage in complex mind and body skills practice repeatedly and often to the exclusion of basics of life. Like learning or re-learning other physical and mental skills (learning a new language, to play a piano or downhill skiing), young and older adults can learn or re-learn to draw. The important thing is not so much the sketching technique or style but focus, reflection and repetition and to embrace the drawing confidently. Studies have shown that practice is the single "major independent variable" in acquiring and honing skills.[15] This is equally applicable for sketching, perception and visuo-spatial thinking. William Chase and Herbert Simon's study of perception and cognitive processes in chess playing revealed that the difference between a master chess player and a novice player came down to one essential variable: the master practiced more. In fact, a master generally practices 10,000 to 50,000 hours to achieve the standing while a novice plays less than 100 hours.[16] Extensive practice helps master players not only to memorize possible moves, but more importantly, helps players discern what moves should even be considered.[17] The masters were, unconsciously, more efficient in ruling out possible alternatives because practice helped clarify their thinking processes.

The aim of practice is to rehearse actions so that they become practically unconscious yet facilitate thinking, expression or problem solving. For instance, a pianist does not practice simply to repeat scales during a performance and a basketball player does not practice merely to perfect dribbling and throwing as end in itself. The pianist, basketball player and others engage in physical and mental practice to better express, interact, resolve or experience more meaningfully the dynamic and relatively unpredictable situations to come. Likewise, design students and practicing designers practice (hence 'practitioners') and engage in design projects (and, I contend, in analytical sketching) to help foster design thinking. The physical, spatial and experiential aspects of sketching inform designers because the sketching act prepares them for the physical interaction with material. Sketching can act as an analogy in terms of a means to thinking and a way to physically interact with that which is being analyzed.

Repeated and frequent practice develops the internal communication between hand (physical) and mind (cognitive). As a physically interactive thinking process, touching and grasping is a way in which we conceive of and visualize form and space. As infants we tested and eventually anticipated location, shape and reaction through physical interaction. By extension, sketching is a way of touching, transforming and predicting spatial and material conditions. It is both communication between the hand and mind and a physical, albeit abstract, transformation of form and idea. It is a kind of proto-design, requiring physical abilities, appropriate code usage and conceptual processes. This is especially true for architects for whom sketching is a way of rehearsing the translation from concept to form. By developing hand knowledge through physical manipulation we can anticipate with some accuracy how things will work or might work.

Learning and practicing specific skills and representational modes helps develop an automatic, unconscious freedom associated with what is commonly known as "muscle memory" or automaticity. In this process, a task is so overlearned through repetition that the task itself occurs automatically and essentially without thinking.[18] Automaticity is a form of what Michael Polanyi refers to as tacit knowledge: a skill becomes secondary or unconscious to the thinking facilitated through the skill. We attend to the more important issue at hand because we can disattend

from the rote skill.[19] In disattending from the more ordinary physical acts "we are attending from these elementary movements to the achievement of their joint purpose, and hence are usually unable to specify the elementary acts".[20] Daily activities such as walking, reaching for door handles, typing on keyboards, operating light switches and even driving automobiles are skills that, due to their repetition and hence familiarity, can be performed without conscious awareness. As Polanyi notes: "We can know more than we can tell."[21] We disattend from rudimentary, even sophisticated actions so that we can focus on the reason of those actions. We walk to explore, we type to express our thoughts, we operate light switches to see, etc. The unconscious actions used to achieve those goals remain tacit. We "know" the skill and we can say that we performed the skill, but we often are not aware of the skill while it is being performed.

Disattending is not only vital for accomplishing or thinking through more pressing issues in our lives but for mental well-being. If we did not disattend from routine skills but attended to every daily action with the requisite, countless and delicate muscular motor skills, even the simplest act would distract us from essential considerations. This is most clear to us when, as adults, we learn new basic skills. For instance, I first started using chopsticks during a trip to Japan at the end of my senior year of college. Because chopsticks were relatively new to me, the first few meals were about training my muscles and mind to hold and work those chopsticks just so that I could eat. While it took mental energy for me just to lift a piece of fish, children who had been using chopsticks exclusively for a few years could pick up individual grains of rice without a second thought. Had I not developed even a primitive ability with those chopsticks, I would have had no time for thinking, conversing or developing a taste for Japanese food.

The same is true for sketching. One goal of sketching is not the sketch itself, but the thinking facilitated by sketching. Holding a pencil, controlling line weights, drawing accurate lines and otherwise getting the sketch on the page are vital to the design process; and yet, as more experienced sketchers and designers, the actual sketching process is unconscious so that the intention of the sketching, the *design*, can dominate. In developing sketching automaticity, the disattended sketching act relieves the mind from the tool and allows it to attend to the idea or the exploration's objective. By disattending from the sketching act we are able to attend to the idea and to exploration, so that we can move beyond thinking *about* sketching to thinking *through* sketching.

Practicing to Practice

Once we develop the sketching act into an unconscious analytical procedure, we can use it in the design process. As essentially an action/reflection process, the design process involves a cyclical consideration of hypothetical propositions or solutions through a series of alternative simulations. Through sketching we can test, re-test and propose through a cyclical formulation and re-formulation.[22] As a continual search of possible solutions, sketching skills amplify design development through strategies within which concepts and solutions might be found through the number and depth of repeated simulations.[23] This amplification through repetition is in a way akin to Emergency Medical Service (EMS) personnel who train repeatedly in simulated catastrophes. A primary goal of EMS simulations is body and mind preparedness for unforeseen events. Even though the exact details of an event can never be duplicated in rehearsals, there is enough in the simulations to instill a particular process that can be called up without thinking in actual events. Likewise, sketching prepares architects for the unexpected (but less catastrophic!) by making familiar those actions and thought processes that approximate unexpected design problems. Unfortunately, practicing ineffective procedures or incorrect skills has the equal effect of reinforcing incorrect actions with equal potency. Or design-thinking habits may unconsciously presume specific solutions. Learning effective sketch procedures is important for helping a designer develop design methods and anticipate design problems.

As sketching is both physical and cognitive, practice also influences unconscious thinking abilities. Sketching exercises allow for thinking through the sketch, so that knowledge and processes can become tacit. Tactile learning informs design modeling by registering information onto paper – or in some cases in the computer and other media – to become automatic or nearly unconscious.[24] While this can be helpful, its adverse effect is developing design-thinking habits that unconsciously presume specific solutions.

4   Gray, Susan (ed.), *Architects on Architects*. New York: McGraw-Hill (2002): 39-40.

5   Wilson, Frank, *The Hand: How Its Use Shapes the Brain, Language, and Human Culture*. New York: Pantheon Books (1992): 7.

6   *Ibid.*: 97.

7   Jeannerod, Marc, *The Cognitive Neuroscience of Action*. New York: Wiley-Blackwell (1997): 21.

8   Wilson, Frank, *The Hand: How Its Use Shapes the Brain, Language, and Human Culture*. New York: Pantheon Books (1992): 96-99.

9   Rose, Sarah E., Jolley, Richard and Burkitt, Esther, "A Review of Children's, Teachers' and Parents' Influences on Children's Drawing Experience", *International Journal of Art & Design Education* 25, 3 (2006): 346-347.

10 Jolley, R. P., *Children and Pictures: Drawing and Understanding*. Chichester: Wiley-Blackwell (2010): 314-329.

11 *Ibid.*: 311.

12 *Ibid.*

13 Boyer, Ernest L. and Mitgang, Lee D., *Building Community: A New Future for Architecture Education and Practice*. Princeton: The Carnegie Foundation for the Advancement of Teaching (1996): 103-105.

14 *Ibid.*: 75-77.

15 Chase, William G. and Simon, Herbert A., "The Mind's Eye In Chess", in: Chase, William (ed.), *Visual Information Processing*. New York: Academic Press (1972): 279.

16 *Ibid.*: 219.

17 *Ibid.*: 257-258.

18 Driscoll, Marcy P., *Psychology of Learning for Instruction*. Boston: Allyn and Bacon (1994): 82-84.

19 Polanyi, Michael, *The Tacit Dimension*. London: Routledge and Kegan (1966): 3-25.

20 *Ibid.*: 10.

21 *Ibid.*: 4.

22 Schön, Donald A., *The Reflective Practitioner: How Professionals Think in Action*. New York: Basic Books (1983): 79.

23 Rowe, Peter, *Design Thinking*. Cambridge: MIT Press (1987): 39-113.

24 Polanyi, Michael, *The Tacit Dimension*. London: Routledge and Kegan (1966): 17-18.

Reflective Practice

Research in fields such as the cognitive sciences, musical performance and sports medicine has repeatedly confirmed what parents, coaches and teachers already know: the single most significant factor separating those who achieve and those who do not comes down to one issue: practice. And not just any practice. To be most beneficial it must be frequent, regular, self-motivated and, most importantly, reflective. For my own part, I fully admit that no barrage of specially designed assignments, readings or drawing tips can equal a student's reflective practice. A student learns more quickly, more effectively and develops skills through a personal decision to practice. If anything, a teacher or coach's job is to inspire while developing exercises that might challenge and develop fundamental and advanced skills.

First, practice must emerge out of a desire to practice. While there are those who must, for their own mental and physical satisfaction, practice continually, even those who are less passionate must develop the motivation to perfect abilities and commit to frequent practice. Discovering that motivation from within or from mentors plays a large role in cultivating that desire. Second, practice must be reflective. Practice is accompanied by evaluative examination of the immediate action and of the results, while articulating improvement methods. It is one thing to know what issues need work, it is another to understand what will be improved by specific changes. Third, practice must be correct. Drawing well requires that you practice so that practice methods match your ultimate use of that skill. When practicing drawing, you must use the same physical techniques that you would use in actually drawing. For example, runners, gymnasts or golfers practice the same way that they perform in competition. Help from coaches or teachers can help develop good habits, both physical and mental, that help you develop your physical and thinking skills. For analytical sketching, it is about methods that develop physical dexterity but also three-dimensional thinking, mapping and transformation. Three simple

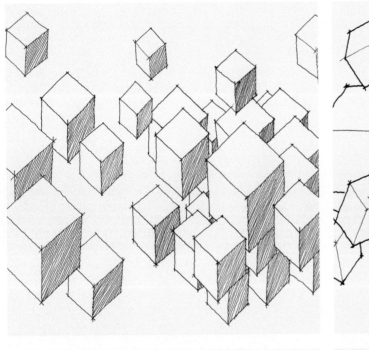

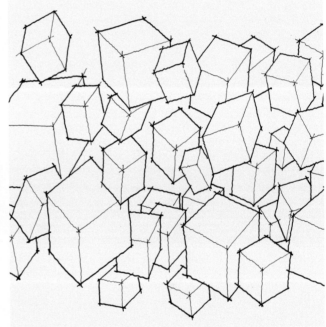

skill-development exercises I often ask of students include simple, complex and household objects.

Exercise 1: Cubes and Cones

The first exercise is drawing cubes or cones in space. Drawn in perspective or axonometric, cubes and cones float, drift, rotate in front, behind, above and below one another with degrees of transparency and opacity, different line weights or shade and shadow. Sometimes the rotations, transparencies and sizes develop from a system or narrative, while at other times they develop slowly and in response to page composition.

Exercise 2: Complex Shapes

This exercise is drawing complex objects that might either "float" in space or are part of an abstract landscape. Additive and subtractive forms interact with one another, linked to a landscape or as part of a larger complex tapestry. As with the cubes and cones, there are rotations, degrees of transparency and opacity with variations in shading and shadowing.

Exercise 3: Household Objects

This exercise is drawing common household objects such as coffee cups, telephones, forks that rotate, float and interact with one another in a void or on a table top. Like with the cubes and cones, the rotations can be part of a narrative or system. For example, a coffee cup might seem to tumble in a counter-clockwise spin from the top of the page to the bottom.

Opposite page:
Top left: Cubes in space on a grid
Top right: Cubes free-floating in space
Bottom left: Doodling as practice
Bottom right: Cones in space

Top left: Spoons in space
Top right: Flashlights in space: 20 minutes
Bottom: Doodling as practice: segmented cones and tartan grids

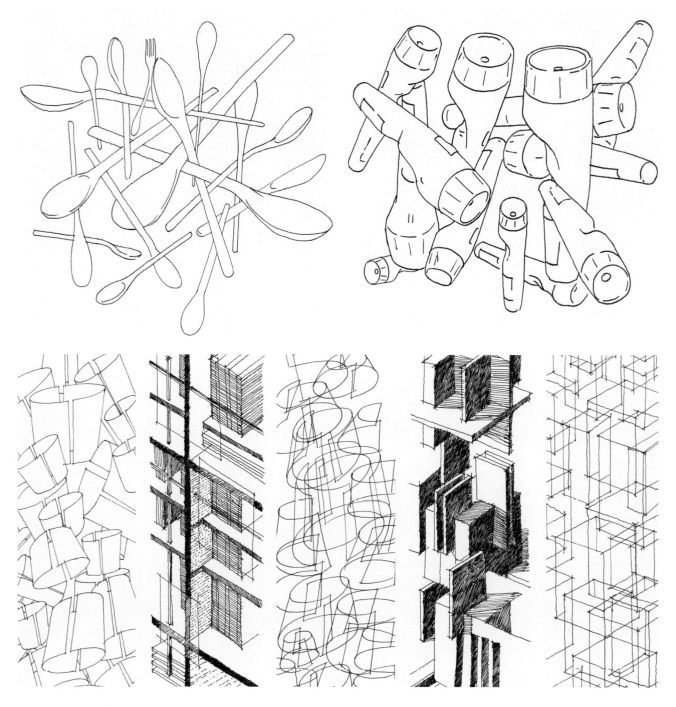

SPQR

When approaching a site, frequent and valid questions include "What do I draw?", "How do I convey so much in a sketch?" or "Where do I begin?". Some answers to these questions begin with the admission that there is no single thing to draw and that things will be overlooked. Specific exercises, diagrams, lenses or topics help suggest a direction, but there will always be other things to draw or to be saved for another visit. Another way to help answer these questions is to simply "start drawing". Drawing itself develops focus and an ability to discern what might be important to sketch and what might be better suited for a photograph or another time. To help develop site drawing there are several site habits that might be summed up as Succinctly-Precisely-Quickly-Rigorously, with the acronym developed in the Rome study abroad program: SPQR.

Succinctly: Tell the story of a site with optimum lines, tones and textures by using the appropriate number of lines. "Appropriate" may be 5,000 lines or one brush stroke.

Knowing the difference and having the ability to reduce that number or raise it according to the intention or place is a key skill. Rather than reductive, it is to understand that if needed, something can be succinct by omitting the superfluous.

Precisely: The drawing should be well-proportioned, clear and accurate so that it corresponds with the subject. Rather than focusing on verisimilitude, capture the arrangement and structure in which there is a clear and accurate relationship among scale, parts-to-whole and dimension. Develop an ability to sketch ideas and designs for a client or craftsperson so as to manifest a drawing's intention. There is a place for imprecision – it is inherent in the medium – but a goal is the dexterity to toggle from imprecision to precision.

Quickly: Often it is impossible to sketch a place without time limits. Buildings close, the sun goes down, trains

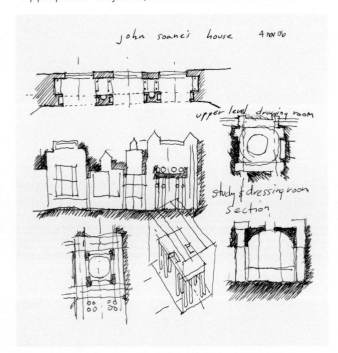

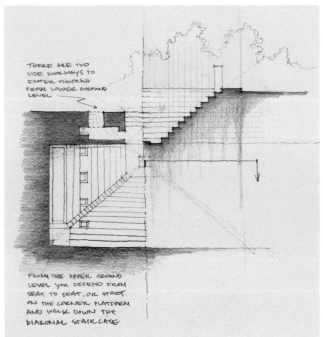

depart or companions want to eat. A key issue is knowing what can be done at the site and what can be done elsewhere. For example, toning or additional line weights might be noted at the site but completed elsewhere.

Rigorously: Lastly, there is a need to develop and maintain rigorous drawing skills. Those who play the piano, kick a ball or balance on a skateboard and make it look effortless and adjust or improvise in unpredictable situations practice their craft for hours a day. Like playing a musical instrument or sport, drawing is a craft nurtured through practice.

Opposite page:
Sketches made during a guided tour:
Bouleuterion, 60 minutes (drawing by Monica Perez)
The Robie House, 15 seconds

Top: Section through the archery range, 20 minutes (drawing by Fred Scharmen).
Bottom left: Study of extrusions and subtractions, 20 minutes (drawings by Mark McInturff)
Bottom right: Elements within the Jubilee Church, 45 minutes

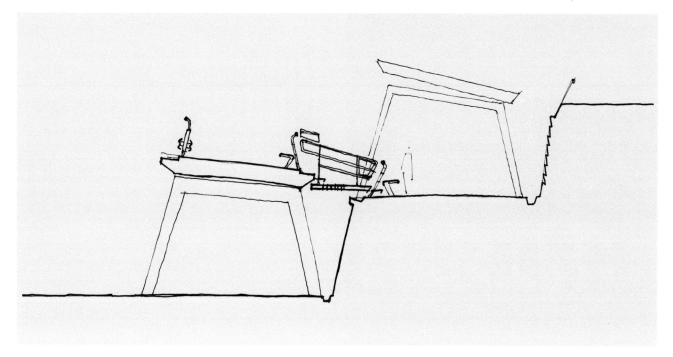

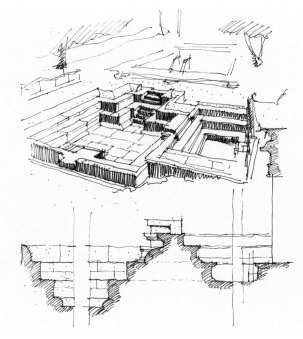

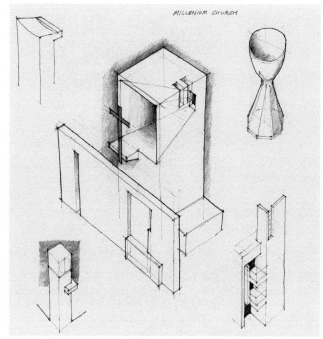

Line and Time Budgets

While traveling to distant cities or simply visiting familiar buildings, there is usually limited time to sit, ponder and sketch. What is required is an ability to grasp and convey as much as possible of the essence of a place – from an overall urban situation to a door handle – within a limited time. In a greater sense, however, line or time budgets can help develop editing skills. Essential for design, film, writing and other creative endeavors, editing is removing, reorganizing or even adding to seemingly complete pieces or processes. Iterative in nature, editing is learned primarily through the editing process as we compare subtractions and additions. As a refined discernment, editing involves understanding, ability and, sometimes, courage to decide what, when, where and how much remains or goes away. In design especially, there is often immeasurable information that must be synthesized into a unified and complex whole. Resolving site forces, materials, program needs, budget allocations and social traditions into a unified whole is more than balance and often involves difficult editing decisions. Discernment is knowing when something cannot be accomplished through a particular medium or process. Quick, accurate and succinct observation and encapsulation is a skill that can be nurtured through varied exercises. Two exercises that are helpful are "Line Budget" and "Timed Sketching".

Line Budget

Use a line budget or a limited number of lines to help discern and convey the essence of the place, façade, space, plan or section. The lines, usually few in number and chosen arbitrarily (you can use one of the 12 months in a year or seven days in a week), are single strokes. Variations might be single strokes that change direction only once or lines of only a limited length. To begin, you may want to start with a larger number (say, 12) and then slowly decrease that number to the point where it may be impossible to convey the building. Can you convey a place using only one line?

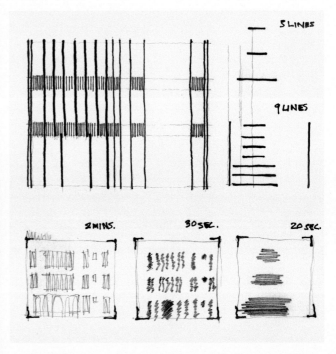

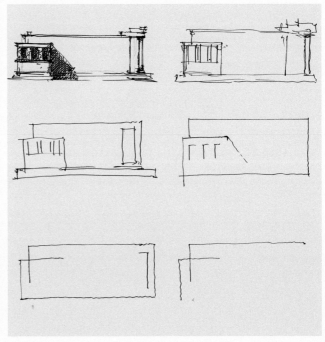

Timed Sketching

With the help of a friend or a portable alarm, repeatedly sketch the same subject within a series of timed intervals. Before you begin, prepare your drawing equipment so that you can focus on the sketching rather than sharpening the pencil or opening a new page. Once set, begin sketching the subject in 30 minutes and then draw four subsequent sketches for ten minutes, two minutes, 30 seconds and, finally, five seconds. The timed intervals can vary but should decrease substantially over the course of the exercise. When finished, think about how the intervals required different drawing techniques and discernment. These exercises are simply that: exercises. They are brief workouts that help nurture thinking and drawing processes that may or may not have a direct link to more extended sketching methods or design processes. Like playing scales on a keyboard, practicing fire drills or kicking a ball among teammates, sketch exercises are not an end but a means to developing tacit physical and thinking skills.

Opposite page:
Top: Ca' d'Oro, Venice, Italy, 1430: Sketches with line budgets (9 and 3 lines) and timed sketches (2 minutes, 30 seconds and 20 seconds) (drawings by Dylan King)
Bottom: Erechtheion, Athens, Greece, 430 BCE: Timed sketches (5 minutes, 2 minutes, 30 seconds, 15 seconds) and line budget (8 and 4 lines) (drawings by Jeff Gipson)

Top: Temple of Hadrian, Ephesus, Turkey, 2nd century AD: Timed sketches (6 minutes, 2 minutes, 30 seconds and 10 seconds) (drawings by John Lang)
Bottom: The Tower of the Winds, Athens, Greece, 2nd century BCE: Line budget (8, 6, 4 and 3 lines) (drawings by Fajer Alqattan)

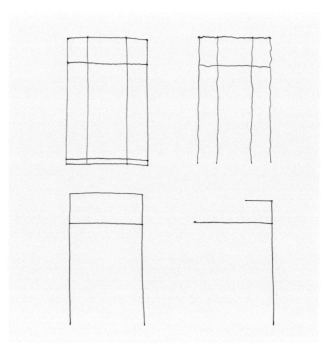

Sketching and Thinking

When one travels and works with visual things – architecture, painting or sculpture – one uses one's eyes and draws, so as to fix deep down in one's experience what is seen. Once the impression has been recorded by the pencil, it stays for good, entered, registered, inscribed. The camera is a tool for idlers, who use a machine to do their seeing for them. To draw oneself, to trace the lines, handle the volumes, organize the surface … all this means first to look and then to observe and finally perhaps to discover … and it is then that inspiration may come. Inventing, creating one's whole being is drawn into action and it is this action which counts. Others stand indifferent – but you saw!

Le Corbusier, *Creation is a Patient Search*[25]

Once we pick up and learn to use a tool what do we do with it? What is the role of sketching in helping develop thinking processes? Simply put, sketching helps understand the world so that we can better work with or, for that matter, against it. Understanding requires that we look beneath the surface of a thing to uncover its essential nature, to make the complex comprehensible and to see that the apparently simple may be more complex. Deliberate and critical sketching can offer a clarifying process in which we translate the complex into the simple and the seemingly infinite into the more finite. A sketch can do that because of its dual nature of clarity and ambiguity and through the notative interaction between sketch and sketcher. Freehand sketching of "what is" is both a tool and process of continuous transformation and, as such, has an essential role in conceptualizing "what may be".

When we sketch, we digest through enzymatic analysis: With questions and lenses and through different drawings or diagrams, a sketch helps disentangle a building or other design system into fundamental components and, as such, links that which is observed to the design act. Digestion is vital: as bodily enzymes transform proteins, carbohydrates, fats and other compounds into nutrients or discard them as waste, we thrive due in large part to the body's food analysis. Essentially, sketching is eating architecture. The sketch (the act and the artifact) transforms what is seen so that a greater design awareness and, possibly, greater understanding of both the world in which we work and of the design process itself may occur. Without digestion, the architectural artifact remains inert. The digestion begins with analysis.

What is Analysis?

Analysis is a process through which we can develop some understanding of complex situations, objects or systems by disassembling them into simpler, fundamental components. Rather than merely separating, compiling or describing individual components or subsets, analysis is an active, exploratory critique of what is observed. Essentially, analysis is asking questions that expose hidden patterns: are there elements – types, categories or taxonomies – within the system? Why are the elements important? How do they contribute to or detract from the whole? In which way are these constituent elements part of a larger narrative? What do the elements mean? What was discovered during the disassembly process itself?

Analyis is essential for fundamental decision making. While we must constantly analyze in daily life – making decisions at the grocery store, choosing what we wear or how to budget time and money – analysis or being analytical is often misinterpreted or sometimes seen as a destructive process that impedes vitality. There is a certain apprehension, perhaps even a fear, that analysis is a kind of vivisection that eradicates meaning, spontaneity or even the object itself. The question: "Must you always analyze everything?" is usually not a compliment. Christopher Alexander's comment in *Notes on the Synthesis of Form* that there is a "good deal of superstition among designers as to the deathly effect of analysis on their intuitions" remains relatively true, especially for students in the design field.[26] The analysis-as-killjoy myth presupposes that any visceral and intuitive satisfaction is mutually exclusive of understanding and knowledge. In fact, analysis can allow for enjoyment of a place, a piece of music or a painting and, at the same time, develop a more in-depth understanding. Learning this double-edge approach is critical.

An analytic methodology must be learned and often in stages. When teaching my analysis course or design studio to beginning design students, I do not expect them to know how to analyze an entire building. Often I ask them to analyze specific elements or sometimes I have them focus on description only. If we recall the examples cited in the Introduction, it can be argued that perspective sketches are processed representations: the mere act of looking at the surroundings and then transferring that image, with some degree of discernment and abstraction, to the sketchbook page is processing. The experienced view has been abstracted into a representative image. That said, for many young students, a perspective sketch remains only one view or is a single way of abstracting and understanding the design environment. The sketching seeks representational alignment or seeks to look the way the view looks. Considered as an analysis, the perspective often remains a singular description rather than critical, multifaceted inquiry. For an architect developing multiple views and seeing through the building, there is a need to develop alternative views of which perspectives are just one.

For the designer who operates within complex systems, the analysis of similarly complex systems can lead to a methodology of conscious and unconscious system mapping and devising. Just as a writer might analyze short stories or essays to help establish and inform the fundamental framework for his or her own work, a designer's analysis translates the designed environment into a form that can help establish and inform his or her own design process. But how do we begin analyzing a complex system such as a building, an urban space or any designed object that not only may be outwardly complex, often overwhelming, but also was influenced by factors both seen and unseen? It is helpful to begin by approaching the design environment from fluctuating points between two, often conflicting, positions: being dependent and being autonomous.

The Context-bound Position

A dependent or context-bound position is one in which objects or systems are situated within, shaped by and continue to be influenced by a social, cultural, political and economic milieu.[27] That is, the systems or objects are contextually determined by external forces and, in turn, those systems and objects themselves reinforce the context and maintain a *status quo*: an object is a product of *x* and in turn reinforces *x*. As instruments of culture, these contextually embedded objects or systems can

include those forces that led to their resolution or current condition.[28] The objects or systems are epiphenomena "dependent on socioeconomic, political, and technological processes" that informed the object's or system's initial form and, in turn, reinforce subsequent social, political and technological processes.[29] The argument is that in order to understand a design, the analysis must investigate those outside forces or contexts that shaped it: a building is more than a building. It is the consequence of those forces within which it was created and, reciprocally, the building continues to influence the context. Just as socio-cultural and economic conditions can shape a designed object, the designed object (architecture, urban design, product design) can, in turn, take on variegated levels of influence within and upon the socio-cultural or economic system. The design environment, by its mere dependence on the economic and social structure and its realities, offers confirmatory authorization of the *status quo*. Architects and their work are supported by patrons and a financial system, built within a given physical and cultural framework (cities, property lines, zoning) and symbolically represent those systems (corporate headquarters, social status, ideas of living, working). At most it might guide society gently when the architectural or urban designer proposes slight alternatives to the existing framework, when he or she offers alternatives to zoning, works within the public sector to shape planning and economic policies or offers alternative organizational strategies.[30] In whatever direction, architecture itself does not bring about radical removal of the *status quo*, but at most its alteration.

The Autonomous Position

An alternative to the dependent, context-bound position is the autonomous position, in which objects or systems are deliberately liberated from cultural, social, economic, historic, material, functional or other external contexts or "authorizations".[31] Autonomy in this sense is based on the conviction that the designed environment "is a self-contained project with its own legible, meaningful forms".[32] The designed object is derived from aesthetic principles that are separate and thus more fundamental than external factors, and therefore objects or systems are examined and analyzed to irreducible, internal principles.[33] These irreducible internal principles are akin to language and, like written language, can be studied in terms of syntax and semiotics. Abstract principles allow for architecture to attain a certain distance from external forces. They can act as a way to critique and develop architecture without those external forces and thus advance architectural production and thinking. The essential difference is that the autonomous object is considered in terms of its own internal language or form. When considered in this fashion, it offers the opportunity to see the form that can carry over and extend beyond current conditions to make more universal inferences. Unlike the gentle affirmation provided by the contextually determined object, the position of some theorists, such as Manfredo Tafuri and Theodor Adorno, is that only the autonomous object, separate from the *status quo* and its interests, can offer radically critical alternatives that challenge the *status quo*. While architectural theorists might agree that given the nature of architectural practice and production there can never be a completely autonomous position or object, quasi-autonomy does offer opportunities for clarification and examination of the object and its possible role within a given system.[34]

Formal Analysis

These two positions play an ever present role in analysis because how the designed environment is shaped, used and conceived parallels how we disassemble components and which analytical tools we employ. In approaching art, architecture or, in general, the designed environment critically, historians, analysts or architects walk a fine line in a critical approach. If the analysis leans heavily on a context-bound critique, the object is seen as a symptom or trace. If, on the other hand, the object is approached as autonomous form, the analysis becomes formalist.[35]

Analysis, as it breaks down complex systems into smaller components, comes to understand the forces that shaped those components (the materials, the culture, the economics), the inverse effect those systems have on forces (how they shape culture, economic and material choices) and the means that we use to understand the system (how we analyze, the methods we employ, the degree of inquiry). Essentially, in order to analyze a complex system we have to ask questions (method) about what makes it so (its nature) and its impact on others (its reciprocal impact). The method is varied and each polar extreme – autonomous or dependent – has its own methodological corollary.

The autonomous position has "formal analysis" as its corollary. Formal analysis, like the autonomously positioned object, focuses solely on the object's form – its organization, shape and patterns. Thus divorced from any external context, its internal language is independent. Rather than examine a designed object that was shaped by a particular economy, social system, technological and material limits or even functional mandate, formal analysis examines the object strictly in terms of its own language of form: instead of considering a house in terms of who built it, the materials that were used or who lived there, formal analysis looks at its abstract organization and language, so that the language of an object can be examined in terms of syntax (how the elements relate to one another) or semiotically (how the language creates meaning).

Developed in the mid-19th and early 20th century by art historians such as Aloïs Riegl, Heinrich Wölfflin and Paul Frankl, formal analysis of architecture came to the fore through Emil Kaufmann, Rudolf Wittkower, Colin Rowe and Manfredo Tafuri. Linked to Kantian considerations of autonomy and the examination of the fundamental opposition between external constraints and personal freedom, the critical analysis of a designed object vacillates between freed autonomy and the forces that constrain or shape it. For Kant, the aesthetic evaluation or critical analysis is one of process, the active process through which we become aware or conscious of the mental activity involved in the analysis. Essentially, any satisfaction or fulfillment we find in critically analyzing an object is not within the designed object itself but in the process of evaluation.[36] If, for example, we say an object is beautiful, the satisfaction implied in that judgment is not that the object is beautiful, but that we were able to actively analyze it. In the mid-20th century architects found that the formal principles in post-Functionalist architecture relied on or developed architecture based on autonomy of architectural language. In the 1960s and 1970s, architects such as Aldo Rossi and Peter Eisenman would embrace the autonomous position and related internalized language and its formal analysis as a means to find some substance in modern architecture, "something more permanent, essential, and universal" in architectural discourse and production.[37]

The formal analysis and linguistic approach to architectural language as separate from specific authorizations and dependencies allows for a focused view on those essential elements and their interrelationships. These languages are syntactical relationships of the elements within the project. Syntactically, the elements, materials, tectonics within a project can develop grammatical relationships between and among each other. Architects often describe a building's language using descriptive relationships that establish clearer divisions of complex systems. Often these relationships, such as "walls that enclose/walls that support", "planes that bend/planes that break" or "prospect/refuge", are relationships that allow the architect to step back and see the building as a series of bigger decisions within which the smaller, often more complex decisions might be made. Materials, for example, may be abstracted as "hard/soft", "natural/artificial" or "wood/metal" so that the architect can determine where types of materials might appear in some consistent or logical system that can be, if needed or desired, broken to embrace or emphasize particularly idiosyncratic moments. While many of these abstractions have an embedded reality and architects are aware of a material's characteristics and properties, the elemental abstraction nevertheless helps the designer filter out the material specifics in an effort to gain a broader sense of the interrelationships among materials, clarify the material palette, and then, often simultaneously, test those emerging abstracted linguistic systems against actual material qualities and assemblies.

Essentially, these relationships are syntactic rule systems, grammatical structures that allow the designer to develop a clear semiotic or symbolic system for the building. Architectural grammar becomes a guide to decision-making. Tadao Ando's work, especially his smaller houses and chapels, are deliberately syntactically clear: all walls are concrete, all metal is black, all floors are black slate, etc. The difficulty is extending a clear grammatical language to larger projects, which must adopt an appropriately complex language.

Context-bound Critical Analysis

The alter ego of formal analysis is context-bound critical analysis. Just as formal analysis has inherently abstract characteristics both in form and process, context-bound analysis is inherently nebulous and less easy to translate into any single analytical method or product. Context-bound analysis considers the dependent qualities of systems more than the formal organization and internal language. Rather than look exclusively at the formal ordering systems or the internal language of the object or system, this analysis converges on historical, cultural, social, economic and material conditions that surround the object. For instance, in order to understand J. R. R. Tolkien's *The Lord of the Rings* we would, the argument goes, have to analyze Tolkien's personal and professional experiences, his teachings, his previous and subsequent research and writing, his colleagues, the physical, political and cultural environment in Oxford or England in the early to mid-20th century and any number of influences both real or provisional. Often this analysis imposes our own interpretations on the work. Even while Tolkien admitted that the World Wars, like any experience, played an inevitable role in his work, he spent much time and effort disparaging those who claimed through their analyses that his three-part novel was allegorical.

Where does the context and its analysis end? Taken to its logical conclusion, analysis could extend to even the most miniscule contexts. In the short essay, "The Metterling Lists", Woody Allen's narrator analyzes the most recent and "stunning" publication of conjured novelist and playwright Hans Metterling: the long-awaited "Laundry Lists". These lists (published as an addendum to a four-volume *œuvre*) serve, the narrator argues, "as a perfect, near-total introduction to this troubled genius"; and he goes on to speculate on, among other facets, the significance of "1 sock" in Metterling's "*List No. 6*".[38] Allen goes fully tongue-in-cheek into the possible extreme of analysis in which even dirty laundry can be the vital context in understanding literary works.

For architecture, context-bound critical analysis can mean a study of those who patronized the architect, the social conditions that existed when the building was conceived, the economic conditions that led to the building or any number of external, albeit highly integrated, conditions. For example, a contextually bound analysis examines Mies van der Rohe's Barcelona Pavilion in the context of pre-Revolutionary Spain, of interwar Germany (the sponsor of the building) at the time of its conception, the role of construction technologies and methods available to Mies in Barcelona and how they contrasted with those in Germany, the value of materials used in its construction, the construction schedule and the economics of the building. Philosophical and theoretical issues such as symbolism in the choice of Mies, issues of reflectivity and mirror image, etc. are also important aspects to understanding the building's final form and use.

Although the manifold external influences and, in turn, the inverse shaping of them by the building (the role the Barcelona Pavilion played in shaping architectural thinking through photographs and sketches) are of great interest, for an architect these issues are usually both a matter of extreme focus and tangential to the design process, in that architectural historians generally focus on one or two of the many possible contexts to the exclusion of others. For the designer who balances formal ordering with the external influences nearly simultaneously there is a need for analysis that balances within an intermediary position and that can, at times, negotiate between formal analysis and context-bound analysis.

Analysis from a Dynamic Intermediate Position

It is doubtful that there is pure "formal analysis" which focuses entirely on an object's internal language, excluding all external forces. Likewise, any qualitative analysis that takes little notice of the formal and internal language is unlikely. Even more formal analyses associated with Colin Rowe or other theorists and architects are inclusive of the functional, environmental, economic and material nature of the built environment. Michael Podro notes in his book *The Critical Historians of Art* that "it may be that it is not possible to conduct the two inquiries independently of each other, but at any one time, any one writer's main concern can lie in one direction rather than another".[39] While both the formal analysis and context-bound analysis offer distinct advantages in discovering the underlying patterns and the forces that shaped those patterns, the separation of the two is, at times, difficult to maintain. Within a quasi-autonomous object there may be forces that play a mitigating role in its formal organization. For example, a mobile phone might be considered autonomously: its dimension, proportion, material, composition and other quantifiable characteristics might be considered with limited reference to outside forces. Yet the designer and manufacturer's choice of dimension, proportion, material and other "quantifiable" characteristics may be highly influenced by interconnected context. An aesthetic refinement and tactile interface may contribute to a positive user experience, but material availability, consumer habits and production costs may greatly inform its final form.

Rather than an "either/or" approach that embraces the polar extremes of pure autonomy or complete determination by context, architecture and its analysis tends toward the middle ground. Critical analysis tends to support a more flexible, "both/and" approach that is, as needed, formal *and* contextualized. To understand an iPad it is important to understand its formal organization just as it is important to study the economic, legal and social systems that contribute to its success. As Michael Hays notes: *"In order to know all we can about architecture we must be able to understand each instance of architecture, not as a passive agent of culture in its dominant ideological, institutional, and historical forms, nor as a detached, disinfected object. Rather we must understand it as actively and continually occupying a cultural place as an architectural intention with ascertainable political and intellectual consequences."*[40]

The analysis argued for in this book is one in which the designed world is both formal, autonomous architecture, but that is ultimately informed by the social, economic and political forces. These forces embed themselves semantically and physically into the architecture. An office building is just as much a system of patterns and proportions as it is a result of the economic, social and political forces. As a start, a building can be understood as a formal, material object separate from other forces. Ultimately, they have to be understood, analyzed and designed within a totality of forces.

Not All Sketches are Equal: Syntactic Sketch Diagrams

Before establishing links to the cognitive sciences and physiological research it is important to establish some understanding of analytical sketching. The focus of this research are syntactically dense, ill-structured and inherently ambiguous sketches that help interpret fundamental formal, spatial and tectonic codes that, in turn, help inform design processes.[41] These are sketches that translate "what is" in order to help formulate "what may be". The intention of these sketches is not completion or illustration, but design processing to help decode and encode while questioning and uncovering underlying systems. In so doing, they transliterate complex ideas into more simplified, mnemonic form.[42]

Syntactic sketches are linguistic doodles or explorations of thought conducive to translation and transformation in the design process. These are distinct from drafted architectural drawings or hard-line illustrations which research psychologist Vinod Goel maintains are types of "well-structured" representations.[43] These "well-structured" representations, Goel argues, are syntactically and semantically differentiated and disjoint, meaning that each symbol corresponds to only one thing (for example, in a drafted floor plan, a "round circle" is always a "column"). Like drafted plans, perspectives aim for correspondent representation and, therefore, are more "well-structured" representations. In contrast, ill-structured syntactic sketches, such as freehand diagrams and analytical sketches, have a greater ability to transform information from one state to another or distill a problem's variegated elements into definite categories.

Syntactic sketching is, fundamentally, an interaction of distinctly human physical and cognitive abilities in which the world is represented in symbol systems. In this representative interaction we project and manipulate material and spatial analogs. Through this physio-cognitive act we acquire knowledge that is both declarative and procedural, declarative knowledge being the "what" we know (such as specific dates, codes or locations), and procedural knowledge, the "how" something is executed (such as how we tie our shoes or use a fork). The division between these

knowledge types becomes ambiguous when knowledge becomes "both/and" – a particular skill and the performance of that skill, for example.[44]

Linking common knowledge to research in cognitive psychology affirms sketching's essential role in design education. With this cross-disciplinary approach, educators might develop pedagogies and methodologies beyond personal intuition and help clarify the considerable role of and, therefore, the need for analytical sketching in architectural design studio. Through the act and practice of putting substantive codes on paper and transforming ideas into a code language, which can then be discussed and eventually transformed into a design drawing, students start to engage in the cycle of action/reflection. In this cycle, physical sketching can be contemplated and revised while the student is engaging in design language in which the physical world is transformed and tested in an architectural coding. This learning by modeling architectural coding is akin to what psychologist Albert Bandura notes is a way of recalling and representing what is learned: "in order for observers to profit from the behavior models when they are no longer present to provide direction, the response patterns must be represented in memory in symbolic form."[45] Students learn the symbolic or representational methods of what they are observing in order for these to be consciously and unconsciously available to them in design practice studio. With a fundamental skill set – specific diagrams drawn with a specific method of line, tone or other pencil technique – the student is able to adapt these symbolic or representational methods to their own methods and their own representation.

Diagramming is something that must be taught not only to understand those things which are analyzed but to take advantage of both the analytical process and the product of the analysis, the diagram itself. Psychologists Jill Larkin and Herbert Simon found that "diagrams are useful only to those who know the appropriate computational processes for taking advantage of them. Furthermore, a problem solver often also needs the knowledge of how to construct a 'good' diagram" in order to benefit from its virtues.[46] Effective diagramming – diagramming that achieves its intended goals with minimal effort – depends upon learning, differentiating and understanding the nature of diagrams. Diagrams and the diagramming process are not as intuitive as they might appear.

What are Diagrams?

"What is a diagram?" While seemingly simple, the question and its answers are complex. This may come as a surprise to anyone who has followed furniture assembly instructions, considered aircraft emergency instruction cards or adhered to street signs. Cognitive scientists, art historians, architects and even diagramaticians have attempted to define a diagram but usually cannot agree on a particular definition nor the criteria to establish a diagram's parameters. For example, Vinod Goel, who has spent a career experimenting with designers and diagrams and is usually quite adept at describing and establishing criteria of research and experiments, endeavors throughout nearly the entire book *Sketches of Thought* to examine diagrams' characteristics and defining criteria.[47]

Any understanding of diagrams begins with an understanding of the nature of symbolic language and how their marks or lines denote particular concepts. This is most clearly explained by Nelson Goodman in his seminal book, *Languages of Art: An Approach to a Theory of Symbols*.[48] It is here that Goodman establishes a way to understand symbols and how those symbols help us see, understand and conceive the world. Essentially, Goodman argues that through analysis and diagrams we can decode experiences so that we can better conceive of and construct places or objects. This decoding is both within the symbol system itself and in the way those symbols imply and we infer meaning.

The fundamental aspect of Goodman's approach is that symbols are references or labels that represent ideas or concepts either directly or indirectly in different modes through *denotation* and *exemplification*. *Denotation* is that connection between a symbol or label and what it symbolizes or labels. Simply put, one thing denotes or refers to another thing: the letter "*x*" refers to object "*y*" because we agree that x denotes y. Denotation is the act of one thing referring to another. For example, an octagonal, red "STOP" sign denotes the concept "stop" because we, as a culture and society, agree to that relationship. While these denotations are labels and sometimes linguistic (letters or numerals), they are also pictorial and can include diagrams, drawings or musical notes that denote particular ideas or concepts. A second aspect of symbols is *exemplification*. Exemplification is a characteristic that refers back to a particular quality possessed by that which is labeled or, as Goodman notes: "Exemplification is possession plus reference."[49] The properties of a particular object determine the meaning of other objects of similar qualities. For example, a wall paint sample is an example of a color (it is a reference or symbol for a particular color), but because it possesses qualities or characteristics of that specific color it is said to exemplify it.

The denotation and exemplification are not static but often vary by context and natural transformation. Context alters the label or reference's meaning in the sense that where or when the label appears can have a great influence on its denotation. For instance, a particular word may mean one thing in one conversation or with one group of people, yet that same word may have a completely different meaning in a different situation. This is especially clear with homographs, which share the same spelling but have different meanings depending on context and pronunciation (e. g. "moderate" and "moderate", "separate" and "separate"), or homonyms, which sound the same but are spelled differently (e. g. "eight/ate", "wear/where"). Likewise, symbols transform and take on new, often unexpected meanings due to circumstance or culture as they combine with other

labels. A benign drawing or word can become inflammatory by an event or use or newly acquired association.

Symbols have syntactic and semantic properties. Properties are syntactical in that the form and arrangement of elements or the symbols represent a particular, even specific concept and any change in that organization or syntax alters their meaning. Semantic properties include how terms of symbols convey meaning. When someone remarks, "It's an issue of semantics", they are saying that it is a matter of how a particular symbol has different interpretations regardless of the way it is organized within a larger syntax. References or labels have varied degrees of specificity, but it is often best to begin with a symbol's most specific meaning. This is described by, among other things, its *disjointness* or the degree of unambiguity in the reading and interpretation of a particular symbol: one symbol means one thing. This is most easily visualized as an unsuccessful Venn diagram in which two or more circles do not overlap. The circles are, in a sense, not joined or are disjoined because each circle is of itself and its meaning is unambigous. Symbol systems have two types of disjointness: syntactic disjointness and semantic disjointness. *Syntactic disjointness* means that each mark aligns with no more than one character and exact differentiation is always possible.[50] There is little ambiguity between the label and its meaning, whereas non-notational systems are vague or ambiguous. *Semantic disjointness* indicates that the meaning is clearly differentiated so that it is possible to know what each symbol means.[51]

Disjointness in both symbols and their meaning becomes important in a fundamental way in relation to freehand drawing: they fail disjointness because freehand drawings, sketches and diagrams, by their nature, are inherently ambiguous or joined. Because they are inexact, they can denote and exemplify the designed environment ambiguously, yet are filled with a great deal of information. The freehand sketch can move from specific to vague with the flick of the pencil and thus offers opportunities for both specific and vague explorations, especially important in both interpretation and design. The line use compounded by freehand characteristics can help analyze complex situations, yet open a range of interpretations. A scribbled line can mean many things including material change, edge or window, and thus the symbol and its interpretation mutate both understanding and conception.

As representations, diagrams are characterized by their notational, procedural and efficiency qualities. First, diagrams are visuo-spatial notational systems (graphic) rather than linguistic notational systems (words, text, sentences). Visuo-spatial notations are, unlike photographically depictive representations, graphically simplified and not always visually similar to what they represent. As such, pictorial sketches, photographs, sentences or even words (including a STOP sign) would not be classified as diagrams. Goodman tries to explain it another way: he notes that the difference between a diagram and a picture (pictorial representation) is syntactic. A picture's structural features – the line types, shading, colors, etc. – cannot be ignored without losing the picture's essential nature.[52] By contrast, he argues, a diagram's features can be ignored and still the diagram can communicate and function. Augment lines or colors in a picture and the picture changes substantially, augment lines in a diagram and the diagram remains effective. Fortunately, Goodman qualifies this argument by noting that much of the difference is an issue of degree.[53] It should be noted that throughout his book, Goodman refers to diagrammatic line charts and graphs rather than design diagrams. This is important to note because much of an architectural diagram's effectiveness lies, in fact, in line types, tones or colors. In other words, an architectural diagram's meaning and effectiveness lies a great deal in whether a line is dashed or solid. The degree that Goodman refers to is indicated by his statement that "what matters with a diagram … is how we are to read it."[54] This implies that knowledge of a diagram's features or code plays a significant role in determining the effectiveness of the diagram and the diagramming process. Second, diagrams are procedural: they "explain how" a thing works rather than illustrating "what it is". Instead of documenting an inert thing with verisimilitude as its goal, a diagram is procedurally intentional. It describes the underlying schema, processes, organization or structure that contribute to the fundamental nature of what is being studied rather that the outward appearance.

Third, diagrams summarize complex systems with optimal effort. A diagram, especially one that is effective, is efficient in the amount of graphic notations, lines, tones or other graphic symbols in relation to the amount of information it explains. It is often frustrating to follow or even use minimalist diagrams. The information embodied and communicated must inform the designer and others without losing critical information and processes. Rather than minimal effort, the goal is optimal effort: the number of lines needed, no more, no less but that can be drawn quickly, repeatedly; yet can communicate to the designer or others without losing their effectiveness.[56]

These criteria could make other non-pictorial representations such as building plans, cross-sections or site plans qualify as diagrams; however, because these tend to be more complex representations, they are more representational than diagrammatic. The diagrams concerned here are those that are analog and graphical. They are graphics that are represented in such a way that they represent systems by analogy. The difference between a complicated diagram (a plan) and a simple diagram (a load diagram in a physics problem) is the number of lines or marks to represent the system. Both a "building plan" and a "plan diagram" represent a building's planar organization; however, a "plan diagram" explains "how it is organized" rather than what is or will be built.

How are Diagrams Used?

Architects encode information into a symbol system so that information can be absorbed, practiced and, in turn, retranslated into physical realties.[57] At a most rudimentary level, architects make plans (symbols), and someone or something (in the case of computer numerical control [CNC] machine tools) transforms those symbols into a built reality. Unfortunately, the information needed to make reality is exceedingly complex, so complex that the encoding symbol system must be only complex enough that it can be accessed and manipulated without extensive decoding. Syntactic sketching achieves this bridging because in diagramming it communicates and explores complex problems more effectively than numbers or words. It does this because a diagram's representational language has implicit meaning and is inherently procedural. The very act and art of diagramming is part of the problem-solving process. Jill Larkin and Herbert Simon note that the "advantages of diagrams, in our view, are computational. That is, diagrams can be better representations not because they contain more information, but because the indexing of this information can support extremely useful and computational processes."[58] Likewise psychologists Pierre Sachse, Winfried Hacker and Sven Leinert note that a significant advantage of sketching is reducing "the perceived difficulty of the problem and [achieving] an increase in the likelihood of correctly inferring relationships between the components."[59] That a sketch can adjust perception is important in architectural education as the demands or forces of a design project often overwhelm students. By assuring the perceived complexity and establishing the understanding that relationships can be found in and through sketching, students can begin to mold relationships among site, program elements and building systems.

Syntactic sketching works well because it links Working or Short Term Memory and Long Term Memory. Thinking and learning is an interchange between Working and Long Term Memory. The predominant understanding of Working Memory is that it is a system that encodes information so that a greater amount of information can be pulled into or stored in Long Term Memory. A predominant understanding or metaphor for Long Term Memory is a mental library where concepts are ordered in terms of interassociations.[60] This interlinked, networked library system has a series of specific nodes, each with corresponding characteristics (e. g. objects, properties). While each of us forms different network patterns and nodes based on personal experiences or associations, there are common predictive patterns, including for example "general to specific" (animal to cat) or "opposites" (small vs. large). While the Working Memory has speed and efficiency, it lacks capacity: it is incapable of holding more than 7 + 2 numbers of information and, even then, for only two seconds if unrehearsed.[61] An outcome of this "limited capacity" is an unconscious and conscious organizing of material into segments or chunks. An example of chunking is the length of telephone numbers and how they are remembered as one continuous number or in a series of numbers such as the area code, the exchange, the individual's specific numbers, then the particular extension. Chunking essentially categorizes information into specific notational forms, such as mnemonic devices, that operate with Working Memory's limited capacity.[62]

The closer the specific chunking method aligns with the way it will eventually be used, the more effective the process will be overall. Larkin and Simon note that we would "be unable to recognize knowledge that is relevant to a situation and retrieve it [from memory] if the situation is not presented in a representation matching the form of existing productions".[63] For example, diagramming existing buildings or sites using varied diagram types is more likely to inform a multitude of design processes that require varied and simultaneous thinking and representations. If we limit the sketch type, we limit the chunking process, our recall ability and thus limit our design exploration. A sketch diagram gives focus because it holds more information that the mind can hold at one time. It is a virtual note card of bite-sized chunks.

Just as sketching encodes and holds information, it also helps resolve multilayered complex concepts and forms nearly simultaneously.[64] This simultaneous processing is necessary in architecture because there are multiple issues, ideas and forces that need resolution in a design problem or, seen from another perspective, because architecture and design is the simultaneous layering of systems, forms and spaces. The design process and the completed design are compositions of simultaneity. Establishing a thinking process that models this simultaneity, therefore, is consequential for the design student. Larkin and Simon write that those who actively use diagrams in a design process "embed" the design procedure into the diagram itself, where "reasoning is carried out 'intuitively'".[65] By learning, developing and working within a sketch, the actual procedure of design becomes increasingly internalized, integrated and intuitive. The diagram sketch moves beyond an issue of skill to an issue of thinking through problems. In architectural design, learning to draw and learning to design is dependent upon the "task domain" used. The manner in which we acquire information shapes the thinking process. Sketching, by its very nature, is simultaneously and ambiguously layered information and transformation and, therefore, uniquely suited for the process involving simultaneity, ambiguity, layered information and transformation that is architectural design.[66] The value of sketching is its similarity to the simultaneous dualities in architecture: legible/illegible, fixed/malleable, opaque/transparent. In essence, it is an ability to oscillate between "both/and" without complex, external moves.

This ability – drawing, reading and transforming complex simultaneities – is in itself so complex that it has become a model for artificial intelligence. Computer software and hardware designers have continued to examine the human process of sketching and working with sketches as a model for artificial intelligence because the concept of simultaneous "both/and" remains unworkable for current computer programs. The ability to conceive of, process and represent simultaneous, multiple and sometimes conflicting data is difficult for a computer.

Developing Spatial Knowledge and Material Analogies

The layered information embedded in diagrams begins to link the drawing to the material and assembly processes, which they denote and exemplify in a kind of material-analog. Establishing these material-analog codes through sketching is especially vital in architectural design because the act of sketching is analogous to the act of material assemblies and systems.[67] The actual sketch process is a series of stages building upon one another so that, ultimately, the drawn form is a complete assembly. By sketching the built environment as an assembly, or disassembly, of form, the student is able to ingest the process and familiarize him- or herself with the process in the design studio. Diagramming a building or other designed object is quasi-mimicry of assemblies – it replicates design and assembly sequences. Alan Parkin notes in *Memory: Phenomena, Experiment and Theory* that "the imageability of material greatly influences how well something will be remembered, and instructions to use imagery greatly enhance retention."[68] With an image of assembly the student is more able to recall and use processes when developing their own layered design systems. Rather than seeing a design as an emerging fully resolved, homogenous form, the architecture student begins to see the design as part of, and linked to, existing systems or emerging from layered systems. For example, a student who sketches structure, program, site, façade, mechanical systems and lighting as fabrication and weaving will internalize this and bring it unconsciously into the design studio. Just as a writer learns style and prose by reading and digesting a book, so can the architect read, digest, take apart, emulate the architecture in his or her own design sketching and design process.

In laying out a sketch, the designer comes to understand the overall organization of parts to the whole, the mapping of designs and the process. The mapping helps students train their eye to see and ultimately produce underlying patterns in design. By seeing how something is complex, composed and ordered, the student becomes familiar with composing and ordering in the design studio. Through the architectural tartans students begin to engage in both declarative knowledge (knowing what) and procedural knowledge (knowing how) for the architectural design process through addition, subtraction and overlay. By taking a building apart and seeing the parts as they relate to a whole, students are able to experience vicariously the design of the building they are witnessing. Although the design act cannot be replicated, by engaging in the work through sketching the student can come to some understanding of the complexity of the solution or the levels of study needed to resolve multiple forces into a unified whole.[69]

This physical mapping continues to inform the design studio because the method used to gather knowledge is likewise the principal way to recall or apply information.[70] When students diagram an observed building, the diagramming method is an analogy to the design drawing. Drawing layered hierarchical tartans mimicks and reinforces the material layering and assembly into a unified whole through "hierarchical representations" that reinforce decisionmaking and procedures.[71] For example, structural systems are assemblies of primary, secondary and tertiary structural elements working in conjunction. Other systems, such as curtain walls, are layered upon the structural system. Like a tartan, these systems are simultaneously interfaced. This fabrication analogy extends to a building's complex, unified multifaceted material and spatial systems.

Within the material system there are the conceptual and literal spatial systems. Spatial or functional zones of paths/rooms, public/private zones, service/served spaces, etc. are often layered upon one another in a shared, interdependent tartan with those of material, structural and environmental systems. There are, of course, exceptions to the layered systems in buildings, but for beginning design students the concept of these as unified systems is fundamental in organizing the complexity of a design project. Diagramming the plans of a building in which the walkways correspond to service/served spaces, to the HVAC duct work and to public/private functions are lessons in how multiple uses or functions are interrelated and unified in a complex building.

Sketching as a Physical Analogy
As mentioned in the Introduction, students often ask: "Why is it essential to sketch a building on site rather than sketch from a photograph?" Though this question has broader implications, including the necessity of travel in design education and spatial awareness, the more immediate answer connects to physical and experiential processes. Since sketching helps us learn from "what is" into "what may be", sketching in situ is a bodily interaction with the building, site or object. We engage the building more than by looking at it from a distance. Because we engage with it we not only see it but interact with it as a real thing. And since we design and eventually build real things it is necessary to learn from the world by engaging in its reality, its material, its volume, its smell, its temperature.

Because we physically engage with drawing in a way that literally touches a stylus to surface, we engage in analog manipulation, identification or transformation.[72] By engaging in the physical act of sketching in situ, students can develop both a conscious and unconscious link between pattern-finding, pattern repetition, symbolic language and the design process as an experience. Mapping "what is" prepares the student for creating new maps of "what might be". When students sketch a designed object or at a site, they engage in a physical act – they are representing thoughts on paper and are interacting with the building or site, and they see and walk through a three-dimensional reality. This reality connects them, through sketching, to a future reality. Students begin to learn, appreciate and feel comfortable with the role of action in the design process while developing muscular facilitation or "muscle memory" so that the act becomes unconscious.

Studies have shown that familiarity with map-making – sketching building plans or neighborhood maps – has a significant impact on developing and tuning spatial knowledge.[73] Those who use and make learn and perform better "in understanding spatial relations within the environment" than those who use no map or, in the case of one experiment, those learning with "walk thru" technology. Though participants that used digital walk-thru programs did develop spatial comprehension, they usually did "not accumulate sufficient knowledge to perform rudimentary tasks, e. g. retracing their routes, giving general descriptions of what they found along the way, telling others how to get from point A to point B without error, or knowing where [places or landmarks] are in relation to other places."[74]

Essentially, map-making not only helps retrace existing conditions, but prepares for anticipating spatial conditions, connecting imperceptible but actual patterns, communicating spatial ideas to others and developing a sense of direction in unfamiliar surroundings.

25 Le Corbusier, *Creation is a Patient Search*. New York: Praeger (1960): 37.

26 Alexander, C., *Notes on the Synthesis of Form*. Cambridge: Harvard University Press (1964): 6.

27 Podro, Michael, *The Critical Historians of Art*. New Haven: Yale University Press (1982): xviii-xx

28 Hays, K. Michael, "Critical Architecture: Between Culture and Form", *Perspecta* 21 (1984): 16.

29 *Ibid.*

30 Nesbitt, Kate. *Thrizing A New Agenda for Architecture*. New York: Princeton Architectural Press (1996): 59.

31 Vidler, Anthony. *Histories of the Immediate Present: Inventing Architectural Modernism*. Cambridge: MIT Press (2008): 55.

32 Osman, Michael, Ruedig, Adam, Seidel, Matthew and Tilney, Lisa, "Editors' statement", *Perspecta* 33 (2002): 7.

33 Podro, Michael. *The Critical Historians of Art*. New Haven: Yale University Press (1982): xviii.

34 Anderson, Stanford, "Quasi-Autonomy in Architecture: The Search for an 'In-Between'", *Perspecta* 33 (2002): 31.

35 Podro, Michael, *The Critical Historians of Art*. New Haven: Yale University Press (1982): xx.

36 *Ibid.*: 10-11.

37 Eisenman, Peter, "Autonomy and the Will to the Critical", *Assemblage* 41 (2000): 91.

38 Allen, Woody, "The Metterling Lists" in: *Getting Even*. New York: Random House (1966): 3-12.

39 Podro, Michael, *The Critical Historians of Art*. New Haven: Yale University Press (1982): xvii.

40 Hays, K. Michael, "Critical Architecture: Between Culture and Form", *Perspecta* 21 (1984): 27.

41 Goel, Vinod, "Ill-Structured Representations for Ill-Structured Problems", in: *Proceedings of the Fourteenth Annual Conference of the Cognitive Science Society*. Hillsdale: Lawrence Erlbaum Associates (1992): 844-846.

42 *Ibid.*

43 *Ibid.*: 846-847.

44 Akin, Ömer, *Psychology of Architectural Design*. London: Pion (1986): 32-33.

45 Bandura, Albert, *Social Learning Theory*. Englewood Cliffs: Prentice Hall (1977): 25.

46 Larkin, Jill H. and Simon, Herbert A., "Why a Diagram is (Sometimes) Worth Ten Thousand Words", *Cognitive Science* 11 (1) (1987): 99.

47 Goel, Vinod, *Sketches of Thought*. Cambridge: MIT Press (1995): 145.

48 Goodman, Nelson. *Languages of Thought: An Approach To A Theory of Symbols*. Indianapolis: Hackett Publishing Company, Inc. (1976): 59.

49 *Ibid.*: 53.

50 Goel, Vinod, "Ill-Structured Representations for Ill-Structured Problems", in: *Proceedings of the Fourteenth Annual Conference of the Cognitive Science Society*. Hillsdale: Lawrence Erlbaum Associates (1992): 844-845.

51 *Ibid.*

52 Goodman, Nelson, *Languages of Thought: An Approach To A Theory of Symbols*. Indianapolis: Hackett Publishing Company, Inc. (1976): 229.

53 *Ibid.*: 230.

54 Goodman, Nelson, *Languages of Art: An Approach to a Theory of Symbols*. Indianapolis: Bobbs-Merrill (1968): 170.

56 Larkin, Jill H. and Simon, Herbert A., "Why a Diagram is (Sometimes) Worth Ten Thousand Words", *Cognitive Science 11* (1) (1987): 98-99.

57 Akin, Ömer. *Psychology of Architectural Design*. London: Pion (1986): 20-22.

58 Larkin, Jill H. and Simon, Herbert A., "Why a Diagram is (Sometimes) Worth Ten Thousand Words", *Cognitive Science* 11 (1) (1987): 99.

59 Sachse, Pierre, Hacker, Winfried and Leinert, Sven, "External Thought – Does Sketching Assist Problem Analysis?", *Applied Cognitive Psychology* 18 (2004): 415.

60 Driscoll, Marcy P., *Psychology of Learning for Instruction*. Boston/London: Allyn and Bacon (1999): 93-106.

61 *Ibid.*: 88-93.

62 *Ibid.*: 89.

63 Larkin, Jill H. and Simon, Herbert A., "Why a Diagram is (Sometimes) Worth Ten Thousand Words", *Cognitive Science* 11 (1) (1987): 70-71.

64 *Ibid.*: 78.

65 *Ibid.*: 81.

66 Goel, Vinod, "Ill-Structured Representations for Ill-Structured Problems", in: *Proceedings of the Fourteenth Annual Conference of the Cognitive Science Society*. Hillsdale: Lawrence Erlbaum Associates (1992): 849; and Fish, J. and Scrivener, S. A. R., "Amplifying the Mind's Eye: Sketching and Visual Cognition", *Leonardo* 23, no. 1 (1990): 118-120.

67 Parkin, Alan J., *Memory: Phenomena, Experiment and Theory*. Oxford: Blackwell (1993): 105-109.

68 *Ibid.*: 118.

69 Do, Ellen Yi-luen and Gross, Mark D., "Thinking with Diagrams in Architectural Design", *Artificial Intelligence Review* 15 (2001): 135-136.

70 Driscoll, Marcy P., *Psychology of Learning for Instruction*. Boston: Allyn and Bacon (1994): 85-87.

71 Parkin, Alan J., *Memory: Phenomena, Experiment and Theory*. Oxford: Blackwell (1993): 105-109; and Wilson, Frank R., *The Hand: How Its Use Shapes the Brain, Language and Human Culture*. New York: Pantheon Books (1998): 167.

72 Jeannerod, Marc, *The Cognitive Neuroscience of Action*. New York: Wiley-Blackwell (1997): 119-121; and Wilson, Frank R., *The Hand: How Its Use Shapes the Brain, Language and Human Culture*. New York: Pantheon Books (1998): 164-181.

73 Golledge, Reginald G., Dougherty, Valerie and Bell, Scott, "Acquiring Spatial Knowledge: Survey Versus Route-Based Knowledge In Unfamiliar Environments", *Annals of the Association of American Geographers* 85, no.1 (1995): 154-155.

74 *Ibid.*: 154.

Sketching in Axonometric

An effective method to analyze the designed environment is through axonometric drawings. Axonometrics are three-dimensional representation that, unlike perspectives, maintain all the dimensions and proportions of the space. In axonometrics, at least three sides of a space or form can be seen simultaneously. For example, the floor and two walls are drawn at the same time. This simultaneity has a great advantage in that it promotes three-dimensional thinking in the analytical and design process. As a three-dimensional Cartesian framework, complex shapes can be mapped as points and then connected with lines to form planes. For example, circles can be mapped within the x-y-z grid to generate cylinders, spheres, domes, arches or cones. Likewise diagonals, curved planes, steps, subtractions and additions. While there are several types of axonometric drawings, the two most common are the plan oblique and the isometric.

A plan oblique is an axonometric in which the plan or the horizontal plane remains true to its geometric shape:

things that are square, circular, oval or of another geometry in the horizontal plane remain square, circular, etc. yet are rotated 30 to 45 degrees from the vertical. Once rotated, vertical lines project up and remain parallel to shape the volumetric form. Isometrics are similar to the axonometric; however, the horizontal plane's interior angles are obtuse to give the illusion of perspective or a more life-like view. If it is square, the plan becomes a parallelogram. For example, a square plan or horizontal plane in an isometric "flattens" so that its interior angles are between 110 and 120 degrees. As in the plan oblique, the plan rotates and verticals remain true and vertical and parallel, as do all lines parallel to the horizontal plane's geometry.

Once the fundamental rules are understood, the plan oblique and isometric can be used to study complex spatial forms and three-dimensional objects through addition, subtraction, superimposition and point-line-plane mapping. The important things to recall are that the

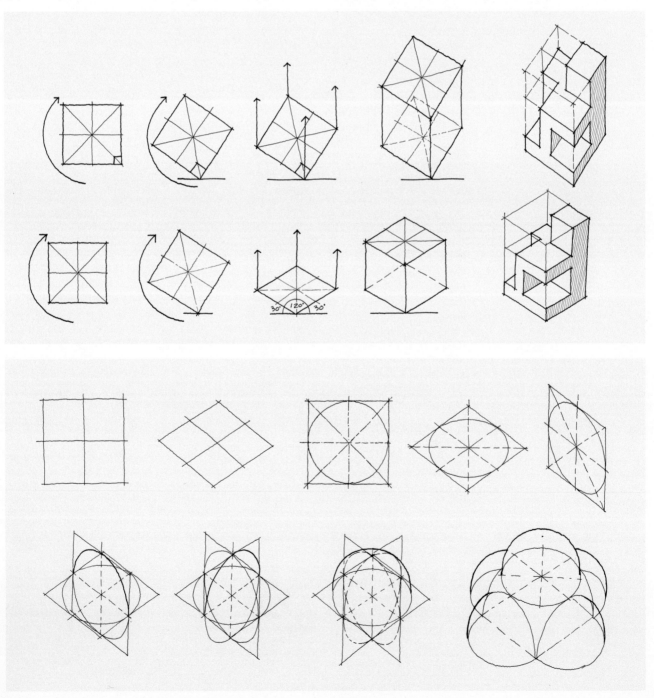

axonometric is a three-dimensional Cartesian grid with the corresponding fundamental geometry: circles are superimposed on squares; cylinders are extruded circles; vaults are bisected cylinders; cones are cylinders that taper to a single point; domes and spheres are rotated circles. Cubes are extruded squares; pyramids are cubes that taper to one point. More complex shapes such as curved or undulating surfaces simply require mapping out the nadir and apex of sine curves or connecting fundamental shapes with diagonals.

Axonometrics are often confusing and disorienting. It is sometimes difficult to discern up from down or front from back. Additionally, while a circle is superimposed on a square, if the square is a parallelogram, then the circle is an oval. Once mastered, however, the thinking behind the process is enhanced and the drawing as a tool of transformation, abstraction and communication is valuable.

Opposite page:
Top: Plan oblique (upper range) and isometric (lower range)
Bottom: Isometric construction of a dome and half domes

Top left: One quadrant of a dome in plan oblique
Top right: Plan oblique
Bottom left: Isometrics of a mixed-use apartment building
Bottom right: Transparent and exploded isometric of a barrel-vaulted townhouse

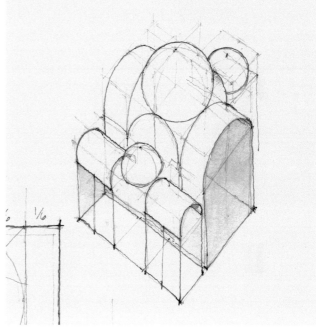

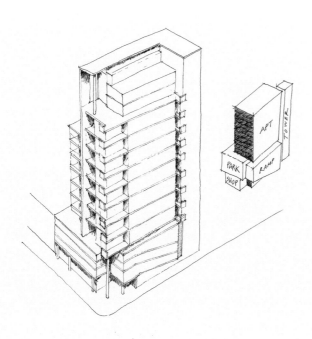

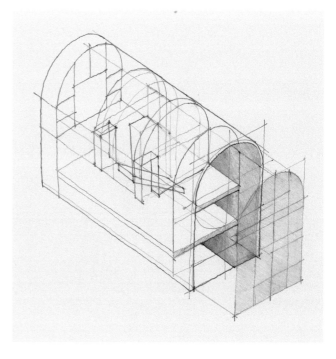

Putting Things in Perspective

Perspectives are contrived representations just as plans, axonometrics or other planometric drawings. Like planometric drawings, perspectives offer particular, two-dimensional depictions of existing or imaginary reality that, seemingly, closely approximate how we perceive the world. In linear perspectives, lines and masses diminish toward the horizon and in aerial perspectives things nearby seem clearer while things farther away appear increasingly pale. Like planometric drawings, perspectives can be the basis for analytical studies and diagrams. The significant caveat, however, is the tendency, especially for novice designers, to use perspectives to imitate or replicate rather than abstract reality. Perspectives can be a naive, if unintentional, way to recreate the world rather than examine and interpret it. Verisimilitude or literalness can dominate and interfere with processing, decoding and otherwise diagramming complex systems.

That is not to say perspectives are inherently un-analytical. Experienced designers use perspectives to study, decipher and propose yet, more than likely, use them in combination with other analytical tools. When used as one tool among many they can cultivate the interchange between literal and abstract. There is an understanding that the perspective is a tool that offers the illusion of three-dimensional space and has, like other tools, inherent limits. Essentially, it is the difference between those who mimic consciously and a parrot that is unaware that it is mimicking. Likewise, just as perspectives have an inclination toward literalness, planometric or reductive diagrams generate dominating abstraction, a distancing from the sense or character of place or, at worst, a dehumanizing of experience. Formal patterns and their unearthing become self-referential and indifferent to human experience.

The benefits of perspective diagramming are within that caveat. Studying volumetric fluctuations, shade and shadow, textures, scale or changes in aerial and linear perspective can bridge the gap between formal and experiential analysis. For example, entering the Acropolis

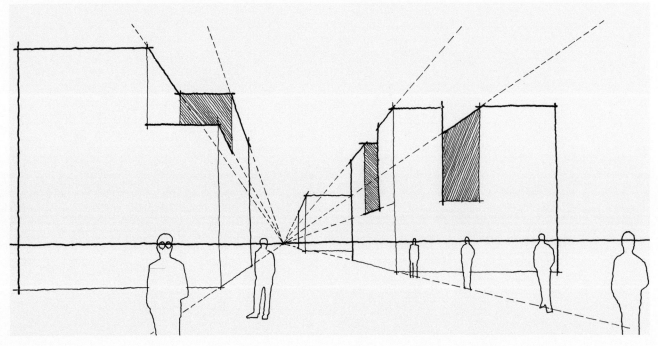

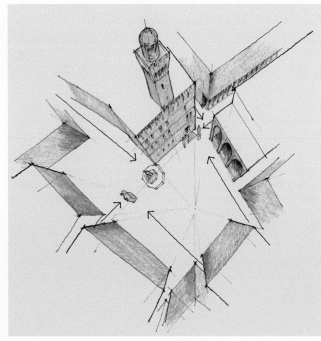

in Athens is (or was) through a series of spaces of changing vistas, partially obscured views and frames. Studying these in plan alone would not uncover the way in which the temples were designed and arranged. Additionally, a façade's or room's perceived proportions are influenced by the observer's point of view. Movement through Peter Zumthor's Therme Vals bath complex is highly dependent on reflectivity, light and atmosphere that a perspective diagrams would help both appreciate and comprehend. When sketching perspectives, it is good to remember the connection to other constructed representations. They have specific rules that, once understood and practiced, can help transfer or imagine three-dimensional space onto a two-dimensional surface and, likewise, help decode and encode the design environment. I recommend other texts on the theoretical underpinnings or accurate perspective construction, but below are tips for sketching freehand perspectives in the field.

Opposite page:
Top: One-point perspective. All lines are perpendicular to the view diminish to one vanishing point. Lines parallel to the view remain orthogonal
Bottom left: A street framing Florence's Duomo
Bottom right: Diagram of enclosure and entry alignments

Top: Two-point perspective. Horizontal lines diminish to two vanishing points on the horizon. Vertical lines remain vertical
Bottom left: Sketch of a street corner in Prague
Bottom right: Massing analysis (drawing by Todd Ray)

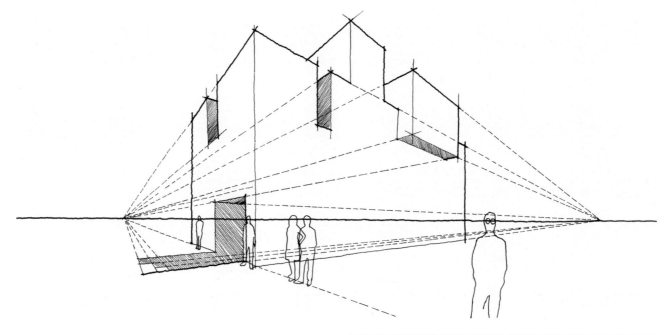

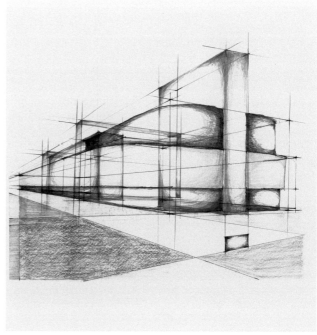

Sketching and Learning

With sketching and thinking comes learning. Learning would be said to have occurred when specific acquired knowledge can be effectively applied to otherwise unexpected conditions. Learning can also be characterized as the realization through reflective interrogation that, indeed, learning has occurred and that lessons are in fact helping to solve problems, resolve questions or raise further questions. Essentially, we know we have learned something when we realize we have learned it.

By its tactile, physical and mental nature, syntactic sketching helps move us into reflective interrogation in which we speculate and question hidden solutions, and in turn supports active participation in a design thinking process.[75] While inherently reflective, syntactic sketching and associated reflection exercises through experience do not come naturally but must be "fostered and coached" so that experience can directly and indirectly inform the design studio.[76] Part of this fostering and coaching is engaging students in questions about architecture that are tangential to their own design process, so that the students become more familiar with design reflection as a thinking process.[77] Although links between questioning and reflecting in field sketching and design studio are not always distinct, establishing a familiar process of reflection is a meaningful step. By promoting and instructing introspective sketching while linking it with a design sketch, the student will begin to associate the two realms. Finally, when students engage in meta-cognitive thinking in which they become conscious of their learning, they begin to see that what they are doing is actually learning. Students who recognize reflective learning through sketching and link questioning to other aspects of their education are more likely to apply gained knowledge to varied and unplanned situations. This meta-cognition, or the awareness or understanding that cognitive development or learning is transpiring, is a level at which reflective learning becomes relevant to other situations. With architectural sketching, the relevance of the reflection process, the declarative and procedural knowledge and the process of layering information become increasing relevant to the design studio. While addressing ideas in the field, students begin to see that the process of discovery and the information they attain is relevant to the design studio process.

A second finding that supports sketching in design learning, especially its early phases, is that by Vinod Goel, who experimented with designers using digital or freehand drawing. Goel's objective was not to critique design quality but understand the design process, so that the development of ideas, the variation of ideas and the stream of development are tests of design processes regarding their potential to promote multiple solutions to complex problems.[78] Goel describes design development in terms of lateral transformation and vertical transformation: "Lateral transformation is one where movement is from one idea to a slightly different idea rather than a more detailed version of the same idea. A vertical transformation is one where movement is from one idea to a more detailed version of the same idea."[79] In the experiment, Goel divided equally adept designers into two groups: one that would use only a digital drawing program to design and another group asked only to sketch, allowing each group ample time to "train" in each tool. Each person in the group was asked to solve a design problem in a given time frame. Goel found that between computers and freehand there was little statistical difference in the number of attempts at design ideas. Essentially, both groups were able to produce drawings and designs. However, and more importantly, there were significant differences in the content and development between those designers who used ambiguous tools (freehand sketching) and those who used computers, most especially in the preliminary stages of design.[80] What Goel discovered was that design explorations and studies of dissimilar variations were much greater in number among freehand designers. Although each team produced a statistically equal number of images, the freehand designers produced nearly five times the number of different design ideas, or lateral design transformations, within sketches. In effect, the computer-based designers established a design early and then repeated and refined their design. The computer drawing tool actually seems to decrease design exploration and development of alternative solutions because the degree of ambiguity in the designs was significantly lower in the computer drawings. The drawings were clearer and more complete and thus gave the misimpression that the design was clear and complete.[81]

With the skill of drawing that is both conscious and unconscious, the student is more able to use drawing as a tool for thinking through design. Drawing becomes part of an internal conversation.[82] As we are aware, the ability to resolve the multiple forces of an architectural design is a mix of experience and flexibility of thinking. Much of it comes from the interaction of both procedural and declarative knowledge. If, therefore, design is about experience and thinking, then drawing what we see is an engagement with experience and possible organizational strategies. Also, given that our short-term memory is only able to recall five to seven pieces or chunks of information at one time, the sketch allows us to note and diagram throughout the process. We are chunking, i. e. noting so we do not forget where we were or where we are in the sketch.[83]

Although it is an act in itself, sketching is also a way of thinking. As such, its usefulness is its ability to be part of the action and reflection cycle – sometimes nearly simultaneously. Schön describes this as a conversation with the drawing, an aspect developed by David Kolb into an "Experiential Learning Cycle".[84] In this cycle the learner's (or in the case of practicing, the ever-learning designer's), ideas and studies flow in a continuous loop of abstract conceptualizing to active experimentation, to concrete experiencing of the experience, to reflective observation and back to abstract conceptualizing. The significant point is that divisions between action and reflection blur: observation, recording, reflecting and design are continuously informing each other, allowing for a progression of learning and development – a cycle manifests itself in the analytical sketching.[85] The sketch forms what is observed, which in turn informs the evolution of the sketch. The sketching act, therefore, moves from conscious to unconscious action, allowing the designer to think through and explore through the drawing.

Likewise, Bandura's theory claims that learning occurs through an interdependent interaction of environmental stimuli and reactions to those stimuli. His "social learning theory" posits that environment is something with which we interact: we observe it, it informs us and likewise our informed selves influence or shape that environment.[86] First associated with mimicking the actual actions in a social situation, Bandura's theory on Reciprocal Determinism can be extended to learning from observing the results of those actions in which "behavior, other personal factors, and environmental factors all operate as interlocking determinants of each other."[87] This feedback loop extends Behaviorists' arguments of stimulus-response learning by including our thinking, our past experiences and our ability to reflect upon a given situation or stimulus. Unlike the more "fatalistic" Behaviorist point of view according to which we are in a one-way stimuli-determine-action learning operation, Bandura believes interaction more accurately represents how we learn from observation and experience. Moreover, this learning is favorable to unpredictable learning and as a result more self-perpetuating as personal interaction or growth comes from the learner.[88] The key here is that we actively interact with, observe, and in a cyclical fashion learn from our environment. Observation, however, should be understood or employed, as psychologist John Dewey believes, as an "active process" in which "observation is exploration, inquiry for the sake of discovering something previously hidden and unknown, this something being needed in order to reach some end, practical or theoretical".[89] It is through sketching of the designed environment that students engage in this sort of reflection and observation interaction. As teachers who must help students along this path of learning, we must fully engage the students' observational learning. In this light, it is helpful to evaluate Bandura's four-step processes of learning, which are Attentional, Retention, Motor Reproduction and Motivational.[90] Starting with what Bandura termed the "Attentional Processes" wherein the students' attention to what they are learning is a key, if obvious, part of the learning process – the student must pay attention; anything that interferes with maintaining attention is going to diminish the observational learning. Second, students must retain the information or lessons learned. It is at this stage that students use coded language or, in the case of sketching, diagrams or other representation systems to record their observations. At this stage, students chunk or engage in apperceptive activities by organizing material into categories and through this act, digest the material for the next stage: Motor Reproduction. In the Motor Reproduction stage students apply the encoded information to new situations. Students transform

and test the knowledge that in turn incorporates the learned material into active part of his or her thinking or problem-solving process. Finally, and most importantly, there are the Motivational processes. The student must be motivated to learn. Without motivation, students do not have an incentive to participate in the learning process. Moreover, motivation most easily affects success or failure in the students' learning process. Motivation to learn can be positive or negative, stated or internal and must be understood and incorporated into any learning strategy.

The degree of ambiguity plays an important role in design as it allows designers to read drawings differently. Unlike the computer drawing that quickly shows an exact and polished image, the sketch is naturally rough and never really complete. Likewise, the design explored in freehand prevents "early fixation or crystallization" and thus can be interpreted and moved into lateral transformations.[91] Learning is facilitated by the growing ability to balance clear communication skills with the need and use of ambiguity for development of design ideas and design thinking. Essentially, a design education that allows for clarity and skill development must also allow a process that promotes creative development. Sketching does this because it is inherently ambiguous. It must be taught, must be nurtured, must be refined, but it must be open to variation.

75 Polanyi, Michael, *The Tacit Dimension.* London: Routledge and Kegan (1966): 22-24.

76 Moon, Jennifer, *Reflection and Learning in Professional Development.* London: Kogan Press (1999): 9.

77 *Ibid.*

78 Goel, Vinod, *Sketches of Thought.* Cambridge: MIT Press (1995): 211-213.

79 *Ibid.*: 193-195.

80 Goel, Vinod, "Ill-Structured Representations for Ill-Structured Problems", in: *Proceedings of the Fourteenth Annual Conference of the Cognitive Science Society.* Hillsdale: Lawrence Erlbaum Associates (1992): 846.

81 *Ibid.*: 849.

82 Schön, D. A., *The Reflective Practitioner: How Professionals Think in Action.* New York: Basic Books (1983): 79.

83 Akin, Ömer, *Psychology of Architectural Design.* London: Pion (1986): 17-19.

84 Kolb, D. A., *Experiential Learning: Experience as the Source Of Learning and Development.* Englewood Cliffs: Prentice-Hall (1984): 40-43.

85 Goldschmidt, Gabriela, "The Dialectics of Sketching", *Creativity Research Journal* 4, no. 2 (1991): 140. Also see: Tversky, Barbara; Suwa, Masaki; Agrawala, Maneesh; Heiser, Julie; Stolte, Chris; Hanrahan, Pat; Phan, Doantam; Klingner, Jeff; Daniel, Marie-Paule; Lee, Paul and Haymaker, John, "Sketches for Design and Design of Sketches", *Human Behavior in Design: Individuals, Teams, Tools.* Lindemann, Udo, ed., Berlin: Springer (2003): 79-81.

86 Bandura, Albert, *Social Learning Theory.* Englewood Cliffs: Prentice Hall (1977): 24-25.

87 *Ibid.*: 9-10.

88 *Ibid.*: 24-25.

89 Dewey, John, *How We Think.* Boston: D.C. Heath & Co. (1933): 252.

90 Bandura, Albert, *Social Learning Theory.* Englewood Cliffs: Prentice Hall (1977): 22-29.

91 Goel, Vinod, *Sketches of Thought.* Cambridge: MIT Press (1995): 218.

The Exquisite Corpse

Composing a sketchbook page might seem more like an aesthetic or logistical concern, however, composition can be an opportunity to develop observational abilities and drawing skills that, in turn, help relate diagrams to one another within an analytical narrative. More importantly, compositional methods and the related drawing skills can help develop contextual and simultaneous perceptions and complex design processes. Various composition strategies can help with this and more. For example, establishing a consistent underlying grid for the entire sketchbook can help start each page while unifying the entire sketchbook. Or asking identical or similar questions and then drawing related diagrams at each site can help develop a rigorous analytical method.

One compositional method I encourage is the *Exquisite Corpse*. Based on the Surrealist collaborative party game, the *Exquisite Corpse* compositional process embraces accident, ambiguity and organic development to help create a complex and unpredictable whole. The sketch-book page and, hopefully, a more comprehensive analysis emerges from a series of developmental steps or responsive design moves. In the actual *Exquisite Corpse* game, Player One begins by drawing on one edge of a sheet and then, when finished, folds the sheet to obscure all but two small lines of that drawing. Player One then hands the sheet to Player Two. Player Two begins a drawing starting from the two exposed lines and, when finished, folds the sheet and passes it to Player Three and so on. After the last player finishes, Player One unfolds the entire sheet to reveal the composite, if surreal, drawing. Similarly, a sketchbook page can be a gradual accretion of responsive drawings that both generate a more holistic view of place and prompt design thinking.

The sketchbook page develops from reading, analyzing and responding to context: Drawing One prompts Drawing Two upon which is added Drawing Three. Analogous to sites or other existing conditions within which a design responds and develops, the sketchbook page and each

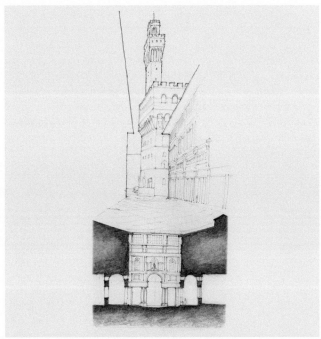

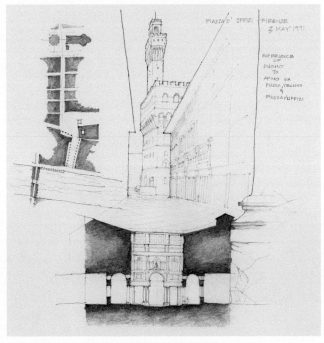

added drawing are particular conditions with noticeable and obscured forces to be studied and analyzed to help resolve often conflicting and complex problems into a unified whole. Even the apparently blank page has its edges, proportion and binding to which a first drawing might relate. For example, a horizontal façade might work better along the page's length. (Usually, guidelines for the first diagram should fit within about one third of a page so that there's room to extend the drawing if needed). Rather than a preconceived total composition, the layout grows organically as each drawing responds to the experience and to the sheet itself.

Deliberately changing the lenses – the drawing type or scale and even the media – helps encourage understanding of a place. Accepting, even encouraging, overlapped and juxtaposed drawings engenders simultaneous "both/and" drawing and thinking. At once clear and ambiguous yet differentiated with subtle line weight, tone or texture variations, simultaneous compositions can help develop a

familiarity and perhaps even comfort with the ambiguity essential for architectural design thinking.

Opposite page clockwise from upper left:
The stages of the page's development

Clockwise from upper left:
Pages with more organic compositions:
Casa Malaparte
(drawing by Christopher Testa)
Ljubljana Fountain
(drawing by Joshua Jacques)
Turkish houses
(drawing by Eric Jenkins) and
Palácio Pombal
(drawing by Josh Humphries)

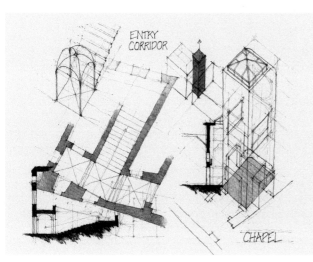

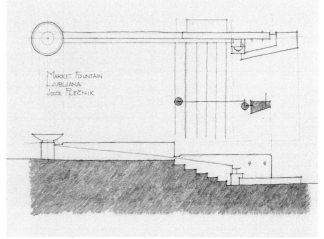

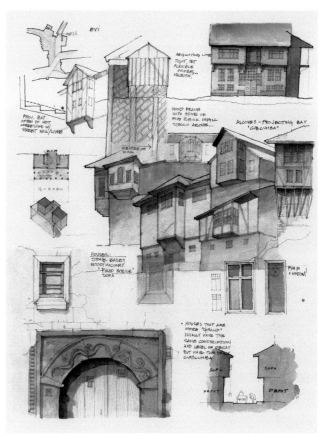

Collage Diagrams

Paul Klee noted that "Art does not reproduce the visible but makes visible."[1] Similarly, it might be said that analysis does not reproduce place, space or things, but uncovers and facilitates discovery. Though the predominant analytical means and ends in this book center on drawing, sketching and diagramming in pencil, ink and brush sketches diagrams, a valuable alternative method are analytical collages. As an assembly of varied materials on relatively flat surfaces, abstract material collages help interpret spatial qualities.

Collage is an effective diagramming tool, owing to an almost inherent abstraction in procedure and conveyance. The elements, gathered from varied sources or on the site, are dislocated from their original context, reshaped and juxtaposed on other materials, often resulting in a disconcerting *non sequitur* that prompts re-thinking. In one respect they are non-objective assemblages the objective of which is not to depict a place, space or thing but to use material as a process. Metal, paper or plastic material and their inherent materiality communicate distinct, sometimes conflicting ideas. More importantly, however, collages are an effective medium in their nature as assemblages in which pieces are selected, sometimes modified, and arranged. It is an active process analogous to the architect as *bricoleur*. A *bricoleur* is a fabricator who uses only the objects and methods available at a given moment to solve problems. The *bricoleur's* material palette is at once everything that is available and those things discerned through observation. Through self-imposed limits (using only a few materials) or external limits (using only materials found at the site) the *bricoleur* selects only those things that can solve the problem. Similarly, collage links analysis to design both conceptually and typologically. As a concept, this is the way in which cities, buildings or landscapes evolve as reactions, accretions interacting with existing fabrics; it is also the way in which collage is the assembly of ideas, forms, images and signs.

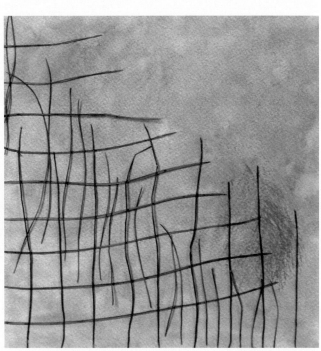

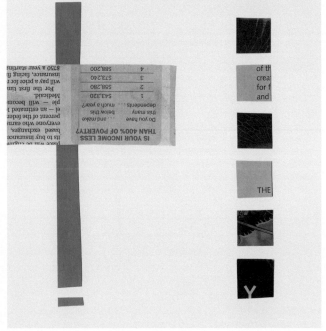

1 "Creative Credo"
("Schöpferische Konfession"):
"Kunst gibt nicht das Sichtbare
wieder, sondern macht
sichtbar." Quoted from Spiller,
Jürg (ed.), *The Thinking Eye:
The Notebooks of Paul Klee*,
trans. Ralph Manheim. New
York: Wittenborn (1961): 76.

Opposite page:
Top left: Impression of Piazza
Cavour, Rome: cardboard,
foam and leaves (collage by
Catherine Simonse)
Top right: Interaction of old and
new on the Gianicolo, Rome: pine
needles, red dust and paper
(collage by Christine Jimenez)
Bottom left: Impressions of the
Pantheon's natural and supernatural
character: pamphlets and wrappers
found beneath the oculus (collages
by Dylan King)
Bottom right: Analysis of scalar
shift through layers within the
atrium system (collages by Sean
McTaggert).

Top:
Biennale interconnections
(collage by Chris Brown)
Impression of Bilbao
(collage by Todd Ray)
Impression of Barcelona
(collage by Todd Ray)

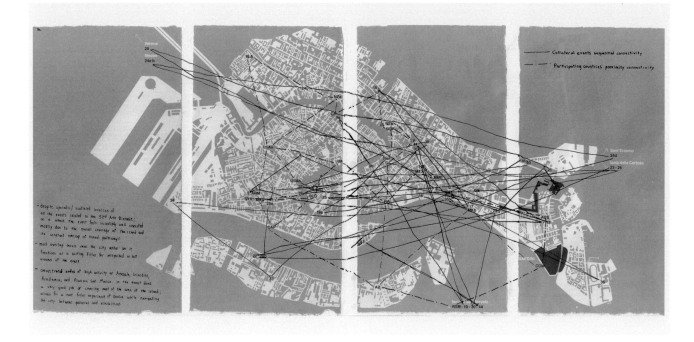

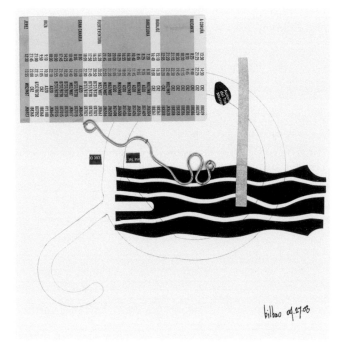

DESIGN ACTS

DESIGN ACTS

The teacher who walks in the shadow of the temple, among his followers, gives not of his wisdom but rather of his faith and his lovingness.

If he is indeed wise he does not bid you enter the house of his wisdom, but rather leads you to the threshold of your own mind.

Khalil Gibran, from "On Teaching" in *The Prophet*[1]

Sitting in a courtyard, smelling a market, peering through a dimly lit vestibule or hearing the echoes inside a mosque are, without a doubt, experiences. Experiences like these are at once spatial, sensual, aesthetic, emotional and intellectual: the *excitement* of moving through a city square, the *pleasure* evoked by familiar aromas, the *anxiety* caused by an unknown and dark street or the *ennui* induced by a beige office cubicle are experiences linked to and facilitated by material conditions. Material conditions are, successively, conceptual, designed, constructed and then experienced. The acts of experience are linked to the past and future acts of design.

This is not to say that all things were designed and built, as we think today; neither are they immune from cultural, personal or material patinas acquired over time. In most cases, however, spaces or things at some point over time were selected, established, recognized, placed and shaped in a particular manner and, ultimately, facilitate experience. Bill Buxton, author of *Sketching User Experiences*, notes that a designer, while working in the material realm, is actually designing experiences. The iPod, the home, the office, the city are material, geometric and functional systems, but more than that they are experiences. Buxton notes that "it is ultimately experiences that we are designing, not things. Yes, physical objects are often the most tangible and visible outcomes of design, but their primary function is to engage us in an experience – an experience that is largely shaped by affordances and character embedded in the product itself."[2] This is a subtle point: without material there would be no experience and without experience the object would be inert. There is, in good design, the interrelational reciprocal material-experience.

This may sound antithetical to material-centric culture: Most designers have been educated and practice designing things. While these professionals do design "things", if the designs are not good experiences (to which function and aesthetics contribute), then they remain inert. Buxton notes that while Apple designers did produce the iPod, the iPod is more than itself. It engages within a reciprocal material-experience: listening to the music, holding the device, wearing the iconic white headphones (and thereby projecting an identity), searching for and selecting songs, looking at (and relying on) its fine craftsmanship, downloading songs and software are greater than the physical thing. An iPod is more than a device or more than listening to music. It is a material-experience.

Examining Architecture as Material-Experience

Understanding that the designer's realm is experience does not reduce the value of material design. Yes, experience can and often is degraded to a manipulative marketing ploy; nevertheless, experience is of fundamental importance to the designed environment and to those by whom it is shaped. By conceptualizing material-experience, the designer becomes aware that the material-experience has more responsibility than expected, because it has to extend beyond itself, beyond function or aesthetics, to comprise the experience that unifies all characteristics and elements into one goal. Material is, for the lack of a better word, arranged to engender experience. This understanding can begin through analysis. Analysis, as explained in Part 1 of this book, is a dynamic examination of both the ephemeral experiential nature and the ordering systems, or other formal patterns or moves, that facilitate experience.

A starting point for analysis is to imagine the designed experience as a narrative: the story of how it engages the environment, how we move through it. The building makes a continued reciprocal contribution to future narratives. The ordering principles, the material organization, the lighting and the sound contribute to experiential narratives of the past, the present and the future. Our experiences of home, library, kitchen, train station, cathedral or pub shape our architectural thinking both consciously or unconsciously. In turn, those experiences shape our architecture that again shapes the experience of those that experience the architecture we helped establish. We, as architects, enter into a type of experiential cycle in which an experience shapes what we think, who we are and what we design, which in turn becomes what others (we can hope) experience and so forth.

These experiences are, for most, unconscious, but they are often examined (or should be) by designers of any kind through specific lenses to help inform conscious experience and thereby the design processes. For instance, that seminal moment in the Turkish madrasa mentioned in the Introduction began as an ineffable personal experience that, while examining it through the lenses or multifaceted analytical methods suggested by my teacher, transformed into a conscious analysis and then awareness of the material place and experience. Essentially, I engaged in a phenomenological investigation of the built environment that contributed to architectural enrichment. More than a library of moves, which I undoubtedly carry with me yet will probably never manifest or transliterate in my design work, the process of examining an experience provides a greater lesson in design process and thinking than any other element. Embedding experience through translation is critical in developing and maturing design thinking.

This phenomenological investigation elicits what Christian Norberg-Schulz calls a "poetic awareness" of the built environment.[3] Rather than limiting the reflection either to experience itself or to a collection of formal ordering systems, a phenomenological analysis coalesces experience and form in order to develop a sensitive attentiveness to the designed world. Architecture, or any design for that matter, interlocks quality with quantity and experience with form to make a complete, multifaceted system. As complex systems, they often cannot be reduced to simpler components without effective analytical approach. Understanding multifaceted systems, therefore, necessitates a multifaceted approach with varied tools. For example, I would need more than one type of tool if I were to truly understand and even interact with a relatively straightforward if multifaceted system – such as trying to understand and repair my bicycle. Essentially, my ball-peen hammer – which in and of itself is an important tool – is insufficient to fully investigate and repair the bicycle. Multiple gadgets, tools and even lateral methods offer greater opportunities for understanding and interacting with complex systems.

Unfortunately, it is difficult to illustrate a multifaceted process without confusing the novice.

Interdependent Design Acts

For the sake of this book and for learning how one might begin to look at the designed environment, it is often necessary to establish a framework. This framework, even one that is somewhat arbitrary and perhaps temporary, helps ground architecture's intimidating or overwhelming nature. Moreover, as architecture is set in physical, historic and conceptual contexts, it is often helpful to see architecture as a series of interconnected systems and decision processes, like for example architects designing a façade incorporate the plan or section and urban designers incorporate issues of zoning or use when examining patterns of the city.

The framework for this book is Design Acts. There are five of them: *Mapping the Plan*, *Facing the Building*, *Traversing the Section*, *Probing the Details* and *Engaging the Context*.

As discussed above, the individual acts ultimately become an interdependent continuum of parts to wholes: from large to small, from inside and outside, from detail to urban design, from personal to social. The intention, ultimately, is that the student be able to see the interrelationship of actions in context and be able to pull out and in to examine the architecture as a continuum without losing sight of the larger, the smaller and the intermediate issues and relationships. A former graduate student noted that what I was talking about was perhaps the experience of playing a trombone. This "tromboning" allows the architect to continuously pull back and forth and in and out to examine the design. A trombone, unlike a piano, has no set stops for each note. The sound produced is *glissando* or *portamento*, a sliding sound in which pitch flows or varies. Whatever analogy might be used, the ultimate goal for architects is to think about the interrelationship of scales, to be able to pull back and look at the big picture yet move in to look at the detail. What the big picture might be is open to discussion: for some it is a site, for others it is actually the detail. The

connection among details within a scale is also important, in the sense that decisions regarding a certain scale are related: the scale of an exterior door is the same as the scale of an interior door, hence the decisions about "doors" are related. It does not mean they have to be the same, but at least considered as related.

By pulling back and forth, the trombonist, to cite the former example once again, is able to hear different scales and notes and take advantage of the sliding sound. Similarly, one can look at architecture in a series of sliding scales that interrelate to one another. Part of the design process is to embrace the act of sliding, to work the piece from the urban scales to the detail. For the sake of writing this book and of learning, somewhat arbitrary stops are inserted here at particular scale. Ultimately, these scales may be abandoned in favor of an ability of looking, thinking and learning about architecture along indeterminate and interrelated scales. By extension, this movement or thinking is not only vertical but also lateral, in the sense that examination prompts re-conceptulizing a problem and perhaps developing unexpected solutions.

Each of the Design Acts – *Mapping the Plan*, *Facing the Building*, *Traversing the Section*, *Probing the Details* and *Engaging the Context* – has at least two interpretations. First, the acts are part of the design process both conceptually and literally. We *act upon*, we *take action*, we *act within or re-act to context*. As we design, we map, enclose, pass through, assemble and link everything to context. While nearly simultaneous, these are distinct acts that help us conceive and construct. Second, these are analytical acts. We *re-act*, *activate* or we see *actors* within a context: separate tools or analytical enzymes for a unified analytical whole. Acting upon the building using the separate acts allows the architect to diagram one particular aspect, to understand that aspect and then see how it is part of a larger holistic vision. Separating acts clarifies the often overly complex building into comprehensible elements. And while this is maybe simplistic (any diagram or discernment runs the risk of reductionism), the intention is for the architect to examine the pieces, see the overlaps and discover the holistic form. These acts are ways to access a building and cross into the threshold of understanding.

Mapping the Plan focuses on the way in which we map buildings in the realm in which things are generally dealt with in plan; *Facing the Building* centers on the overall articulation of a building's exterior, including façade and massing; *Traversing the Section* focuses on the spatial qualities of moving in and through a building; *Probing the Details* involves material assemblies, joints and the interaction of humans with a building; and finally, Engaging the Context involves the way in which buildings interact with the city and landscape but also how those contexts affect design.

1   Gibran, Khalil, *The Prophet*. New York: Alfred A. Knopf (1966): 60.

2   Buxton, William, *Sketching User Experiences: Getting the Design Right and the Right Design*. Amsterdam: Elsevier/Morgan Kaufmann (2007): 127.

3   Norberg-Schulz, Christian, *The Concept Of Dwelling: On The Way To Figurative Architecture*. Milan: Electa (1985): 135.

MAPPING THE PLAN

Mapping establishes a relationship between you and something you recognize. It helps you find out where you are, and it helps describe the overall structure of the place you are in, making it comprehensible and therefore habitable.

Charles Moore, Gerald Allen and Donlyn Lyndon[1]

The plan is the generator.
Without a plan, you have lack of order, and willfulness.
The Plan holds in itself the essence of sensation.

Le Corbusier[2]

Plans, and the act of drawing plans, consolidate and interrelate complex spatial and material information, so that relationships among parts within a whole may be made more explicit. By actively identifying, unifying and clarifying diverse elements in context to an entirety we can begin to understand how spatial and tectonic strategies work and, during the design process, orchestrate and facilitate mapping strategies for those who experience the building.

Plans are ideal for helping others locate themselves in space because they are coded abstractions that represent information efficiently and succinctly. Like other diagrams, a plan holds information that is often too complicated to remember or recall for practical use. A plan does this because it eliminates a great deal of information. Much is left out of the plan diagram, leaving us to infer greater information than explicitly stated. Such an edited diagram allows us to see, at a glance, a room's, a building's or a city's overall organization. We can begin to discern patterns that help us navigate and understand spatial and material arrangements. A street map helps us understand a city's fundamental organization, which is then further informed when we experience that city. The map is not the end of the experience but an important diagrammatic tool for understanding our position in an environment. Moreover, as in a placeholder process, plans have the ability to embody information at varied scales. We can essentially zoom into a plan to understand how the smaller elements of a system relate to the larger scale. As a process of discernment and distribution, composing plans by identifying and developing underlying patterns with spatial, material and structural implications helps us develop our own awareness and appropriate strategies.

It is no accident that self-perception and our social interaction with others relate directly to the way we literally draw maps and plans. Research in both geography and cognitive psychology reaffirms what most architects already know: that those who use and, more importantly, draw maps while they travel or move through spaces establish frames of reference more easily. The constructed maps become critical in developing the "processes of reasoning about space, understanding spatial relations, and in developing configurable understanding."[3] Essentially, mapping relationships, configurations and patterns is integral to acquiring spatial knowledge and to using that knowledge in future, unanticipated circumstances. Those who do not make or use maps are less likely to understand the overall configuration of the systems (a city or a building) and even less likely to articulate where they are, let alone to reproduce the spatial systems and the strategies and patterns generating and reinforcing those systems.

In his seminal article, "The Logic of the Plan", Frank Lloyd Wright notes that plans project their material nature.[4] He argues that when we read plans we are actually reading a building's materiality. The plans telegraph to us the nature of construction and of spaces. By simply reading wall thickness, column spacing and other charged lines, architects and builders are able to understand or map the material and structural systems of the building.

Wright's essay is part of an obligatory caution: plans have three-dimensional implications, but if used improperly or alone, they can take a dominant role in design and analysis and lead to two-dimensional thinking. Being "plan-dominant" or "not thinking in section" are often correct accusations and faults that emerge out of thinking two-dimensionally, yet plans embody three-dimensional spatial volumes and mechanical and structural continuity. With practice, drawing a plan has immediate implications and, after a time, drawing in plan can become a three-dimensional exercise. This practice, however, comes from first drawing plans alongside other drawings and while moving through spaces and working in models. Essentially, plans are not the problem but rather how and when they are used and combined with other representations.

Mapping the Plan involves specific drawing acts that link overall strategies to specific articulations.

Five questions are at the root of the fundamental actions:
How is the building's fabric interwoven?
In what sense is the building a type or part of a typology?
How are the building and its spaces organized? What hierarchies or differentiations exist? Is hierarchy necessary or are there other ways to articulate space?
How are geometries resolved or articulated?
How do materials convey use, continuity and sequence?

1   Moore, Charles, Allen, Gerald and Lyndon, Donlyn, *The Place of Houses*. New York: Holt, Rinehart and Winston (1974): 207.

2   Le Corbusier, *Towards an Architecture*, trans. John Goodman. Los Angeles: Getty Research Institute (2007): 116.

3   Golledge, Reginald G., Gale, Nathan, Pellegrino, James W. and Doherty, Sally, "Spatial Knowledge Acquisition by Children: Route Learning and Relational Distances", *Annals of the Association of American Geographers* 82:2 (June 1992): 223-244.

4   Wright, Frank Lloyd, "In the Cause of Architecture: The Logic of the Plan", *Architectural Record* 63 (January 1928): 49-57.

Clarifying Public/Private

The public/private spatial dichotomy delineates the nearly universal human need for psychological and physical privacy in relation to the community or others. Though often simplistic, mutable or ambiguous as a concept, the public/private division exists as a way to regulate degrees of interaction. The diagrams show both the clear and ambiguous public/private zones in a building.

The diagram of Toshiko Mori's House in Maine II reveals the way the house's overall form is based upon public and private divisions. One half is more private and the other half is more public. Here darker tones indicate more private zones, becoming increasingly lighter toward the more public areas. Medium tones delineate ambiguous areas such as vestibules that for guests affirm entry to a more private realm. The primary circulation path divides the private and public, yet even here there is subtlety:

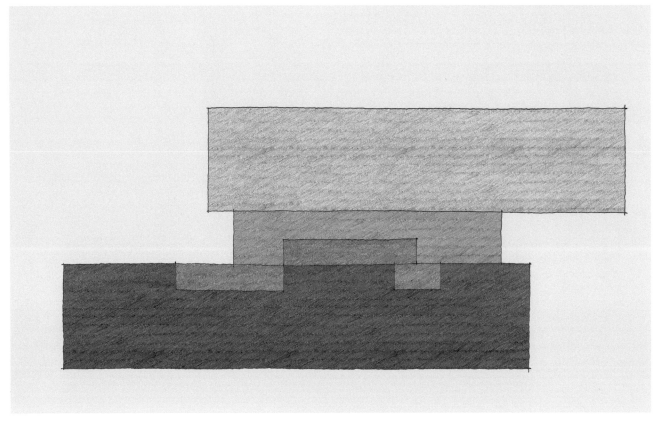

Public and private gradations

Ground level floor plan

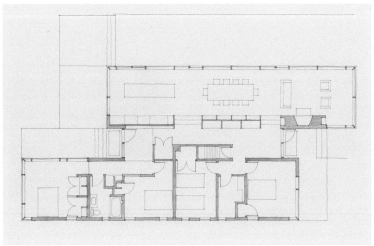

House in Maine II
Penobscot Bay, Maine, 2004
Toshiko Mori House

Where is public and private most clearly apparent?
What architectural elements underscore the separation of these two zones?
How does the architect intermingle public and private?
Does public and private change depending on time or event?

alcoves, storage and the stairway just off the main circulation act as transitions between the public and the private
circulation, while also offering sound insulation. The
diagram of Aalto's Skeppet House, drawn in ink, uses
hatching density to indicate gradations of public and
private zones. The diagram reveals how privacy is often not
limited to specific divisions or lines: some very private
rooms can be within public realms, questioning definitions
and perceptions of privacy and public access. The separate

wing, which might be very private, is the guest wing and
the sauna while the private study, on the upper left, is
adjacent and nearly embedded in the house's public area.

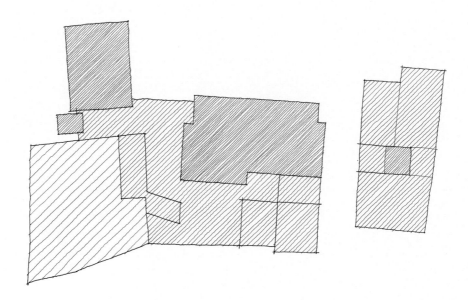

Private and public areas intermixed

Main level floor plan

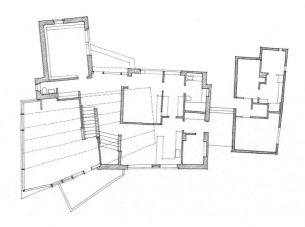

Skeppet House
Tammisaari, Finland, 1970
Alvar Aalto

Delineating Service and Served

A building's organization often hinges on delineating service and served spaces. Service spaces sustain or serve a building's chief purpose. Discreet links maintain the needed interfaces. Occasionally, however, ambiguous segregation of service and served zones may be needed or desired: blurred divisions may actually serve a greater purpose, engender social and economic exchange or generate a particular affect. Likewise, service/served zones often have scalar gradations: a building often has overall central service zones, yet rooms within that building will often have their own local service/served zones. Regardless of scale or segregation degree, delineating and balancing service and served zones remain vital in the life of a building.

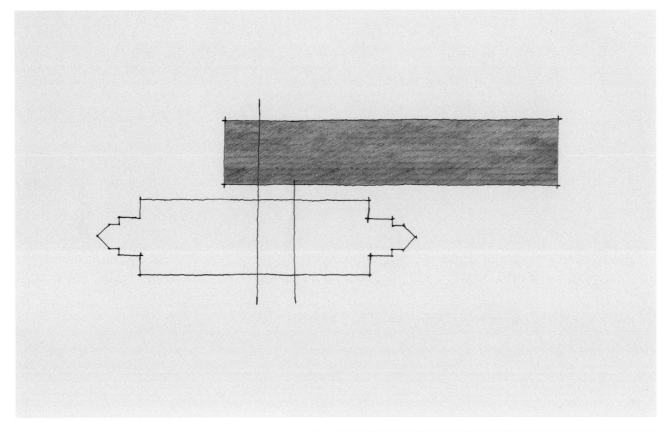

Service and served zones

Upper level floor plan

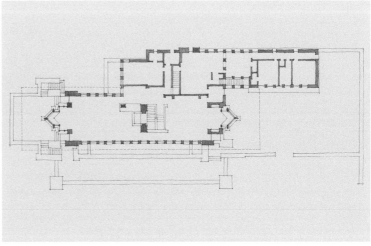

Frederick C. Robie House
Chicago, Illinois, 1910
Frank Lloyd Wright

How is the building divided into service and served zones?

What are the links between service and served zones?

When is mixing or an ambiguous delineation of service and served zones needed or desired?

When is segregation between service and served zones essential?

How does service/served relate to path/room, public/private or other zoning strategies?

Are there subsidiary or smaller scale service/served spaces within the building (e. g. closet in a bedroom; a lab table in a lecture hall)?

In these diagrams, tones and line weights delineate service and served zones within the building. Tones indicate service while line weights show served zones. Like all diagrams, these deliberately generalize the building for momentary clarity. While nuances of service/served may appear in the building, the goal here, at least momentarily, is to divide the building into clear dichotomies. For the Robie House, the diagrams show, primarily through tones, the two parallel off-set wings: one for service (here toned), the other served. The gap between the two is, on the ground level, the house's main entrance, but on the upper levels there is a permeable link between the two wings. Likewise in the diagram of the Münster City Library, the tones illustrate the generalized service zone at the rear of the building that supports the reading room and stacks toward the street. Varied tones delineate these interspersed service and served elements within the generalized dichotomy.

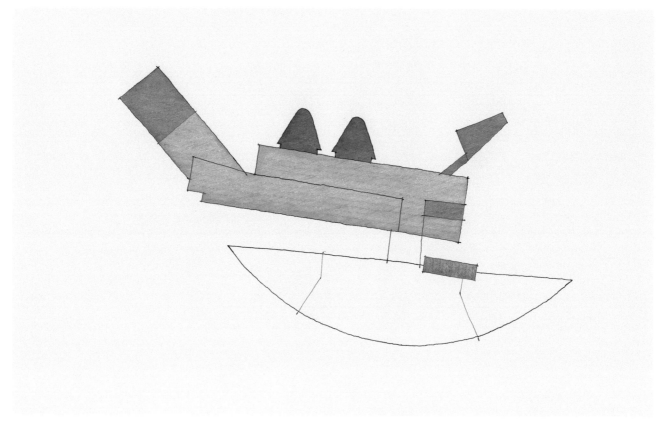

Service and served gradations

Upper level floor plan

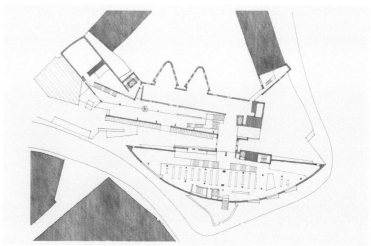

Münster City Library
Münster, Germany, 1993
Peter Wilson and Julia Bolles

Demarcating Profane and Sacred

In his book, *The Sacred and the Profane*, Mircea Eliade[1] describes the sacred as differentiated space. Unlike profane space, which is heterogeneous and unarticulated, sacred space is unusual and singular. While religious "sacredness" is a subset of hierarchical sacredness, sacred can be areligious and include private areas within a home, rare book collections in a library or simply areas associated with a special moment or experience of a particular individual. The sacred/profane dichotomy has less to do with who enters but with the sense of how one behaves in that space. For example, a public library is a communal space yet as a "sacred space", visitors' behaviors reflect its role as a place of quiet reading and contemplation. All may enter but all must act appropriately once inside. Any violations or misinterpretations of that sacredness often lead to social and cultural conflicts.

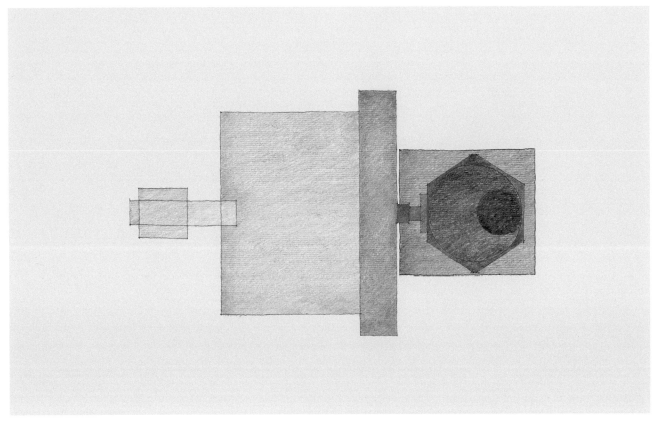

Profane to sacred gradations

Entry level floor plan

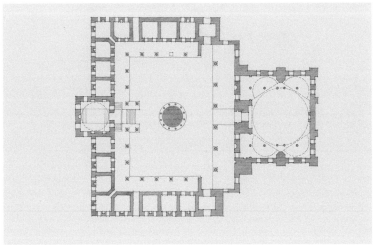

Sokollu Mehmed Paşa Complex
Istanbul, Turkey, 1574
Sinan

Where are the real and perceived thresholds of sacred and profane?

What changes occur at these thresholds (material, section, pattern, geometry, sound, light, scale)?

Does sacred correspond or contrast with a public/private dichotomy?

The diagram of the Sokullu Mehmet Paşa Complex in Istanbul shows the transformation from the street to the mosque's interior. Distinct layers of sacredness are accentuated by thresholds, stairways, porches and porticoes. Drawing and the experience of these layers help reveal a threshold as both a religious and personal experience. Varied tones from light to dark mark increasingly sacred zones. The Phillips Exeter Academy Library is slightly different but retains a sense of sacredness within the diagram. Here there is the idea of moving from the main center atrium through the stacks and finally to the intimate reading carrels incorporated into the windows. The personal private space becomes a kind of sacred space within the library. Changing the hatching density highlights those areas of increased sacredness. The fireplace also is a moment of sacredness as it becomes a place of gathering within the library that obviously is not about everyone but about a few, reading or discussing ideas.

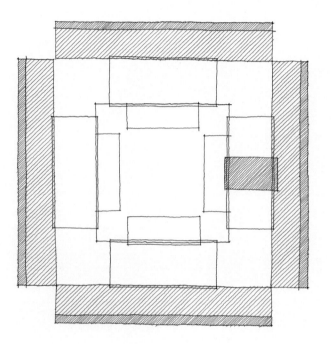

Profane to sacred gradations

Typical upper level floor plan

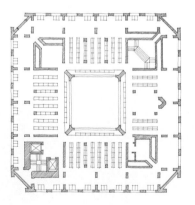

Phillips Exeter Academy Library
Exeter, New Hampshire, 1971
Louis Kahn

1   Eliade, Mircea, *The Sacred and the Profane: the Nature of Religion*, trans. Willard R. Trask. New York: Harcourt, Brace (1959): 20.

Relating Materials

Floor material, form and pattern often demarcate or correlate with specific rooms, functions or spatial experiences. Stone, carpet, tile and their innumerable types and patterning fulfill both functional and symbolic roles specific to a particular room's purpose and significance. A floor type can mark a room's purpose and telegraph meaning to those who tread, or cannot tread, upon it. Similarly, floor types can act as a code for similar room types. For example, all floors in wet areas might use one stone type while all sacred rooms might be in a particular wood. Diagramming these allied material and spatial relationships helps develop a sense of how the floors can imbue meaning, signal a change or simply accommodate specific use.

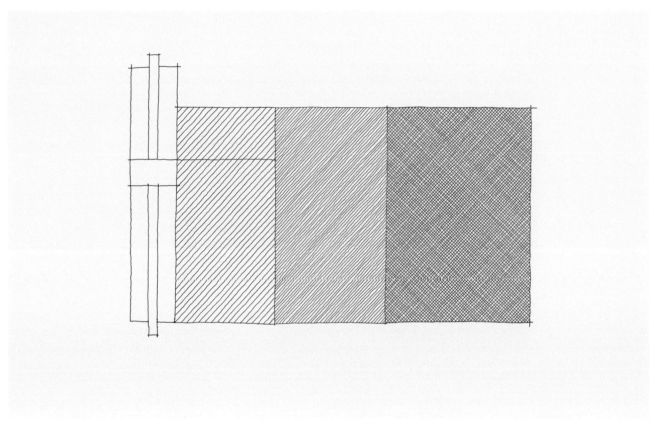

Material changes in sacred and enclosed zones

Ground level floor plan

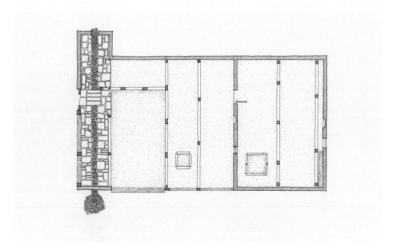

Mosque
Kamu, Afghanistan

How does the floor change from one room to another or from outside to inside?
Is there a system to the floor types and locations?
If the floors are different, are there any connections at all?

The diagram of the mosque in Kamu shows, first, that as the space becomes increasingly sacred (from exterior, to ablution to the mosque's external and internal prayer areas) the floor changes accordingly. The rough stone floor near the ablution area leads to the outside courtyard, to an exterior "summer" prayer area and then finally into the "winter" prayer area, with each zone having a different surface. Hatch densities and cross-hatching delineate particular zones within the buildings. The diagram of Carlo

Scarpa's Querini Stampalia Foundation shows how the floors emphasize a spatial experience accentuated by steps, change in stone, thresholds and patterns as well as the intermingling of other materials. The diagram uses nearly the same tone to delineate the varied rooms; however, two darker tones are used to delineate or emphasize the juxtaposition of varied floor types and levels.

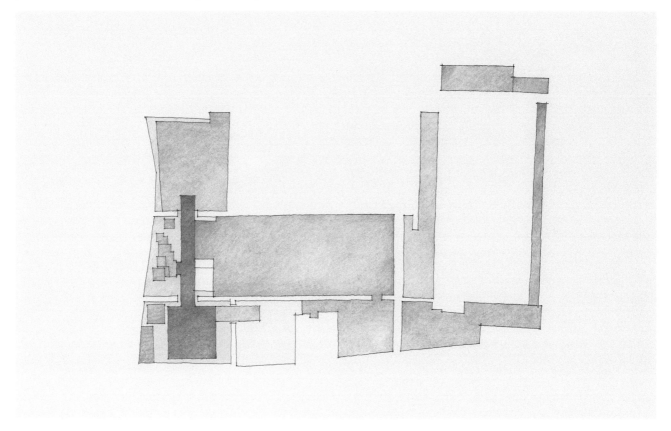

Floor types highlighted

Garden level plan

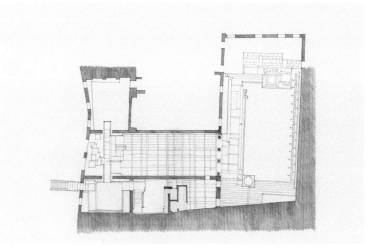

Fondazione Querini Stampalia
Venice, Italy, 1963
Carlo Scarpa

Filling Walls

Storage, mechanical equipment, plumbing and other service elements are often corralled into zones or walls. These necessities, however, can be more than just contained but can help define rooms and accentuate spatial sequences, to enhance a sense of privacy between rooms.

The diagram of Richard Meier's Royal Dutch Paper Mills Headquarters uses tones to delineate the occupied walls between offices and other rooms along the double-loaded hallway. Cabinets, storage, services and other support functions are treated as thick walls that divide spaces. This has a double result in keeping services in specific areas yet also creates a sense of entry to the rooms as one passes through the zone, increasing privacy between the offices and hallway. Likewise, the diagram of a traditional Turkish

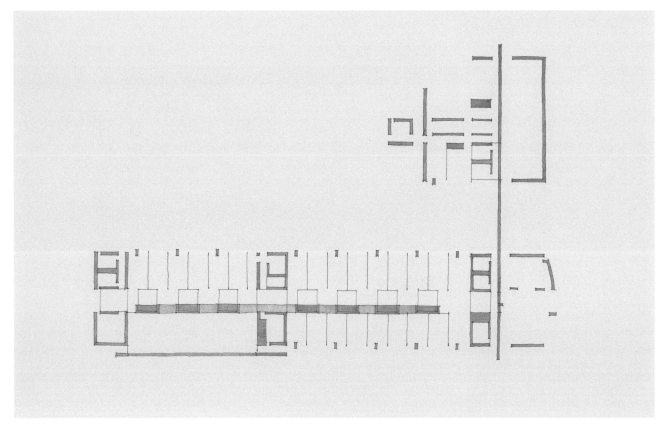

Wall types highlighted

Typical floor plan

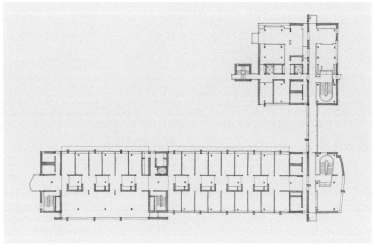

Royal Dutch Paper Mills Headquarters
Hilversum, The Netherlands, 1993
Richard Meier & Partners

Do the walls contain use?

When and how are service zones articulated as walls?

How would a room improve if the wall incorporated use?

house shows how the walls incorporate functions. Most of the walls contain various things, not only for compactness but also for insulation and privacy. Walls are generally for storage/entry, for heating, for view and for built-in "couch" or divan. The specific feature of these diagrams is that they shows how service and served zones are scalable: the idea of areas of service and areas that are served supports a more efficient distribution on a room scale.

Zones associated with walls

Living level floor plan

Traditional Turkish House

Responding to Light

The modulation of light and situating rooms to it is of critical concern. Diagramming natural light helps understand how architects respond to areas that must have, should have or may have natural light. Though ideally all rooms should have natural light, this is often impossible or perhaps undesirable. Therefore, applying "must-should-may" criteria can help orchestrate a plan's organization. For example, knowing that bedrooms must have natural light, but bathrooms may have natural light can help

determine a room's location within an apartment block. While diagramming a plan's organization in relation to natural light is necessary, it is often difficult. The difficulty arises due to light's changeability through filtration (full sun, clouds, overcast), location (e.g. color variation due to land or water) and direction (from the side, above, below, indirect, direct and with reference to the angle throughout the day and year).

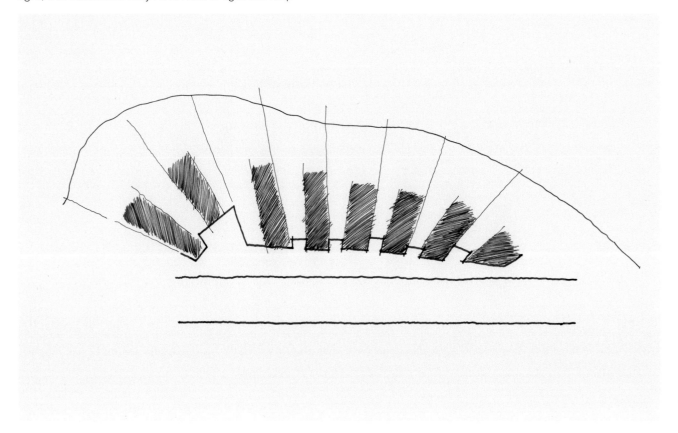

Areas of light and dark

Typical floor plan

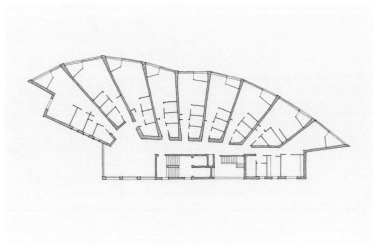

Neue Vahr Apartment Block
Bremen, Germany, 1962
Alvar Aalto

How does the building form or react to sunlight?

How does the north side differ from the south side?

How is light modulated? Is there a change in form, skin, overhangs or other devices?

The diagram of the Neue Vahr Apartment Block shows how a building is organized according to light as one of its primary goals. Aalto's splayed floor plate opens wide toward the light, while areas in which light is not essential are set back. The diagram of the National Air and Space Museum shows how the regular systemized and organized building responds to light by enclosing the southern side while opening to the north for indirect display lighting and toward the National Mall.

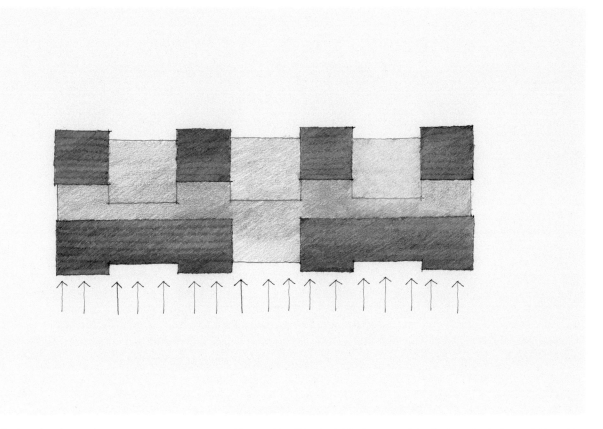

Interior organization related to southern exposure

Main level floor plan

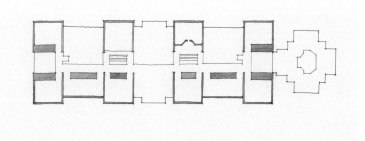

National Air and Space Museum
Washington, DC, 1976
Hellmuth, Obata + Kassabaum

Connecting Rooms and Paths

Transitional spaces and paths within buildings function both as necessary environmental and spatial transitions but can also have symbolic and social roles: as an airlock between outside and inside, to reduce sound transmission or mitigate a change in direction, to underscore degrees of sacredness and help increase privacy between zones, or to accentuate or heighten a spatial sequence. The series of transitions are myriad thresholds that enrich the building's spatial experience. Similarly, differentiating path and room demarks areas of movement from areas of rest so that those who are relatively stationary do not impede those who enter, pass through or exit a room. To avoid (or perhaps encourage) physical and even psychological collisions involves orchestrating "places of rest" together with "places of movement" within a room, a building or in a city. A "place of rest" allows for static activities (contemplation, meeting, conversation, presentation) while a "place of movement" allows for circulation into, from or

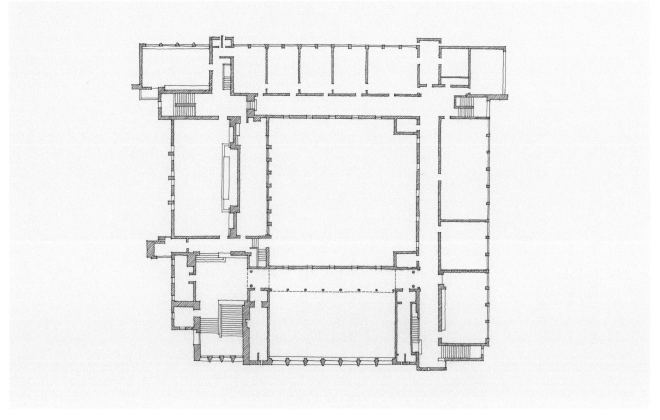

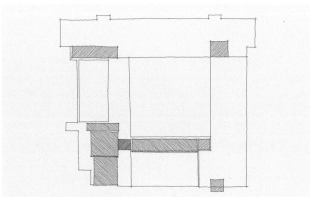

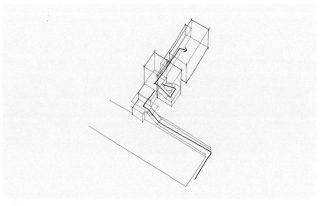

Main level floor plan

Connecting rooms

Movement from outside to inside

Hilversum Town Hall
Hilversum, The Netherlands, 1931
Willem Marinus Dudok

Is the transition from one room to another abrupt or is there an interstitial space?
Where is path in relation to room? Where is movement and where is rest?
What is the proportion of path (movement) in relation to room (rest)?
When is the path deliberately intermixed with room and why?

within a place of rest. One differentiation strategy is to create an *enfilade*: circulation is placed eccentrically yet juxtaposed on a room, creating a path/room overlap. *Enfilade* movement can be discreet and informal yet interactive. In contrast, juxtaposing path on center or *en suite* enables a more direct, confrontational interaction of the mobile and static; it also suits more ceremonial situations (for example, entering a courtroom or mosque).

The diagrams of Dudok's Hilversum Town Hall highlights a series of spatial gaskets that allow for deliberate transitions from room to room. The plan's hatching indicates lobbies, anterooms and interstitial spaces that accommodate the interaction of the public with civic functions. The transparent axonometric shows the path through connecting volumes to the main meeting room. The diagram of the Pallath House shows toned pathways that define the areas of rest within the house, underscored in "good room" diagrams.

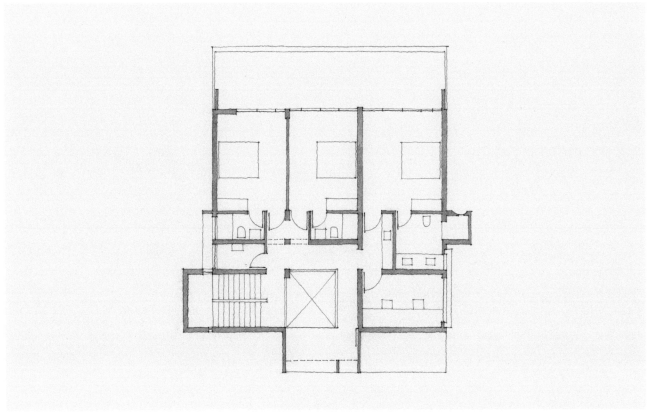

Upper level floor plan

Path/room relationships

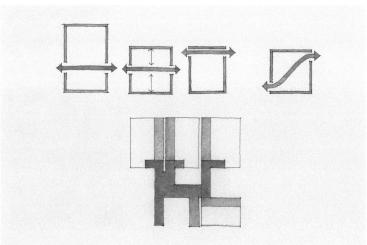

Leslie Pallath House
Cochin, India, 2005
Klaus-Peter Gast

Uniting Connections

Like gaskets between two machine parts or hyphens joining two words, architectural gaskets or hyphens are identifiable elements that connect pieces of a building. These connections – between two buildings or between new and existing buildings – are interstitial spatial and material links that allow the two elements to co-exist.

The diagrams of the Cantor Center for Visual Arts high-light the inserted hyphens that connect the existing building and the new addition. Hyphens extend from the two most logical existing linkage points: the central bay and the center of the octagon wing. Tonal gradations underscore how a hyphen interpenetrates that which it connects. In the diagram of Lutyens' British Embassy, a dark tone highlights the transition from the embassy's more public zone, which is oriented toward the street, to

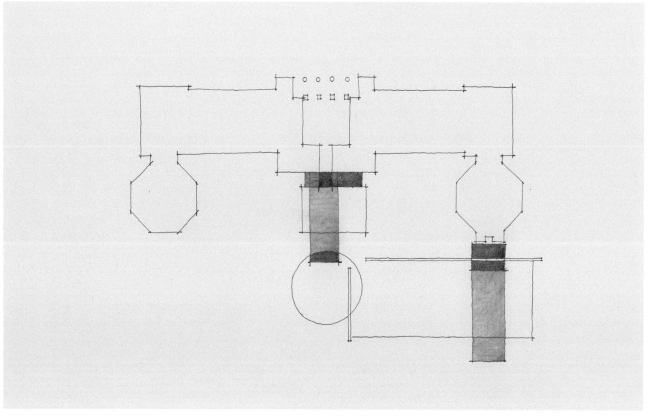

Connections between old and new

Ground level floor plan

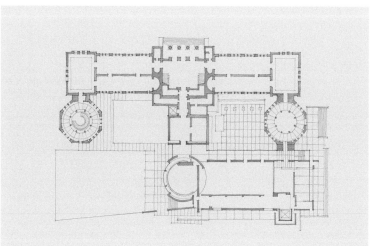

**Iris & B. Gerald Cantor Center
for Visual Arts at Stanford University**
San Jose, California, 1998
Polshek Partnership Architects,
renamed Ennead Architects LLP

Is the hyphen simply connected or does it extend into the two parts?

How is the hyphen programmed? Is it circulation, entry, service, a void?

How does the hyphen or "third thing" also manifest in smaller details or connections?

Where is the hyphen located? Are there natural "linkage points"?

What receives the hyphen? Is there a "third thing" for the hyphen itself?

the ambassador's private residence, which is oriented to the south. Here the hyphen, distinct architecturally from the two halves of the embassy compound, is in reality and appropriately a meeting room.

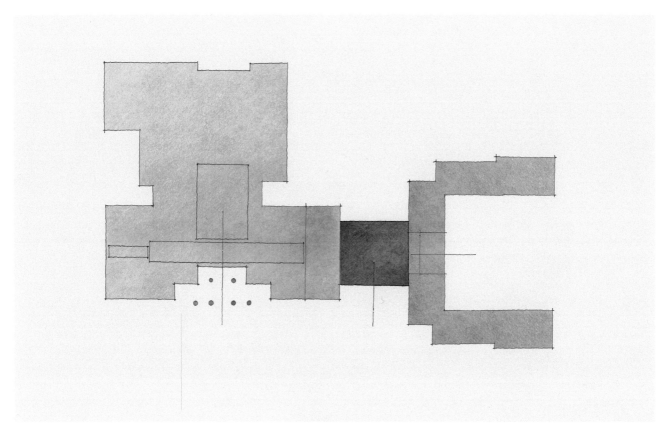

Pavilion connecting public and private

Main level floor plan

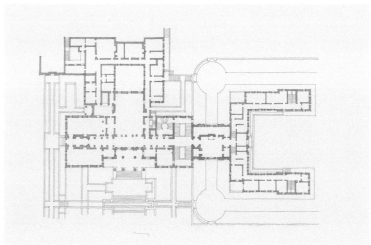

The British Embassy
Washington, DC, 1928
Edwin Lutyens

Aligning Edges and Centers

Centerlines and edges are imaginary lines used to orchestrate plan composition and spatial transitions. While these lines can mark axes between points, they often correspond to movement or pathways through a building, garden or city. As compositional devices, centerlines are those about which space and form are symmetrically disposed, while edges are where spaces and forms are asymmetrically disposed. Though centerlines often remain clear, the interchange of these two – when a center becomes an edge and vice versa – may lend itself easily to augment the plan composition. Beyond spatial and formal composition, center and edge alignments and their interchange help organize and relate a building's interior to a tectonic system so that columns and walls interact with and reinforce room and path.

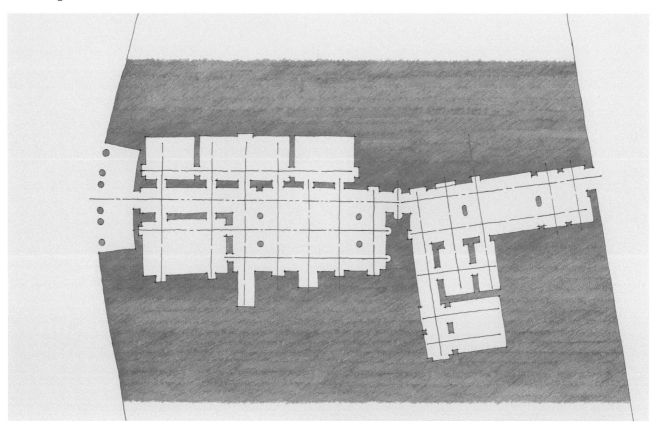

Edge and center lines

Ground floor plan

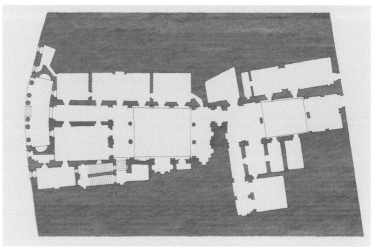

Palazzo Pietro Massimo alle Colonne
Rome, Italy, 1538
Baldassare Peruzzi

What, if any, are the primary axes?

At what scale can these be found? In the overall plan or in specific rooms?

Where do centerlines become edges and edges centers?

From the diagram of Palazzo Massimo we can see how
Peruzzi begins with a primary centerline to organize the
street face, yet just behind the entry portico that centerline
becomes an edge-line. From there, edges and centers
alternate to mark primary, secondary and tertiary relationships. Likewise, in the diagram of Loos' Villa Müller, which
only highlights the planes defining the centers and edges,
we can see how Loos created dynamic movement within
the villa.

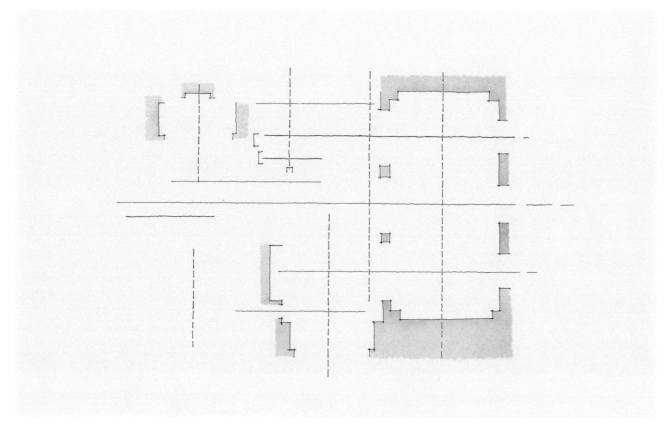

Edge and center alignments and interchange

Main level floor plan

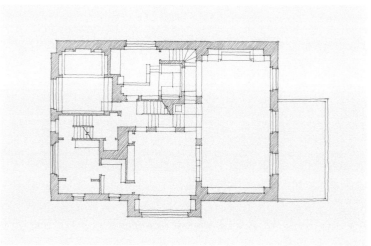

Villa Müller
Prague, The Czech Republic, 1930
Adolf Loos

Stitching Tartans

Tartan patterns – patterns akin to those ordinarily associated with plaid textiles – are complex hierarchical grid patterns communicating varied scales, layers, depths and rhythms simultaneously through a hierarchy of line type and through the varied colors and values of background, foreground and overlapping field tones. Understanding and applying these conceptual and literal tartan patterns is essential for the design student, as architectural and urban tartans are themselves three-dimensional spatial, mechanical and material systems. Architectural tartans can also include the façade assembly, urban design or landscape design or any designed object that unifies complex systems into unified wholes. Layered and interdependent, these systems and spaces can be dislodged and recognized as separate elements within a totality.

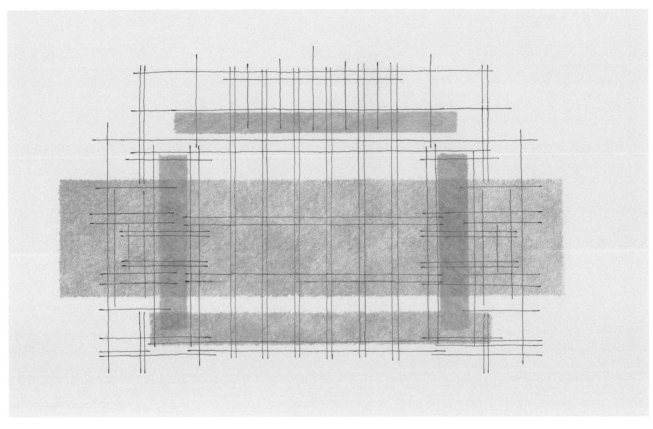

Underlying tartan pattern

Entry level floor plan

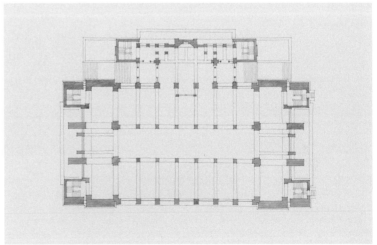

Larkin Building
Buffalo, New York, 1904
Frank Lloyd Wright

What is the building's underlying tectonic grid?
How are spatial patterns overlaid on this grid?
How are programmatic dichotomies (service/served, path/room, public/private) integrated into this tartan?

The tartan diagram of the Larkin Building shows how the plan is a complex weave of tectonic elements and space. Wright's rigorous tectonic grid coincides with spatial patterns in a way that the great hall interlocks with the stair tower bays. The building's entry – formed from a gap between the building main mass and the ancillary tower – and lateral circulation zones are delineated as tones that overlap with the great hall's spatial volume. The tartan diagram of Rick Mather's Dulwich Gallery addition shows the interlinked patterns of the existing site and of the addition. Mather mapped the existing structures in order to mesh the new project within the historical structure.

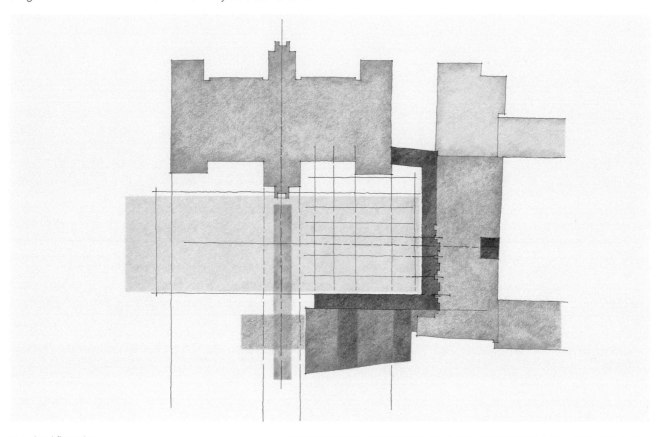

Entry level floor plan

Underlying tartan pattern

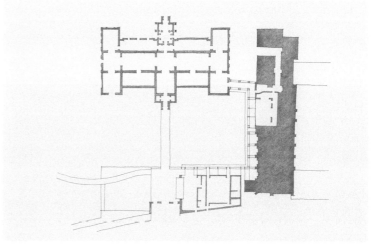

Dulwich Picture Gallery Addition
Dulwich, England, 2000
Rick Mather

Shifting Geometries

The orthogonal grid's ubiquity throughout time and across cultures is due in part to its ability to scale, expand, contract or transform, either in part or as a whole, without necessarily affecting other fragments of the same grid. A grid can accommodate complex forms, sizes and hierarchies yet maintain continuity and simplicity. In buildings, grids transform most often as they accommodate circulation, rooms or courtyards and their interaction. One way a grid accommodates differences is shifting on the x, y or z axes. These shifts, which can occur within predetermined modules, maintain an overall order yet adapt to local needs. Rather than a homogenous grid, these shifted patterns start to resemble overlapping, semi-transparent plaids or tartans. The plaids intensify or subside to accommodate complex systems.

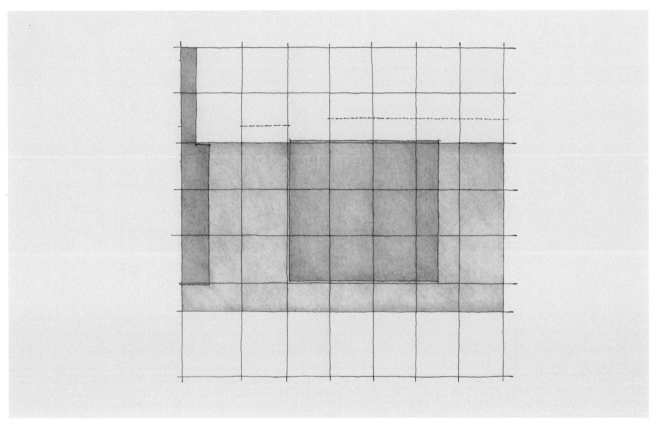

Grid and spatial shifts

Entry level floor plan

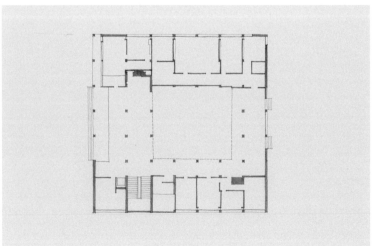

Casa del Fascio
Como, Italy, 1936
Giuseppe Terragni

What is the fundamental floor grid?

How is the grid shifted, augmented or otherwise transformed to accommodate complex situations?

Is the grid shift articulated in structure and enclosure? When are these coincidental or in opposition?

The diagram of the Casa del Fascio shows how Terragni shifted and varied the column grid to accommodate varied programmatic and spatial needs. The tones show how these moves allow for multiple spatial readings in which the interior atrium relates to the defining walls and columns. Rather than a homogenous room, the shift of walls and columns produces a complex interwoven spatial experience. The diagram of the Hôtels de Crozat and d'Évreux illustrates how one, albeit shifted, grid helps link the two distinct courtyards yet allows for the two to interact. Both Terragni and Bullet did not follow the grid slavishly but instead used sophisticated grid patterns to develop complex, three-dimensional tectonic systems and powerful spatial arrangements. This is especially apparent in the Casa del Fascio's internal volumes and façades, to be examined later in this book, which hold invaluable lessons for architects working with the ubiquitous grid.

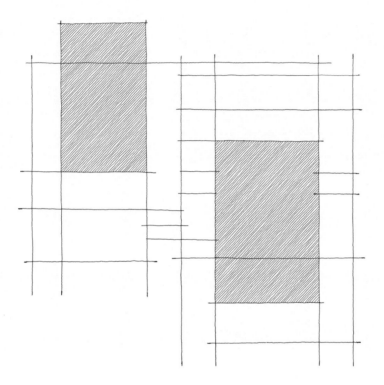

Shifted courtyards linked by a common grid

Main level floor plan

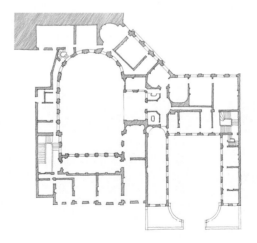

Hôtels Crozat and d'Evreux
Paris, France, 1706
Pierre Bullet

Overlapping Spatial Patterns

Multiple readings and spatial overlaps reinforce a sense of interlocking continuity from room to room and from inside to outside. Accomplished either as alignments or as overlapping vistas, these spatial extensions can help overcome limited dimensions. For example, two rooms or a path through a room can be coincidental having both a clear identity but also a duality created by overlap.

The diagram of the ground floor of Sir John Soane's Museum shows a series of overlapping tones that represent the paths as well as the real and implied spatial slots. Soane's nascent modernist spatiality is best seen in those moments when a room, which at first seems clearly enclosed by walls or columns, extends beyond a threshold to interact with other rooms: a parlor extends into a sitting area across a courtyard and into the gallery. Likewise, the diagram of Mies van der Rohe's Barcelona Pavilion shows

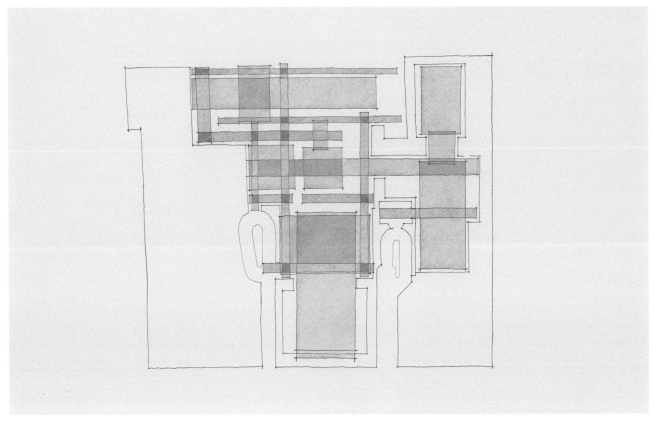

Overlapping spaces and views

Entry level floor plan

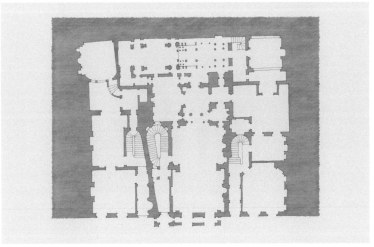

Sir John Soane's Museum
London, England, 1827
John Soane

How is space defined explicitly or implicitly?

Where are shared views?

Where do spaces overlap? When is a path both separate from yet part of a room?

both Soane's nascent modern spatiality but is also an
example of the role of ambiguity in architecture in that the
room's edges are indistinct. Containment is implied rather
than explicit, with more of a "sense" of enclosure or of
boundary. In both diagrams, the intention is to illustrate
unconfined space through the use of overlapping tones.

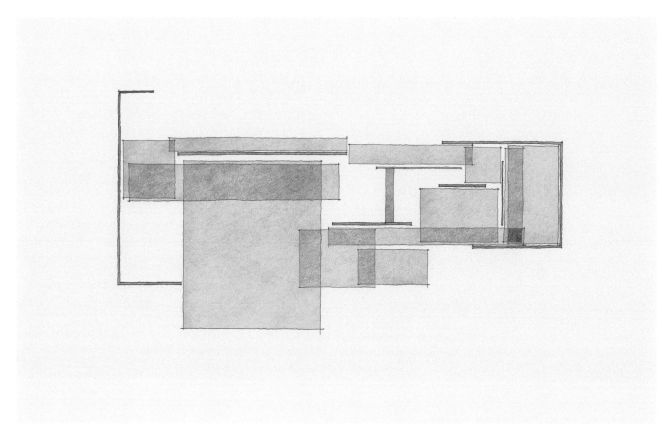

Overlapping spaces and views
Ground level floor plan

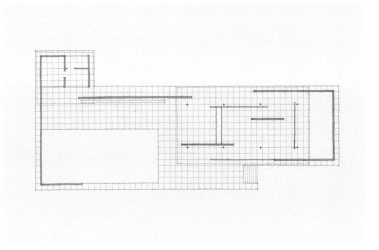

View of Pavilion as of 2008
(reconstruction 1986)

Barcelona Pavilion
Barcelona, Spain, 1929
Ludwig Mies van der Rohe

Engaging the Landscape

Engaging with the landscape is a relationship of building to site, yet it is also part of a much larger attitude of a building's link to its context. How a building reciprocates with its context or is, by contrast, indifferent to context (with gradations in-between) reflects a greater attitude about the environment and society.

The diagram of the Schindler-Chase House, drawn in pencil, describes the overlap of the spaces and views from the house into the landscape and helps articulate the ambiguity between the two. Intermixed with the primary structural walls (dark tones) and landscape elements (lighter tones) within the compound are rectilinear spatial frames where the interior rooms extend beyond the glass enclosure to the exterior garden rooms. These spatial frames are often part of shared views, which are delineated

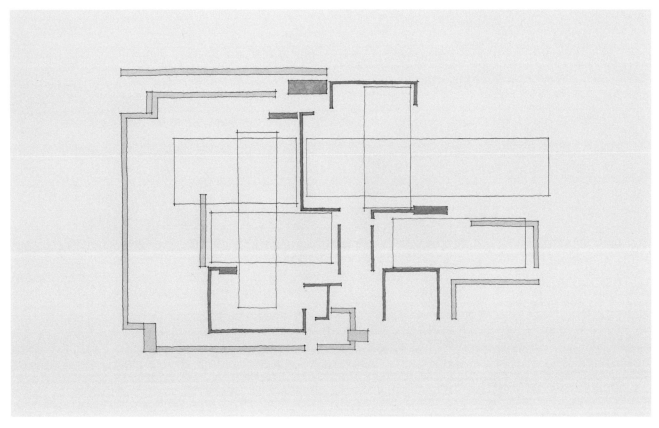

Overlapping inside and outside spaces and views

Ground level floor plan

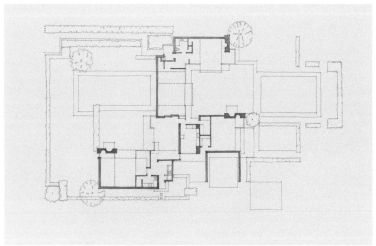

Schindler-Chase House
West Hollywood, California, 1923
Rudolph M. Schindler

How does the building relate to the landscape? What would change if the landscape were changed?
Is there a clear or indistinct line between "landscape" and "building"?
Where does the sun rise and set? Where is the sun at mid-day?
Where is north?

as overlapping rectangles. The diagram of Palladio's Villa La Rotonda, drawn in ink, shows the building as well as its subtle and complex relationship with the landscape. The bilaterally symmetrical villa, set at one end and to one side of a plinth, provides the occupant with four distinct relationships with the landscape. The views from each porch are quite different and thus evoke different villas in different landscapes. Toward the southwest the view is into a wood. To the northwest is a more urban view of the entry lane and chapel beyond. The views to the northeast and southeast are similar; however, the southeast is partially framed by trees while the northeast view is seen, one would suppose, during most of the day and year with the sun to the viewer's back. Of course, diagramming the villa with north up immediately reveals that the villa is situated 45 degrees from north, allowing sunlight on most of the four façades during the summer months.

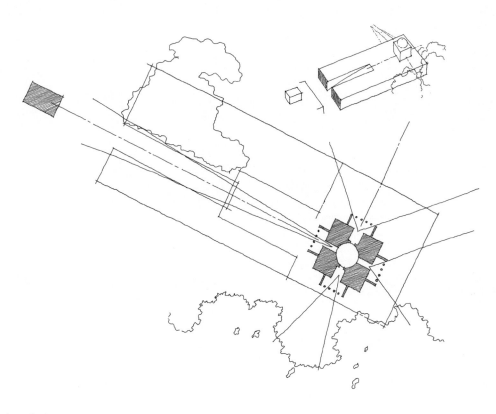

Different views through similar frames

Main level floor plan

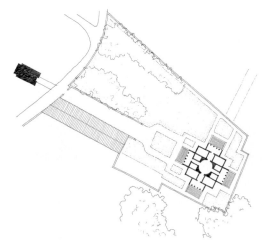

Villa La Rotonda
Vicenza, Italy, 1570
Andrea Palladio

Fashioning Order and Disorder

Fashioning order and disorder is an essential balancing act in architectural design. There will always be a need for order, regularity and consistency, yet there will always be disorder, irregular conditions and inconsistency. That is the nature of things. For example, embracing variety and change within the consistency is essential when designing an organized and unified bookshelf that must accommodate a variety of published and yet unpublished books. These diagrams are ways to help understand in what way complex design is actually simple, by focusing on the building's essential geometric order or essential programmatic elements. The key is to draw reductively in order to simplify the plan to an almost simplistic ordering. Although plans may appear complicated, more often than not there is an underlying order.

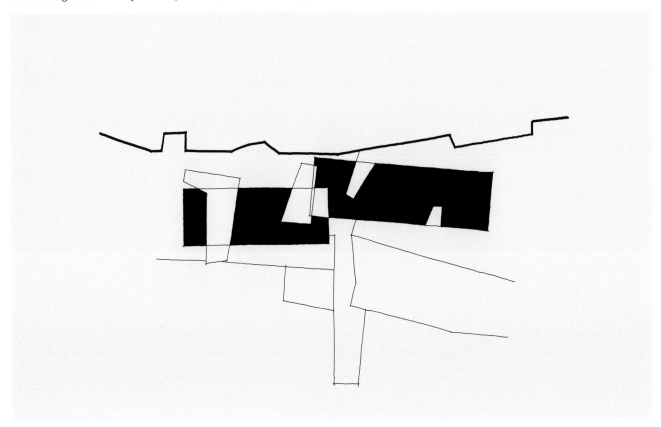

Rectilinear form transformed

Main level floor plan

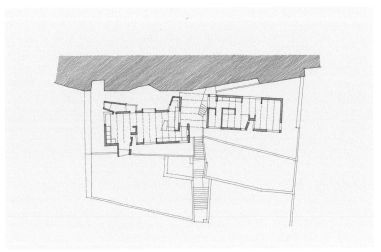

Casa en Bunyola
Bunyola, Mallorca, Spain, 2006
Francisco Cifuentes

Leaving aside the geometric patterns, how is the building organized programmatically?
How might you diagram the plan so that it does not have a geometric pattern?
What elements of the plan are continuous and what are discontinuous?
What is the rule, what is the exception?

The plan of the Casa at Bunyola is, at first sight, complex; yet a quick diagram reveals underlying straightforward patterns. Essentially, the diagram reduces the building to a fundamental geometric form (a bar divided into two), which is then augmented with angular subtracted and additive voids. The diagram of the Guggenheim in Bilbao is, in some ways, astonishingly reductive as it removes all aspects of the dynamic space. When looking at the plan, and even experiencing the building, its organization may be difficult to perceive. However, Gehry's design has, at its basis, his work prior to the 1980s. Reducing the building to a geometric pattern allows this straightforward organization. In both of these diagrams, the nature of black ink helps clearly delineate "either/or" relationships; yet subtleties are possible using different line weights and types, textures and hatching. The black-and-white drawing uses solid black to indicate the original, now displaced mass, while a thick, jagged line indicates the landscape hillside.

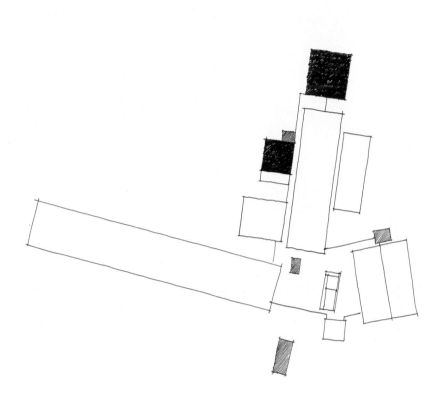

Organization within the complex form

Gallery level floor plan

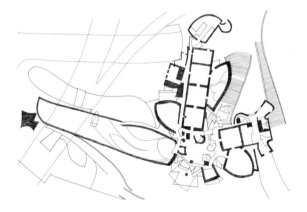

Guggenheim Museum Bilbao
Bilbao, Spain, 1997
Frank Gehry

Resolving Geometries

Design is often about resolving conflicts. This is especially evident when resolving two or more geometries found in cities, sites, rooms or details. The most common conflicts occur within the surrounding context, for example by introducing orthogonal structural systems into a trapezoidal site or implementing square prefabricated cabinets in a room whose walls are neither plumb nor square. Other demands might include accommodating specific, pre-determined room shapes, like a concert hall, or orienting a building to a specific cardinal direction. Solutions can range from explicit to veiled. Exaggerated geometric overlaps accentuate elemental differences in order to emphasize intention, composition or ambiguity. Each element maintains its integrity, yet the new, overlapping arrangement can prompt composite readings. Alternatively, tangential transitions can blur the boundaries between one geometry and another. Lastly, tertiary elements or zones like gaskets accomodate the conflict for the larger, unified whole.

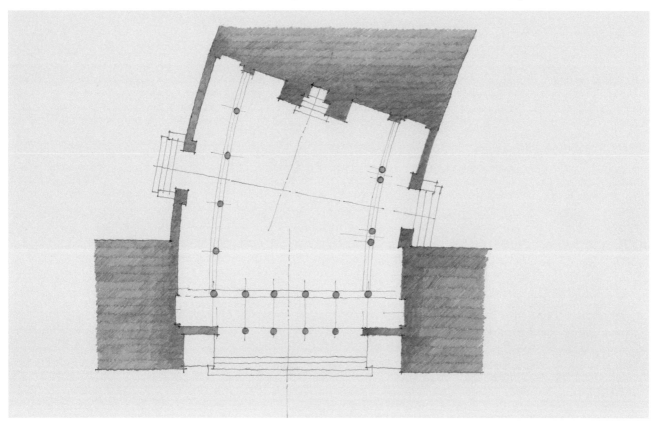

Ground level floor plan

Solution through circular geometry

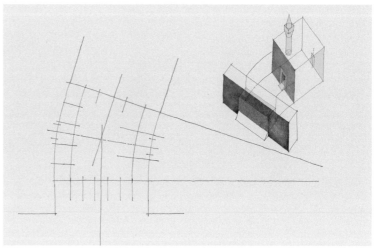

The Islamic Center of Washington
Washington, DC, 1957
Mario Rossi

Why are there two or more geometries? What is their meaning?
Does one geometry dominate another?
Are the different geometries juxtaposed or resolved in a third geometry?
What are the underlying orders of both geometric systems?

The diagrams of the Islamic Center of Washington explore the nearly hidden transition between the geometries of city and mosque. Curved courtyard walls and colonnades, each segmented arcs with the same center point, meet the straight walls of the street and of the *qibla* perpendicularly. The diagram shows the street plane and the *qibla* plane in two tones to emphasize the difference. The arced courtyard acts as a hyphen between the linear building along the street and the cubic building of the mosque. It creates a subtle transition, as a solution that remains tangential to the other buildings and isolated to this specific zone. In the Museum für Kunsthandwerk, the juxtaposed geometries are identified and isolated in the paths, which adds to a certain dynamic in the movement as the galleries remain orthogonal. The architect's decision to correlate particular geometries with specific uses helped resolve not only the site conflicts but also the site and building circulation.

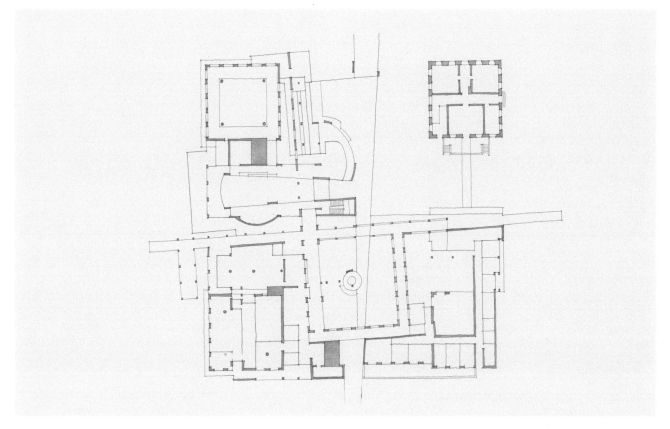

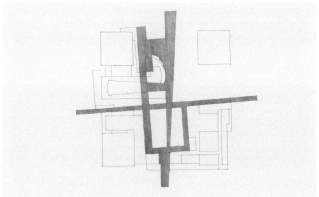
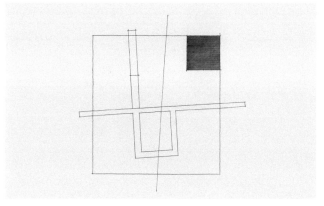

Ground level floor plan

Circulation within the rotated geometry

Existing villa within the new geometric order

Museum für Kunsthandwerk
Frankfurt am Main, Germany, 1985
Richard Meier & Partners

Extracting Voids from *Poché*

Inserting identifiable voids or objects within their irregular opposites is an essential exercise in resolving hierarchical relationships. These relationships are at once between the designed and the residual, but also between old and new, between furniture and room, between that which is inserted and that within which things are inserted. More-over, they are less about irregular/regular but rather about the relationships of elements to context and the rules that govern these relationships.

The diagrams of the Hôtel de Beauvais show how the irregular, polygonal (eleven-sided) site can accommodate a clear yet complex plan. Using tones of gray to differentiate or extricate the primary and secondary figural rooms, the diagrams show how the tertiary spaces are held within all that remains. The diagram helps identify and outline the primary space, which remains untoned, and the secondary rooms, which are lightly toned, while the tertiary spaces are completely unified into an encompassing dark-tone *poché*.

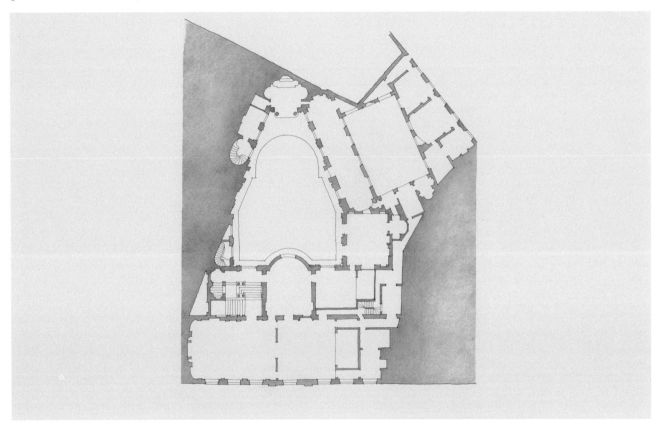

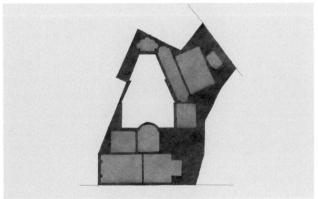

Upper level floor plan

Primary and secondary rooms within the *poché*

All major rooms with the surrounding context

Hôtel de Beauvais
Paris, France, 1656
Antoine Le Pautre

Is there a primary figural void in the building?
What is the relationship of the primary void to the secondary and tertiary voids?
What constitutes the primary, secondary and tertiary spaces?
In what respect is this a model of other design problems?

This type of diagram can be even further clarified or simplified by outlining only the primary spaces. Similarly, the diagram of the Institut du Monde Arabe uncovers how Jean Nouvel seems to have formed a pure cubic room in the center of the larger building mass. The exterior form is shaped by street edges and existing site lines. Unlike the diagram of the Hôtel de Beauvais, this diagram only shows the primary figural void. Interior secondary rooms merge with the *poché*.

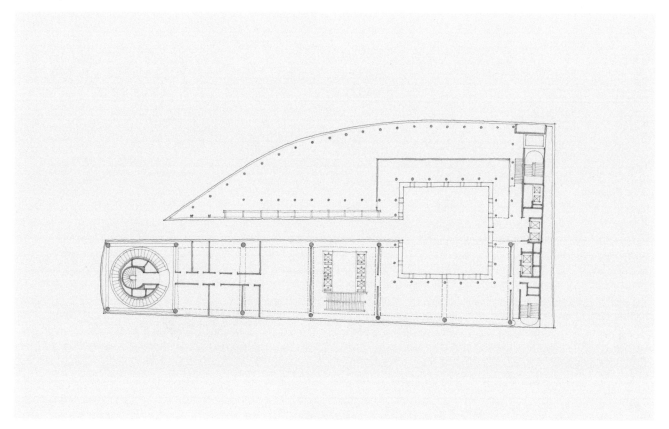

Upper level floor plan

The main figural courtyard within the *poché*

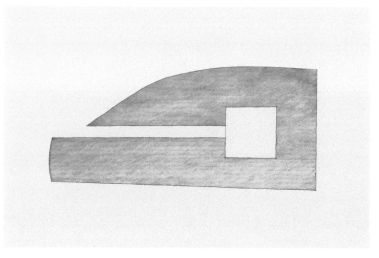

Institut du Monde Arabe
Paris, France, 1980
Jean Nouvel and Architecture-Studio

Composing Tectonic Order

The building process is a careful and systematic assemblage of elements to form a total complimentary ensemble. Assemblies often form a series of layers, one on the other: the skin, for example, in itself a series of layers, can be built only after the skeleton is complete. To clarify and realize this layered assembly, architects often establish formal compositional rules to guide material and assembly relationships. Proportional systems or hierarchical patterns help the architect develop and maintain a sense of order even as the project increases in complexity. While not all buildings employ landmark geometric proportional systems such as Golden Rectangles, in most cases there is a consistent underlying system that helps unify and coordinate the assembly process. These underlying patterns may be based on standardized construction modules, manufacturing processes or shipping limitations.

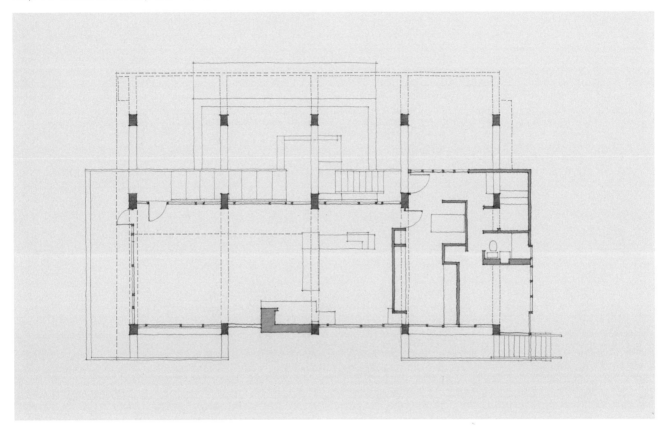

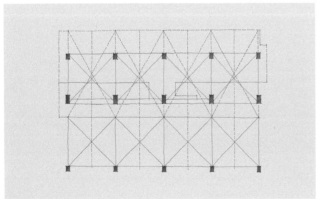

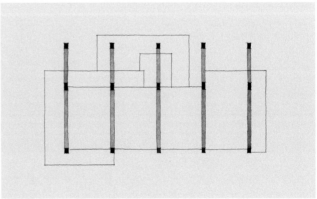

Upper level floor plan

Underlying geometric order

Highlighting the structural bents

Lovell Beach House
Newport Beach, California, 1926
Rudolf Schindler

How is the structure organized or composed?

Do the structural bays have a rhythm or proportional system?

How do different systems maintain a clarity yet work with other systems?

How do materials meet?

The diagram of Lovell Beach House shows how Schindler composed the structural frames, using squares and double squares that weave in and out to accommodate entry, balconies, rooms, etc. For the diagram, overlaid on the lightly toned bents are outlines of the floors, that highlight how the bents are a datum upon which the floors seem to shift. The diagram of Patkau Architects' Agosta House highlights a structural order in which primary parallel masonry walls contrast perpendicular L-shaped and

J-shaped masonry walls interconnected with secondary and tertiary glass planes. These diagrams are particularly relevant to the design and construction process that has to synchronize tectonics, interrelated systems and underlying organizational patterns into a hierarchical fabric.

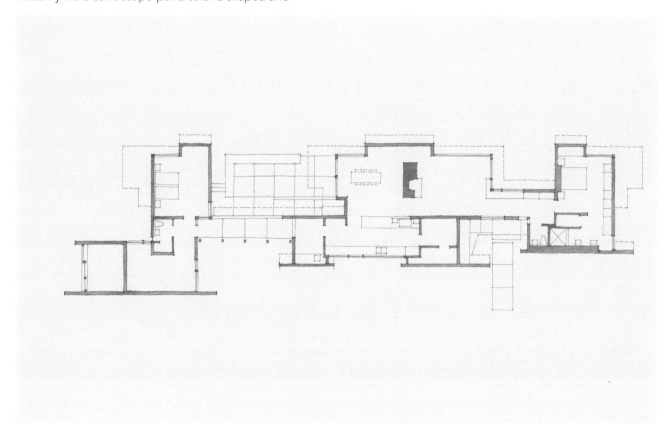

Main level floor plan

Highlighting the masonry walls

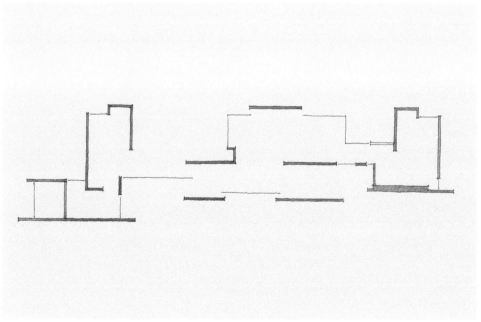

Agosta House
San Juan Island, Washington, 2000
Patkau Architects

Reconciling Structure and Enclosure

The relationship of structure and enclosure is one that reflects how we build today. Generally, when we build we raise a structure – columns and beams, columns and floor slabs, walls and beams, etc. – and then we slowly layer upon this structure the enclosing walls, glass or fabrics. How these two systems interact is an essential issue in developing not only a clear construction process but an understanding of the nature of that which supports and that which encloses.

The diagram of Le Corbusier's Villa Stein reveals how free-standing, non-structural enclosing walls as well as the additive and subtractive volumes play against the structural A-B-A-B-A grid that defines and regulates movement through the house. The diagram highlights primarily the structural bays and columns, with enclosing walls drawn in lightly. As a point of contrast, the diagram of Albert Kelsey's and Paul Philippe Cret's Pan American Union Building (now the Organization of American States) shows how spaces

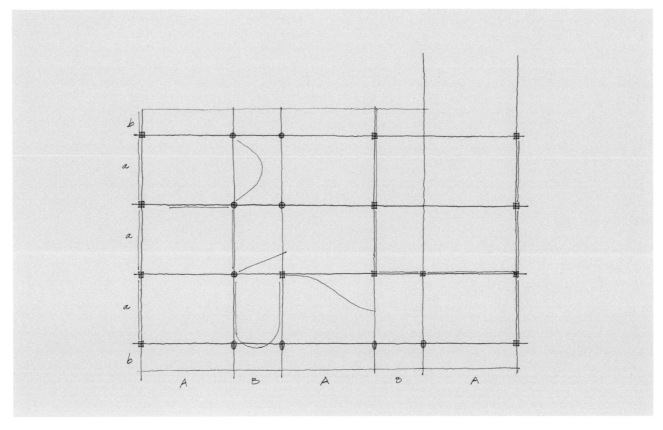

Main level floor plan

Columns independent of enclosure

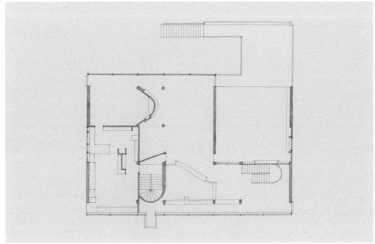

Villa Stein-de Monzie
Paris, France, 1928
Le Corbusier

What is the building's underlying structural pattern or system?

How does the enclosing system complement or contrast the structural system?

How are service/served, public/private, path/room and other organizational dichotomies related to the structural system?

correspond with the structural system: that which is structure is also that which is enclosure. Here the building's tectonics – its columns, beams, walls, floors and overall material articulation – are a kind of language of material use, type, size, orientation and location that corresponds to specific functions or is used to convey and reinforce meaning. For example, a simple tectonic language might be: "round columns in areas of movement / square columns in areas of rest." This language, while simplistic,

can accentuate or obstruct a spatial sequence. Moving through a space formed by polished, round concrete columns, set on a tight grid perpendicular to movement, is quite different from moving through a space with rough, square concrete columns set on a neutral grid.

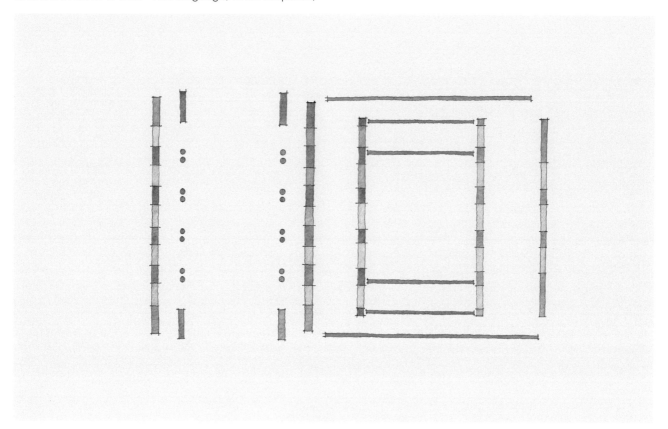

Walls as enclosure

Composite plan

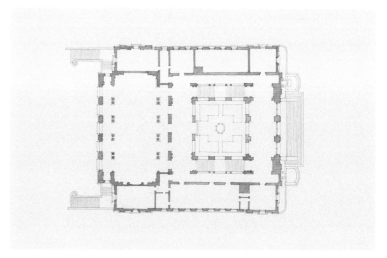

Organization of American States
(Pan American Union Building)
Washington, DC, 1913
Albert Kelsey and Paul Philippe Cret

Disposing Walls

Masonry walls are essential elements of architecture. Their organization, thickness, height, transformation and interplay with other architectural elements can develop a sophisticated architectural language. Walls, by their nature as solid and long-lasting, often attain symbolic meaning – we need only think of the Berlin Wall, the battered walls in Beijing's Forbidden City, the Western Wall in Jerusalem or even the metaphorical walls that we erect among ourselves.

The diagrams of Moneo's Museo Nacional de Arte Romano show the museum as series of parallel brick walls augmented through carving (archways) and insertions (mezzanines) to introduce spatial hierarchy into the plan similar to Roman basilicas and baths in which occurred the activities of Roman life. While the repetitive bays, which are superimposed on the ruins found on the site, offer a distinct order they also act as a datum to random movement and light washing in from the upper levels. In a

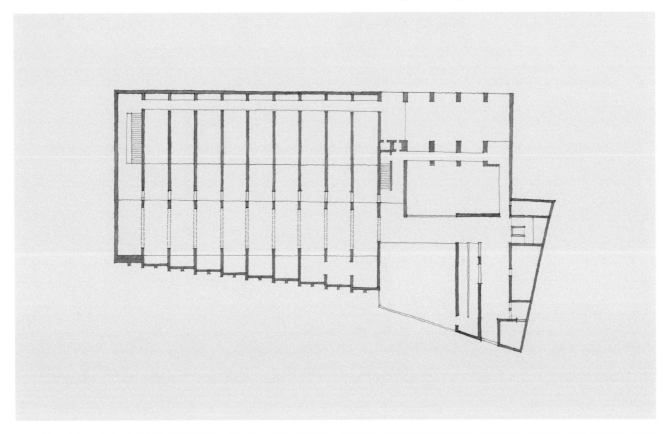

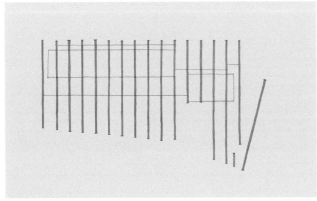

Ground level floor plan

Wall organization

Walls with openings and inserted mezzanines

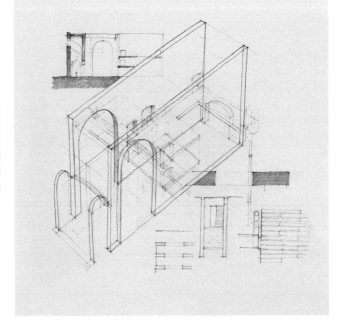

Museo Nacional de Arte Romano
Mérida, Spain, 1986
Rafael Moneo

What is the langue of the walls?
Where do specific wall types occur?
In what way are the walls hierarchical?

different manner, the diagram of the Sonsbeek Pavilion shows how, unlike Moneo, van Eyck incorporates curved walls of varied dimensions to introduce hierarchy to the plan.

Ground level floor plan

Underlying grid and circular geometries

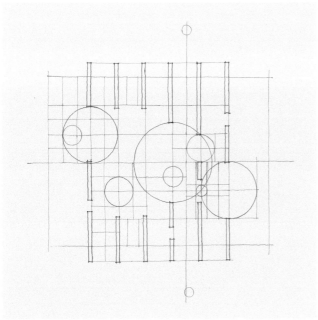

The Sonsbeek Pavilion
Arnhem, The Netherlands, 1965
Aldo van Eyck

Classifying Type: the Infill

The party-wall or infill-building type is an efficient and flexible organizational strategy in which perimeter rooms have access to light and air while services, such as stairs, toilets and storage, concentrate toward the darker center. Asymmetrically disposed horizontal paths and centralized stairs optimize the usable floor area and, at the same time, allow for maximum internal flexibility. For example, by simply "closing a door" an infill house can accommodate multiple family types within a simple framework.

The two plan diagrams and the two transparent isometric diagrams show typical spatial organizations. The floor plan diagrams employ tones to delineate service/served, light/dark and path/room spaces and to show how the spatial concentration creates a clear, yet flexible layout in which the open or closed doors, insertions or removals of walls at any level can accommodate varied functions. The transparent isometrics show how circulation weaves along the edge and center, leaving the perimeter free for living spaces.

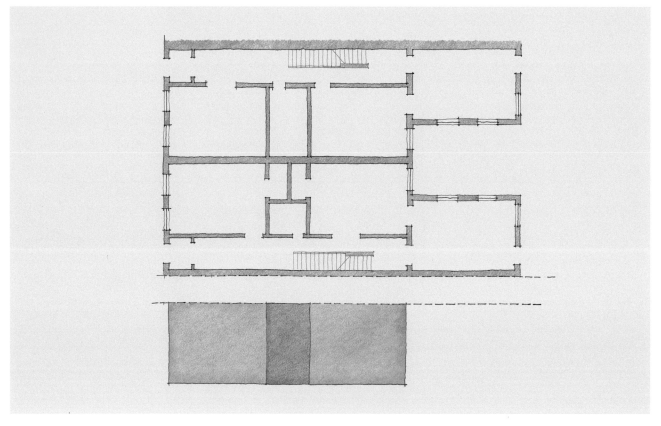

Typical floor plan

Service core with linear stairs laterally disposed

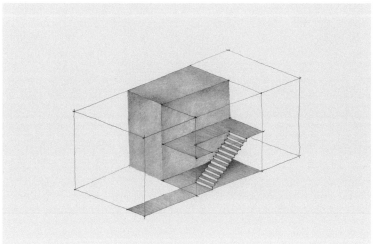

Rowhouse 1

Where is horizontal and vertical circulation concentrated?
How is the roof used to pull light into the building's center?
In what way are upper floors similar to or different from the lower floors?

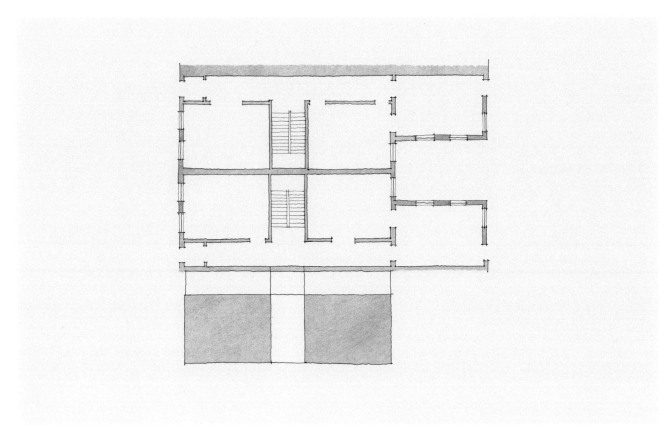

Typical floor plan

Service cores enclosing a wrapping stair

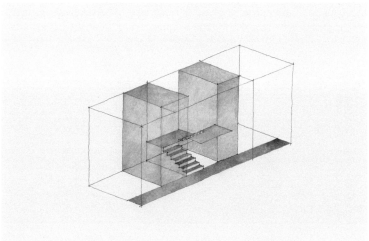

Rowhouse 2

Classifying Type: the Bar

The linear bar as a building type is a simple, flexible and efficient organizational strategy with varied spaces arranged along horizontal internal or perimeter paths with distributed or centralized vertical cores. Relatively narrow floor plates, supported by often simple and repetitive structural systems, allow ample natural light penetration and cross-ventilation. While simple and adaptable, a bar cannot adapt to all program needs and therefore is often supplemented with ancillary elements to the sides or ends.

The diagram of Le Corbusier's Steel-Frame House in the Stuttgart Weißenhof Estate reveals the access to flexible private/public and service/served zones along a linear pathway with prominent stair towers that serve other floors. Similarly, the Glasgow School of Art diagram, drawn with tones to indicate levels of public and private space, shows how the horizontal circulation separates the building into service/served and light/dark zones: to the north are classrooms and studios with exposure to the relatively

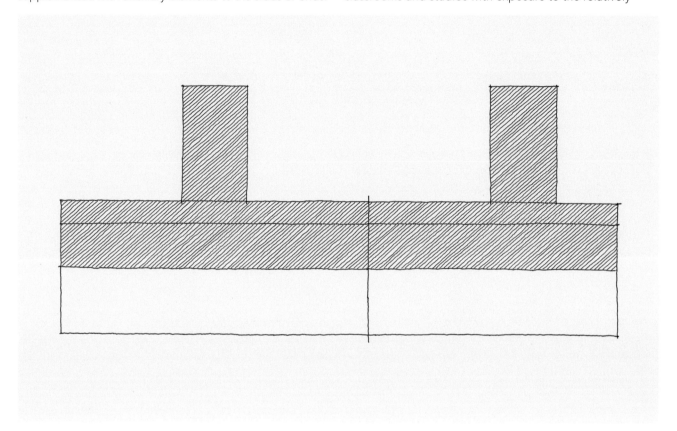

Service and circulation to one side, rooms to the other

Upper level floor plan

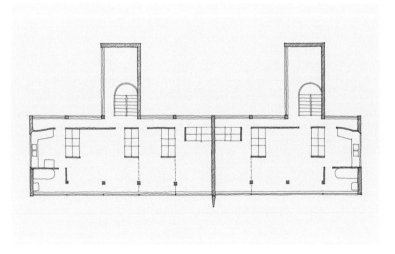

Steel-Frame House
Weißenhof Estate
Stuttgart, Germany, 1927
Le Corbusier

How do service/served, public/private and light/dark dichotomies work with circulation?
How does the bar type accommodate varied programmatic needs?
How does the type accommodate needs that do not fit within the bar?
Does the horizontal circulation change from floor to floor?

uniform natural light; on the opposite side are the service spaces adjacent to interior service alley.

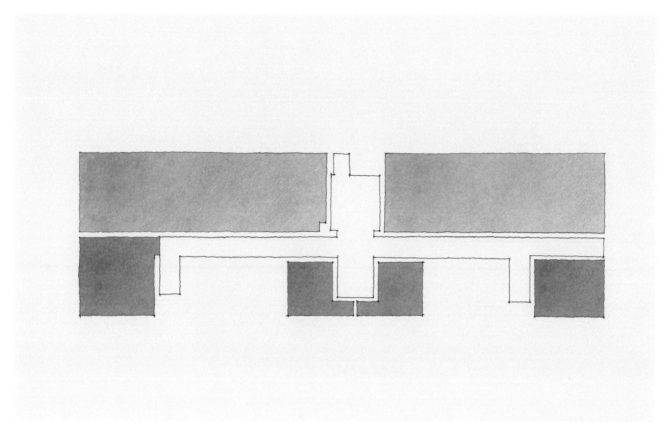

Service to one side, served to the other

Main level floor plan

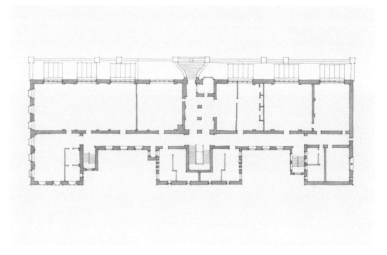

The Glasgow School of Art
Glasgow, Scotland, 1899
Charles Rennie Mackintosh

Classifying Type: the Courtyard

The courtyard type, found throughout the world regardless of time and location, owes its ubiquity to the way in which it organizes many rooms, which need access to light and air, within an enclosed, identifiable and internalized private realm accessed by a compact circulation system. Further solidifying its universality, from huts grouped around a bonfire to an Andalusian patio, the courtyard type reflects the desire and need for centralized communal space.

The diagram of the Palazzo Farnese, drawn in ink, shows a rather typical courtyard building that is at once compact, with a well-ventilated and lighted center accessed by horizontal and vertical circulation. Although the surrounding rooms vary in width and length, the internal courtyard is an identifiable and unified external form. The diagram of the Säynätsalo Town Hall, drawn in pencil with tones to indicate circulation and program distribution, shows how the courtyard type adapts to climate, site and program.

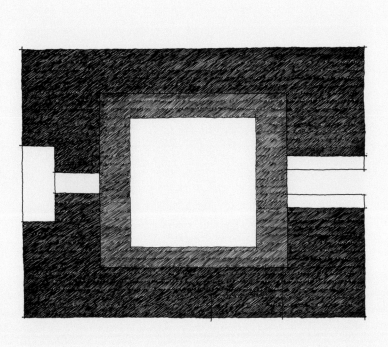

Rooms wrapped around a central court

Ground level floor plan

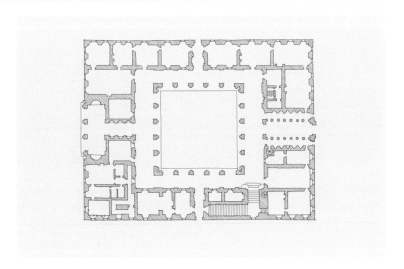

Palazzo Farnese
Rome, Italy, 1515
Antonio da Sangallo

How is the type transformed?

Where does the circulation most often occur?

What is the deepest part of the plan?

Is the courtyard open to the elements or conditioned? If the courtyard is open to the sky, how is the circulation enclosed or exposed to the elements?

Here, Aalto augmented the courtyard type by pulling away one wall, thereby allowing the public to "slide" into the courtyard and toward the main entry that is highlighted by the larger meeting hall, yet still creates a compact and identifiable public building.

A courtyard with articulated elements

Courtyard level floor plan

Säynätsalo Town Hall
Säynätsalo, Finland, 1951
Alvar Aalto

TRAVERSING THE SECTION

The employment of masses and cavities together in effective contrast leads to works which lie in one of the peripheries of architecture, close to the art of the theater and at times to that of sculpture. But still they belong under architecture.

Steen Eiler Rasmussen[1]

Space, in contemporary discourse, as in lived experience, has taken on an almost palpable existence. Its contours, boundaries, and geographies are called upon to stand in for all the contested realms of identity.

Anthony Vidler[2]

The plan is organization. The section is experience.

Mark McInturff[3]

Traversing the section – ascending stairs, stepping across thresholds, meandering through rooms – is at once the act of moving through space and the experience that informs our understanding of place embodied in space. Beginning with rudimentary and varied definitions, we can begin to understand the connection between and transformation of quantitative (dimension, material, texture) and qualitative (place, sense, feeling) phenomena through architectural analysis.

Space, explicitly or implicitly defined and enclosed by boundaries or perimeters, is more than a three-dimensional Cartesian x-y-z matrix, but a material and immaterial identifiable entity, the existence of which depends on variegated material and immaterial boundaries: material boundaries, such as walls, floors or ceilings, and immaterial, such as imaginary, yet definitive lines implied by edges, columns or other frames. Variations of these abound: when does a row of columns become a solid wall or an implied plane?

Like philosopher Lao Tzu's bowl, the essence of a bowl is not the bowl but the void formed by the bowl: its usefulness is in absence.[4] Even essential ethereal voids would be unusable without the "clay" defining it. This interdependent material-void relationship is one in which the awareness of both void and solid as essential helps us see that the design of architecture is at once material and spatial. We build using materials, but the ultimate goal of these materials is to shape space. This conceptual shift relieves the predominance or focus on material to a balance of the two. The significance of a piazza, concert hall, bedroom or alcove has as much to do with its void as with its material and immaterial limits.

And with significance begins the sense of place. The nature and definitions of place are myriad and often paradoxical. From the Heideggerian interrelationship of the building act as a means to and result of place-making, to more phenomenological examinations in which place itself emerges from the deliberate act of engaging with space, place is that ineffable character that we use to differentiate from other spaces. In these acts of defining, describing and differentiating place, we engage in place personally and intimately so that place emerges out of what we bring to the space. By introducing time, marked by changes in position, light or temperature, three-dimensional space transforms into four-dimensional place.

Diagramming Place

Architects, theorists and philosophers including Christian Norberg-Schulz, Juhani Pallasmaa and David Seamons have searched for an understanding of place and how looking, observing and engaging with the world relates to architectural education, thinking and design – moreover, how the study, analysis and representation of place can help architects shape place. Understanding the dynamic of multi-dimensional place through diagrams is inherently challenging. How is one supposed to draw something that is ephemeral, phenomenological or experiential? That is what architects do: they produce representations that will, it is hoped, result in a built environment that achieves experiential goals. In a sense, architects design place indirectly. They suggest through drawings and text the materials, dimensions, orientations and other quantifiable aspects that, when combined and built, will result in a particular qualitative and sensual experience. Architects essentially provide instructions that will, if they are clearly phrased and accurately followed, result in place. Learning to correlate instructions to outcomes is learned not only through repeated attempts or studying previously successful representation-reality relationships, but also through studying three and four-dimensional space through drawing. Essentially, reversing engineering experience into possible instructions will help an architect to become a better instruction writer.

This does not mean that a diagram will uncover intentions or that drawings will guarantee poetics. As Juhani Pallasmaa observes, "Analysis of the formal structure of architectural work does not necessarily reveal the artistic quality of the building or how it makes its effect."[5] Fortunately, Pallasmaa offers us some hope by suggesting that analysis that incorporates experience can, in fact, help us examine and question the interaction of material, dimension and conveyed meaning. The diagram in particular and the architectural drawing in general must try communicate intentions, and those intentions, prosaic, poetic or otherwise, must be incorporated into the drawing itself so that others (builders, contractors, artisans) can decipher and then construct those "intentions" into three-dimensional realities.

To help develop three-dimensional thinking and, in turn, four-dimensional results, the diagrams in Traversing the Section focus primarily on decoding a building's quantitative attributes. By examining a volume's dimension, scale and its relationships among volumes or by examining the floors, walls, ceilings and their role in shaping volume and their relationships to one another will, it is hoped, develop an understanding of how these come together in a way that can at least inspire a particular spatial experience. Moreover, the diagrams focus on the way in which volume is experienced in terms of procession, movement, path and sequence. While a particular experience cannot be predicted, it does not hurt to know what contributes to a particular experience.

Like a plan, elevation or other nominal drawing type, a section is a two-dimensional representation based upon an imaginary vertical slice through a three-dimensional space. As an abstraction, we really do not experience a section as much as we experience a milieu of volumes, materials, temperature and light represented in a section. Added to this is the fallacy that a section is somehow more spatial than a plan or other two-dimensional representations. A plan and elevation are spatial in that they follow one particular convention of defining space in two dimensions. At the same time, digital models are no more three-dimensional than two-dimensional drawings. Three-dimensional models are still projected onto two-dimensional surfaces.

Toward Understanding Place
The focus of many of these diagrams is on quantitative and compositional characteristics, with the ultimate aim of offering methods to engage with varied interpretations of space. While diagrams are often interrelated and difficult to reduce into separate categories, this is the essence of diagramming.

The first overriding diagrammatic lens is movement through a building: sequence, in the sense of how we articulate that sequence, how we guide people through the building, how room is designated differently than paths. The relationship of path (space of movement) to room (space of rest) and how each complements the other, how both can be clear yet overlap seems one of the most critical.

A second common lens is the nature of volumes of a building, including the solid mass, the roof, the *poché*, subtracted volumes, interlocking volumes and scale. The fluctuation or articulation of volume as we move from entry into the building has an incredible impact on our perceptions and our senses: compression and expression, orchestrated in ways that bring sense of excitement, of calm or other feeling.

The third lens is that of surfaces that define volumes: floors, walls, ceilings, roofs, and how these participate in the spatial definition. The floor as it moves from flat to sloped to ramped to steps is another important aspect – the floor not only as a flat plane but as the surface upon which we walk. Rather than viewing it as a floor, it might be better to view it as the plane of walking or stepping. If it is considered a plane of stepping or walking or treading, then it becomes consciously considered. The plane of stepping as it transforms from relatively level to sloped or to stepped then becomes a critical part of the spatial sequence.

Questions at the root of this action include:
How is this place manifested through dimension, scale, enclosure, material and texture?
How might I, as an architect, represent and communicate a sense of place so that others might build it?
What did this architect draw to make this place? What was not drawn but is only a patina?
What diagrams can help me understand this place?

1   Rasmussen, Steen Eiler, *Experiencing Architecture.* Cambridge: MIT Press (1962): 82.

2   Vidler, Anthony, *The Architectural Uncanny: Essays in the Modern Unhomely.* Cambridge: MIT Press (1992): 167.

3   Mark McInturff, The Catholic University of America, Washington, DC (September 10, 2009).

4   Lao Tzu, *Tao Te Ching.*

5   Pallasmaa, Juhani, "The Geometry of Feeling: A Look at the Phenomenology of Architecture", *Skala: Nordic Journal of Architecture and Art* 4 (June 1986): 22-25.

6   Venturi, Robert, *Complexity and Contradiction in Architecture.* New York: Museum of Modern Art (1966): 22-23.

7   Moneo, Rafael, "On Typology", *Oppositions* 13:23 (Summer 1978): 27.

Orchestrating Sequence

Orchestrating sequence is at one moment part of a larger functional need, yet may be an effort to provoke a particular mood. Sequence can instill a sense of rebirth or transformation, heighten expectations or support a particular ritual or tradition. Examining the way in which architects orchestrate space helps reveal the way architecture can be more than a functional layout but rather something that can enliven both mundane and special events.

The diagram of Tadao Ando's Chapel on Mount Rokko reveals how the chapel's covered walkway is part of a procession from an adjacent hotel to the actual chapel and, moreover, coincides and reinforces the part of a marriage ritual. Correspondingly, it begins to show how Ando uses a variety of methods to orchestrate the sequence including geometric shifts, views and movement around a wall, changes in geometric form (circle to square), elongated and focused paths, unbounded views, rotation,

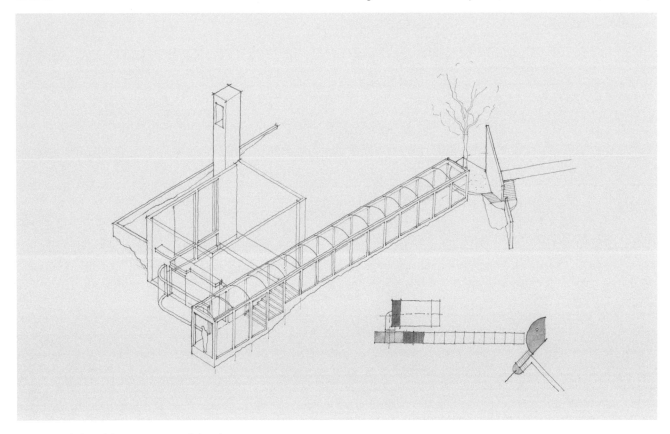

Isometric and plan of the passageway and chapel

View down toward the chapel

Chapel on Mount Rokko
Kobe, Japan, 1986
Tadao Ando

What dimensions, directions, materials or scales help orchestrate movement?
How did the architect extenuate movement into and through the building?
What orchestration seems forced and what orchestration is hardly noticed?

compression and finally openings. The diagram of Flagg's
Corcoran Gallery of Art shows how a relatively short and
straight path to a small rotunda, which seems relatively
simple, is actually highly articulated. Passing through
several volumes, the visitor climbs a stairway, passes
between a bisected atrium counter to the cross-axis, into
a larger stairway, through a threshold and finally into the
rotunda.

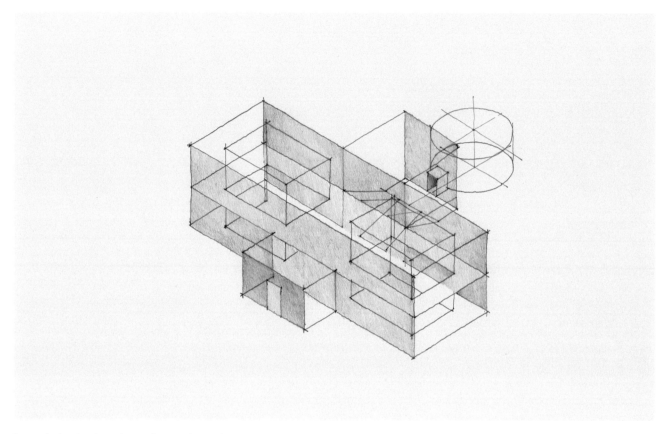

Isometric showing the atrium, stairway and rotunda

View through the atrium to the main stairway

Corcoran Gallery of Art
Washington, DC, 1874
Ernest Flagg

Entering the Building

More than just opening and passing through a door, entering a building is part of the journey from one state of mind to another. As a journey, even the most rudimentary entry is a series of thresholds or a complex layered system of beginnings that begin well before the door. It is difficult to say when one "enters" a building in the sense of moving through a street or neighborhood.

The axonometric diagram of Asplund's Stockholm Public Library reveals how the very straight stairway moves through the plinth and under the drum's edge to emerge nearly in the center of the library's main hall. This nearly straight path is dynamic and transformative as it cuts through and interacts with a variety of spaces. By contrast, the entry sequence of Ando's Church of the Water requires movement up, then down and around to the final sanctuary. The chapel sits within a resort area, and with the help

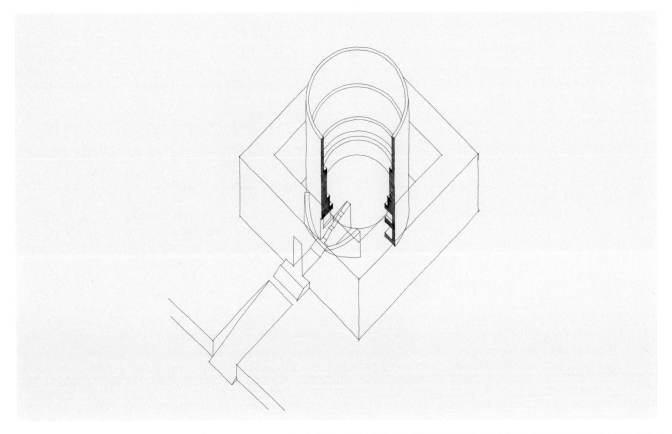

Section plan oblique showing the primary volumes

Section through the entry sequence to the central hall

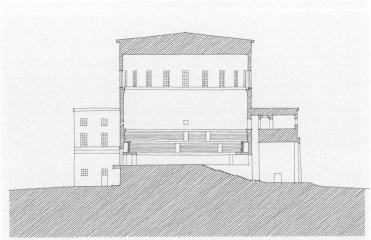

Stockholm Public Library
Stockholm, Sweden, 1926
Erik Gunnar Asplund

Where does the entry "begin"? At what point are you "entering" the building?
What kind and how many thresholds do you penetrate as you enter?
What material, spatial or dimensional changes occur as you enter the building?
How is entry marked in section?

of walls, columns and piers, it is clear at the end of this sequence that the visitor is in a sacred world. Its diagram tries to examine this sequence that is otherwise difficult to understand in section or plan.

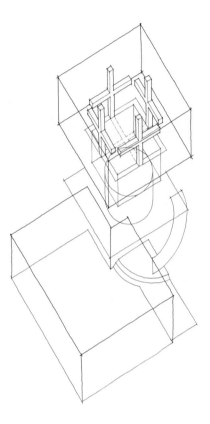

Plan oblique of the entry sequence

Plan of the chapel and surrounding landscape

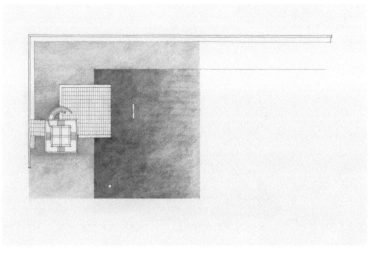

Church on the Water
Tomamu, Japan, 1988
Tadao Ando

Passing through Buildings

The interface of public and private realms at the urban scale remains an important concern in architectural design. The public-private boundary involves concerns including a public's right of entry versus security concerns or the interaction between those who visit and those who labor there, to give just two examples. Buildings in which public pathways interlace through a private building have particular importance, especially in how public and private can have a more complex, ambiguous "both/and" relation-

ship: for instance, a private building accommodates a public path that, in turn, contributes to the urban fabric and experience.

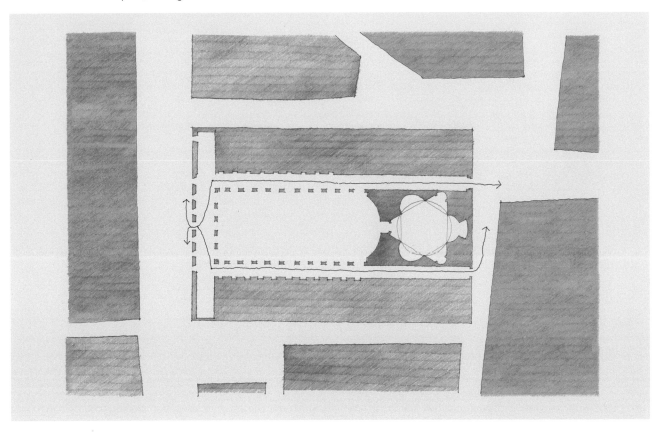

Nolli plan of the complex within the urban fabric

Plan oblique showing the path through the site

View of the courtyard

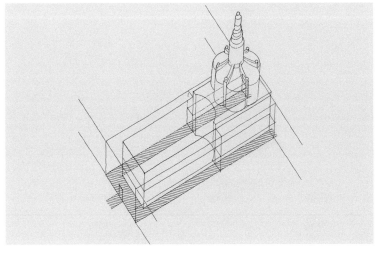

Sant'Ivo alla Sapienza
Rome, Italy, 1650
Francesco Borromini

How does a public path participate in a private building?

How is the private realm maintained even if overlapping with a public path?

Are the public and private zones clear or ambiguous? Why is that so?

The transparent axonometric of Sant'Ivo alla Sapienza highlights paths through the building from one side of the block to the other. The axonometric shows the volumetric, spatial experience afforded by the move from the street to the portico, along either side of the courtyard, past the chapel and, finally, out to the rear street. Likewise, the diagram of the Neue Staatsgalerie highlights the ribbon-like link from the one side of the neighborhood to the other. Moving from higher elevation to lower allows the public to engage with the museum's interior while on a path that has unique, nearly paradoxical characteristics: it is "within" the building but clearly outside and while it is integrated it is also separate from the building.

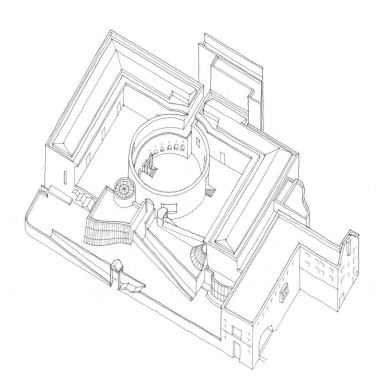

Plan oblique of the museum

Plan oblique highlighting the path through the site

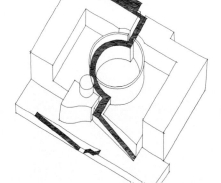

View of the courtyard

Neue Staatsgalerie
Stuttgart, Germany, 1983
James Stirling

Articulating Path and Room

Paths through a building or room are typically differentiated from areas of rest. This differentiation may be made explicit by changing floor plane materials or level changes or by walls or colonnades, or it can be implied through aligned doorways. It is the ceiling plane, however, that allows for the best opportunity for path/room differentiation. Simply put, while a floor remains level, a ceiling can fluctuate.

In the diagrams of Sir John Soane's Museum, the section through the rear gallery illustrates the highly articulated ceiling along the gallery and above those paths that cross the gallery perpendicularly. While each room and pathway has its own articulation, the floor, or the paths across the floor, remain level just as views penetrate and link the multiple spaces. There is both continuity and articulation. The first diagram clearly maps out the mass and void relationship, while the second uses minimal lines to

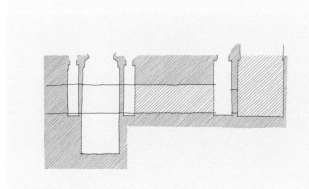
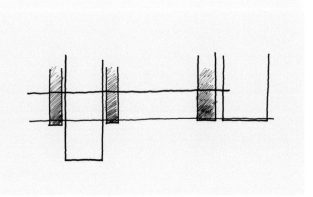

Section through the galleries

Section diagrams of separate and continuous spaces

Sir John Soane's Museum
London, England, 1824
John Soane

Where is the zone of movement and where is the zone for rest?

How is movement or path marked or highlighted?

When in the zone of rest, where is the focus or foci?

When is the clarity or the ambiguity of path/room differentiation needed?

communicate the consistent view of corridors and paths even as the ceiling heights fluctuate. Contrasting these diagrams, the diagram of Palazzo Strozzi's paths and rooms shows that the floor remains level while the paths, articulated as an arcade, and the rooms remain distinct, giving a sense of either inside or outside.

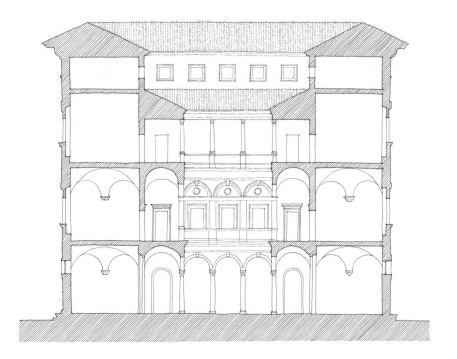

Section through the courtyard

Section diagram showing the separate paths and rooms

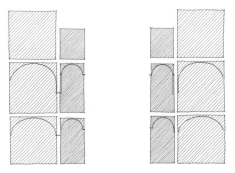

Palazzo Strozzi
Florence, Italy, 1538
Benedetto da Maiano/Simone del Pollaiolo

Ascending Stairs

In buildings with more than one level, stairs are the obligatory moment when a floor plane transforms into a succession of miniature floors, allowing vertical movement without mechanical means. Conceived or reconsidered as a place for ascension, the idea of a stair can easily move beyond the prosaic to, perhaps, the poetic. As such, these moments are opportunities for spatial dynamics that, when diagrammed, both demand and, at same time, promote considerable three-dimensional thinking.

The transparent isometric diagram of the Boston Public Library helps reveal how the stair is part of a series of compressed and expanded rooms, culminating in the oblong, vaulted reading room located above the main entry. The diagram shows that the stairs emerge out of a vaulted passageway into the stair hall and double back toward the main floor. There the person enters a loggia, moves through a doorway and finally into the main reading room. In comparison with the section, the isometric reveals

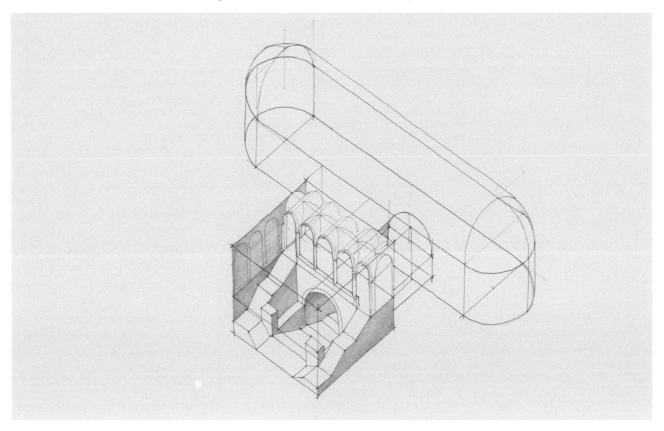

Isometric of the sequential volumes

Section through the entry and reading room

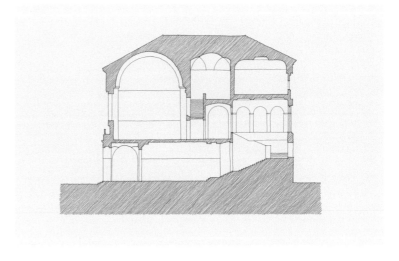

View of the central stair hall

Boston Public Library
Boston, Massachusetts, 1888
McKim, Mead and White

How is the stair contained? Is it in its own "room" or is in part of another room?
How does the stair begin, change direction and end?
What role does the stair play in facilitating transition?

the spatial layers inherent in the path from street to reading room. Unlike the Boston Public Library, the diagrams of the Unity Temple reveals how the complex stair towers enclose and hide the visitor until the last moment. This is especially advantageous to those arriving late for a service, who can remain hidden until they emerge at the desired seating area. These diagrams, which were particularly challenging, help untangle the complexity of the stairway and of the Unity Temple as a whole.

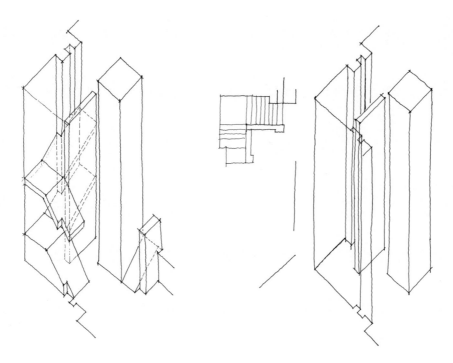

Plan oblique diagrams of the stairs and the tower's structure

View of the main hall with stair tower in the corner

Unity Temple
Oak Park, Illinois, 1908
Frank Lloyd Wright

Stepping with the Landscape

Interlinking architecture with landscape necessitates harmony or consonance of elements. The elements can remain distinct yet combine to create a new, more complex whole. While there are countless examples of landscape and architecture interfaces, the topic is especially apparent in buildings that step with the landscape. This can take the form of a series of terraced rooms connected by paths that both work with and are in opposition to the land. The land retains its natural descent, yet acquiesces to help form distinct spaces by extending, diminishing, wrapping, rising, falling or staggering.

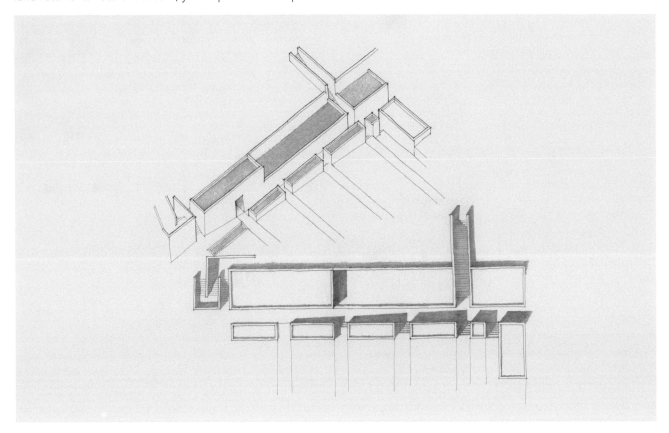

Isometric and partial plan of the theater

View toward the stage

Generalife Amphitheater
Granada, Spain, 1952
Francisco Prieto-Moreno

To what extent is the terracing regular and irregular?
How is hierarchy and differentiation incorporated into a regular system?
What are corresponding moves? If the width increases, what happens to the height?
How do stairs change within the terraces?

The diagram of the Generalife Amphitheater shows how a continuous series of terraces incorporates a complex system of entries and stairs, including connections to a linear service wing. Here the terraces and retaining walls help shape the variable slopes into a harmonious whole. Likewise, the diagram of the Şelale Tea House garden near Priene, Turkey shows how its terraces combine and vary to make a series of outdoor rooms. Increasing floor widths, corresponding high or low retaining walls and wider and

narrower paths help create a varied, yet comprehensible outdoor setting. Diagramming terraces such as these helps develop a greater awareness and understanding of contours, slope and grade change because it requires that you walk around, up and down the site to see how land can integrate architecture.

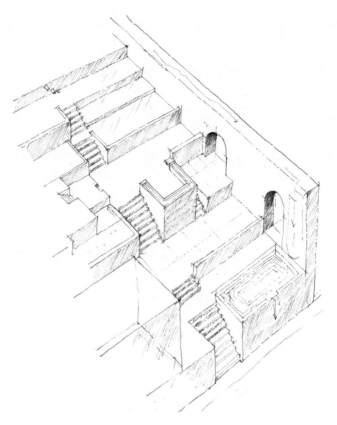

Plan oblique of the terraces with aqueduct

View of the terraces

Priene Antik Şelale Restaurant
Güllübahçe, Turkey

Considering Circulation

As might be expected, the complexity of a building's circulation systems generally corresponds to the complexity of its functional and spatial organization. The more varied the spatial organization, the more challenging is it to circulate to and around those spaces. Such complexities can be especially common in housing that has varied unit types contained within a single structure. Vertical and horizontal movement outside and within units can be simplified sections or complex three-dimensional studies.

The diagram of Le Corbusier's Marseille block housing shows how an alternate level corridor with "skip-stop" organization, in which horizontal, double-loaded corridors occur at every third level, allows for a complex spatial structure as well as through-unit air ventilation and light to two sides of any apartment. The diagram of Sert's Peabody Terrace housing complex shows a variation on this system: while the elevator stops at every third floor, local stairs go up or down to varied apartments types.

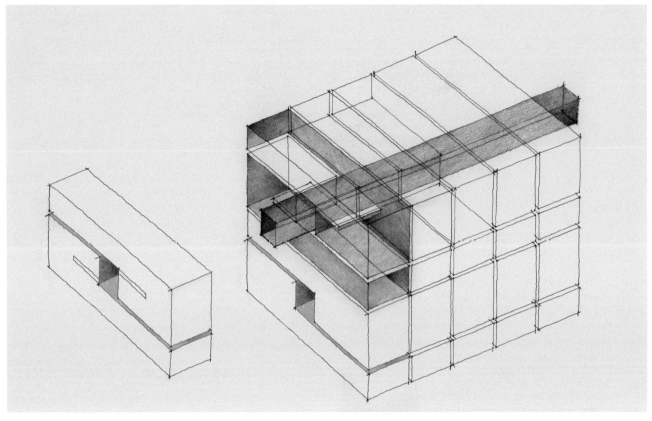

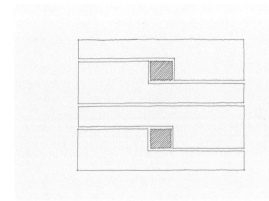

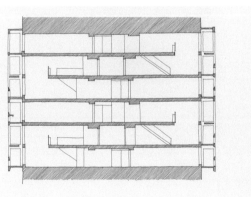

Sectional diagram showing interlocking flats

Transparent isometric showing interlocking flats and horizontal circulation

Partial section

Unité d'Habitation
Marseille, France, 1952
Le Corbusier

What is the public circulation in the building?

How did the architect accommodate varied units within one large building?

What is the simplest way to diagram this organization?

How are access to light and air improved through a complex circulation system?

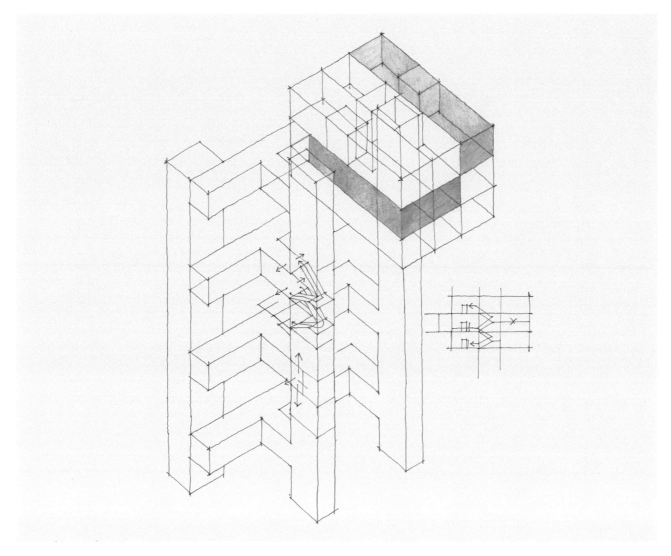

Transparent isometric showing apartment types linked to local circulation

View of the exterior revealing
the apartment types

Peabody Terrace
Cambridge, Massachusetts, 1965
José Luis Sert

Compressing and Expanding Sequences

Spatial compression and expansion within a building highlight the transformation from one space to another. The compression is, at one level, practical and relates to the functional distribution of larger and smaller rooms. For example, volumetric meeting rooms are most commonly surrounded by smaller support spaces that must be traversed. At another level, it is deliberate manipulation: augmenting compression and expansion through a building heightens the spatial experience.

The section diagram of the Sokullu Ismihan Sultan Complex shows the spatial compression and release from street to entry to courtyard through the porch and doorway and finally into the domed mosque. The smaller isometric diagram of the entry-courtyard stairway shows how, at a short distance, the spatial sequence is dramatic within a relatively confined area. The diagram of Rome's Termini rail station shows, through pen and felt-tip pen, the idealized compression and expansion, which has been compromised

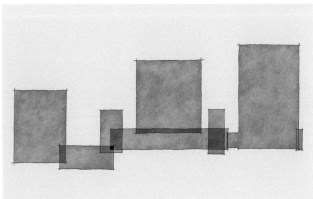
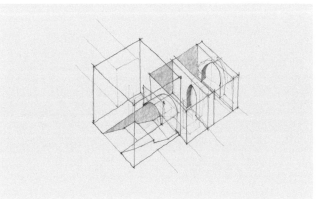

Section through entry, courtyard and mosque

Sectional diagram showing spatial compression and expansion

Transparent isometric of the entry stair

Sokullu Ismihan Sultan Complex
Istanbul, Turkey, 1512–1520
Sinan

How did the architect articulate the section to emphasize movement and transition?
How many ceiling heights are in the building's entry sequence?
What is the ceiling profile of that sequence?
Where and why does the ceiling change or stay the same?

over the decades that visitors experience as they exit the station (or, perhaps more accurately, enter Rome). There is a series of compressions and expansions from the train platforms through the main concourse under the shops and offices, and then the expansion outward toward the bus and taxi plaza and to Rome.

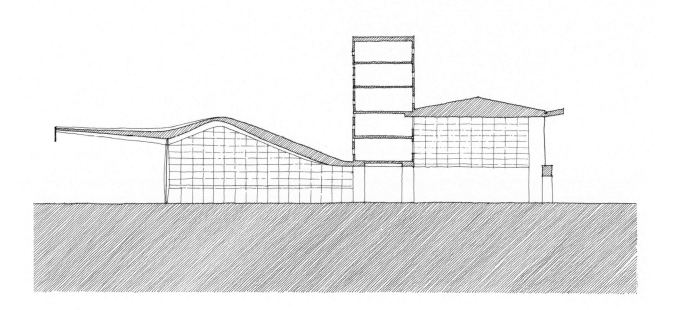

Section from platform to entry hall

Diagram showing sectional profile

Roma Termini
Rome, Italy, 1950
Montuori Vitellozzi Group

Walking beneath Portals

Portals, porches, porticoes and overhangs play both functional and social roles. Delineating the boundary between interior and exterior, they offer protection from sun and rain and mitigate movement to separate domains. In this latter respect, they amplify the procession both from the public to the private domain and between inside and outside. This in-between zone is in fact neither completely inside nor completely outside, it is necessarily a "both/and" precinct. Gradations of public/private often fluctuate with occasion, purpose and affiliation. For example, a room or portion or area of a building that is "public" at one time of day, may be very "private" at another. Likewise, moving from public to private is less through an "either/or" portal, but usually a series of layers in which bidirectional exchanges might occur. Transitional spaces, established by material, volumetric and tectonic change, help define the varied and critical transitional moments where public and private interact.

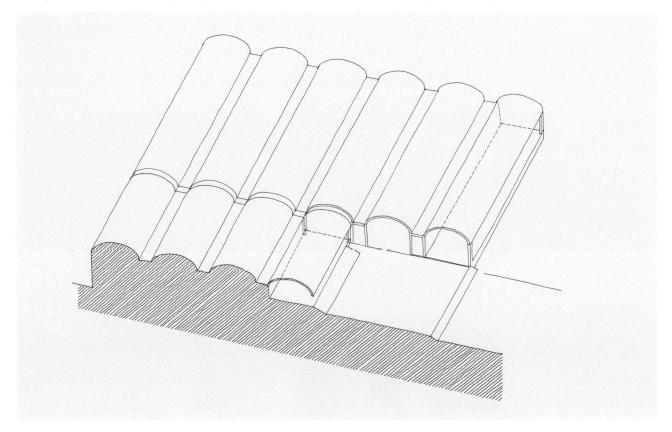

Section isometric through the entry courtyard

Section through the entry to the auditorium.

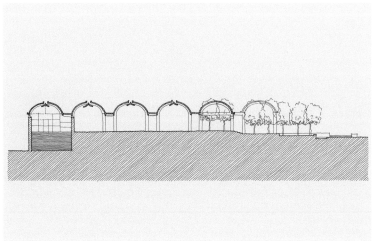

View from under the elongated portico toward the entry courtyard

Kimbell Art Museum
Fort Worth, Texas, 1976
Louis Kahn

How does a porch or portico function in terms of public/private relationships?
What architectural moves hint of decreased publicness and increased privacy?
Is the porch a separate unit or is it linked to the building's internal structure?
How would the building be different if there were no porch?
What changes in floor level, room width, material, columns, ceiling and height help indicate private zones?

The diagrams of the Kimbell Art Museum show how its porches, which are the unenclosed cycloid vaults weaving throughout the building, help guide the visitor along the length (parallel) and then across the vault's grain. The continuation of these vaults from exterior to interior further links the building to the landscape. The axonometric diagram of the Altes Museum reveals movement from the more public to the more private zones. In this case, the diagram illustrates how museum visitors move through a series of layers into increasingly private zones comprised of colonnades, doorways, stairways, passageways and ultimately into the domed inner sanctum. The pathway is nearly linear as it moves from perimeter to interior.

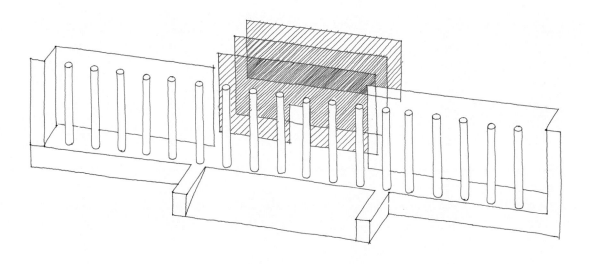

Isometric diagram of entry layers

Section through the entry hall and central rotunda

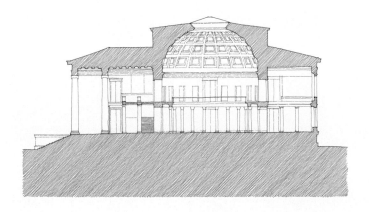

Altes Museum
Berlin, Germany, 1830
Karl Friedrich Schinkel

Moving through Layers

Changes in function or levels of privacy within buildings frequently manifest themselves as physical and spatial layers through which a visitor may pass or be prohibited. The layers also delineate transformations between or among conditions that require more than an abrupt change. For example, moving from outside to inside normally involves a series of steps that are both functional and experiential. Environmental airlocks, security points, calming, noise or light control or inculcating a sense of arrival are just a few examples of the many layers encountered when entering a building. While these layers may be veiled or implied, they can also be made explicit in the changes in material, section, light or direction of movement.

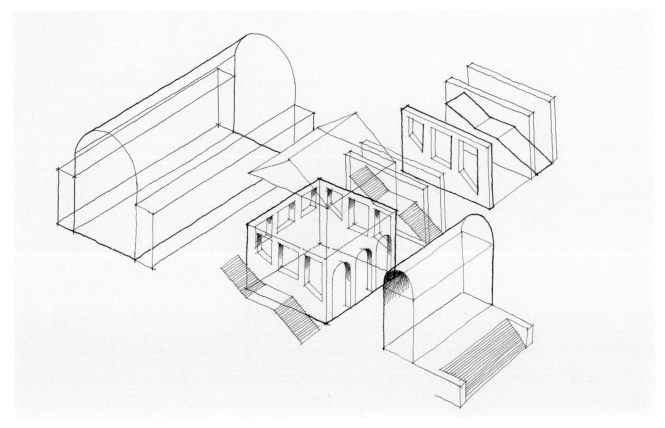

Exploded isometric showing the layers and volumes

Isometric diagram showing the interior layers

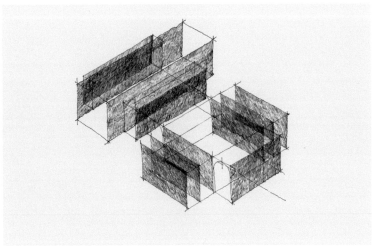

View through the atrium's layers

Organization of American States
(Pan American Union Building)
Washington, DC, 1913
Albert Kelsey and Paul Philippe Cret

How is the building composed of a series of layers?

How are those layers made?

How is the experience different from or similar to a tectonic sequence?

The diagram of the Organization of American States building shows a complex series of layers across and along which the visitor moves through the building. An exploded isometric shows how walls, stairs and vaults are elements that come together into a complex weave, which is further simplified in the tone diagram in which only the planes are shown. The diagram of the Museu d'Art Contemporani de Barcelona shows how Meier designed a series of literal planes through which the visitor moves into and along with the building. Here, planes act both as a diffusing mechanism of the bright Barcelona light but also as a series of screens that reveal the interior.

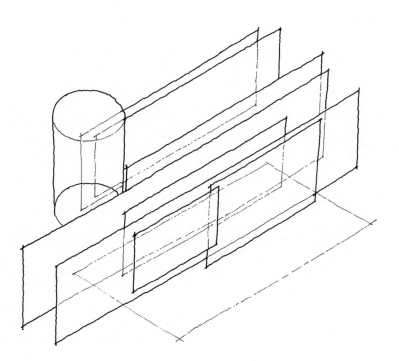

Isometric diagram showing the layers

View through the ramp toward the plaza

Museu d'Art Contemporani de Barcelona
Barcelona, Spain, 1995
Richard Meier & Partners

Linking Profane with Sacred

The role of section in moving from profane to sacred, which is not limited to religiousness, is often highly articulated: that which is sacred is distinct from that which is profane. For example, placing four sticks to form a room on a sandy beach differentiates an otherwise neutral sandy plane. While sacred and profane, like phenomena of public-to-private or compression and expansion, are sometimes gradated, they are more often clear in their division and have a distinct architectural expression.

The diagrams of the House of the Temple show how the spaces increase in size and scale toward the final ceremonial room. Its horizontal entry hall, constructed with black stone and stout Doric columns, gives way to the more vertical stair hall, which redirects movement by 180 degrees to the final and lofty ceremonial room. In a much different fashion the diagram of the Bagsværd Church, drawn using ink and brush, shows how the ceilings are a series of undulating biomorphic shapes that accentu-

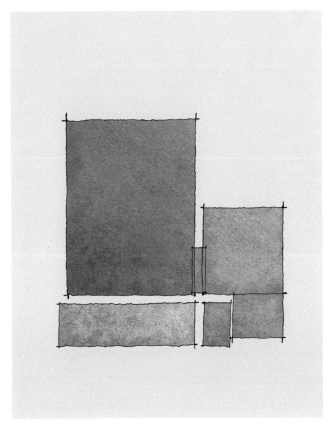

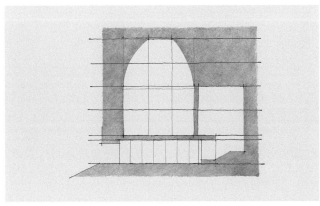

Sectional plan oblique of the profane to sacred volumes

Section diagram of the entry and the main hall

The House of the Temple
Washington, DC, 1915
John Russell Pope

How are thresholds of sacredness marked or accentuated?

What changes in material, form or scale help delineate sacred zones?

How does the floor remain the same or undulate to achieve sacredness?

ate procession toward the more sacred sanctuary, hide the light source and give ambient light to the space. The floor remains a datum to these shapes: a relatively consistent white mass only changes in undulation pattern and height.

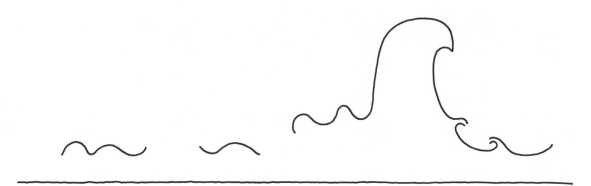

Sectional diagram showing ceiling clouds

Diagrams in ink and brush to study the ceiling clouds

View of the sanctuary from the upper level

Bagsværd Church
Copenhagen, Denmark, 1976
Jørn Utzon

Interfacing Public with Private

Like plant tendrils or an amoeba's pseudopods reaching out to interface with the environment, a building can, in a sense, reach out to link with a site and interface with the public domain. These links can be as simple as a building's joints aligning with those of the paving, low walls extending into the landscape or overhangs protecting an entry. When extended in these ways, the surrounding context is not residual but part of the building. This is especially true for a building's threshold: by extending outward, the

building's "entrance" can begin to occur long before a door is actually opened. Rather than a hermetically sealed or taut skin, a building that extends into the public realm helps engender a public and private exchange while providing a richer spatial experience alongside and into the building.

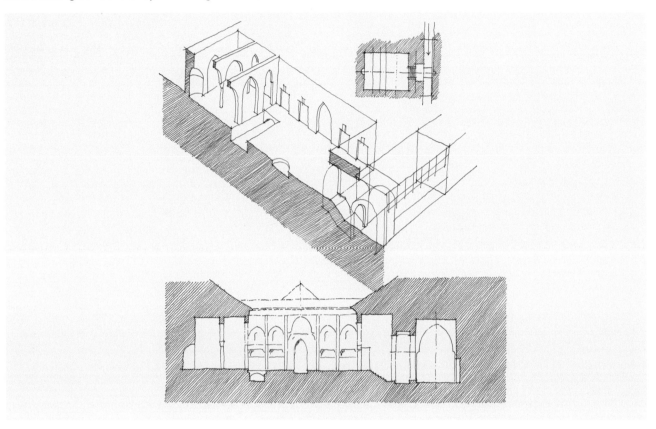

Sectional isometric and section showing the relationship of street and building

Plan of the complex and its relationship to the street

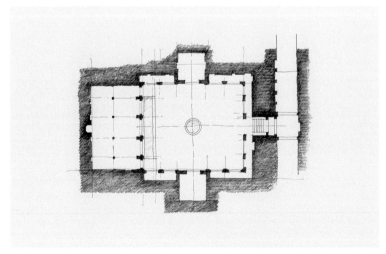

View of the madrasa's water channel separating the courtyard from the mosque's interior

Madrasa Bou Inania
Fes, Morocco, 1355

How does the private realm overlap with the public realm?

At what point is the private realm distinct?

What spatial or material changes help in the public/private overlap?

The plan and section diagrams of the Medrese Bou Inania reveal how the building extends beyond what might be considered the actual building and into the public realm. Here the building begins outside with the street wall that transforms into a water clock that then engages with a domed entry portal that bridges across the street to mark both the entry to the medrese and to a building related to the medrese. The building extends to engage the city. The diagram of the Frank Thomas House shows how a series of planes parallel and perpendicular to the street extend beyond the house's actual enclosure to articulate the private and public realms. Here, the diagram shows how the walls are a series of layers beyond which is the main door.

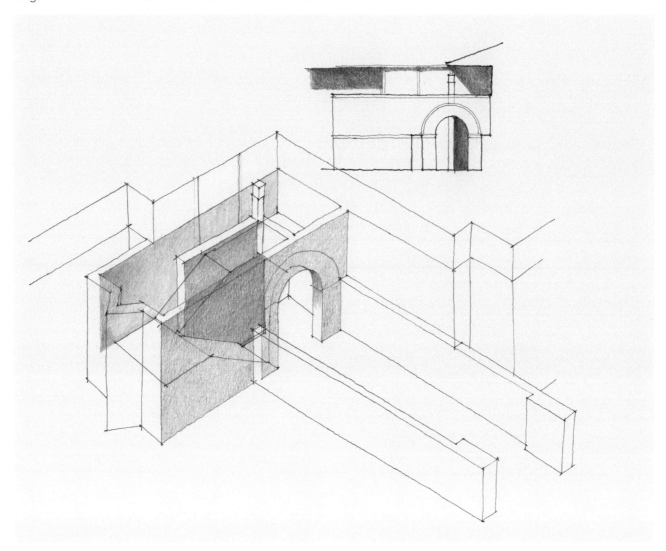

Isometric and elevation diagram of the entry sequence planes

View of the entry path and doorway

Frank Thomas House
Oak Park, Illinois, 1901
Frank Lloyd Wright

Interlocking Sections

In his book *Complexity and Contradiction in Architecture*, Robert Venturi extols architecture of "both/and", in which "contradictory relationships express tension and give vitality".[6] This notion of tension and vitality, while both a conceptual and architectural polemic, is most spatially apparent when an architectural double entendre animates a building or room's section. In these "both/and" sections, buildings extend into the landscape or public space, or small scales interact with larger scales.

The **diagram** of the Yeşil Madrasa reveals a spatial and perceptual overlap of the interior arcade and the exterior courtyard. Unlike a typical courtyard-arcade relationship, in which the courtyard's floor level matches the arcade's floor level, here the courtyard's and arcade's floor levels coincide until half way beneath the arcade, where the latter drops about half a meter to the floor of the arcade. Because of this drop inside the arcade, there is a sense that the floor "slides" beneath the columns to make a grey

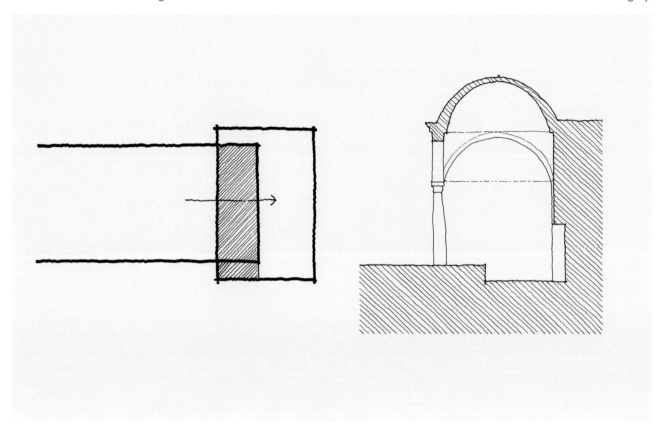

Sectional diagram showing overlaps

View of the arcade and courtyard floor

Yeşil Madrasa
Bursa, Turkey, 1424
Haci Ivaz bin Ahi Beyazit

In what respect is the section clear or ambiguous?
Where are the overlaps in the section?
Do any parts of a section share a space? Do any rooms share one element?
Are there any spaces in which you are in two rooms at the same time?

zone between inside and outside. A similar idea, but more about mass than volume, shows the diagram of the Plot 18 House in Amsterdam: inserting a mass into a large volume clarifies a particular hierarchy within the building, yet at the same time the resultant rooms around the inserted mass produce a new double reading of large and smaller volumes.

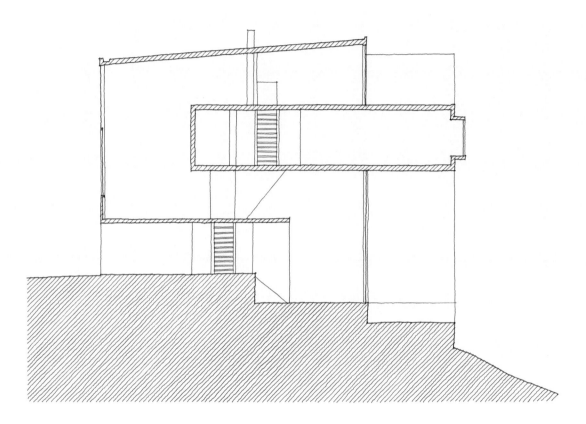

Section showing private areas inserted into public zone

Sectional diagram showing interlocked volumes

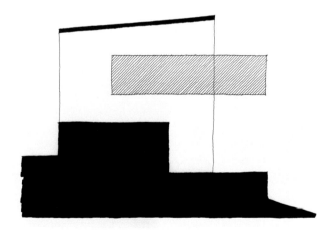

Plot 18 House
Amsterdam, The Netherlands, 1999
MVRDV

6   Venturi, Robert, *Complexity and Contradiction in Architecture*. New York: Museum of Modern Art (1966): 22-23.

Carving Voids

It is rare indeed to carve rooms out of solid stone, yet carving, in architecture, remains an essential conceptual position in which, through literal or figural subtraction, void is conceived of and enclosed within a mass. In an experiential sense, "carved" space elicits a contrasting spatial attitude that space fashioned with assembled elements. A room embedded in solid, albeit assembled, walls connotes a feeling very different from a room shaped by assembled sticks.

The diagram of the Muradiye Mosque shows how the niches along the rear wall become refuges from the larger mosque's interior space that seems carved out of the mosque's surrounding walls. The slightly raised floor of the niche also contributes to this feeling of a void carved into a wall. Using transparent oblique drawings at different scales and a large section reveals how this carved form helps elicit a particular feeling. The diagram of the housing at Santa Caterina Market shows how the architect subtracted

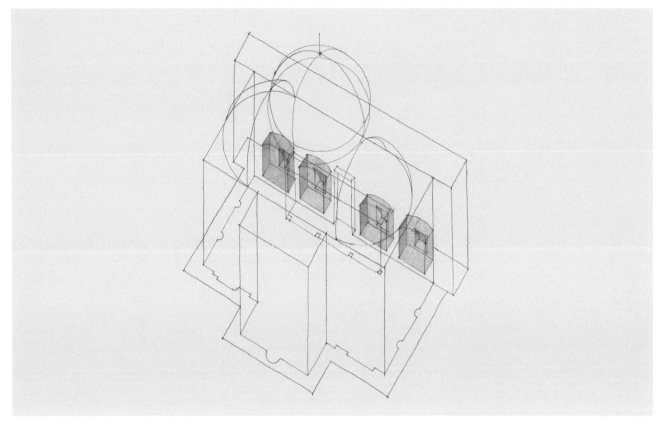

Transparent plan oblique showing niches in relation to the mosque

Detail section and isometric showing the niches "carved" into the wall

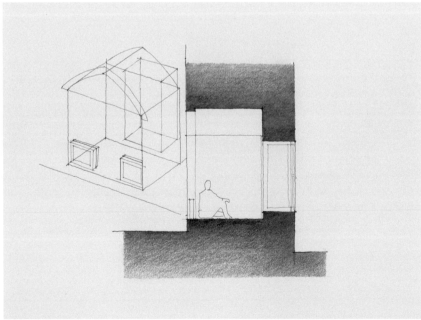

Muradiye Camii
Manisa, Turkey, 1592
Sinan

How does a room seem "carved" from mass?
What has the architect done in terms of material and dimension to convey "carving"?
What is the difference between a "carved" room and an assembled room?
How is a building carved from a mass versus assembled in a composition?

balconies, courtyard and entries to articulate the mass, to create spaces within and around the small building to allow light to penetrate into the mass. Added elements such as wood louver window bays add contrast to the heavier stuccoed "solid".

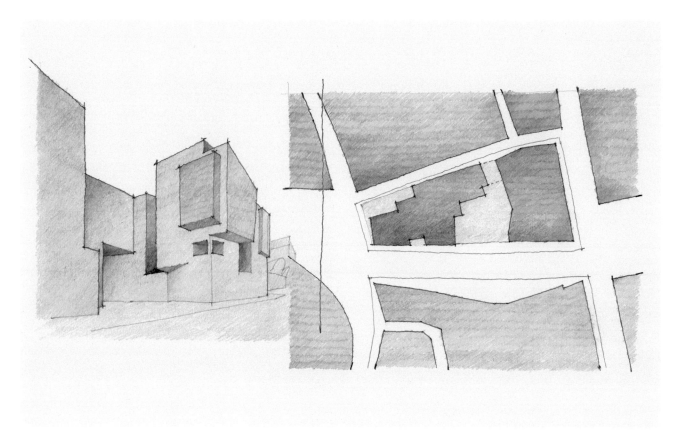

View and plan of the market in its urban context

Exploded isometric showing voids as solids

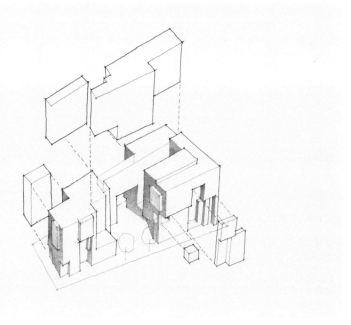

Housing at Santa Caterina Market
Barcelona, Spain, 2003
Bravo and Contepomi

Shaping the Floor

Through change in height, step or slope, floors can delineate use and telegraph meaning. A floor plane raised above a surrounding plane can designate importance, sanctity or privacy, while a recessed floor can isolate activities from its surroundings. A plaza below or above street level communicates very different ideas about the plaza's use and those permitted to enter, either explicitly or implicitly. The number and rhythm of steps incorporated into the floor or the floor's slope can determine pace or pause.

The diagram of Le Corbusier's crypt chapels delineates levels within a complete volume. Its floors are a series of sloped terraces that help modulate the space into seven chapels yet give a sense of subterranean enclosure, because of the relatively flat ceiling punctured by three oculi. The diagram of Tate Modern's entry sequence shows how the extended, if gently sloped ramp leading to the entry and building core seems to connote a descent into the building's bowels. An isometric shows how the ramp

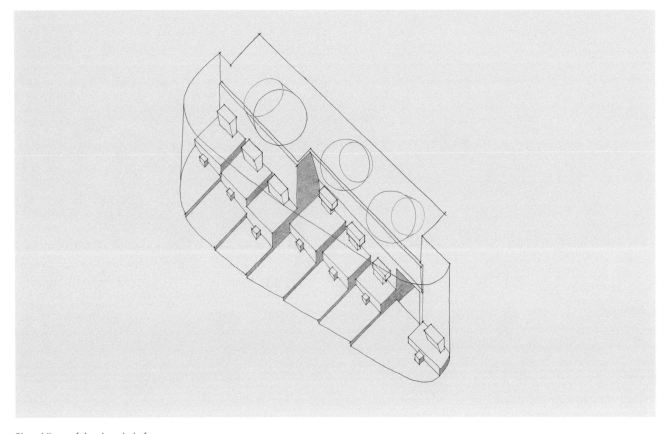

Plan oblique of the chapel platforms

View of the chapels

Sainte-Marie de La Tourette Crypt Chapels
Lyon, France, 1960
Le Corbusier

Does the floor remain a neutral element or does it become an active element in the building?
Where does the architect slope or step the floor? Why at those points?
How does the floor elicit a particular feeling or evoke a particular atmosphere?
How does height, step or slope convey a particular use, movement or feelings?

extends from the outside under a low entry and down toward the building's center, while the main floor remains level. As it slopes, it slowly reveals the museum shop while a bridge from the first level extends over the entry area to mark the ticket area, internal entry and core.

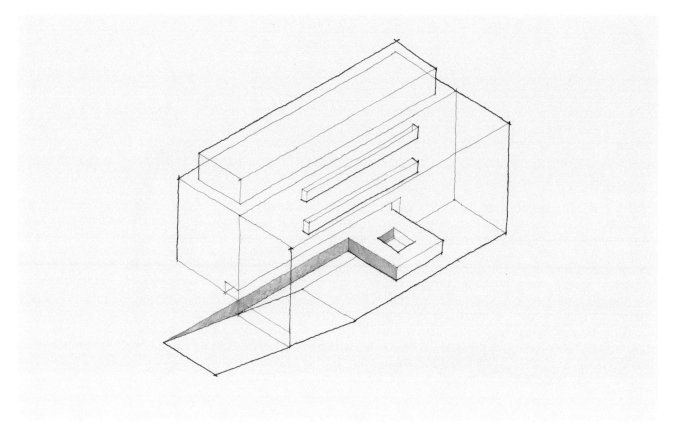

Isometric showing the ramp and entry bridge

View up the ramp toward
the main entry

Tate Modern
London, England, 2000
Herzog & de Meuron

Reinforcing with Tectonics

The tectonic form of a building comprises the relationship of structure to enclosure, of column to wall and the wall-to-wall types; however, it can be simplified as a description of a building's bones. These bones – columns, beams, piers, walls, arches and vaults – may be isolated systems or intermixed to form complex tectonic systems. This skeletal system can orchestrate sequence or mediate scale.

The diagram of Union Station's main entry hall shows how tectonics help mediate scale and orchestrate movement from the public plaza into the Great Hall. Much of this is accomplished by intermixing a smaller-scale tectonic system among the larger piers. The result are bays that support the vaulted roof, while the smaller columns and entablatures weave between the vaults to mediate the scales and create entry doors and other, smaller elements in the room. An isometric diagram of the Rüstempaşa

Exploded isometric showing intermixed scales
(drawing by Fajer Alqattan)

View of the main entry hall's side vaults

Union Station
Washington, DC, 1908
Daniel Burnham

What is the building's tectonic? Is it explicit or implicit?
How do the tectonics change in relation to movement?
How are varied tectonic systems linked or separated?

Mosque uses degrees of transparency and opacity to illustrate how the tectonics help orchestrate movement. Smaller columns give way to larger columns, which then lead to thick walls and finally to piers in the building's interior.

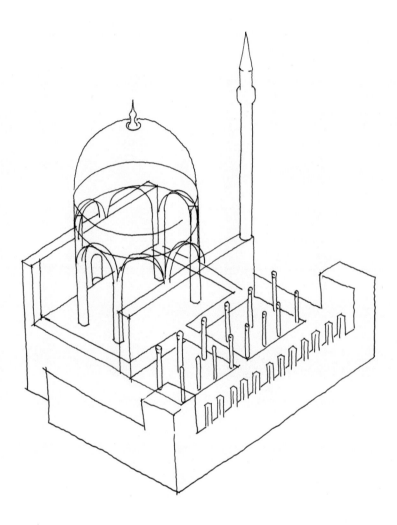

Isometric showing the relationship of tectonics to volumes

Upper level plan of the mosque in its urban context

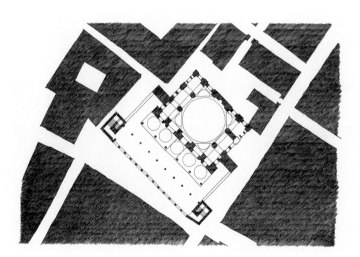

Rüstempaşa Camii
Istanbul, Turkey, 1561
Sinan

141

Expanding Atria

Atria are focal points for the building's occupants as they admit light and air into a building's center. As a focal point, an atrium can link a building's levels into a common center, coordinate circulation or act as a landmark for the users. More than simple extrusions from ground to sky, atria can also form complex, multilevel, sculpted volumes that accommodate varied uses and scales.

The diagrams of the Casa del Fascio study how the atrium can be more than an extrusion but a stacked volume with different articulations along its edges. Here, Terragni makes a enclosed central atrium serving the lower two floors and above an open courtyard serving the upper levels. The axonometric is especially helpful in understanding the complex volumes. Similarly, the isometric diagram of the Museum of Modern Art's new atrium shows how its complex volume coordinates the many rooms beneath and

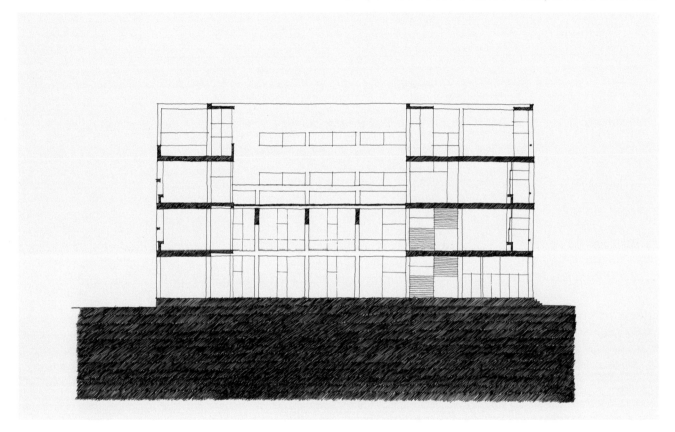

Section through atrium

Section diagram showing atrium and upper courtyard

View of the atrium toward
the front entrance

Casa del Fascio
Como, Italy, 1936
Giuseppe Terragni

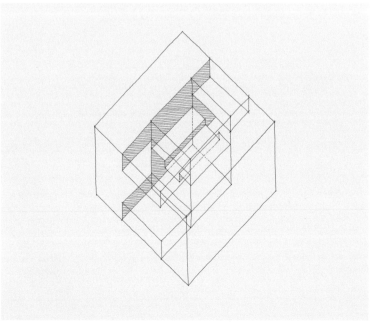

In how many ways is the atrium experienced?

Is the perimeter continuous or shaped?

How are the varied levels connected spatially, materially and formally?

along its edges. As a kind of volumetric datum, the atrium organizes varied added and subtracted elements, allows views over and across, and can be traversed and encircled on many levels.

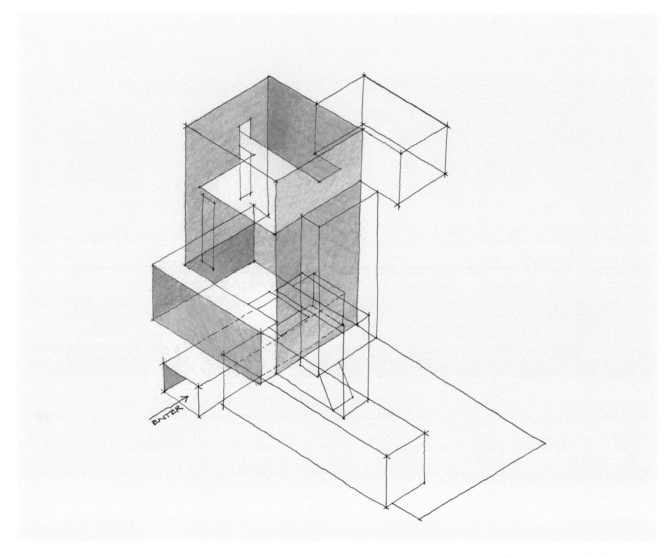

Transparent isometric showing
added and subtracted elements

View of the atrium and bridges

The Museum of Modern Art Extension
New York, New York, 2004
Yoshio Taniguchi

Sensing Scale

Scales within rooms, especially public rooms, frequently shift between a scale suited to an overall room as a grand gathering space and the scale of those who inhabit it. Large public room, such as lobbies, concert halls or public meeting rooms, often must have elements that are scaled to the room as a public space – ceiling, stage, podium or stairway scale – for the room's greater significance. People who use these rooms, however, are often at a much smaller scale, requiring much smaller dimensions such as stair risers, counters, chairs and tables. Reconciling or at least relating these scales remains critical to ensuring that both scales are satisfied.

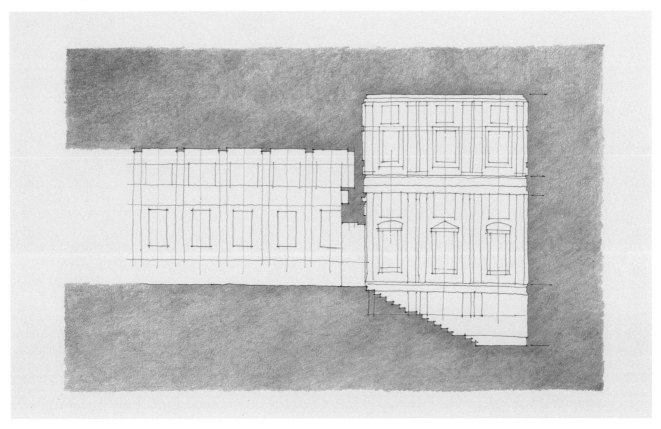

Section through entry vestibule and library

Plan oblique and isometrics of the entry vestibule

View of the vestibule

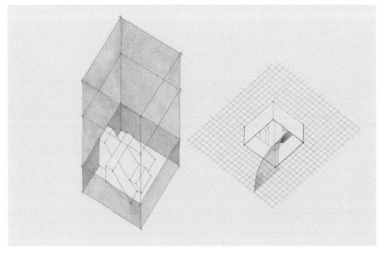

Biblioteca Medicea Laurenziana
Florence, Italy, 1534
Michelangelo Buonarroti

Is there a scale for the room and a different scale for humans?

Where do the two scales meet?

What material or dimensional moves accentuate the scale shifts?

The diagrams of the Laurentian Library vestibule show how Michelangelo divided the volume into two levels, each with its own scale. Its lower level, which contains the stairway, is a zone in which the stairs are scaled more to the visitor, while the upper levels that help establish the grandeur of the entire vestibule are at a larger scale. A second diagram attempts to convey the impression that the stair seems to spill out of the upper levels into the vestibule. The diagram of Sullivan's National Farmers' Bank shows the distinct difference in scale between the lower portion and the upper portion of the bank by using two hatches divided by a single line. The scales of material, surface articulation, elements and color are distinctly different between each zone. Its lower level, scaled to the human being, seems to support the more lofty upper area in which the arches and the corners of the pendentives imply a lofty and grand bank in a small building.

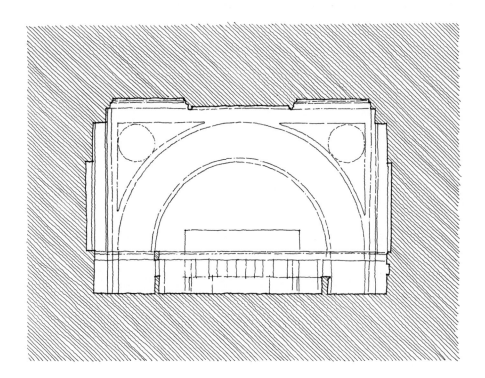

Section through the banking hall

Section diagram showing the two scaled zones

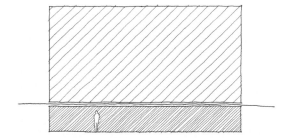

The National Farmers' Bank
Owatonna, Minnesota, 1908
Louis H. Sullivan

Reconciling Ideal and Real

Typological studies are at once a process of understanding types but also a way to develop systematic analytical habits. Typological knowledge is a way to understand both the role of a form's *Gestalt* in heuristic problemsolving and how idealized forms adapt to or accommodate forces. As Rafael Moneo notes, types can be "thought of as the frame within which change operates, a necessary term to the continuing dialectic required by history. From this point of view, the type, rather than being a 'frozen mechanism' to produce architecture, becomes a way of denying the past, as well as a way of looking at the future."[7] More than a way to serve architecture in terms of solving problems, augmentation of idealized forms offers lessons about the way in which forms mutated to idiosyncratic forces, such as site or program. Beyond design lessons, typological studies help develop a systematic categorization and synthesis – methods that, in turn, help train the eye to discern and understand the relationship between ideal and real in other situations.

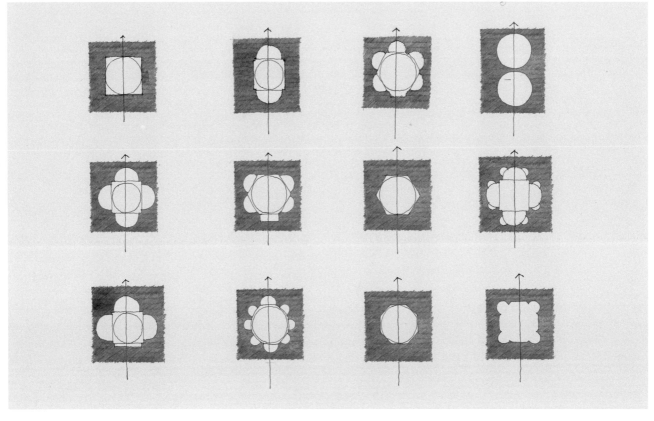

Plans of various Ottoman mosques in Istanbul

Transparent isometrics showing the varied spatial conditions

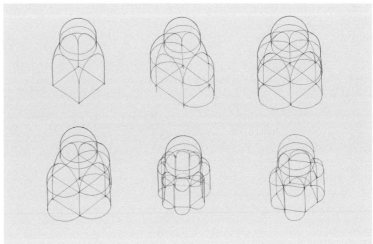

Ottoman Mosques

What is the fundamental typological organization of the building?
What would be the "purest" version of the plan and volume?
What drawing will be repeated in every analysis?
What changes and what remains the same in the buildings?

The diagrams of Ottoman mosques, developed during several trips to Istanbul, began with a similar diagram at each site: a diagrammatic plan organization with the qibla (direction to Mecca) superimposed, in most cases, with a central dome. A variation on this systematic diagramming method are the isometric studies of the dome and the myriad of support structures. We can see through this study that directionality, movement and the structural system offer dramatic and subtle transformations of a common type. Likewise, the diagrams of churches in Italy, also done over many visits and years, study how the ideal centralized church responds to liturgical needs such as the congregation's participation, the hierarchy of the altar and, like in the mosque, entry.

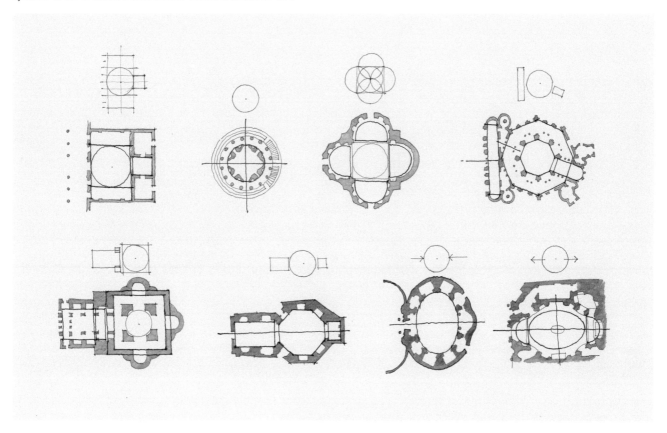

Plans of various centralized churches

Plans oblique showing various spatial conditions

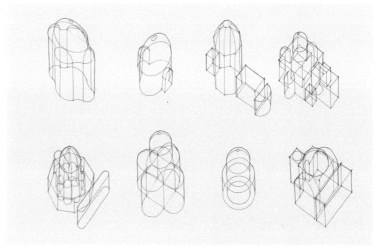

Italian Centralized Churches

7   Moneo, Rafael, "On Typology", *Oppositions* 13:23 (Summer 1978): 27.

Arranging Voids

Ranking a building's spaces into primary, secondary and tertiary categories is a way to describe and conceive succinctly its essential components. For example, a house may have primary public and private rooms (living, dining, bedroom) that are supported by secondary rooms (bathrooms, kitchen, hallways, foyers) which, in turn, are supported by tertiary spaces (closets, pantries). Arguably, this tripartite division is limited, yet it does help clarify complex buildings for better comprehension.

The diagram of Santa Maria della Salute reveals how the primary, secondary and tertiary categories involve volume, location and context. While the surrounding ambulatory would be considered tertiary to the dome and sanctuary, the relationship of the dome to the sanctuary is unclear: is one or the other primary or secondary? The diagram of San Clemente in Rome reveals the volumetric procession from tertiary to secondary to primary. The axonometric is especially helpful because it combines several drawing

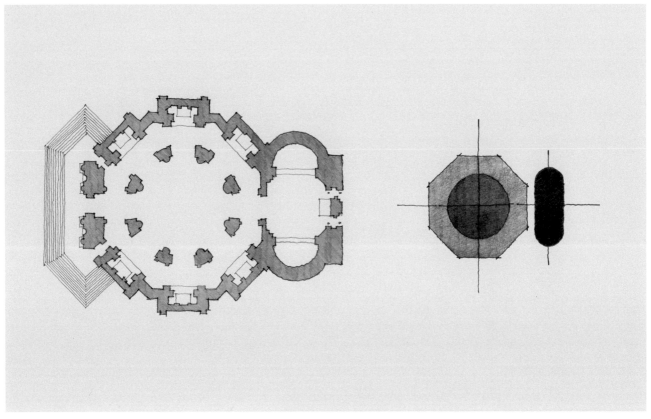

Plan and plan diagram showing spatial hierarchies

Plan oblique in line and in tones showing
spatial hierarchies

General view

Santa Maria della Salute
Venice, Italy, 1687
Baldassare Longhena

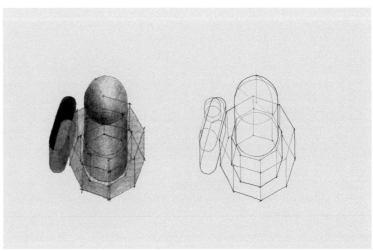

What are the primary, secondary and tertiary spaces of the building?

How does the section correspond to these spaces?

Are there sub-spaces within primary, secondary and tertiary spaces?

types: plan, section and transparent axonometric. This
drawing compels the observer to link all aspects of the
building into a unified representation. Its plan begins to
show how the primary, secondary and tertiary organization
may have more complex readings.

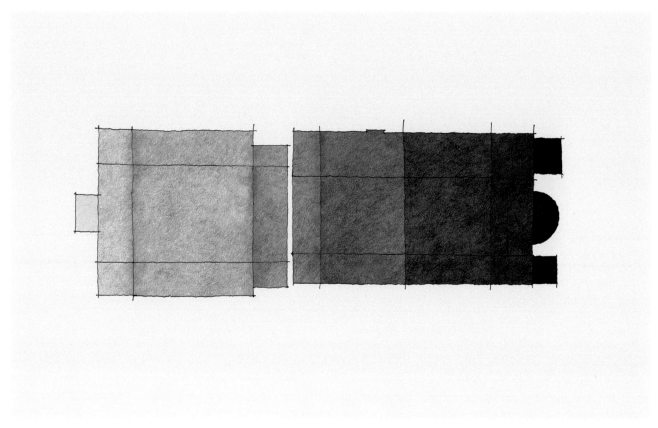

Plan showing spatial hierarchies

Section and plan oblique showing spatial sequence

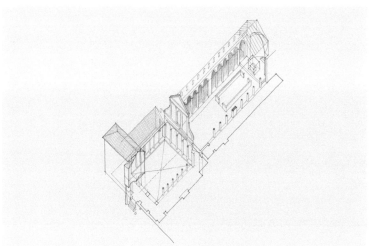

Basilica di San Clemente
Rome, Italy, 1123

Sculpting Light

Light in a building is necessary for human activities but essential for human well-being, both psychologically and emotionally. Its modulation can therefore influence how we feel, behave, think and know. This is especially true for natural light, which is difficult to diagram because of its variability. Sunlight changes considerably throughout the day and year: the sun's nearly imperceptible movement or the change in weather will offer a myriad of spatial experiences.

The diagram of Le Corbusier's chapel at Ronchamp tries to capture the subtle wash of light in the side chapels. These studies show a view of one of the chapels but also try to show how light enters and washes down the curved walls with the overall intention to show the surface rather than the source. Another goal of these diagrams was to understand how light helps manipulate feeling or spirituality or a sense of the sublime. Similarly, the diagram of the Treptow Crematorium begins to show how light interacts with the

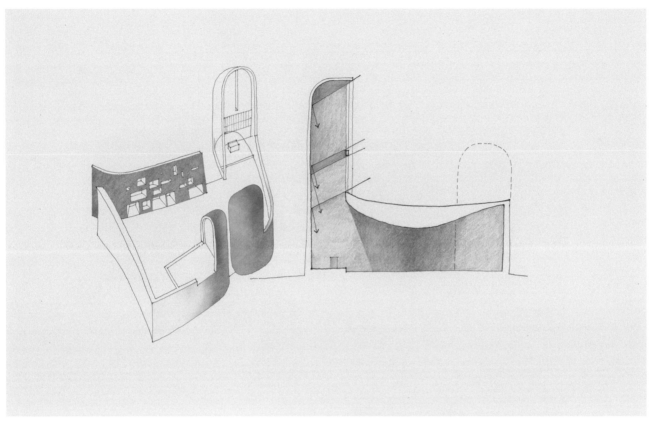

Plan oblique and section showing play of light

Perspective showing light washing on surfaces

View of the chapel's sculpted light

Chapelle Notre-Dame-du-Haut
Ronchamp, France, 1954
Le Corbusier

How is light seen? Do you see the source or the surface touched by light?
How does the light help elicit emotion?
How would the room be different if the light were changed?
If you stayed in the room for an extended period, how did the light change? What were the differences?

tectonics. Columns are delineated as a series of posts supporting a dark plane with the light linked directly to the structure. Again, this study tries to diagram the sublime light rather than to show how it entered. The goal is not so much to break it down into a typical diagram of function or order but to understand the unspoken aspects of light.

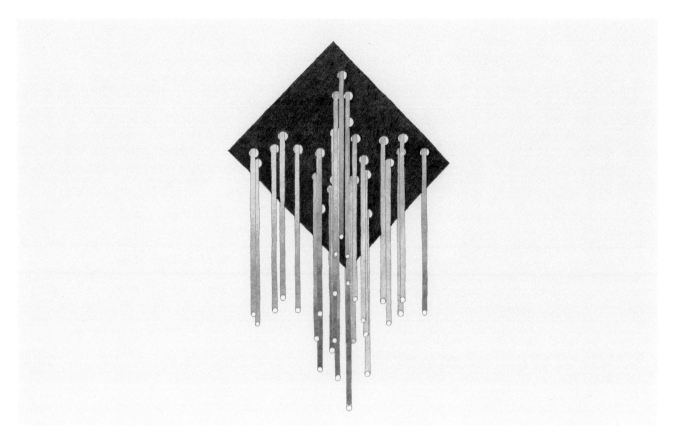

Diagram of light washing on the columns

View of the crematorium's central hall

Treptow Crematorium
Berlin, Germany, 1998
Axel Schultes

FACING THE BUILDING

The façade of a building is in many ways like the surface of any container. We often compare it to the skin or the shell of an animal, and it may also be likened to the external surface of a box or crate. Like a box, the building's façade must protect its contents, the rooms or spaces and the inhabitants within. Like a box, a façade usually tells us something about its contents. How this is done, either via corporeal form or through some graphic indication, is often the subject of debate amongst architects and theorists.

Thomas L. Schumacher[1]

A building's exterior is almost certainly its most experienced feature. While we might enter and experience many building interiors in a lifetime, the ratio of buildings entered to those merely encountered is nearly astronomical. One afternoon, while walking through Rome's historical center, I counted the number of buildings that I passed by, not including those just seen from across the street or from afar. I entered five, but passed 110. Although Rome is compact, even in least dense settings a person may pass dozens of houses, churches, garages or shops that they will see but never enter. As a primary way in which we encounter the designed environment, it makes sense that its exterior design be of some importance.

The focus of this chapter is the study of a building's most visible characteristic: its face. A building's face, like that of a human, is not just its two-dimensional frontal view or elevation but its three-dimensional overall external form: its masses, corners, voids, additions, fenestration and entries and how these unite in scale, proportion, rhythm and other formal ordering systems.

Vis-à-Vis
The term "Facing the Building" takes advantage of intrinsic multiple definitions and readings. On the one hand, when facing the building, we approach it, stand in front of it, observe it from specific or from multiple vantage points, and move toward it and, in some cases, enter through its skin. On the other hand, facing the building is also how we design it and how we construct it. More than an *appliqué* of false façade or mask, building faces are, regardless of construction method or technologies, enclosed by layered systems that are taut or loose, thick or thin, spatial or flat. A building's "face" has its own meaning as a physical thing like in "that is the building's face" or as a face that is implied, for example in "putting on a happy face", or inferred as a *facie* (a medical mask-like condition of those suffering from Parkinson's disease). The multiple meanings, depending on a particular point of view, greatly affect the way we diagram a building's face.

Façade Fallacy

A building is like a soap bubble. This bubble is perfect and harmonious if the air is evenly distributed and properly ordered from the inside. The exterior is the result of an interior.

Le Corbusier [2]

In his article "The Skull and the Mask" Thomas Schumacher discusses how Le Corbusier's soap bubble analogy, in which internal forces project outward to a building's form, remains a recurring myth within architectural design and debates. There is no doubt that an interior speaks to the exterior, but the exterior does not always listen with rapt attention. Façades are not inevitable or pre-determined by the interior but are, in fact, designed as much as any other part of a building. The external design accommodates a number of forces to become part of the building, in sync with the other parts, but also responding to external forces and compositional forces: the relationship of a building to its neighbors, the more durable materials that meet the ground, protection from sun and heat, one surface meeting another and resolving internal forces, to name a few of the façade's jobs.

The relationship of internal and external forces shaping a façade is similar to the forces that shape a human face. This is especially apparent with identical twins whose faces may be very similar at birth, yet, as the twins age and each has different experiences or engages in different lifestyles, their faces slowly deviate from one another to reflect those different external forces. Without significant changes to the skull or other internal structures, the faces do ultimately and appropriately reflect the outside. Likewise, even though two buildings or two sides of one building may have an identical interior, other external forces can help differentiate the form. Even a single building may have different solar orientations, different features for those who walk past it on the lowest level, changes from one floor to another, different connections to neighboring buildings. And yet the entire building is one building. If the façade were merely a projection of internal function, in most cases façades would be a hodgepodge of windows, misalignments and patterns.

The intention of the diagrams in this chapter is to see the building as a totality, understand the façade as a critical part of that totality designed and integrated within the whole to offer ways in which the whole and the pieces might come together. The thrust of these diagrams, then, is about facing the building in the broadest sense of the phrase and attempting to understand why a building looks as it does.

When discussing a building's face, students tend to have an especially difficult time abstracting the usually massive form into or through diagrams. Standing in front of a building and trying to understand where to begin and what to consider is a daunting task for almost any architect. The diagrams here, like those in the other divisions of the book, help in that beginning.

While the building's face is often the most experienced, it is also often the least discussed in design studios. Regardless of holistic BIM software or other three-dimensional design software, the building's skin remains the last item on the list. Photorealistic renderings of an interior often supplant design drawings and if shown, plans continue to dominate, sections usually run second and façades bring up the rear. While there are many publications on façade construction, there are few on façade design.

Facing the Building involves specific drawing acts that help answer questions of overall strategies of a building's exterior.

Questions at the root of this action include:
How does the building respond to its context?
How does the building touch the ground and is it different as it moves upward?
What are the compositional rules or systems used in the façade design? Are there alignments, proportions, material or other rules of the game?
What are the overall guiding lines or tartans that unify and differentiate the façade?
Can you speculate, from looking at the façade, on how the interior is projected or not projected on the building's face?

1   Schumacher, Thomas L., *About Face: On the Architecture of Façades, Classic and Modern*. Unpublished manuscript, University of Maryland, College Park (2009): 8.

2   Le Corbusier, *Towards an Architecture*, trans. John Goodman. Los Angeles: Getty Research Institute (2007): 216.

Revealing Tartans

The intention of these diagrams is to study a building's underlying organizational hierarchical pattern or tartan patterns. Tartan patterns – patterns akin to those ordinarily associated with Scottish clan textiles – are complex hierarchical grid patterns communicating varied scales, layers, depths and rhythms simultaneously through a hierarchy of line types and through the varied colors and values of background, foreground and overlapping field tones. Understanding and applying these conceptual and literal tartan patterns is essential for the design student, as architectural (and urban) tartans are simultaneous three-dimensional spatial, mechanical and material systems. Architectural tartans can also include the façade assembly, urban design or landscape design or any designed object that unifies complex systems into unified wholes. Layered and interdependent, these systems in these forms and spaces can also be dislodged and recognized as separate elements within a totality.

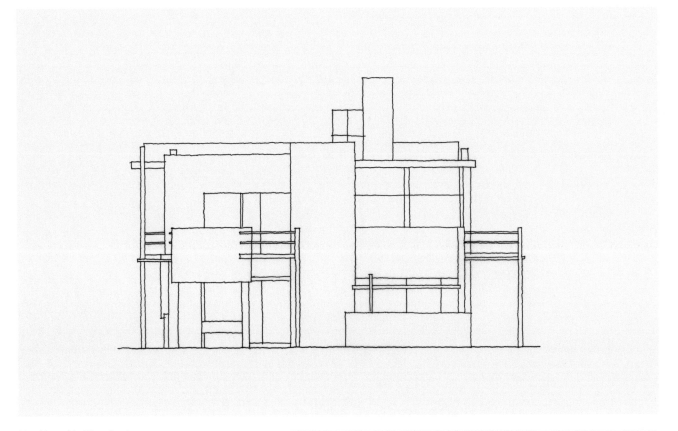

Non-hierarchical line drawing

Tartan patterns

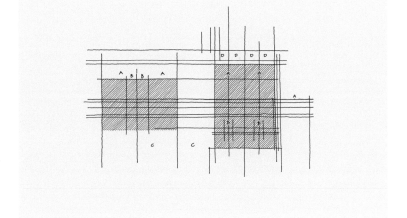

Southeast façade

Rietveld-Schröder House
Utrecht, The Netherlands, 1924
Gerrit Thomas Rietveld

What are the underlying primary, secondary and tertiary lines on the façade?
Do primary, secondary and tertiary lines transform into other lines?
Are there local symmetries or independent systems in the patterns?

This diagram type is especially relevant when applied to the Rietfeld-Schröder House, because this building does not seem to have an underlying grid or tartan. While the de Stijl patterns are orthogonal, in the Schröder House it appears that the arrangement and compositions are more overlaid with one another, without underlying grid pattern. A tartan grid study, however, reveals that elements are actually interrelated across the façade: horizontal lines disappear and reappear, vertical lines link elements, and even local symmetries and overall balance can be found in the composition. In Terragni's Casa Rustici, there is a more overt tartan grid pattern, but even here the tartan grid reveals that the project is a complex two and three-dimensional weave of patterns with alternating rhythms and multiple readings. The tartan, as a three-dimensional implication, is especially relevant in the building's fenestration, railings, masses and voids.

Southwest façade with shadows

Underlying patterns revealed

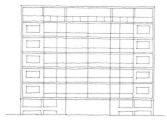

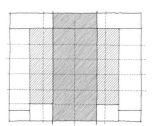

Southwest façade

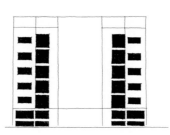

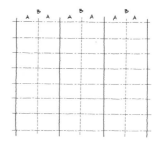

Casa Rustici
Milan, Italy, 1936
Giuseppe Terragni

Disposing Symmetry and Asymmetry

Similar to the diagrams of edges and centers in plan, these diagrams help reveal how a balance of symmetry and asymmetry mitigates and resolves complex forces. In any design project there will always be a need to balance asymmetrical forces into a unified whole. Varied and often conflicting internal forces such as program or room size, or external conditions such as site, scale or setbacks must intermingle with one another. In these examples, elements that are symmetrical in themselves, or more precisely symmetrical compositions of smaller-scale elements, are placed with larger asymmetrical compositions. Known as local symmetry, these secondary compositions can highlight elements in an asymmetric façade. For example, an architect might employ local symmetry to highlight an entrance that is, in fact, off-center in the overall façade.

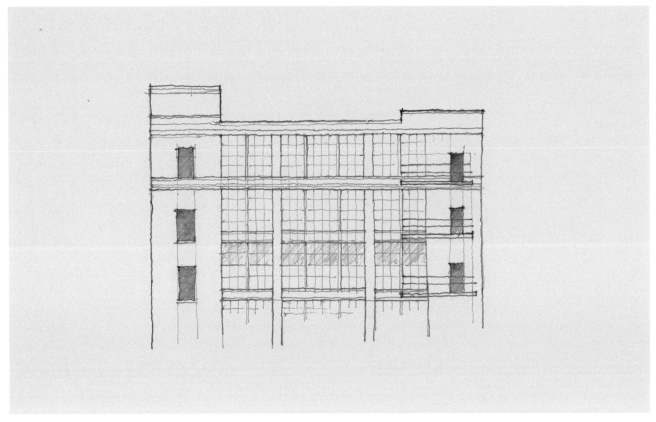

Elevation

Local symmetries and overlapping bays

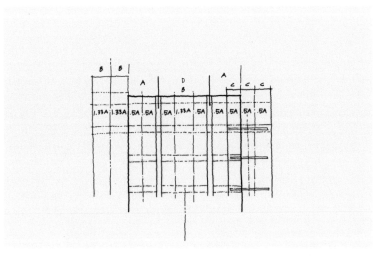

Upper levels

Young, Smyth, Field & Company Building
Philadelphia, Pennsylvania, 1902
Field & Medary Architects

What is the primary underlying rhythm or pattern?

What are or where are the A, B, C, etc. orderings of the façade?

How, when and why do these systems transform and overlap?

The diagram of the uppermost floors of the Young, Smyth, Field & Company building uses line weights and types; however, added to this are letters of the alphabet that augment the lines to help identify the complex ordering. For example, the letter "A" signifies the primary underlying pattern or bay – in this case, the two large plate glass windows on either side of the central window. The primary pattern "A" is then either multiplied or subdivided to show how it links the entire façade or how it works with other patterns. Multiples become "B" = "A1.33"; "A0.5" = "C" and so on. Similarly, in the Güneş apartment building diagram, line weights combine with dashed and discontinuous lines to reveal how local symmetries interlink with one another and then, in turn, link to an overall asymmetrical, yet balanced composition. The tone diagram reveals, as rhythms continue yet transform, how the overlapping elements and voids imply a degree of transparency and spatial hierarchy.

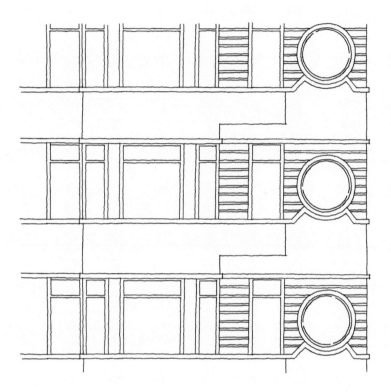

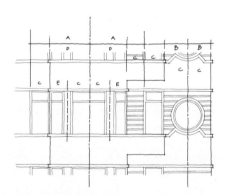

Typical bay

Güneş Apartment Building
Istanbul, Turkey, 1936
Seyfi Arkan

Non-hierarchal line drawing

Local symmetries and overlapping patterns

Addressing Entry

Just as a musical composer establishes complex rhythms, architects establish and then alter rhythm to help emphasize important moments such as entry or movement. The intention of these diagrams of building entrances is to examine the way in which entry might be inserted and marked within a façade. They reveal how a building's order slowly transforms to introduce hierarchy while maintaining overall cohesion. Essentially, entry is an anticipated and integrated element in the façade's overall pattern.

The pencil diagrams of the Scuola Grande di San Marco delineate the façade's overall horizontal bay rhythm with a series of regularly spaced vertical lines. On this basis, secondary lines reveal the fenestration rhythm that anticipates the primary and secondary entries. Tones help reveal the layered primary, secondary and tertiary forms that add another variation to the complex beat. By changing the tone value, the façade has been interpreted as a series of planes superimposed upon one another to

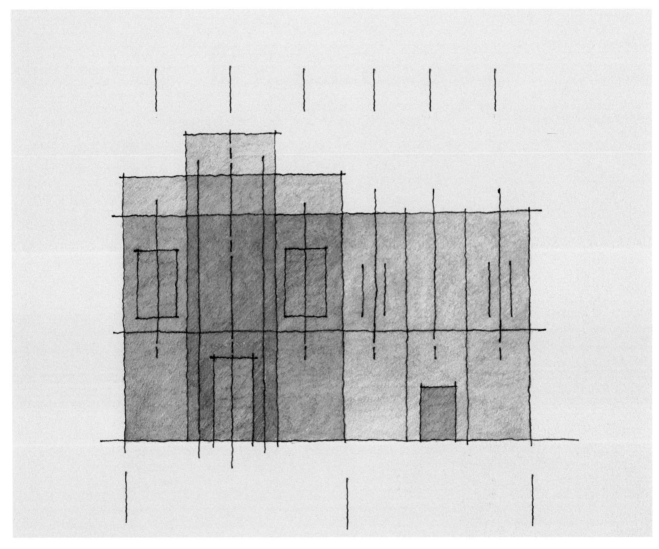

Overlapping patterns and layers

Southern façade

Scuola Grande di San Marco
Venice, Italy, 1495
Pietro Lombardo

What is the overall order of the façade? How is that order augmented at the entry?
How is hierarchy created? Is it through emphasis or a new system?
How is the entry highlighted?
Is the entry "anticipated"? Is the entry an anomaly or a more subtle transformation?

give hierarchy and mark the primary entry. For the diagram of Bohlin Cywinski Jackson's Wallace Hall, inked line weights and limited shading help uncover a similar move. Secondary and tertiary beats of the offset window and panel joints augment the primary structural bay rhythm. A canopy anticipates the entry, which is a void one and a half bays from the left and extends toward the void just as the window sill continues half a bay from the right to form a low wall that partially encloses the void.

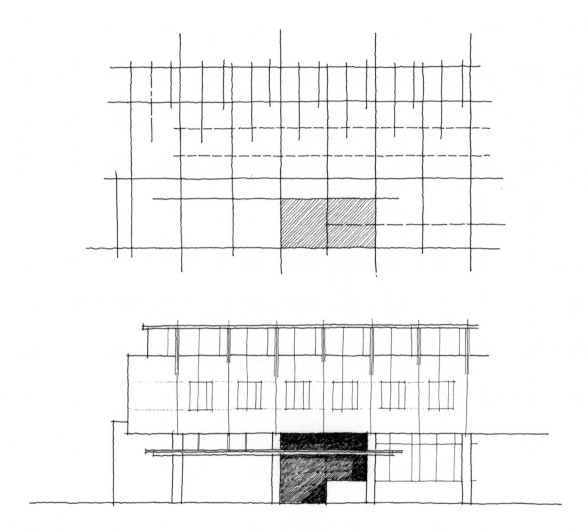

Patterns established and broken to mark entry

Northeastern entry

Wallace Hall
Princeton, New Jersey, 2000
Bohlin Cywinski Jackson

Alternating Edges and Centers

In most buildings, the design must orchestrate varied elements or forces into a unified and complex whole. One way to do this, without homogenizing the entire building into one mass, is unifying the exterior and its elements by alternating edges and centers. This interaction allows each section of the building to remain distinct yet related to other sections and to the entire building. The Raadhuis' massing, fenestration and surface articulation lend themselves particularly well to this type of investigation.

The diagrams use both tones and line weights to help reveal the underlying interaction of edges and centers. Lines vary to show how edges of a smaller mass align with the center of a larger mass or how window edges align with the edges of larger masses. Tones gradate to indicate that transparent masses are organized around edges and centers. The two diagramming methods reveal slightly different shifts: line weights focus attention on the alignments mentioned but also on fenestration and other

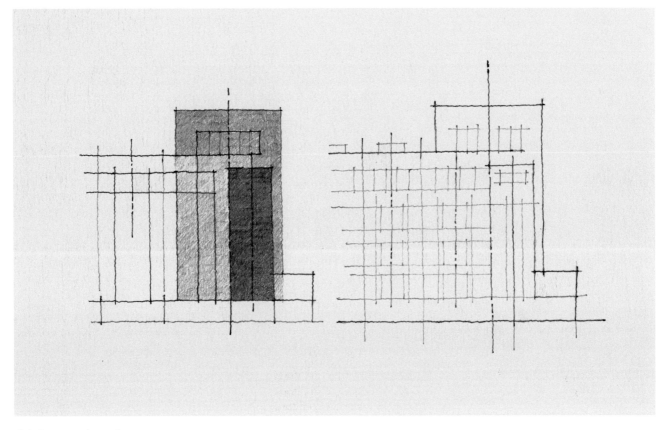

Shifts between edge and center

West façade

Raadhuis (Sofitel Hotel)
Amsterdam, The Netherlands, 1926
Nicolaas Lansdorp

Do any elements of the building alternate from edge to center?
How do different masses interlink through alternations of centers to edges?
If there is no alternation of center and edge, how does the architect compose mass and scale?

smaller elements that are aligned on edges and centers. Likewise, in the Can Jaumandreu façade diagram, line weights and types reveal how much of the shifting of edges and centers occurs not with massing but with fenestration, panels and the structural bays.

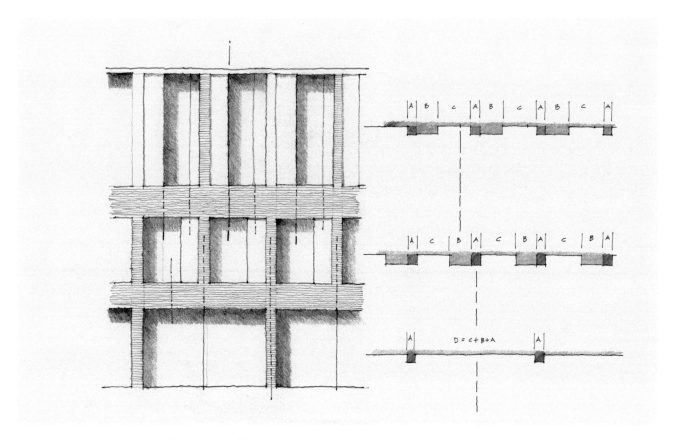

Façade and plan diagram showing edge and center shifts

South façade

Can Jaumandreu
Barcelona, Spain, 2006
Josep Llinás Carmona

Establishing and Then Breaking Order

How does an architect establish and then break the façade's ordering system? The process of drawing these diagrams is to help understand how the ordering systems might break in order to accommodate varied systems or to articulate the façade. Essentially, the ordering and its breaking help anticipate and resolve conflicting forces. The theme provides the order upon which variations can occur.

The diagram of Scarpa's Banca Popolare di Verona attempts to reveal the façade's underlying system that at first seems straightforward but upon closer examination is a complex transformation of ordering systems. The diagram first identifies the regular rhythm of the façade and another rhythm of circular apertures. Within these two rhythms, Scarpa shifts edges to centers, varies aperture size and window spacing. Short vertical lines above and below the façade establish the primary and secondary

Line and tone drawing showing façade depth

Overlapping rhythms and syncopations

North façade

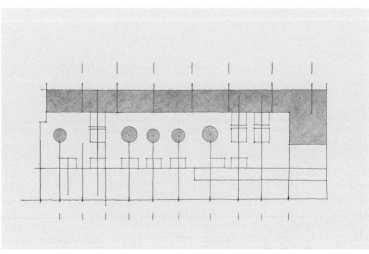

Banca Popolare di Verona
Verona, Italy, 1973
Carlo Scarpa

What are the underlying vertical and horizontal orderings?

How can one describe order and breaking of order using only two line weights?

How does an order transform from one side of the building to the other?

What role do the windows play in the façade?

rhythms. Then vertical lines within the façade help bring the rhythms together and overlap. The diagrams of the Casa del Fascio are various ways to investigate the façade's complexity. Each diagram explores different interpretations of the façade's order and breaking of order. Beginning with the regularly spaced bays, Terragni introduces a complex grid system, which appears or disappears to facilitate windows, doors, railings or, in the case of the two bays to the far right, to nearly fade altogether, only manifesting

itself in the stone veneer joint lines. While three of the four diagrams are similar in technique, each diagram attempts a different approach to unravel the hidden order and disorder. The "fenestration only" diagram, drawn using ink, shows how the order breaks to give variety to the façade.

Façade with shadows

Various orders established and broken

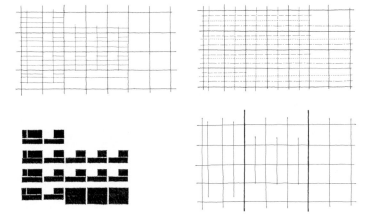

Southwest façade

Casa del Fascio
Como, Italy, 1936
Giuseppe Terragni

Diagnosing Proportional Systems

These diagrams illustrate how proportions are often drawn over a façade by using varied line weights. Identifying façade proportions is important, first, for finding and documenting the façade's underlying proportions, which act as a foundation for a more complex drawing. Once the underlying proportions are established, more complex information such as details or shading may be added without losing the overall drawing quality. Second, and perhaps more importantly, the discovering of the underly-

ing proportion is about the search itself: it is not so much about finding one particular proportional system that the architect may or may not have used, either consciously or unconsciously, but rather on deliberately analyzing a building to discover complex order.

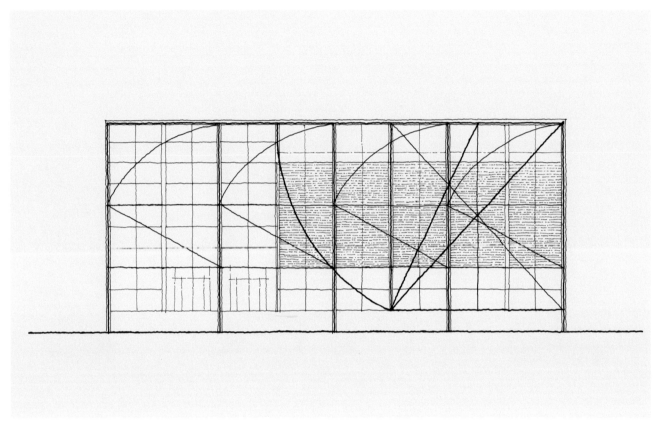

Underlying Golden Rectangles

East façade

Carré d'Art
Nîmes, France, 1993
Foster and Partners

What might be the façade's underlying proportional systems?
How do parts relate to the whole?
Are there rectilinear, scalar or linear relationships?

In both diagrams, the darker line weights and line types highlight the real or speculative proportional systems over the ghosted façade drawing. The underlying ghosted image is established through a careful mapping before the identified proportional system is laid on top of this. Like in other diagrams, information is limited in favor of the diagrammatic information. Detail, shadows, textures and other features are removed to emphasize the proportioning and regulating lines. The diagram of Foster's Carré d'Art reveals the underlying and overlapping Golden Ratio proportional system (1:1.618) that helps orchestrate and unify the façade and, in some way, link it to the Roman era Maison Carrée, which shares this proportional system. Likewise, the diagram of Le Corbusier's Maison Planeix reveals how the façade might be interpreted as a series of stacked and overlapping squares.

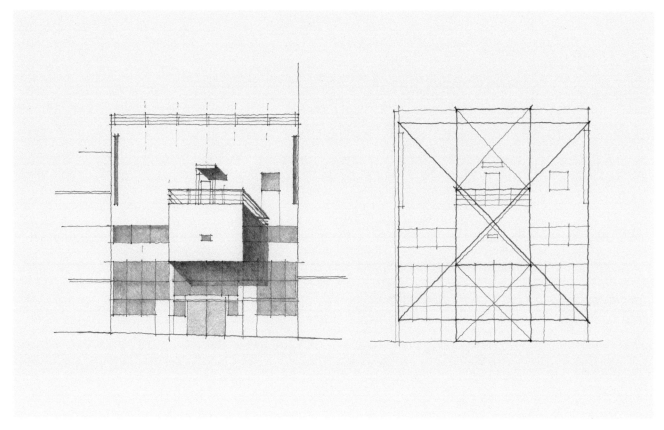

Elevation with shadows and underlying squares

Street façade

Maison Planeix
Paris, France, 1928
Le Corbusier

Connecting Scales

Generally, buildings are part of larger civic settings ranging from dense urban fabric to a more rural landscape. Yet, in a greater sense, a building is part of a larger social, spatial and historical setting beyond its own site. How a building participates in this setting depends on its sensitivity to material, type, use, meaning and culture. One important participatory act is the way in which a building accommodates multiple scales: civic scale, street scale and human scale. This ability to work at multiple scales simultaneously obliges the architect to understand how details such as doors, windows, sills and other small-scale elements integrate into a building's larger scale. Working at multiple scales simultaneously necessitates a balanced interweaving in which the large and the small co-exist yet remain distinct. Drawing them integrated and isolated and at multiple scales can help clarify each scale's integrity.

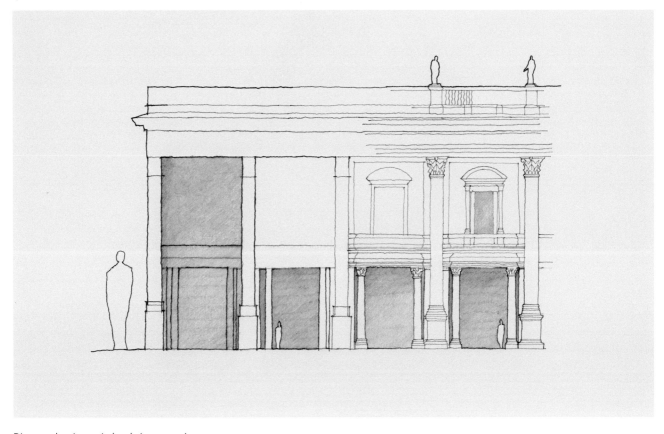

Diagram showing varied scale interpretations

Piazza façade

Palazzo Nuovo
Rome, Italy, 1537
Michelangelo Buonarroti

How does the building accommodate the urban and human scales?
What helps achieve this scalar shift?
How are different size and scale elements interrelated?
At what instances does a building shift from large to small scale?

The diagram of the Palazzo Nuovo shows how Michelangelo is able to make the building adapt to different scales by the interweaving of elements at two scales. One part of the diagram highlights different aspects through tones that emphasize and de-emphasize elements in order to see them independent of one another. Inserting scale figures, one at actual size and the other at an extremely large scale, shows how different elements can work at varied scales. Likewise, the diagram of the Equinox Fitness Center shows how the building is at once at the scale of the city with larger openings and patterns, yet is able to accommodate the smaller human-scale issue of entry and fenestration with a smaller grid behind the larger-scale plane.

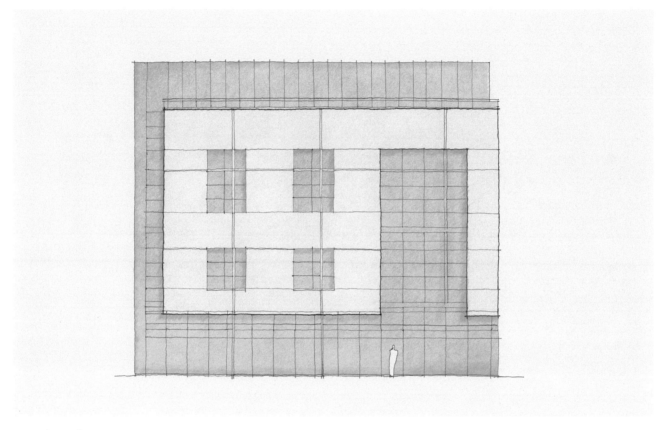

Line and tone elevation

Diagram proposing two scales

East façade

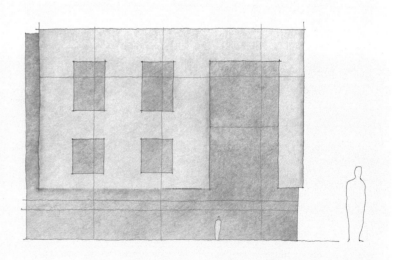

Equinox Fitness Center
New York, New York, 2001
Platt Byard Dovell White Architects

Understanding Continuity

Akin to "blind contour" drawings, these diagrams are formed by one continuously moving line in which a pencil or pen remains on the page. The viewer can choose to look at or not to look at the sheet (thereby making this a truly blind contour drawing). The benefits of this drawing are twofold. First, as a quickly drawn diagram in which there is little planning or caution, the façade's fundamental order must be quickly assessed and communicated. There is little time to map, measure or debate but only time to set the essential moves. A second, perhaps more important, benefit of this diagram type is the technique itself. Keeping the pen or pencil in constant contact with the sheet and constantly moving forces helps train the eye and hand to read a building quickly and succinctly. The results are often not beautiful or perhaps even accurate, but the process that leads to this and the thinking that can result are beneficial in the long term.

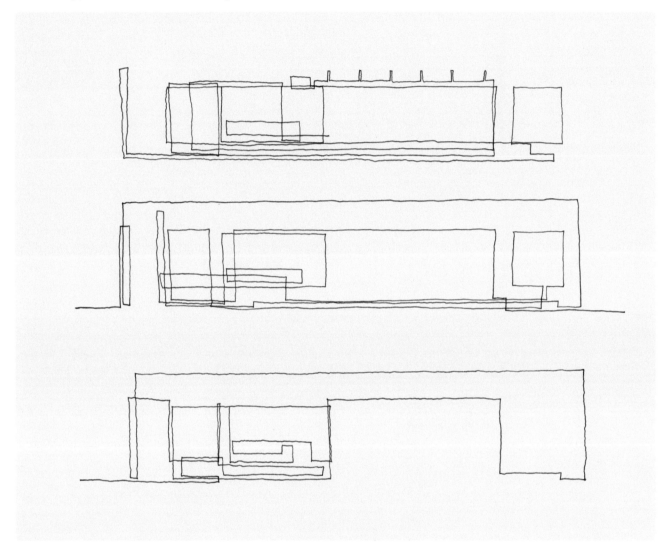

Three continuous line drawings

Main façade

Museu d'Art Contemporani de Barcelona
Barcelona, Spain, 1995
Richard Meier & Partners

How or where do you begin the blind contour drawing?
What part of the building continues to be difficult to draw?
Can you describe the entire building or only parts of the building?
What lines overlap and what are the similarities between different drawings?

The diagrams of both Meier's MACBA façade and the Freer Gallery, drawn in ink, reveal how the drawing type is distinctly procedural rather than declarative: the diagrams help to see, but they are unable to record all information without muddying the outcome. Essentially, it was difficult to "record" all aspects of the buildings without repeatedly superimposing lines on those already drawn. Ultimately, this difficulty helped clarify the building and induced other iterations and experimentations.

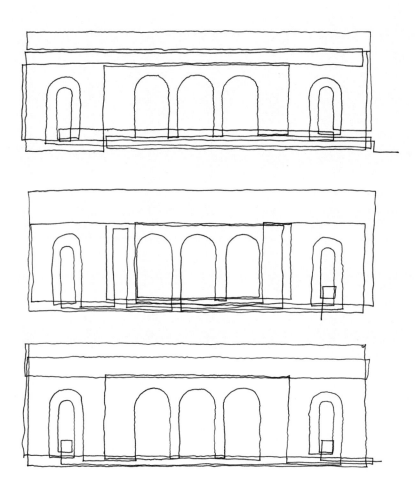

Three continuous line drawings

North façade

The Freer Gallery of Art
Washington, DC, 1923
Charles A. Platt

Attaching to Context

A key task in any design project is connecting to context – not only in terms of physical attachment but as greater connection to historic fabric, urban and street scales and to a cultural fabric – while maintaining the new or refurbished building's integrity. Rather than slavish attention on context, new buildings inserted into existing contexts contribute to the ever-evolving city without either dominating or ignoring the past.

The diagram of the Massachusetts Bay Transportation Authority Operations Center reveals how a contemporary building responds to the surrounding context in massing, material and rhythm without taking recourse to an artificially historical decoration. The elevation diagram uses line types to show how the building mass and material adjust to existing adjacent buildings to either side. The diagram of the Am Kupfergraben 10 gallery shows how the building adjusts to the two different existing building heights with

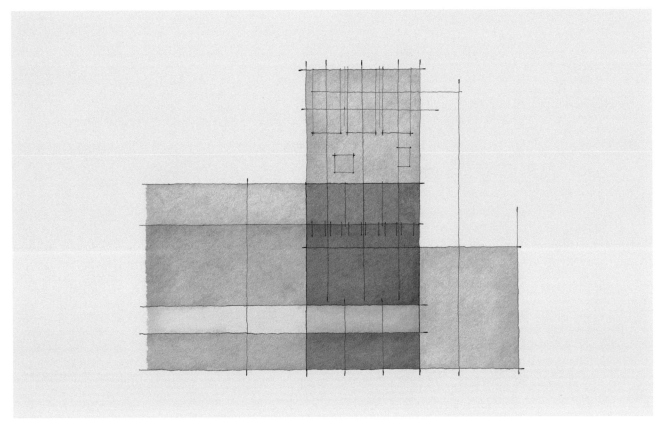

Diagram showing lines of force from neighboring buildings

South façade

Massachusetts Bay Transportation Authority Operations Center
Boston, Massachusetts, 1993
Leers Weinzapfel and Associates

What lines carry through from the context into the building?
To what degree does the new building contribute to, imitate or ignore the fabric?
How does the building adjust the change in scale, massing or fenestration?

continued horizontal banding yet does not duplicate the historic façades. The large window on the building's front aligns with the pilasters on the neighboring building. Additionally, the diagram reveals how the façades wraps from the higher neighboring building to adjust slightly to the lower neighboring building on the side street. Horizontal banding, stepped massing and fenestration are linked to patterns and dimensions on the adjacent buildings.

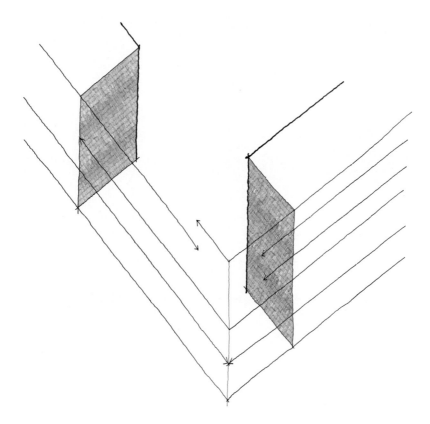

Plan oblique showing lines pulled from the neighboring buildings

Plan oblique showing the general massing and façade lines

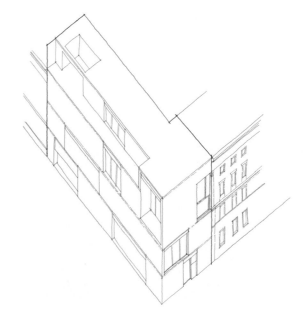

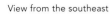

View from the southeast

Am Kupfergraben 10 Gallery
Berlin, Germany, 2007
David Chipperfield

Harmonizing Forms

A fundamental aspect of any architectural design project is harmonizing forms. These forms may be the varied internal spatial volumes or varied contexts such as changes in neighboring building heights, scale or marking an important element. These diagrams take two very different approaches to explore form harmony.

The diagrams of Hilversum Town Hall combine more pictorial representations with a more abstract massing study. The intention of these diagrams is to study the building quickly and succinctly by using ink and brush – an inherently imprecise medium that requires speed and agility. The brush must move quickly to delineate the essential lines. When doing these diagrams, it is often beneficial to work within self-imposed limits to help focus attention on the essential elements while disciplining the mind and hand.

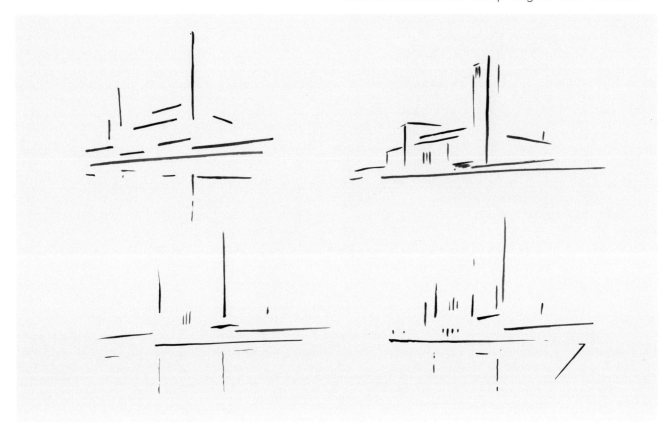

Variations on ink-and-brush gestural massing diagrams

View from the southwest

Hilversum Town Hall
Hilversum, The Netherlands, 1931
Willem M. Dudok

What are façades' varied scales, elements or moves?
Does the architect use alignments or perspective to help balance the building?
How would the building change if one portion or element was diminished or removed?

172

One limit is time. For example, complete the diagrams in five to ten seconds each. This almost unreasonable time limit compels succinctness of study and representation. A second limit is a "line budget", by assigning a limited number of lines to convey the maximum of information. By contrast, the Henry Rabe House diagrams are studies of how several individual masses might be harmonized through slow and steady transformation of alignments. Bay, garret and spire come together through regulating lines.

Elevation, diagram and elements pulled apart

South façade

Henry Rabe House
Washington, DC, 1891

Arranging Mass

Hierarchy or differentiation helps the building to become readable, in terms of what elements are more important than others or to mark specific elements within an overall unified composition. For example, a secondary or tertiary mass can help identify the entry or a particular program element within the overall composition. This legibility also helps organize a building's complexity in the design: distributing program in separate elements or pieces can help organize a building's functional layout.

The diagram of the Pavilion of the City of Brno reveals how a secondary platform, distinguished both in size and material from the primary mass, helps mark an entry, while the stair tower is juxtaposed on the planar rear wall. The tripartite composition is further distinguished by material choice and language: the terracotta brick-like mass, the white concrete plane and the sinuous tower each play a distinct role in the overall composition. The Erectheun diagram uses three tones to show the primary, secondary

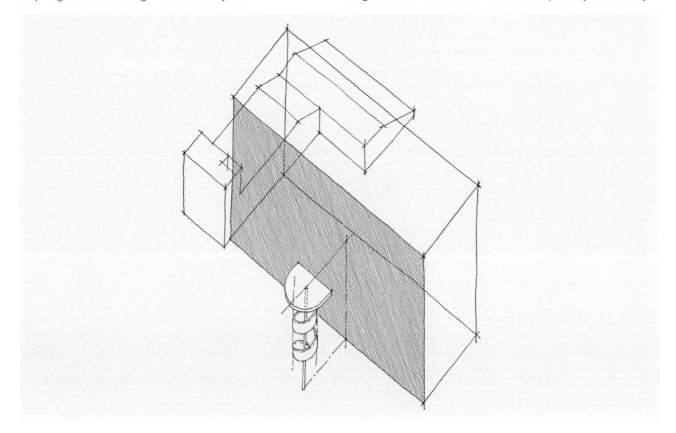

Transparent plan oblique showing individual elements

Southeast façade

Pavilion of the City of Brno
Brno, The Czech Republic, 1928
Bohuslav Fuchs

What are the primary, secondary and tertiary masses?
How do material and form coordinate with primary, secondary and tertiary roles?
How do primary, secondary and tertiary elements respond to specific forces?

and tertiary elements. While the building as it appears today is actually incomplete, the effect of the three masses offers an important lesson: as they remain distinct depending on the viewer's point of view, the three masses help mitigate the grade change and work together to make a unified whole.

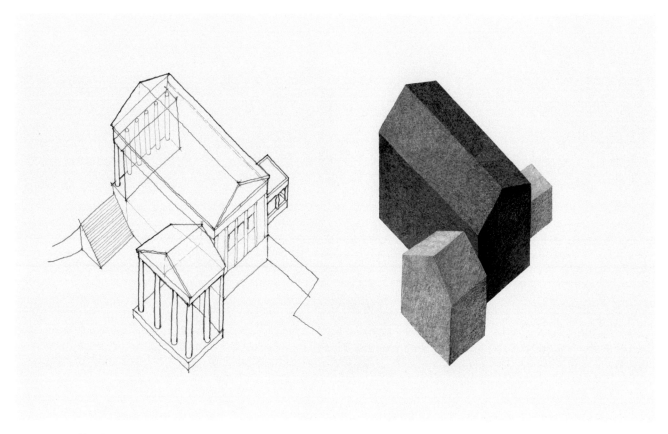

Transparent and highlighted plan obliques

View from the southeast

Erectheun
Athens, Greece, 427–424 BCE
attributed to Kallikrates

Balancing Mass

A building is often comprised of varied internal volumes or external masses that must be orchestrated into a comprehensible whole. Large open volumes work together with smaller-scale volumes and larger masses come together with smaller-massed elements. Varied elements are nearly inevitable in any building design. Embracing and working with this inevitability involves understanding that any unity or balance emerges from each element's location, size, proportion, color and material.

The **diagram** of Mackintosh's Hill House uses three tones to highlight the side elevation's massing composition. While in reality these elements are superimposed and somewhat unified by a stucco surface, by drawing them as three distinct elements we can start to see how these three autonomous elements are part of a more sophisticated composition that interweaves entry and fenestration. The diagram of the Metropolitan Community Church shows how the building's masonry wall wraps the glass sanctuary.

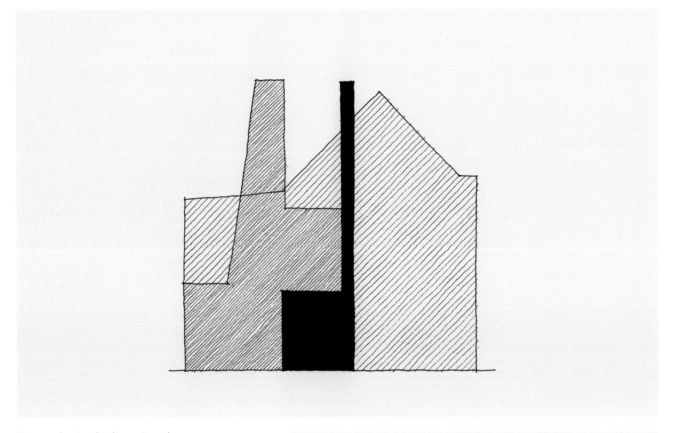

Diagram showing the three primary layers
Lines and windows

West façade

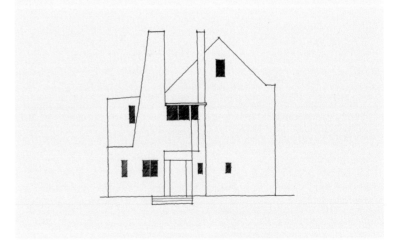

Hill House
Helensburgh, Scotland, 1904
Charles Rennie Mackintosh

What are the primary, secondary and tertiary masses of the building?
How are the varied volumetric scales articulated?
How are varied volumes and masses orchestrated to make a cohesive whole?

The diagram reduces the project to its essential nature: a "wall" begins as a mass or "inhabited wall" on the main street façade and, as it turns, transforms into a perimeter wall. For both of these buildings, the size of the individual elements plays an important role; however, material, location and proportion also contribute to the balancing act.

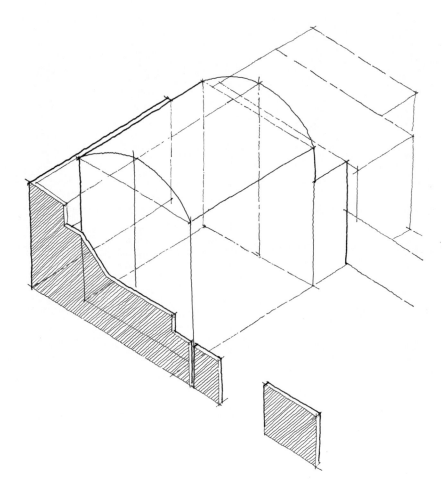

Wall enclosing the sanctuary

View from the southwest

Metropolitan Community Church
Washington, DC, 1993
Suzane Reatig

Subtracting Voids / Adding Figures

A building's mass is often a combination of added elements and subtracted voids. Added elements are those elements added to a buildings mass, while voids are those elements that appear to be carved into the building mass. These are essential ways to assemble buildings and also ways to shape space: adding, or assembling, versus carving.

The diagram of the Villa Müller shows how elements have been both added to and subtracted from the house's primary mass. Loos adds balconies, bays and garden walls, yet subtracts window voids and, on the upper level, removes a wall to open the uppermost terrace to views of Prague and, when it was built, the landscape. The diagram of Siza's Meteorological Service Building in Barcelona, drawn in pencil, shows how a primary mass has been augmented to create voids for fenestration and entry as

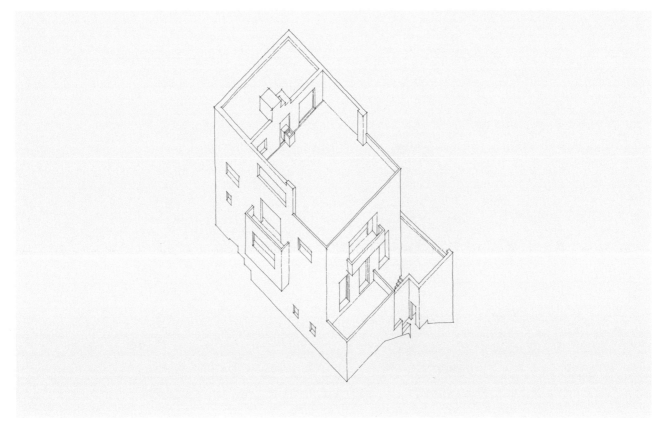

Plan oblique showing the villa's overall form

Exploded plan oblique showing added and subtracted elements

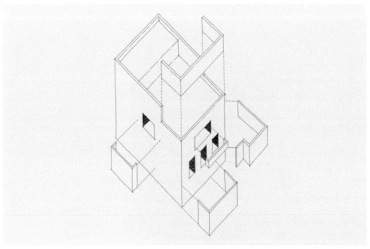

View from the southeast

Villa Müller
Prague, The Czech Republic, 1930
Adolf Loos

What is the building's primary mass?

Where and how are volumes subtracted from that mass?

How did the architect subtract sufficient void yet maintain the primary form?

well as to accommodate movement along the building's edge. While Siza does not add to the primary mass to make spaces as Loos does at Villa Müller, he does carve more deeply into the mass to create layers and voids for offices and laboratory windows. Both designs establish and maintain a pure and identifiable building mass yet add complexity through secondary and tertiary subtractive and additive elements.

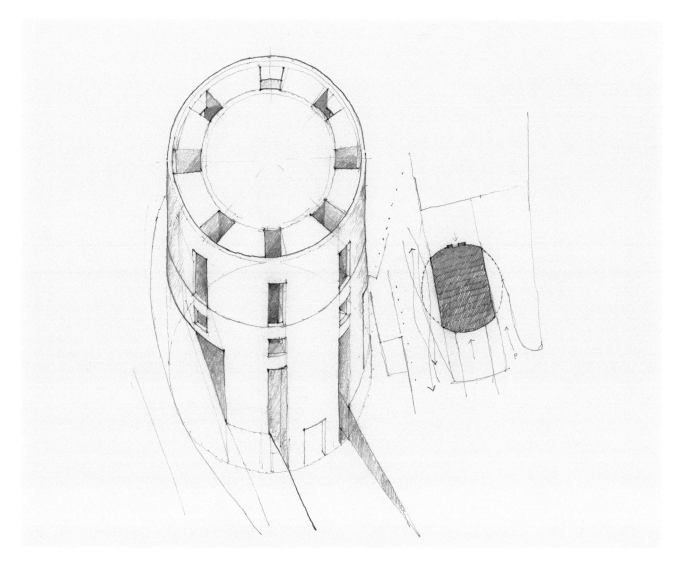

Plan oblique and plan diagram showing carved voids

View from the south

Meteorological Service Building
Barcelona, Spain, 1992
Álvaro Siza

Expressing Planes

Architects often use material and spatial layers to articulate a building entry. This is not only a technical matter, but also helps engender a sense of threshold where the visitor moves from one world to the next. On a conceptual level, moving through layers is about the interstitial layers necessary in any spatial sequence; more importantly it is a spatial experience that speaks to a metaphysical transformation.

The diagram of the Phillips Exeter Academy Library reveals how the building's exterior is expressed as four enclosing walls. The axonometric diagram "slides" one wall aside to reveal the interior layers, while emphasizing the planar and spatial quality, yet also articulating the façade openings. In comparison, another exterior wall is drawn using only tones and lines to further express these layers on a more fundamental level. Diagrams like these help reveal how the library, as a receptacle of knowledge, encloses onto itself;

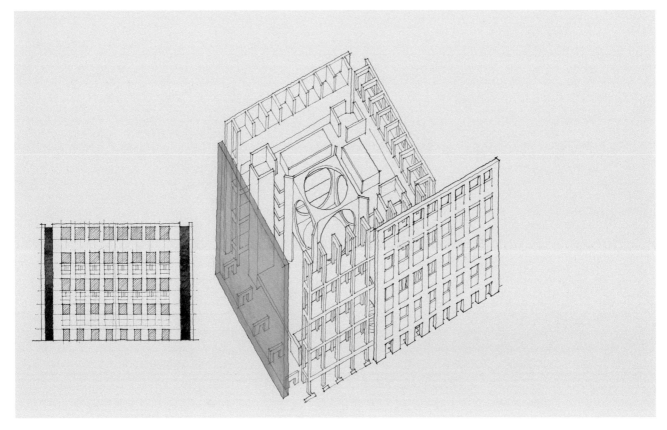

Plan oblique diagram showing planes

General view of the library's exterior

Phillips Exeter Academy Library
Exeter, New Hampshire, 1971
Louis Kahn

How are the planes made clear? Are the planar edges visible?
When or where are the planes penetrated?
What roles do transparency, translucency or opacity play in the building?

at the same time, they reveal how movement back and forth through various layers plays a role in conveying a greater intention. Tones in the Newseum diagram clarify the building's varied layers beneath which a visitor enters or looks out through the building. These layers decrease the building's depth and protect it from the southern solar exposure, also mitigating the setbacks from the Pennsylvania Avenue street wall to the face of the neighboring Canadian Embassy. Lighter tones indicate planes closer to the street edge, which increase in density as they move farther away from the street. This diagram might also underscore the building's more conceptual framework: the varied transparent and translucent layers reveal an interior that seems to symbolize the transparency of the government, freedom of the press and freedom of speech.

Tone-only drawing showing the various planes

View from the southwest

Newseum
Washington, DC, 2008
Polshek Partnership Architects, renamed Ennead Architects LLP

Weaving Structure and Enclosure

An essential nature of contemporary architecture is the differentiation of structure and enclosure; or more generally, differentiating those things that hold up the building versus those things that enclose the building. With the advent of the concrete and steel frame systems, structure no longer needed to correspond exactly with enclosure – a differentiation discussed by Semper and Laugier. Best exemplified by Le Corbusier's Maison Dom-ino diagram, structure became a skeleton around or within which curtain or free-standing walls would enclose space. While other systems, such as load-bearing walls in which structure is enclosure, structure and enclosure are now primary systems within which architects work. Essentially, a "skin-and-bones" duality is a fundamental principle in contemporary architectural design and production: understanding the constituents of this duality and how they interact is an essential design lesson.

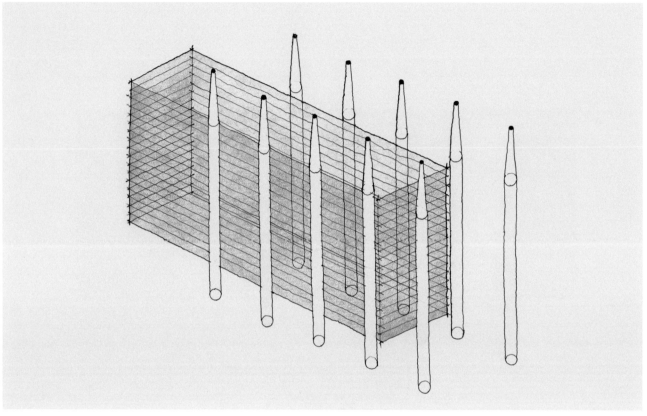

Isometric showing structure and enclosure

Tone and line drawing showing structure and enclosure

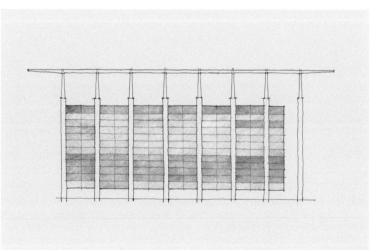

View from the southwest

Nederlands Architectuurinstituut
Rotterdam, The Netherlands, 1993
Jo Coenen & Co. Architects

Can the structure (skeleton) and the enclosure (skin) be identified from the exterior?
How are the structure and enclosure separate or unified?
If the structure is regular, is the skin then regular or irregular?

The diagrams of the Netherlands Architecture Institute show how this system plays a significant role in articulating the façade. Essentially, the NAi remains nearly diagrammatic in its clearly articulated structure and enclosure. The round columns support the virtually floating enclosing box, while the structure continues above the roof to support an enclosing frame. The diagram of the Office of Thrift Supervision shows how the columnar system moves from outside to inside and outside again, to help articulate the building mass. Here the outer wall is articulated as a screen, with the row of columns located behind it. Both sets of diagrams differentiate structure from enclosure to better clarify the nature of these two interdependent systems. While the difference is not always this distinct, the simplified "skin-and-bones" principle is a fundamental design and construction consideration.

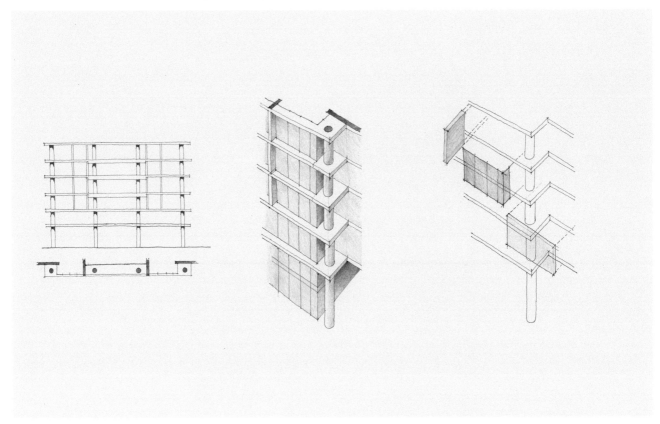

Diagrams of structure and enclosure

Elevation with shadows

View from the south

Office of Thrift Supervision
Washington, DC, 1977
Max O. Urbahn

Viewing Layers

Similar to the discussion about moving through layers, these diagrams examine how a façade is composed by a series of compressed layers. While these might remain conceptually spatial, the overlapping, superimposed and compressed layers often mitigate scale, by taking different scale elements, and articulate the often varied layers inherent in façade building. The notion of a building's layers is both literal and conceptual: the façade is constructed using layers, yet the layers are autonomous, interdependent elements.

The diagram of Café De Unie starts to suggest how Oud superimposed layers to imply that the façade is a series of planes. Here, the elevation diagram shows how layers overlap through lines and assigned tones that increase in darkness as they move toward the rear. Similarly, the diagrams of Palladio's Palazzo Valmarana Braga peels away each superimposed layer to reveal the unmolested, complete layer beneath. For Palladio, the layers carry their own burden: the giant pilasters address the overall

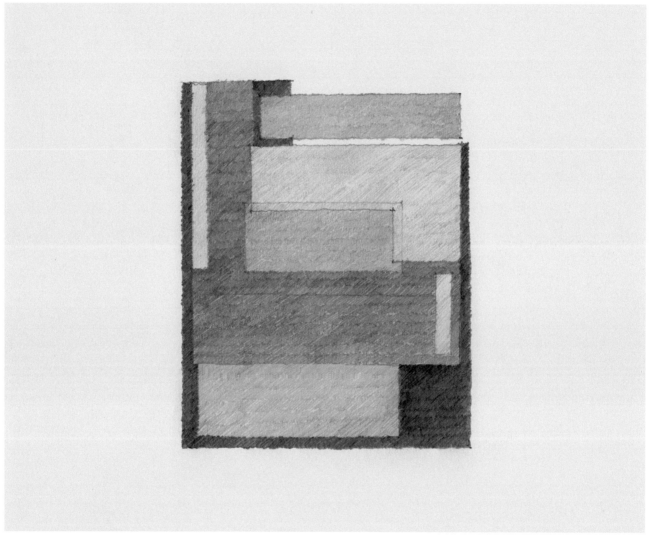

Tone-only diagram showing layers

View from the south

Café De Unie
Rotterdam, The Netherlands, 1925
J. J. P. Oud

How are perceived layers different from spatial layers?
What lines appear, disappear or move "behind" or "in front of" other layers?
How deep, literally, is each layer? How does this differ from perceived depth?
How do the layers help mitigate the scales of the site, of the building, of windows or doors and of people?

street scale, the layer beneath addresses the connection to the floors and to the adjacent building, and the layer beneath that adjusts to a more human and detailed scale of masonry joint lines. While these are layers not in the literal sense, they are nevertheless conceptually complete. Layers "slide" behind one another and are only revealed at critical moments. The exploded axonometric reveals how these layers might look if peeled away from each other. The tones are assigned to further reveal the distinct layers.

These types of diagrams remain important when designing a façade, simply because a façade is layered system: a façade is built using elements that often must be assembled in a particular order one on top of the other. Moreover, as the façade must adapt to changes and conditions, the building may have to add or remove elements in a layered manner.

Exploded elevation oblique showing layers

Detail of the pilasters layered upon one another

Palazzo Valmarana Braga
Vicenza, Italy, 1565
Andrea Palladio

Relating Base-Middle-Top

The tripartite division that transforms a façade from base to top, although often understood as a purely compositional approach, is more about connections. The tripartition of base, middle and top is an articulation of the often necessary differentiation in a building as it sits on its site. As it touches the ground, there are obvious differences that must be addressed so that it can sustain water, maintenance, physical wear and human interaction. Subsequent vertical striations address more typical vertical changes from program. The top of the building must address issues of roof, cooling towers, elevator towers, etc. While all of these can sometimes be discarded (and often should be discarded), the issue of tripartition of base, middle and top is often more about composition than it is utilitarian.

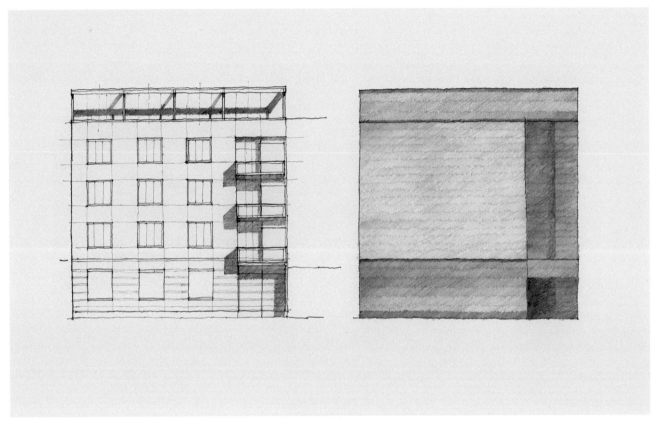

Façade with tones showing the tripartite divisions

Isometric of the façade

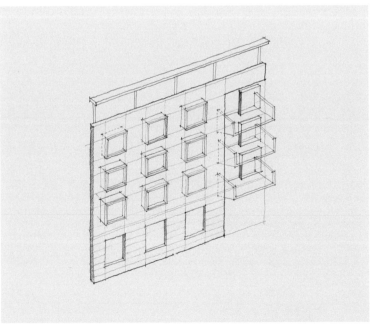

Casa Pedraglio Apartment Building
Como, Italy, 1937
Guiseppi Terragni

How is the building's façade articulated into base-middle-top?

To what extent, how and why is base-middle-top not articulated?

How does the building touch the sky versus touch the ground?

Is there a base-middle-top within each part?

The diagram of Terragni's Casa Pedraglio apartment building shows how the base-middle-top tripartition is quite clear. The base, with its darker and heavier stone, connects the building to the street, while its uppermost terrace is light and distinctly fragile to connect to the sky. The diagram clearly indicates the tripartite order as well as the interconnecting vertical bay. The diagram of the St. Paul Companies office building base reveals how base-middle-top is both scalar and overlapping. To allow for the connections between the lower levels and upper levels and to adjust from street scale to city scale, the design introduces elements that support the transition with a scalar overlap. While the overall building has a base-middle-top organization, each of these elements has its own base-middle-top, so that there are three of these altogether.

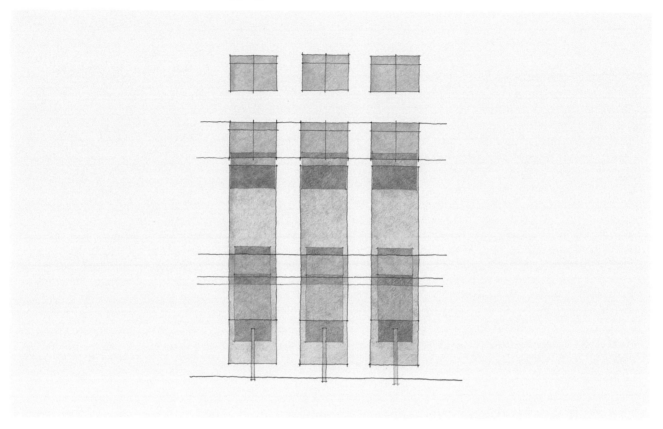

Tones used to show tripartite divisions and overlaps

Line and tone elevation

View looking southwest

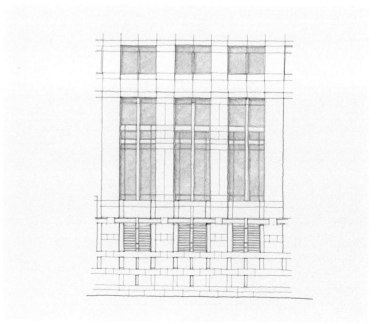

St. Paul Companies
St. Paul, Minnesota, 1991
Kohn Pedersen Fox Associates

Topping the Building

These studies investigate how a building touches the sky or, perhaps less poetically, how vertical surfaces transition to horizontal ones. Generally, these transitions revolve around practical issues of the way in which a roof attaches to or is incorporated into a wall, but it also deals with the issue of what distinguishes upper floors from other, lower floors. These may be attenuated transitions or abrupt transitions. While the abrupt transitions simply stop the façade and embody a minimalist allure, the focus of these diagrams is the attenuated transition. The transition begins well before the actual roofline, further down the building. To prepare for that transition, anticipate that transaction, aesthetically, in a foreshadowing that prepares you for the end. Look at how a building transitions from top to bottom, almost oblivious of the transition.

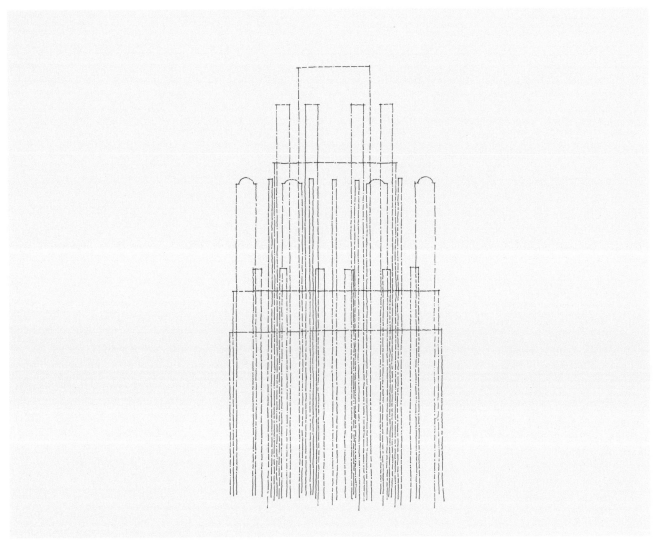

Line drawing showing lines and massing diminish toward the top

View from the south

The Tribune Tower
Chicago, Illinois, 1925
John Mead Howells and Raymond Hood

What lines continue from the base through to the top of the building?
How do lines transform as they move toward the top?
How is the building's top significantly different from or similar to its vertical surface?
How does the design anticipate the building's top?

The diagram of the Chicago Tribune Tower examines how the architect slowly linked the building's base and shaft to the building's top. Drawn with a fountain pen, the diagram uses only lines to delineate those vertical elements that steadily disappear to reveal the building's uppermost layers and core. Drawing all the lines the same way as at the bottom, but then dropping them off near the top, reveals the line continuity. The diagrams of the uppermost floors of the Bay State apartment building use two meth-

ods to examine the transformation from surface to sky. First, line weights and types show how the underlying grid manifests into hierarchically ordered horizontal and vertical panels. Lines appear and disappear "behind" layers. Then the diagram with tones helps reveal how the three layered masses essentially "fade", so that the center element emerges out of other elements, in a layered system.

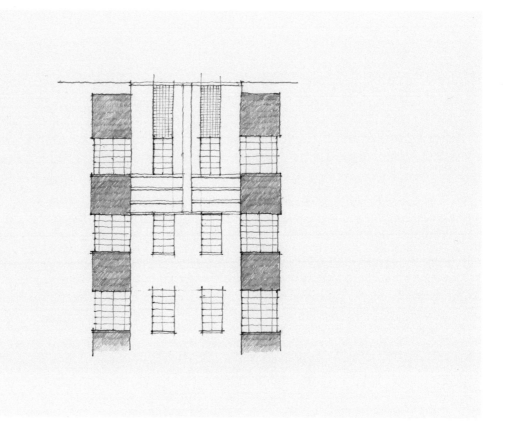

Line and tone drawing of the upper floors

Diagrams showing overlapping elements

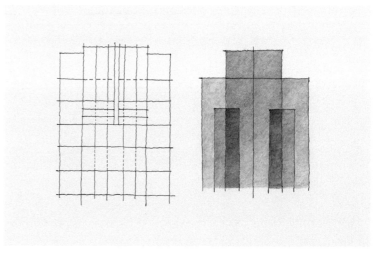

View from the south

Bay State Apartment Building
Washington, DC, 1939
Robert Scholz

Turning the Corner

Turning the corner or making the transition from one direction to another is a significant, if underrated, move. The corner is one moment when the façade must transition from one direction to another. Like the previous diagrams that show how a building might touch the sky, these diagrams show how a corner might be anticipated. This is similar to turning a bicycle around a corner. A bike rider must contemplate and anticipate the turn well before the actual change in direction. When making the turn, it is

often a gentle arc that begins and ends with the bicycle moving in a different direction. Likewise, when turning a building, rather than simply turning at the corner, the turn or change in direction is anticipated or planned for early on the façades.

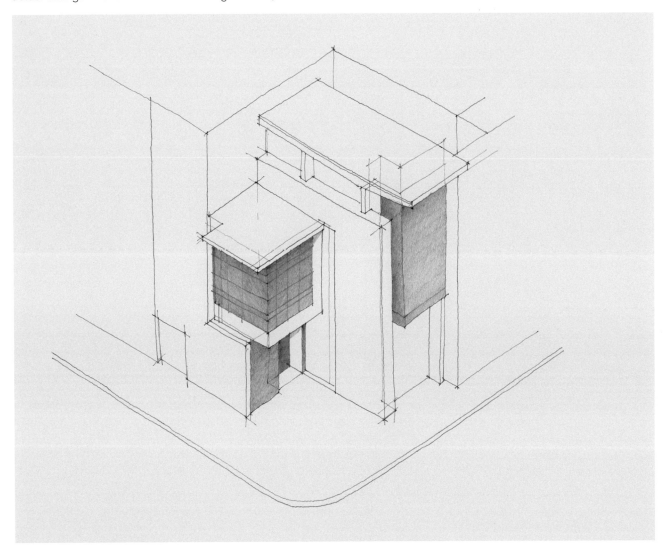

Diagram of interlocking elements

View from the northeast

Walter E. Washington Convention Center
Washington, DC, 2003
Thompson, Ventulett, Stainback & Associates

What lines help anticipate the direction change?
When does the corner start? How far back along the façade does the turn begin?
Does massing transform at the corner?
Is there a primary and secondary plane or are both planes equivalent?

These corner diagrams highlight two ways architects might turn corners. The diagram of the Walter E. Washington Convention Center shows how the architect introduced smaller building elements such as stairways, lobby and meeting rooms to alleviate the potentially massive corner. The design anticipates these changes with an underlying grid that slowly transforms as it meets the corner. Likewise, the diagram of the Budapest apartment building, drawn using ink pen, shows only the façade lines that transform as they slide toward the corner: sills and lintel lines fade out or transform into railings and balconies and then, after the turn, reappear or revert to sills and lintels.

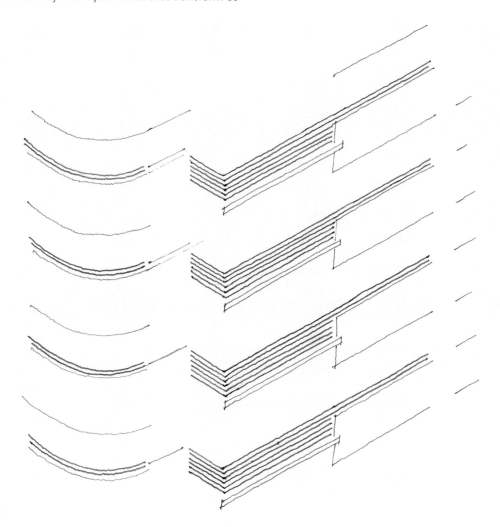

Diagram of continuous and discontinuous lines

View from the south

Apartment Building
Budapest, Hungary, 1935
Hofstätter and Dományi

Seeing Windows

For many buildings, window size and variety are often dictated by economies of scale, combined with spatial and visual experience. The economics of windows often force the architect to think around the window size variation by varying the window spacing or gaps between windows, window grouping (in pairs or sets) and altering the framing context such as sills, lintels or the surrounding wall surface.

The diagrams of the 2929 Connecticut Avenue apartment building, drawn using pencil, first document the elevation with its windows, balconies, projecting bays and horizontal banding. It is lightly shadowed to help articulate the surfaces. This is paired with a drawing that shows the windows only. The windows-only diagram helps reveal the influence of context. When looking at the façade of the building, one does not realize that all the windows are the same generally; this is revealed when the windows' context

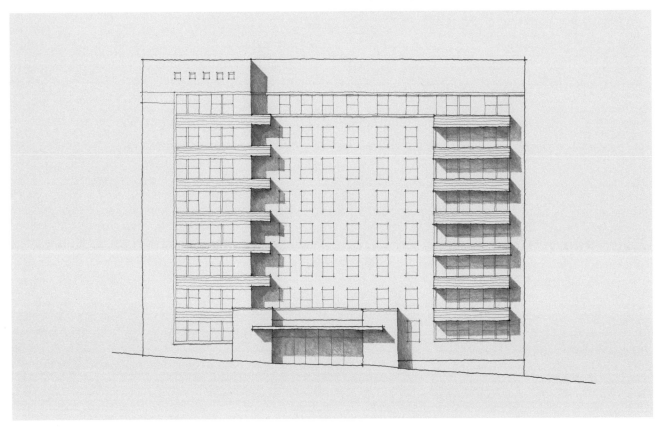

Façade with shadows from balconies and projections

Façade showing only the windows, which are all identical

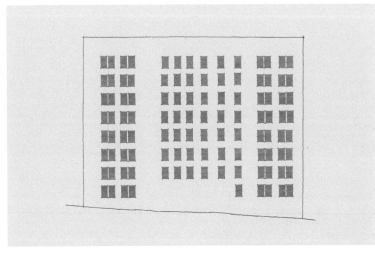

View from the southwest

2929 Connecticut Avenue NW
Washington, DC, 1936
Dillon and Abel

What are the primary window types in the façade?
How is the primary window augmented or duplicated?
How does the context change around the windows?
How is the fundamental order altered?

– the balconies, frames and massing – are removed. In comparison, the diagrams of the Dessau Bauhaus dormitory wing, drawn using ink pen, reveal how one common element can remain uniform yet produce a dynamic façade. The façade's unrelenting repetition is part of its strength; however, through diagramming it becomes clear that unrelenting repetition is insufficient. The design breaks the seemingly unrelenting order in simple ways and brings complexity to an otherwise simple façade. The

tripartite window uniformity organizes the overall façade, yet the introduction of a door and balcony to one side shifts the balance slightly to one side. Rather than context, it is in this case the individual unit that transforms the façade.

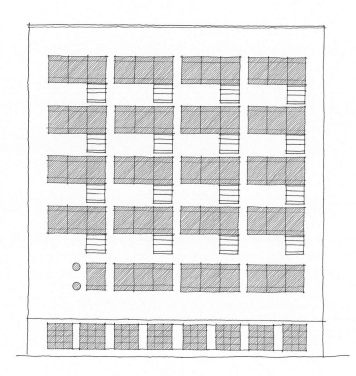

Façade in lines and hatching

Diagrams showing the façade shift and variation
in the window module

View from the northeast

Dessau Bauhaus Dormitory Wing
Dessau, Germany, 1926
Walter Gropius

Highlighting Shadows

Rather than drawing all the elements, drawing only the shadows implies all things that produce the shadows. This diagram type is a simple way to reveal a building's façade both quickly and succinctly. In so doing, it has the added benefit of indicating, when there are no shadows, that shadow-producing elements may be necessary. Like other diagrams, shadow-only diagrams highlight one particular issue by selectively and temporarily eliminating information. Like black-and-white "figure/ground" diagrams, shadows-only diagrams reveal one clear aspect of the building, so that one can briefly and temporarily see the building for its overall composition. This diagramming method is a lesson in editing essential for any design pursuit. As designer we must use refined discernment combined with understanding, ability and, sometimes, courage to decide what, when, where and how much remains or goes away.

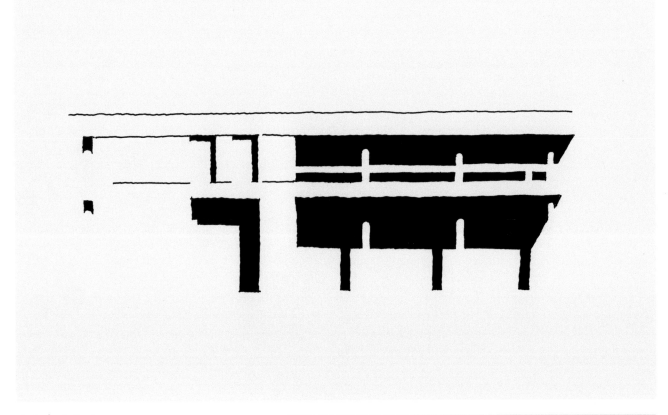

Shadow-only drawing

Line and tone elevation drawing

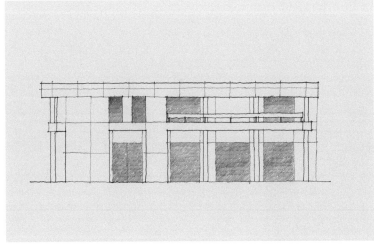

View from the west

Engine Company 2 Fire Station
Washington, DC, 1978
Keyes Condon Florence

Where are the shadows?

What is revealed when there are few or no shadows?

If the building has no direct exposure to the sun, how can one still draw "shadows"?

The **diagram** of the Engine Company 2 Fire Station, done using felt-tip pens, shows how drawing the shadows quickly and succinctly reveals a building's patterns, but also how a building modulates shadow to provide hierarchy but also to protect the particular parts of the building. In this case, the shadows reveal the protected truck bays and public entry. The diagram of Palladio's Basilica, done using ink pen and brush, shows the contrast between solid and void, while suggesting detail through extremely abstract marks. Additionally, it underscores the basilica's white marble shell enclosing a darker-stone medieval building core. In both diagrams, there is a deliberate decision not to draw everything. This decision arises not only from the diagram type but also from the media. The qualities of brush and ink, markers or even soft pencils encourage discerned focus.

Shadow-only drawing

View from the north

Basilica Palladiana
Vicenza, Italy, 1549
Andrea Palladio

PROBING THE DETAILS

We attain to dwelling, so it seems, only by means of building. The latter, building, has the former, dwelling, as its goal.

Martin Heidegger[1]

The quality of the finished object is determined by the quality of the joints.

Peter Zumthor[2]

Architecture is made up of details, fragments, fabrications. And the very idea behind it can be captured in a fragment, in a detail.

John Hejduk[3]

Probing the Details concerns, on one level, smaller things from rooms and entries to furniture and door knobs as well as the joints, seams and material assemblies in architecture. While the literally small are important, a second concern are the relationships among different scales: large things joined by small things, grand rooms linked by diminutive ones or elements that link human scale to larger situations. For the latter, it is a matter of context. For instance, in its context, a 30-story office building's entry canopy is a detail, although it may be the size of a small house. Yet, beyond the small and the scalar relationships, the chapter's topic concerns dwelling through the act of making: dwelling in the sense of how we might fully engage with architecture through the act of assembling and interacting with materials.

In his essay, "Building Dwelling Thinking", Martin Heidegger examines the intrinsic relationship of dwelling to the building act by linking it, ultimately, to technique (*techne*), noting: "To the Greeks *techne* means neither art nor handicraft but rather: to make something appear, within what is present, as this or that, in this way or that way. The Greeks conceive of *techne*, producing, in terms of letting appear."[4] In Heidegger's definition then, dwelling is linked to assemblies that can reveal and celebrate the nature of building. By engaging with the nature of how we build, we engage with a site, with space and ourselves. It is through making that we dwell. Yet, Heidegger seems to complicate this narrative with a paradox: while he notes that through making we can grasp dwelling, he later notes that only after we are "capable of dwelling, only then can we build".[5] This apparent paradox might be resolved if we conceive of the design process as an action-reflection sequence. If dwelling-building becomes part of an action-reflection process, both building and dwelling are part of a cycle leading to greater understanding. It is in this context that Probing the Details concerns both a systematic process and a scalar relationship in which we build, reflect upon and occupy place.

From Suppositions to Propositions

As systematic analog processes, diagramming assemblies and places parallels the building process in which drawings are mock assemblages. Like building or making, the principle of drawing a detail is systematic layering of one element with others into a complete assembly. In fact, a crucial lesson for many young architects is learning the difference between *drawing a detail as a graphic and drawing a detail as an assemblage* – a distinction that is at once subtle and dramatic. As a graphic, details only represent assemblies while, by contrast, a detail as an assemblage is rooted in sequence: while drawing, pieces are assembled in systematic succession with the drawing following a gradual internal narrative – "this goes here, then that attaches there, and eventually this wraps around that". Essentially, the drawing, to be a more successful detail, is a constructed act mimicking the anticipated constructive act. The drawing is assembled step by step, much like the constructed assemblage. In fact, during the drawing process, a detailing error or misstep appears when there is a realization that the assembly does not work. Therefore, at this point, architects often begin the drawing again, if from a slightly different point, and then diverge at particular moments until the details or the assembly come together. Rather than a "how to" of construction details, the diagrams discussed here are suppositions on the nature of assemblies, suppositions that can help develop design propositions. Essentially, diagrams that un-construct or reverse-engineer partially or completely obscured assemblies are informed guesses of how hidden elements *might have been* assembled, and they parallel the process of how things *could* be assembled. Through systematic analysis and synthesis of an existing assembly may arise a systematic understanding of future assembly processes and, perhaps, invention.

Diagramming Place

These diagrams also explore the ways we can transform parts of a building. Opening windows, touching railings, turning knobs are ways in which we physically encounter architecture on a personal level. The tactile qualities of this interaction are important because of the nature of what is touched, how the hand grips, turns, moves along material and how that material and its form correspond to the human hand. On another level, these diagrams explore how we interact with architecture through scale or how a building helps connect us to the others, to context and to history: the way in which the human body engages with architecture in terms of furniture, entry, scale and room. At this scale, the human interacts with the building to make the building a place. The architecture accommodates the human body by incorporating its scale. Walls that are benches or rails that are tables are a part of architecture in which we are intimately involved in the building. Likewise, architecture is about how a building plays a role in framing our intimate and personal relationship with our surroundings. For example, it explores how a window or seat helps extend us beyond the moment into the surrounding landscape, and even to our past. This even extends to *impromptu* places within rooms, buildings or cities that we occupy more than likely unforeseen by those who designed and built them. Fences for display, fountains for napping or stairs for reading are those places in which we find dwelling within the designed environment. A building's details, from how a floor meets a wall to how one enters and moves through a space, are concerned with subconscious perceptions. Attending to details in the design process is also about the joints, but mainly about the subtle, even small moves in the context of the larger project, that play a larger role in the design. For example, at the Institut du Monde Arabe in Paris, Jean Nouvel introduces distinct material changes at thresholds and wall-floor intersections. While details in the sense of how to resolve a joint, they seem to imply or refer 20th-century interpretations of Middle-Eastern architectural traditions of threshold and layering. In a sense, the larger meaning of the building and its overall success is in its details, both in how it is made and conceived.

Ultimately, an aim of looking at details is to understand them not as just small or just details but how they are part of a larger engagement and larger understanding of architecture. They are about how to engage with the scale with which we are most familiar: the scale of ourselves; how we literally assemble materials, how we touch a building, how we dwell within architecture; about respecting the nature of materials so that when they are assembled they not only work together but that the materials are used in an appropriate situation or that the materials' nature is not denied but expressed.

Questions at the root of this action include:

How does the object conform to the human body or to the human hand?
What is mobile within architecture? What can mutate, transform and otherwise move?
How are things joined? What is the "third thing" in the assemblage?
What accommodates human scale?

1 Heidegger, Martin, *Poetry, Language, Though,* trans. Albert Hofstadter. New York: Harper & Row (1971): 143.

2 Zumthor, Peter, *Architektur denken.* Basel: Birkhäuser: 14. Transl. here by Eric Jenkins.

3 Hejduk, John, "The Flatness of Depth", in *Judith Turner Photographs Five Architects.* London: Academy Editions (1980).

4 Heidegger, Martin, *Poetry, Language, Thought,* trans. Albert Hofstadter. New York: Harper & Row (1971): 157.

5 *Ibid.*

Finding Rooms within Rooms

While most rooms generally match the scale of activities occurring within, there is sometimes a need to establish subsidiary spaces within a room to accommodate varied spatial needs or scales of interaction. Like interior canopies, such as church baldachins or wedding chuppahs, rooms within rooms can frame particular moments or simply offer a greater sense of dwelling within a larger framework.

The diagrams of Sir John Soane's Breakfast Room, which include a plan, section and axonometric, help show how a smaller room is, like a Russian doll, nested within the larger room to define the breakfast area. The dome, set on pendentives, does not touch the four walls but seems to hover above the table like a canopy. By pulling the dome away from the four walls, Soane allows indirect lighting in from the gaps beneath the floating dome and allocates pathways through the room yet along its edges. This

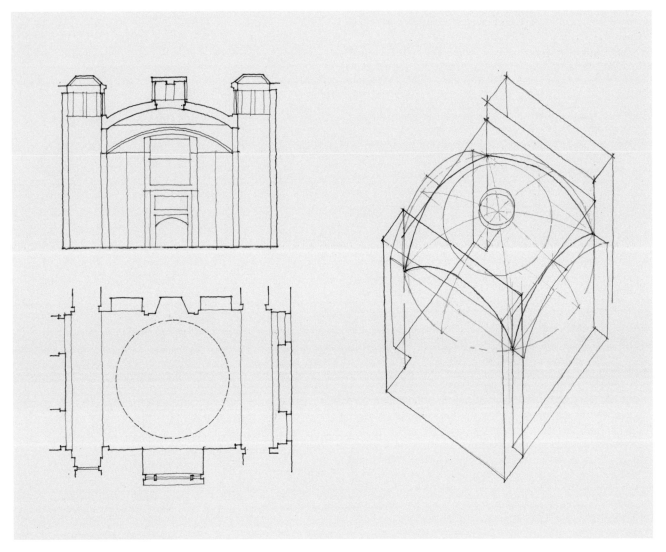

Section, plan and plan oblique diagrams

Ceiling and alcoves of the Breakfast Room

Breakfast Room in Sir John Soane's Museum
London, England, 1824
John Soane

Are there rooms within rooms?
How are these rooms defined?
What makes the difference in forming rooms within rooms?
What are other benefits of defining rooms within rooms?

axonometric diagram began by drawing the dome's circular form that, once set, helped frame the rest of the drawing. The diagram of the Sea Ranch Condominiums is a single isometric that highlights the small pavilions or aedicules that form more intimate rooms within the larger, and here ghosted, space. This undifferentiated surrounding area is left nebulous, because unlike Soane's Breakfast Room, the Sea Ranch rooms-within-rooms are more like pavilions within a larger void.

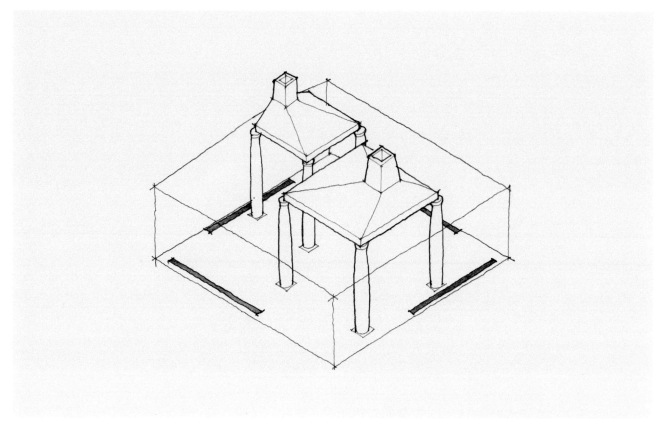

Isometric of the pavilions within a larger room

Condominium plan

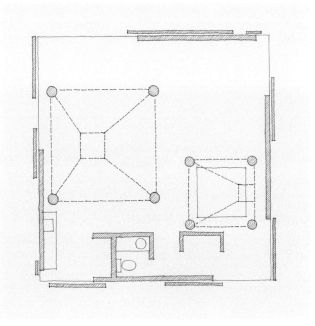

Sea Ranch Condominiums
Sea Ranch, California, 1964
MLTW (Charles Moore, Donlyn Lyndon,
William Turnbull and Richard Whitaker)

Sheltering within a Room

Like engaging with windows or finding rooms within rooms, there are moments when elements in a building such as desks, bookcases, balustrades or stairs become intermediary dwelling places by accident or design. In these places, the elements become places that act in their original intention yet provide a secondary meaning or place.

The diagram of Alvar Alto's Rovaniemi Municipal Library shows how, in section, a reading table is also a ledge between upper level book stacks and a lower-level reading area. While a simple railing would have sufficed, Aalto provides a place to read and, because of the desk's depth, additional privacy to both levels. Likewise, the diagrams of Bramante's Santa Maria della Pace Cloister shows how its railing, like Aalto's library, can also be a place for reading and contemplation. Instead of a simple balustrade,

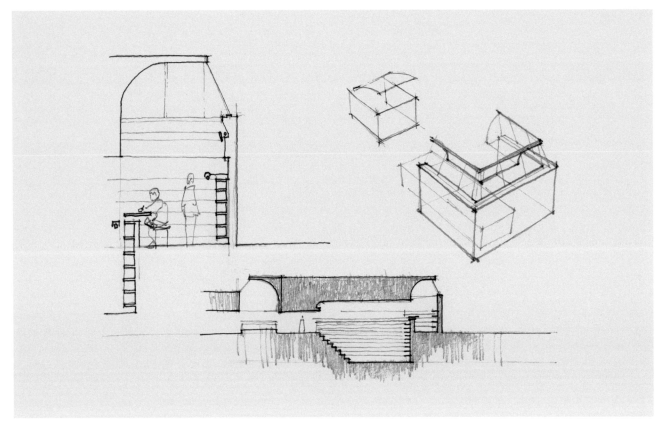

Diagrams showing the various zones within the larger room

View of the reading areas

Rovaniemi Municipal Library
Rovaniemi, Finland, 1965
Alvar Aalto

How can a railing, desk or bookcase act in two capacities?
How does the intermediary element improve the relationship of two spaces?
What is the zone created between the two rooms?

Bramante creates a third, occupiable moment. These diagrams may heighten an awareness of occupied interstitial zones within rooms and, by extension, gardens and cities. Rather than separating room from furniture, occupied interstitial areas allow for a window, a garden wall or a street edge to become more than edges but places with multiple readings: a window can be bench and a curb a place to rest. As such, shelters within a room are opportunities for architecture to embrace the human body.

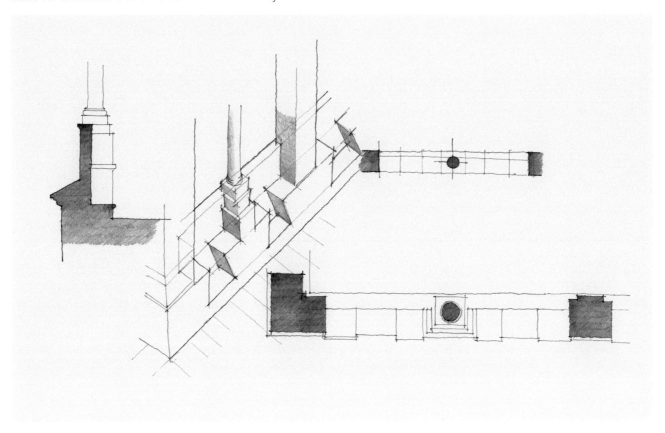

Diagrams showing seating zone within the cloister parapet

View of the upper level cloister parapet

Santa Maria della Pace Cloister
Rome, Italy, 1483
Donato Bramante

Opening Doors

Opening a door is at once a physical and a metaphysical act: gripping the handle, pulling or pushing the door, stepping over a threshold mark a change from one state to another. Regardless of its triviality or its momentousness, the spatial experience of opening a door is a moment of change. Considering all doors in this way reconceptualizes what might be a utilitarian moment into a moment of opportunity.

The semi-transparent diagram of the Castelvecchio Museum doorway shows in isometric and plan of how the actual single door is integrated into a pavilion inserted behind an archway. The free-standing pavilion, comprised of folded planes, allows the door to be part of a larger threshold between inside and outside but also forming the connection between contemporary and historic. Likewise, the diagram of the University of Virginia's Pavilion IX illustrates how Jefferson framed the door using volumes

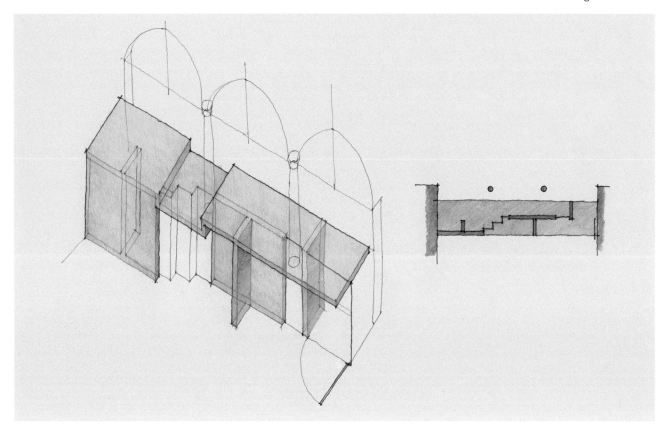

Diagram showing the threshold framework

Exterior view of the courtyard doorway

Castelvecchio Museum
Verona, Italy, 1973
Carlo Scarpa

In what way is the door part of a threshold?
Is the door more than a "hole in the wall", is it part of a larger system?
How would you describe the door's frame and immediate surroundings?

and light. The half-dome protrudes above the colonnade's roof, allowing ambient sunlight to illuminate what might otherwise be a dark door. These diagrams examine and can help reveal the ways in which entry can be more than a door. If conceived only as a door, the entry is liable to remain a hinged panel, but conceived as a threshold, even the most mundane entry or door celebrates and participates in a more profound human phenomenon.

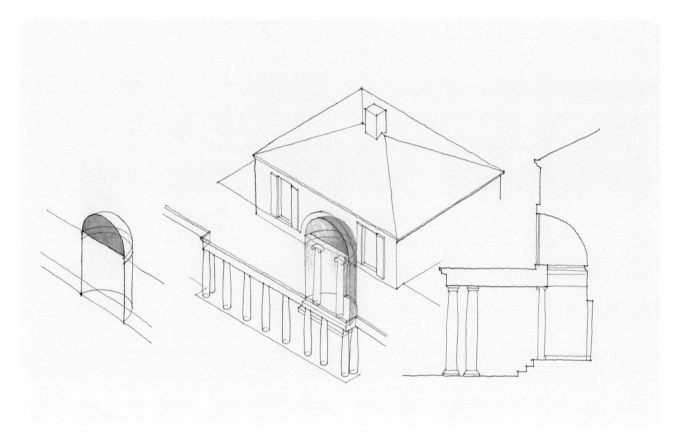

Diagram of the doorway and arcade

View of the pavilion
doorway and light scoop

Pavilion IX
Charlottesville, Virginia, 1820
Thomas Jefferson

Framing Views

Buildings can be, and often are, linked to a site or context through massing, proportion, material and other large-scale moves, yet links can also be at a more personal scale. Visual alignments with particular landmarks, vistas framed by windows or doorways, or openings marking the sun's path often integrate a building and its context at a personal level. Moreover, discovering links that are noticeable only at specific times or from particular vantage points can be part of a transcendent experience.

Diagramming Kahns' Phillips Exeter Academy Library reading carrels with an isometric helps uncover how a window can be a place for private contemplation and personal views to the surrounding campus. Part of Kahn's idea was that a student would take a book and move toward the light, so in that respect the window becomes a piece of furniture. The student engages with the window. In a simple and elegant way, Kahn creates a space that is, metaphorically, a window to learning through contem-

Isometric of the reading carrels

Diagrams of carrel and window interface

View of the reading carrels

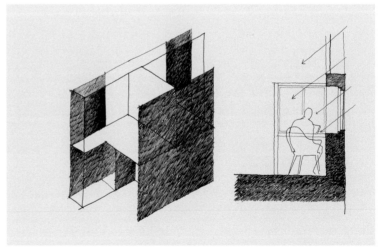

Phillips Exeter Academy Library
Exeter, New Hampshire, 1971
Louis Kahn

In what sense is the window a spatial experience?

Do windows, doorways or other gaps frame particular views?

In what way does the context become a personal experience?

plation. Contemplation also plays a role in the diagrams of the Mountain View Cemetery. Here, plans, sections and isometric diagrams show how the architect links the new columbarium walls and at the same time connects visitors to the site, both physically and historically, by mapping the site and then aligning gaps within the walls with existing and historic headstones and trees.

Section showing relationship of bench to view

Diagrams showing how the voids align with surrounding context

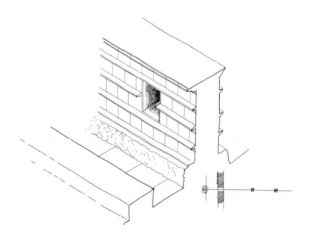

View through the columbarium
aligned with tombstones

Mountain View Cemetery
Vancouver, Canada, 2008
Phillips Farevaag Smallenberg Landscape Architects/
Birmingham and Wood Architects

Shading Glass

Traditional shutters, often associated with more picturesque settings, are actually complex, layered systems that are models for contemporary environmental systems. Like other traditional and vernacular systems, there are lessons to be learned from devices that have developed in response to environmental, technological, material and social needs over thousands of years. A shutter's asset is the way it prevents sunlight and thus heat to reach a surface through louvered, multi-axial hinged panels that mitigate light, view and ventilation through multiple configurations. More important, however, is that analyzing and learning about the traditional shutter is one example of how vernacular or historical traditions can help us solve contemporary design problems. Many vernacular forms and elements have as their basis the same energy concerns that we have today. Overhangs, evaporation, insulation and natural ventilation were ways to use less or no energy for keeping cool.

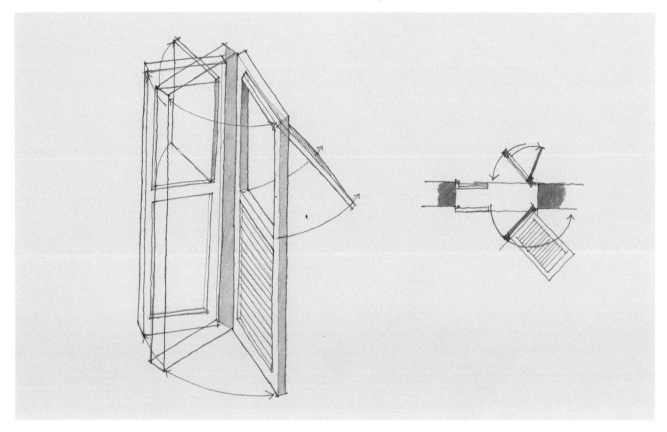

Diagrams showing the many configurations

View of shutters at midday in Rome

Traditional Italian Shutter
19th–20th century

How are shutters manifested in more contemporary buildings?
What is the degree of variability? How many configurations are possible?
What is the shutter dimension in respect to the window dimension?
How are the shutters stored when open?
How many layers are part of the window system?

The diagram of a typical Italian shutter shows the possible configurations that accommodate varied conditions or needs. Upon closer examination, after sitting and drawing carefully, the shutter is actually part of a three-layered system that includes the shutter, the window and an interior. The shutter itself has inset louvered panels that rotate and pivot while the window and interior panels can rotate independently. The diagram of the shutters at the Senior Common Room at St. John's College shows a contemporary interpretation of the traditional shutter. Here, panels on a free-standing framework protect the glass curtain wall from the morning sun and act as a privacy screen during special events.

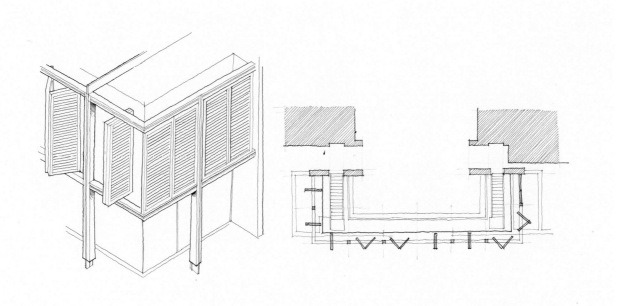

Diagrams showing the shutter configurations

View of the shutter framework

Senior Common Room at St. John's College
Oxford, England, 2005
MJP Architects

Adjusting Panels

The maxim "the only constant is change" is a kind of paradox with which architects continue to struggle. How can architecture, being inherently permanent, also change? How can a building or a room adapt quickly (or slowly) and dramatically (or subtly), avoiding to become a "multi-use" space that serves no one function well?

The plan and isometric diagrams of the Storefront for Art and Architecture show varied stages of opening the façade. Rectangular, T-shaped, U-shaped and L-shaped planes rotate and pivot to open and transform both the gallery and the street. At most times, the gallery's wall remains shut or only partially open (which required a guess at the rotations that were later verified in publications). The axonometric diagrams of Gerrit Rietveld's Schröder House are, likewise, attempts to understand how the upper-level

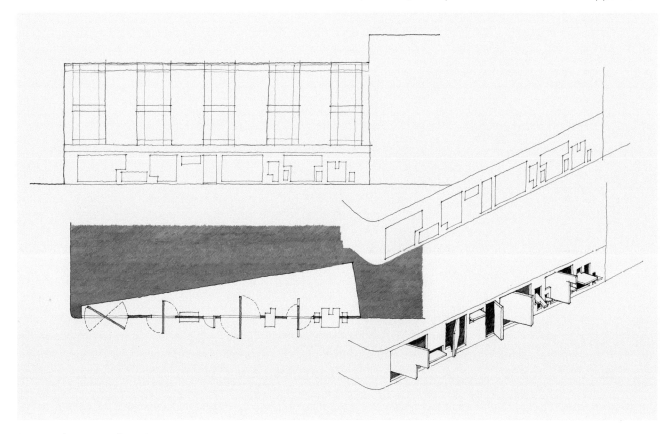

Diagrams showing transformations

View of the Kenmare Street façade

Storefront for Art and Architecture
New York, New York, 1992
Steven Holl Architects

How does the building or room adapt to varied uses?
What changes and what stays the same?
Are the changeable elements simple or complex?
Do the changes occur in one way or many?

room completely transforms through sliding and rotating panels. Only the movable panels are darkened to clearly highlight that which is fixed and that which is mutable. While ever-changing or completely flexible, architectural ideas may not always be possible or practical. Examining the ways in which architects addressed or attempted flexibility can help raise an awareness that parts of rooms, buildings or civic spaces need not always to be fixed but can adapt and re-adapt as needed.

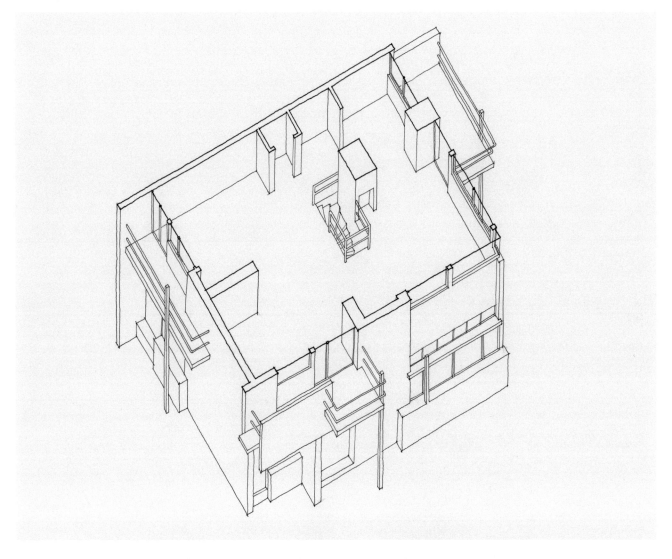

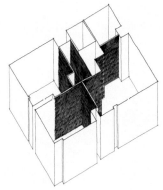

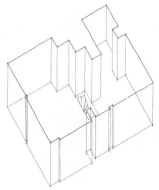

Rietveld-Schröder House
Utrecht, The Netherlands, 1924
Gerrit Rietveld

Plan oblique of the upper level

Plan oblique of the panels extended

Plan oblique of the panels stowed

Incorporating Furniture

Incorporating furniture, such as cabinets, benches, panels, bookcases or desks, into a room has the benefits of efficiency and of framing activities. Efficient, custom-fitted elements alleviate some of the residual spaces resulting from mobile furniture. Linked and attached to the room's fundamental form, the integrated furniture can also frame activities by linking furniture to architecture. Establishing zones with the integrated systems helps concentrate particular functions while freeing the rest of the room for

unanticipated or more mutable purposes. Like the interstitial zones and the flexible panels examined earlier, these diagrams examine how furniture becomes part of a room's identity. In this case, furniture both interweaves with the room and becomes an active participant in its use. It becomes as critical as the floors, walls and windows in shaping the room.

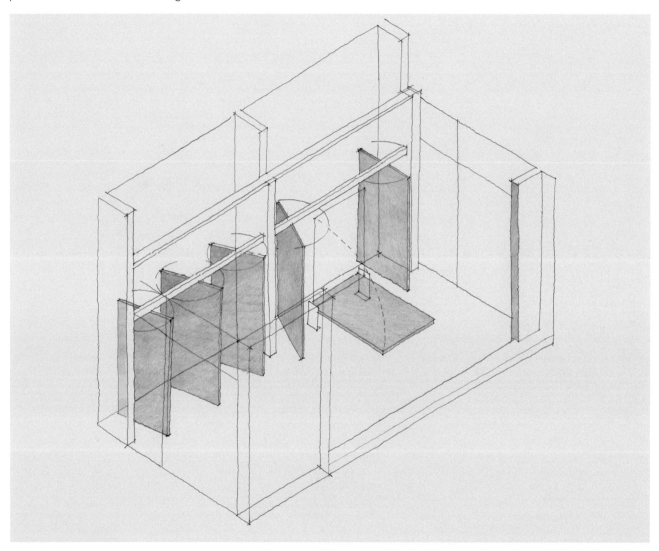

Isometric showing the movable panels within the jury room

Multiple exposures showing table rotation

University of Virginia Victor and Sono Elmaleh East Wing Jury Rooms
Charlottesville, Virginia, 2008
W.G. Clark

Is furniture integrated into the room? Is the furniture fixed or mobile?
How does the furniture help make smaller rooms within a larger room?
Can you identify zones within the room where furniture might go?

The diagrams examine two particular types of integrated furniture: moving elements and static elements. In the diagram of the University of Virginia's jury rooms, panels pivot to make smaller sub-spaces and allow students to change presentations quickly or, in one case, to rotate horizontally to make a discussion or presentation table. These panels also fulfill a third role by providing a degree of privacy to make the otherwise glass room feel more enclosed. To show these actions, the diagram shows only the panels themselves, while the room as such is ghosted in. The diagram of the boudoir in Loos' Villa Müller is, on the contrary, about integrating furniture that does not move but helps divide the room into smaller zones. The inglenook bookcase, day bed and bookcases are distributed to make a series of spaces within the room.

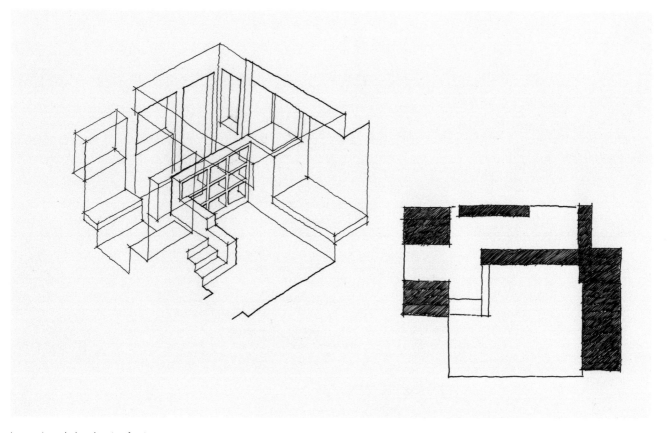

Isometric and plan showing furniture incorporated into the room

Plan and section showing furniture incorporated into the room

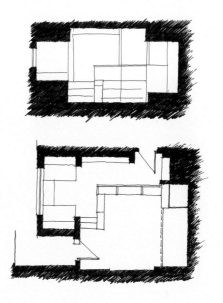

Villa Müller Boudoir
Prague, The Czech Republic, 1930
Adolf Loos

Categorizing Joints

In his 1931 book, *The Construction of Architectural and Machine Forms*, Russian architect and educator Iakov Chernikov describes seven fundamental construction joints that, when fully studied and understood, would help architects develop a sophisticated and logical approach to construction. This typological study remains helpful in that describing ways in which elements come together helps establish a clear systematic approach to building assemblies.

The first set of diagrams are, from left to right, three of the Chernokov's types: "Embracing", "Clamping" and "Integration", each of which is paired with examples of the respective types of construction joints. A column detail by architect Mark McInturff shows how the steel angles embrace a railing and a table support; the detail of Richard Rogers' truss shows how the forked end of a cable rod clamps onto the central circular plate; the link between a Doric capital and shaft is more of an integrated system

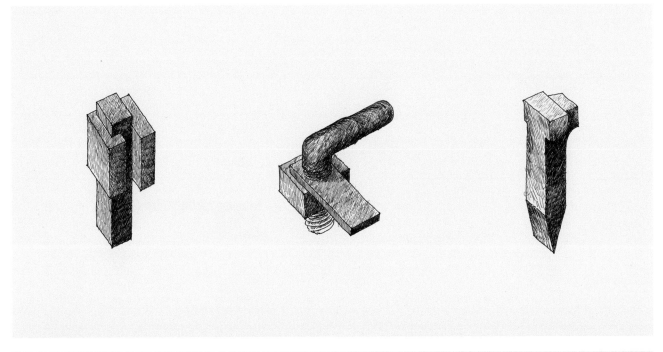

Diagrams of "Embracing", "Clamping" and "Integration"

Diagram of a column detail, truss plate and Doric column

Assembly-Type Diagrams
Iakov Chernikov

What is the detail type? Is this clear or ambiguous? Why?

What is the hierarchy within the assembly?

with a gradual transition from shaft to capital. The second set of three diagrams, from left to right, are "Penetration", "Mounting" and "Interlacing". These three types are paired with those in the diagrams of built examples. "Penetration": a stairway by Mark McInturff, in which a wall seems to penetrate a bridge/stair composition; "Mounting": Le Corbusier's rooftop walls and pavilions are essentially mounted to the pure form; "Interlacing": the rods supporting the stair at Frank Lloyd Wright's

Fallingwater interweave with the concrete steps. The seventh joint – "Coupling" – does not appear here because, as Chernikov notes, it differs from other joints in that it allows many combinations with no direct link. He uses a chain to illustrate this type of joint without direct connections.

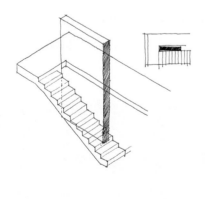 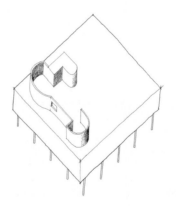 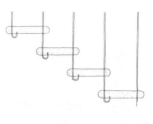

Diagrams of "Penetration", "Mounting" and "Interlacing"

Diagrams of a stairway, rooftop walls and stair

Assembly-Type Diagrams, 1931
Iakov Chernikov

Expressing Connections

Smooth transitions from one condition to another – from bottom to top or from side to side – are often achieved by clearly recognizable overlapping elements. In these transitions, elements interweave with one another yet maintain much of their autonomy to form new amalgamated systems.

The diagrams of the Barnsdall House's hollyhock-inspired columns and piers help reveal Frank Lloyd Wright's methods used to link varied amalgamated elements into a unified composition. Elements seem to slide behind and in front of one another and give a sense of overlap, interlock and transparency. One diagram shows the overlap through changes in tone, while the other shows each element or group pulled away from one another and drawn separately to see, for a moment, how the elements are discrete and

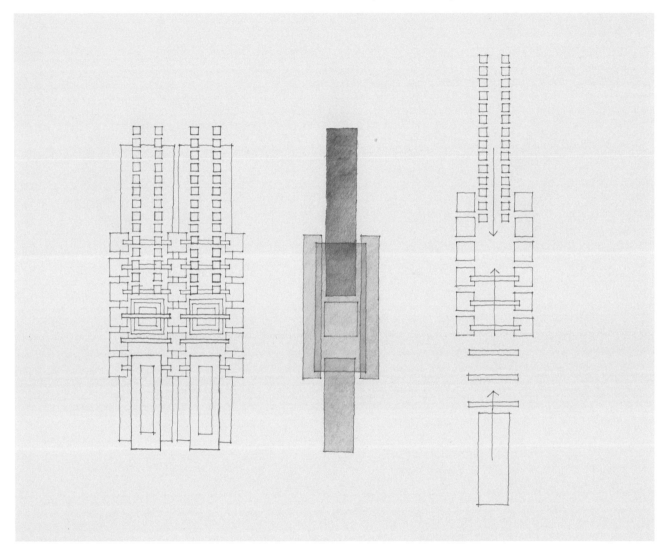

Diagrams showing elements engaged and disengaged

Light post base

Barnsdall House/Hollyhock House
Los Angeles, California, 1921
Frank Lloyd Wright

What are the discrete systems of the composition?

How and where do they interact?

What does the connection help join?

214

complete systems that then interact with other systems. Similarly, the diagram of a façade detail at the 920 H Street office building shows how the architect activated an otherwise blank service alley wall by pulling lines from the façade above and from elements to each side to interact with one another. The patterns remain distinct, yet combined, creating a new overall composition.

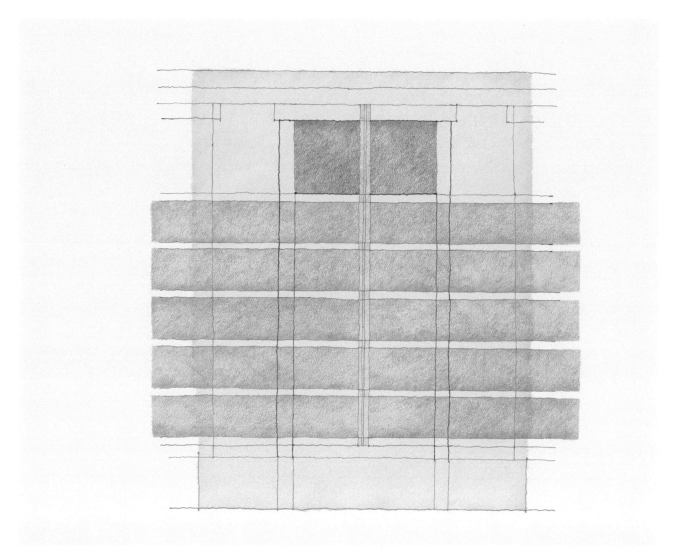

Diagram showing the meshed elements

View of a typical bay

920 H Street NW
Washington, DC, 1998
HOK Architects

Joining Wood

Wood construction remains a widespread system because, among several reasons, wood can be cut and joined using minimal tools. Moreover, complex connections can be incorporated into the wood itself: mortise and tenon, dovetails, lapped, mitered and tongue-and-groove joints are but a few of the strong yet flexible joints that exploit wood's inherent structural qualities.

The first set of diagrams are studies showing traditional Japanese and traditional Western joinery methods. Suppositions are based on published examples, however; *in situ* these internal configurations are often hidden and, therefore, difficult to guess but, upon careful observation, it is possible to reveal the joints. This reverse-engineering process helps not only in understanding the system but also helps designers think about assembly. The second diagram is of a gateway in Turkey. This sketch is a thorough

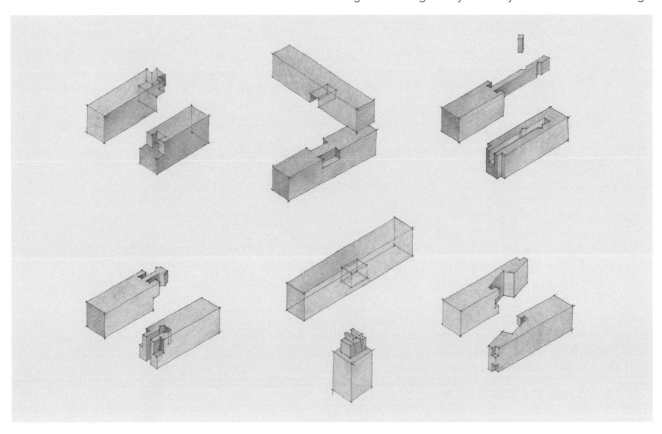

Japanese wood joinery methods

Various wood joints

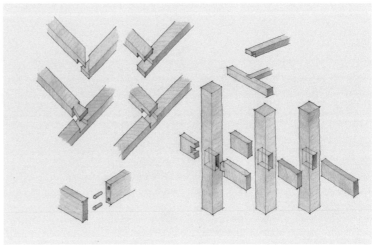

Types of Wood Joinery

What can you see without literally taking the joint apart?
What do you suppose is happening inside the joint?
For what reason is the joint stronger when stressed?
What are the primary, secondary and tertiary elements in the joint?

study of the gate's assembly through drawn disassembly. Each element is pulled away with suppositions or speculations on the internal assembly. The sketch, made by Douglas Pettit, a former boat designer studying architecture, links his interest in boats with that of architecture.

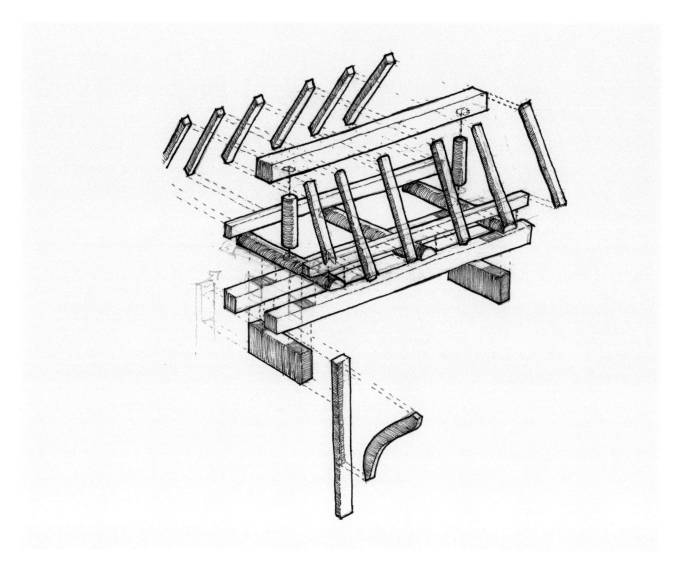

Exploded isometric of the gateway's assembly

View of the gateway

Gateway Roof Assembly

Assembling with Third Things

In *Timaeus*, Plato notes that two things "cannot be well joined without some third thing". While his argument centers on the nature of the physical and metaphysical universe, his observation remains true in our everyday assemblies. Joining two elements both generates and involves a connector element. These connectors or "third things" are the fasteners, clamps, pivots and hinges of all assemblages and assemblages within assemblages. Often distinct, the third things can also be integrated and indistinguishable. The third-thing transition does not necessarily require an element of its own: it may be achieved just by a material thickening or a slight geometric change to mitigate one condition to another. What is more, third things often scale: two elements connect by a third thing, yet that third thing has its own tripartite connective system that, in turn, has yet another three-part connection and so on.

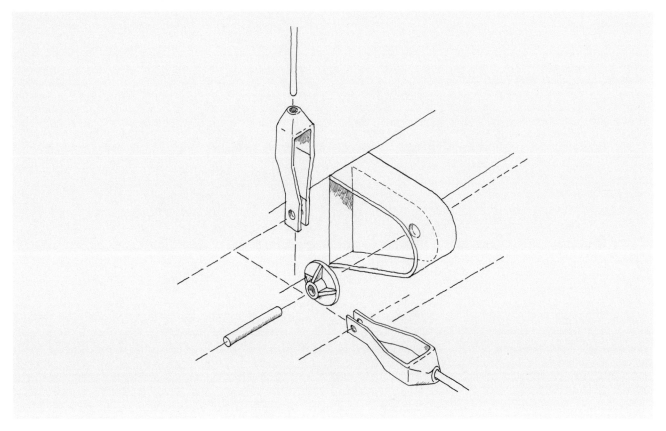

Exploded isometric of the elements showing "third things"

View of the walkway cable support structure

Vancouver International Airport
Vancouver, Canada, 1998
Patkau Architects

What are the two things and what is the third thing?
Is the third thing distinct or integrated?
How does this triad scale up and down?

The exploded isometric diagram of a suspended walkway tension support reveals how individual pieces are joined through third things. Each element is analytically separated and pulled apart from others, much like in an instruction manual. As such, we can start to see that these two connected by a third, scale downward and upward: to connect a cable to a walkway requires a plate; to connect the plate to the cable requires a swage socket; to connect the swage socket to the cable requires a turnbuckle; and

so on. The diagrams of the Bilbao Guggenheim Museum glass wall support, drawn by student Scott Gillespie, includes an exploded isometric but also a section through the connector. Combining both section and axonometric helps understand the connection assembled and separated.

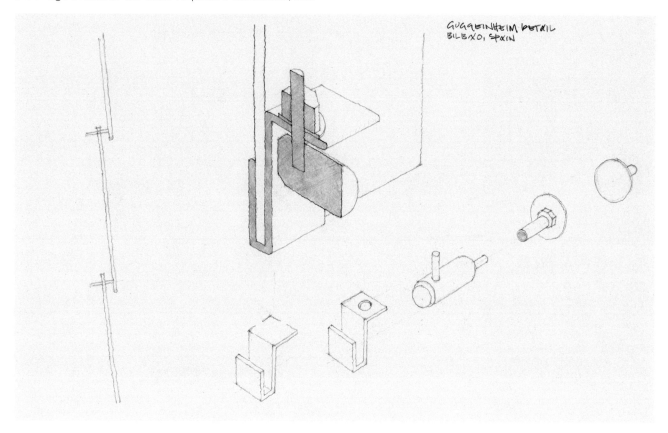

Exploded isometric of the curtain wall's individual elements (drawing by Scott Gillespie)

View of the interior curtain wall system

Guggenheim Museum Bilbao
Bilbao, Spain, 1997
Frank Gehry

Aligning Seams

Seams, those lines created where two materials come together, are most often associated with clothing; yet they play as great a role in buildings, furniture and other manufactured things and, like clothing seams, are design opportunities. Essential elements in material assembly and movement, seams are linked to an overall composition through alignment, placement, size and articulation. Based on function yet sponsoring ornament, building seams can become part of the underlying assembly system and unify the overall design. Joints, seams, links and other connections are significant and often form the most visible elements in design. For example, an office building's windows and fascia panels are essentially about seams. We see the lines that connect the windows and the panels as much, if not more, as we see the actual surface material. Ignoring or oversizing these seams may add unanticipated visual weight to the entire façade.

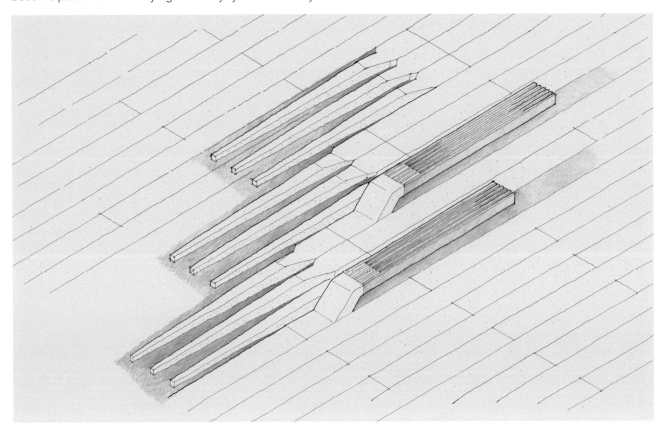

Drawing of bench and decking transformation

View of the benches and decking

The High Line Park
New York, New York, 2004
James Corner Field Operations/Diller Scofidio + Renfro

How are the seams articulated? Are they expressed or denied?
How do the seams extend and transform beyond a particular area?
How are seams coordinated with a larger module?
To what extent do seams play a role in proportion and rhythm?

The diagram of the High Line Park shows how the repetitive module creates a series of linear seams along the entire length of the park. Drawing the fabric-like modular pavers, laid on the former track bed, helps reveal how the pavers transform into benches, planters and other elements. The first step in drawing these is to document the standard module's length and width. Once established, breaks in the pattern are more easily mapped. The diagram of Scarpa's fountain and door at the Querini Stampalia

Foundation reveals how the stone and metal are linked together with seams. Rather than drawing only the fountain's plan, it helped in this exercise to draw only the fountain's joints.

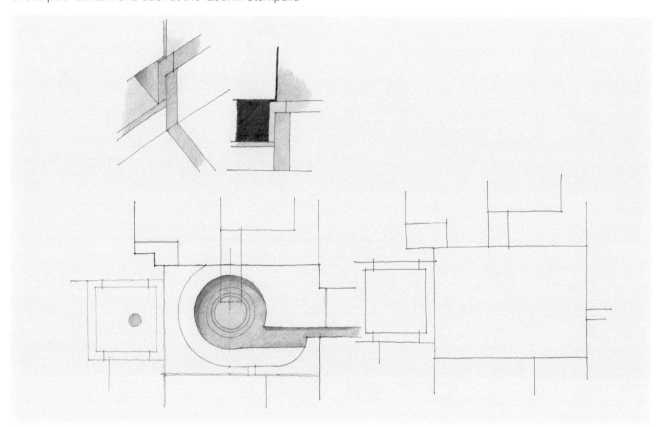

Diagram of the cut stone and seams

View of the fountain

Fondazione Querini Stampalia
Venice, Italy, 1963
Carlo Scarpa

Changing Material

Attentiveness to a ground plane's material, pattern and undulation helps manipulate what might be thought of as a fifth wall of spatial enclosure. Continuity or alteration of its qualities can help emphasize meaning and use both consciously or unconsciously in those that experience the space.

The diagram as plan isometric of the New England Holocaust Memorial examines how the architect Stanley Saitowitz augmented the ground to mark important moments. To those who approach, he announces hallowed ground by extending the memorial's stone walkway beyond the edge of the site into the quotidian brick-paved sidewalk. Once on the memorial's stone path, he switches to steel grating, which incidentally emits heated air, to mark one of the memorial's towers. The stone, grate and

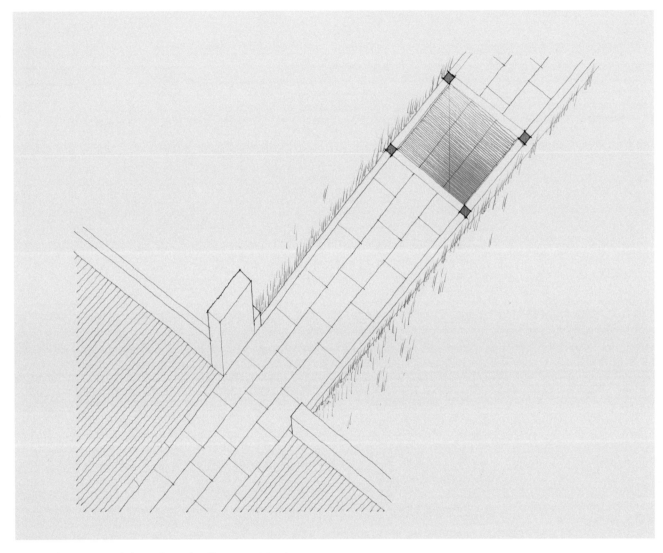

Diagram showing material change from sidewalk to memorial pathway

View of a tower floor grate

New England Holocaust Memorial
Boston, Massachusetts, 1995
Stanley Saitowitz

What are the materials, patterns and topography of the ground or floor?
Where do these change or continue and why?
How do the materials interact or contrast with columns and walls?

heat heighten the experience to help engender a change in thinking from the normal to the sacred. Similarly, the diagrams of the Pentagon Memorial, which include a plan and isometrics, map out how ground materials underscore the memorial's striations that parallel the aircraft's plunge. Parallel bands of stone, steel and gravel along and across which to walk remind the visitors of individuals who perished.

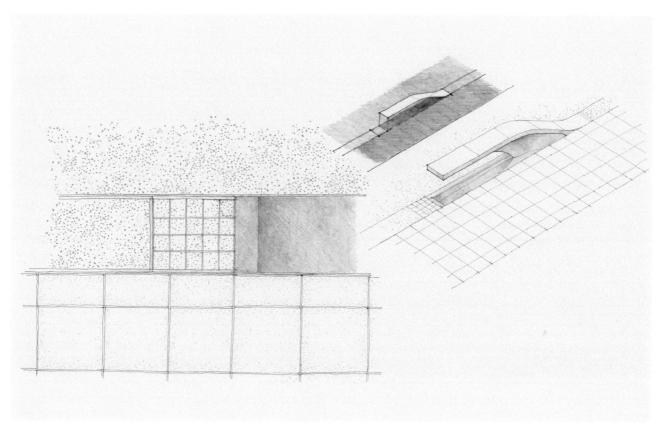

Diagrams of material changes

View of the benches and walkways

Pentagon Memorial
Arlington, Virginia, 2008
KBAS Studio

Interlocking Masonry

As an assemblage of interlocking elements, masonry construction follows definite rules in order to maintain internal structural integrity. As a result, masonry walls completely reflect the way they are assembled. Understanding the rules helps make the assembly not only work but appear as well-crafted. It is one reason that most appliqués or veneers intending to appear authentic will look very artificial because they are not considered as assemblies but only as arrangements.

The diagram of the brick cornice of Washington, DC's Eastern Market shows the three-dimensional brick assembly. Because it is an assembly of rotated, interlocking modules, the most effective diagrams incorporated three-dimensional volumes with degrees of transparency and opacity. These are challenging diagrams as they require a degree of speculation and often repeating the same diagram to see the assembly. In contrast to the three-dimensional brickwork studies are the stone wall

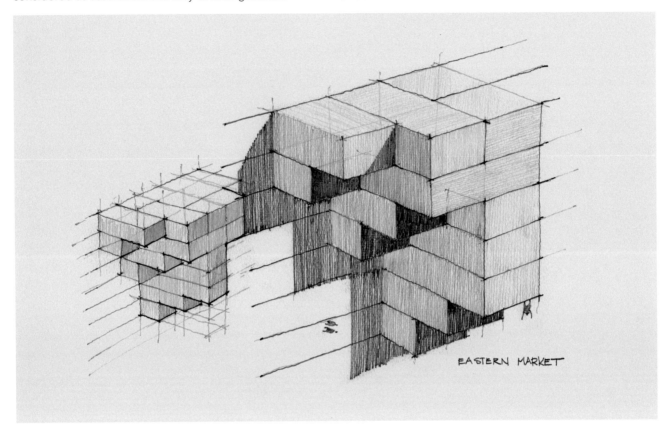

Isometric studies of brick corbelling (drawing by Elizabeth Wiersema)

View of the brick corbelling

Eastern Market
Washington, DC, 1873
Adolf Cluss

To what extent is the masonry a three-dimensional assemblage?
What is the module for brick or manufactured stone?
For natural stone, can you identify types or a taxonomy?
Can you speculate on the assembly's logic?

diagrams, which took systematic hour-long drawing just to record the wall's face. Rather than analyzing how identical modules come together in a three-dimensional grid, these diagrams began with questions about the distinctive qualities of dry stack walls, in which stones fit together without mortar. The fundamental questions are: Why do authentic dry stack walls look very different from faux stacked walls? Why can I immediately tell the difference between the two? After carefully drawing the wall in

elevation and section and then diagramming the patterns, one can discern specific assembly rules such as the battered wall's slope, stone sizes and continuous and discontinuous joint lines.

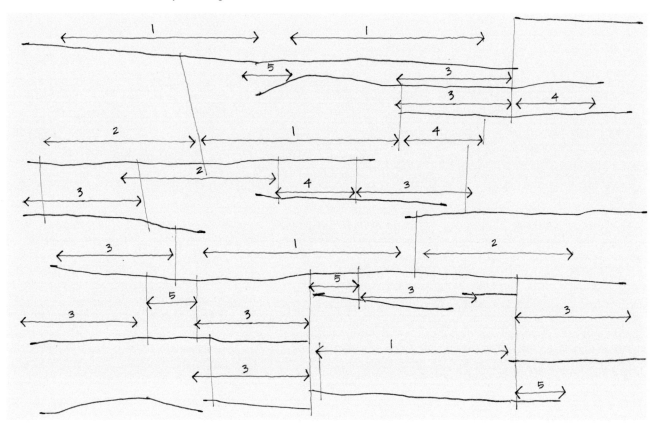

Analysis of continuous lines and stone types

Drawing of the wall

Retaining Wall
Washington, DC
19th century

Organizing Geometries

Resolving two or more geometries involves developing strategies that are simultaneously geometric and hierarchical. Geometrically, these resolutions require a thorough understanding of each geometry's rules – dimension, edge, center, angle. Hierarchically, the question is how and which geometries takes on specific relationships to one another.

The plan diagram of the new stair and walkways at the Market of Trajan shows how the architect resolved two geometries by assigning specific material and patterns to each geometry. In the horizontal path, wood remains rectilinear while steel is irregular. The diagram of the National Gallery of Art's East Wing reveals how the circular planters interact with the triangular floor grid through edge, center, radius, circumference and arc segments. When starting this diagram, most of the time was spent

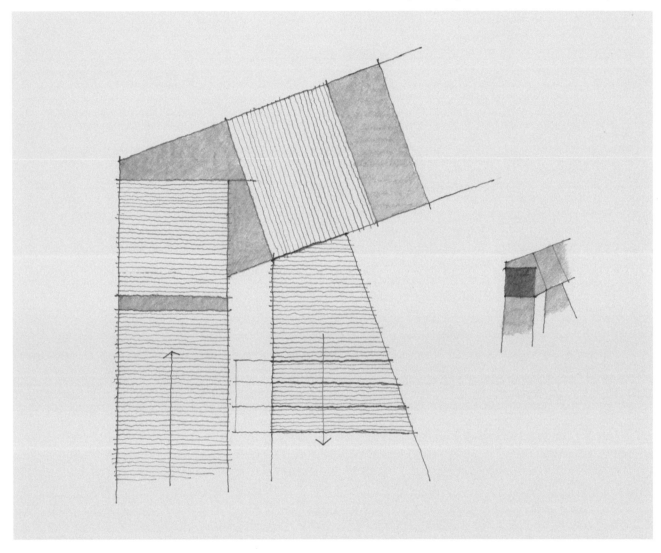

Diagram showing the order of steel and wood material

View of the walkway intersection

Mercati di Traiano
Museo dei Fori Imperiali
Rome, Italy, 2004
Nemesi Studio

What are the fundamental patterns and rules of each geometry?
How do these independent patterns and rules interact?
Did the architect assign hierarchy to each of these systems?

mapping the grid pattern to determine Pei's rule system. Once revealed, these underlying geometric patterns help establish a system that both links the two geometries and limits the hybrid pavers – pavers that are both circular and triangular – to a specific and symmetrical hexagon around each planter.

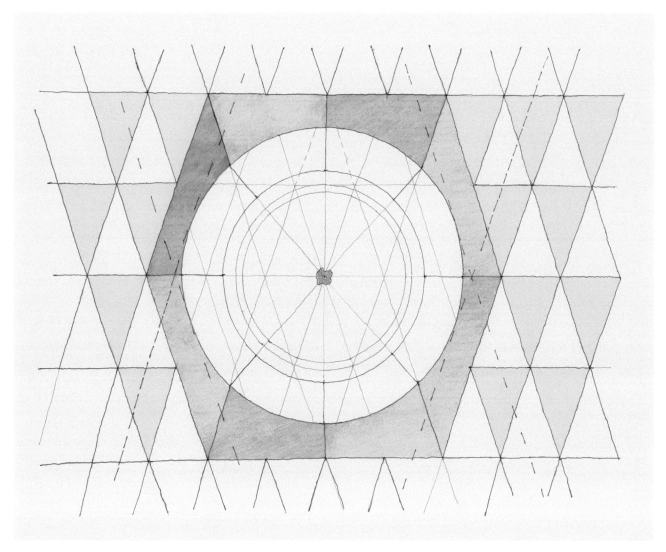

Diagram of the triangular and irregular stone pavers

View of the atrium floor

National Gallery of Art East Wing
Washington, DC, 1978
I. M. Pei

Gripping the Rail

As connections to the floor or wall, railings and their assembly are opportunities for lighting, enclosure and material interaction. Yet they offer more. In addition to physical support, they can also perform a greater role in providing a reassuring link between the hand and the building. Like a door knob or handle, a hand rail in a stairway, along a corridor or at a precipice offers a reassuring moment in which a building links directly to the human hand.

The diagram at the Pope John Paul II Cultural Center explores the hand rail and baluster assembly. In this additive assembly each element and how it is assembled is clearly articulated as pieces slide, overlap, attach and weave together to form a complete ensemble. In the composition, each material has its own unique role to play: steel supports, glass encloses and wood accepts the hand. The diagram disassembles the pieces to reveal how the parts are at once autonomous yet interdependent.

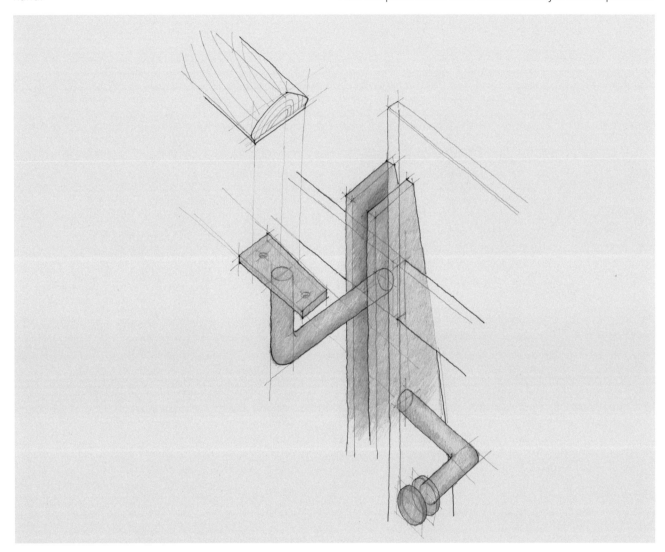

Exploded transparent plan oblique of the rail assembly

View of the hand rail and balustrade

Pope John Paul II Cultural Center
Washington, DC, 2000
Leo A. Daly Architects

Is the material for the hand different from other materials?
How is the hand rail connected to a wall, post or banister?
Is the rail integrated or added?

In contrast, the diagram of the hand rail at the Tate Modern explores a more subtractive design in which the rail and the lighting seem to be "carved" out of an enclosing mass; the hand moves in a continuous gap that winds and wraps its way up the stairway. While the railing was obviously constructed with pieces, these are unified and perhaps hidden through gluing, sanding and painting.

Diagrams of the rail system

View of the stairway
hand rail and lighting

Tate Modern
London, England, 2000
Herzog & de Meuron

Grasping Knobs

Finnish architect Juhani Pallasmaa observed that a "door handle is the handshake of the building": turning a knob and opening a door is one of those personal moments in architecture.[1] Touching, turning and pulling or pushing a door handle or knob is an intimate physical interaction with a building. The design of this moment balances formal composition with accommodating human touch and action.

The diagram of Mies van der Rohe's Tugendhat House door handle studies formal composition and quantitative dimensions of circles, rectangles, alignments, centers and edges with the help of a small measuring tape. The diagrams of handles designed by Johannes Potente and by Antoni Gaudí attempt to understand how ergonomics plays a role in design by mixing quantitative studies with more qualitative analysis: measuring tape, tones and gestural lines try to capture the knobs' underlying patterns.

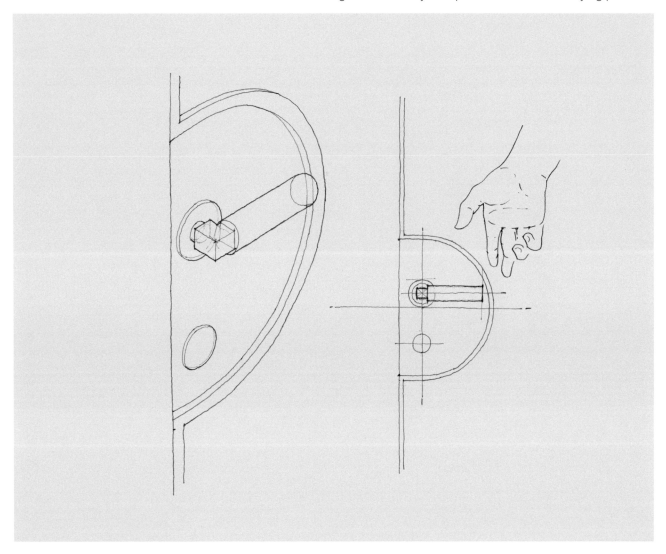

Isometric and elevation of the door hardware

View of the door handle

Tugendhat House
Brno, The Czech Republic, 1930
Ludwig Mies van der Rohe

Is the handle a more formal composition or a response to human touch?
To what extent did the designer take into account the hand?
What are the formal attributes of the handle?

Emulating the human hand's grip, Potente's handle corresponds to thumb, forefinger and palm, while Gaudí's knobs reflect exactly the human grip: cast from molds of malleable material gripped by a hand, these positive forms reflect those volumes created by human fingers.

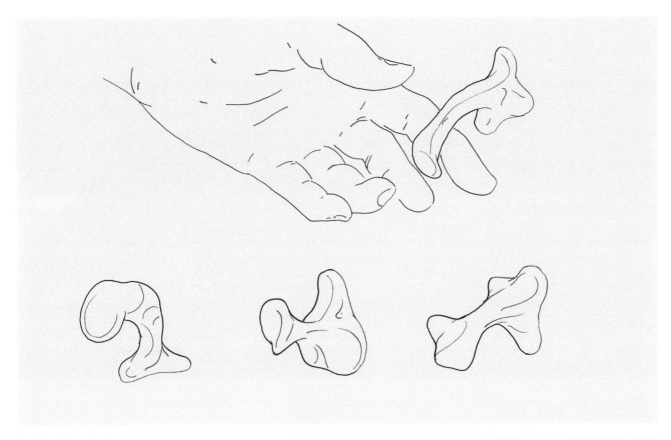

Details of shaped knobs

Details of the handle

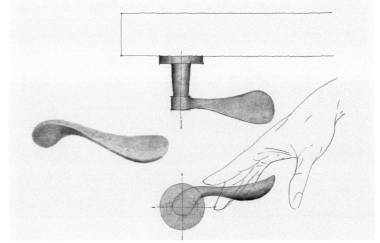

Knobs
Knobs from Casa Mila and Batlló
Antoni Gaudí, 1910

Door Handle 1020
Johannes Potente, 1953

1 Pallasmaa, Juhani, *The Eyes of the Skin: Architecture and the Senses*. Chichester: Wiley-Academy (2005): 56.

Studying Unintended Consequences 1

These diagrams drawn by Gregory Pray are a selection from over 100 studies completed over several years and eventually transformed into part of his Master's thesis. In these studies, which Pray started simply out of curiosity, he recorded the *impromptu* use of spaces in Boston, New York and Washington, DC. An initial impetus for these diagrams was to record the humorous, ingenious, clever and sometimes awkward ways in which people expropriated spaces. Gradually, Pray became interested in uncover-

ing and understanding any rules for how and why people occupy or use things. This, in turn, helped him develop urban design and architectural design strategies that could encourage ad hoc use. Of course, he could not fully predict the future appropriations but knew that certain qualities could engender community and social interaction.

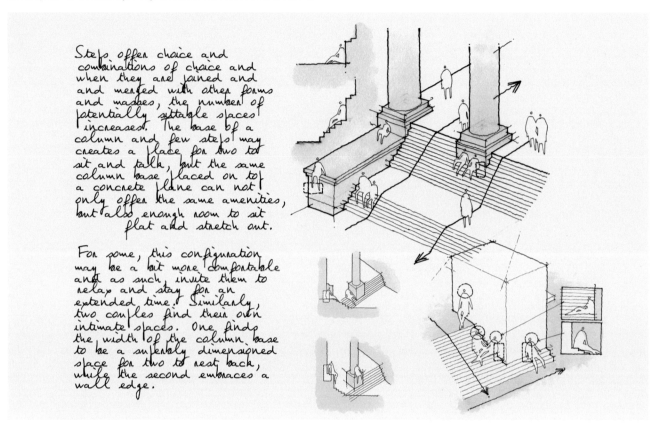

Study of the steps and varied uses
(drawing by Gregory Pray)

View of library steps

Stairway and Columns
Widener Library
Cambridge, Massachusetts

Where do people make *impromptu* places?
What was the original intention or purpose of the place?
What allowed for the *impromptu* use?

The first series of diagrams, mostly in isometric, show people and their rest and movement with ink and light gray marker, and demonstrate how designed places are used in ways probably not considered by the original designers. For the stairway at Harvard's Widener Library, Pray notes how the stairs, columns and piers offer varied experiences or opportunities for different gathering. Each offers a different place for solitude or intimate discussions, for watching people from a more enclosed space or in contrast fully exposed. Additionally, he speculates in his notes on how and why people gravitate to different parts of the stairway. The second set is from Boston's Copley Square, where Pray studied how the fountain offers a respite from the city and even how a tourist uses a shopping bag as a makeshift pillow. Here again, Pray uses a variety of drawings to help document and understand the places.

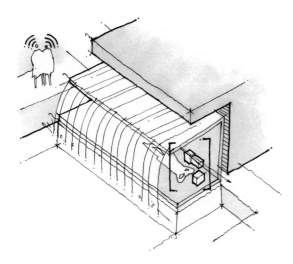

The stone may appear to be a bit uncomfortable, but as noted in many circumstances – people are adaptable. As seen, a bag can be a makeshift pillow, other belongings can also be arranged to protect the head and enclose from the top.

Study of the fountain as a cool retreat
(drawing by Gregory Pray)

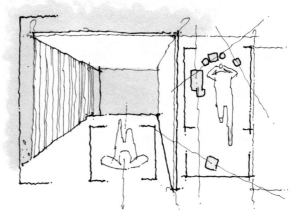

The underside of this fountain appears to be the ideal getaway, a sheltered area where one can stretch out.

While the shelter itself promises a substantial shade, the water fashions a strong enclosure on the left side. The enclosure is a successful one, slightly recess, slightly protected, yet still very open and even quite airy on a cool day.

You can still hear the birds!

View of the underside of the fountain

Fountain
Copley Square
Boston, Massachusetts

Studying Unintended Consequences 2

These two studies show how utilitarian elements or things have been appropriated for unanticipated use. Unlike Pray's previous set, these spaces were, in all likelihood, never conceived as "places" but more as necessities. Unlike the Harvard library steps or Copley Square fountain, the loading dock and the chain-link fence were utilitarian solutions.

The first diagrams show how merchants at a local weekend flea market have adapted a schoolyard's chain-link fence as an *impromptu* display stand. Here Pray notes how the fence, because of its height, transparency and multiple apertures, offers the merchant a way to display the coats at different levels to those on the street and those inside the market, to hang the coats above the crowd and to move the display to different positions. The diagram of the loading dock in New York shows how dimensions and scale

> The chain link fence establishes a protective boundary. Its a hard edge - it contains and keeps the unwanted out, though people tend to walk along it and on this note, it is a rather suitable display wall, the coated wire patterns creates perforations ideal for hanging goods, for instance, fur coats.
>
> The coats transform a rather unsightly edge into an attractive and rather approachable market place. Though it establishes a strong physical disconnect, it is a permeable and visually unifying periphery. Those passing by on either side are able to see the merchandise and each other. A distinct connectivity exists between potential consumers.
>
> Strangers are drawn together on either side of the periphery.

Study of the playground as a sales room
(drawing by Gregory Pray)

Detail of the fence used as a display stand

Fence
Eastern Market
Washington, DC

How has something utilitarian been appropriated for other uses?
What makes the object or space adaptable?
What is the role of material or surface articulation in its adaptation?
What would prevent the space from being appropriated?

offer an opportunity for sitting and watching people without disrupting the movement in and out of the warehouse. Moreover, the indentation of the loading dock door offers a type of niche in which those resting on the dock might feel a bit more enclosed or protected.

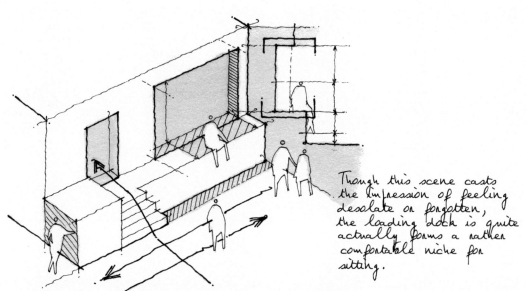

Though this scene casts the impression of feeling desolate or forgotten, the loading dock is quite actually forms a rather comfortable niche for sitting.

The height of the concrete short wall creats a seat which keeps the feet off of the ground, it invites to commit to it and relax. The void of the loading door itself includes a small, but ample recession. Sitting towards one side can offer a humble cover, a sense of feeling protected.

Study of the loading dock as a framework of many activities
(drawing by Gregory Pray)

View of the loading dock

Loading Dock
New York, New York

ENGAGING THE CONTEXT

Always design a thing by considering it in its next larger context – a chair in a room, a room in a house, a house in an environment, an environment in a city plan.

Eero Saarinen quoting his father, Eliel Saarinen[1]

To me, the presence of certain buildings has something secret about it. They seem simply to be there. We do not pay special attention to them. And yet it is virtually impossible to imagine the place where they stand without them. These buildings appear to be anchored firmly in the ground. They give the impression of being a self-evident part of their surroundings and they seem to be saying: "I am as you see me and I belong here."

Peter Zumthor[2]

Urban design is a synthetic, inventive mapping of physical conditions which establishes and explores whole areas of the city. In other words, it is architecture – but encompassing more in scale, intention and technique.

Steve Peterson[3]

Engaging the Context considers designed environments larger than buildings: urban form, urban spaces, gardens, landscapes and building sites within which buildings are situated and to which perhaps they contribute. Examining these and other contexts is a study of how individual design projects might extend into and relate not only to context but also link to a greater sense of place, society, culture and environment.

A fundamental step in understanding a greater situation are diagrams that examine the physical fabric within which buildings interweave. Like a tapestry's underlying structure, patterns of the designed environment are a kind of weft and warp that form the complex weave of the city, landscape and the physical environment. This fabric also includes types that are formed from cultural, material or social conditions, for instance the building types that emerge from environmental, social or construction traditions specific to a particular region, city or even neighborhood. The New York Brownstone, the Berlin Hof or the Moroccan Riad are just as much a fabric of the respective cities as the streets and public spaces.

Diagramming and analyzing fabric helps understand the nature of fabric, especially urban fabric, as a layered system, as a spatial tradition and as organizational strategies. Examining fabric is to decipher how a building interacts with its context, from the greater setting to the immediate site or situation. And examining fabric is even more than the mere practice of searching for and letting patterns inform design. Rather it constitutes a design ethic or a set of design values in which context is part of greater ethical and moral principles – principles through which we begin to understand and respect the ways in which site, building, room, garden interrelate to one another both physically, environmentally, culturally and socially.

While the diagrams in this chapter focus primarily on tangible fabric, the latter can also help understand the less tangible, fundamental social, cultural and economic fabrics within which buildings, spaces, gardens and even the greater physical fabric integrate and from which they emerge. These intangible elements may seem, in and of themselves, difficult to diagram yet they are unmistakable in the artifacts within which they are manifested. For instance, it may be difficult to diagram an economic fabric *per se*, yet diagrams can help reveal economic artifacts such as residential, commercial, religious or other types, artifacts that reflect a particular economic condition.

Just as situational diagrams link the concrete and ethereal, they can also extend across scales. Situations of a city or landscape can apply to or help analyze a building, a site and a room as interrelated microcosms and macrocosms. Diagrams of landscape or urban space can apply to and inform analyses of neighborhood, a site, a building or a room. For example, diagramming a city using Kevin Lynch's five elements of the city – path, edge, district, node and landmark – helps develop a clearer image of place in the city; it can also clarify the spatial organization and place within a building or even a room. Like fabric diagrams, Lynch's elements are a universal process of how we orient ourselves in space, a process which can then be applied to nearly any space or place.

Diagramming tangible conditions and, by extension, the intangible properties that are explicitly or implicitly embedded in the physical surroundings, is part of a design ethic in which there is an openness to what exists and what will exist long afterwards. Architecture is, by its very nature, intrinsically embedded in settings that exist before and will exist after the construction concludes. Buildings, even temporary buildings, are set in landscapes and subject to the natural environment; they are part of building traditions, informed by economic conditions, related to historical settings; they work with the human scale and belong to existing tangible and intangible fabrics that have or will in some way inform or shape a design. Since a building will contribute to its context and their common future, there is an obligation and larger responsibility beyond the site, beyond the building and beyond the present. As such, design involves ethical decisions. Only in that knowledge of context can ethical considerations inform decisions and judgments.

In other words, analyzing a site, city, neighborhood or landscape is that vital step of gathering information that might inform ethical design acts. These acts, by their nature, are part of a larger ethic of how to act in a given situation. A goal of drawing, therefore, may be to develop a way of gathering information and attaining knowledge that encourages acts which respect that knowledge and information. To respect, however, does not necessarily and simply mean to capitulate. Contributing with respect entails knowing when and how today's work is part of a greater cultural or historical tradition and context. Additionally, to respect does not necessarily mean submitting to context with a loss of identity. Like a lively and civilized discussion, there are respectful responses and give and takes in which there may be points of agreement or disagreement but ultimately a debate with understanding. Even a challenge to the fabric can and perhaps should occur if it is informed and capable of subtleties. In informed engagement with context, there is the obligation to work within what was given and to respect those givens, examining that context to understand to what degree the fabric might be copied or augmented.

The intention, here as in all chapters, is to develop analytical methodologies that inform design decisions. By understanding and contributing to the patterns with informed acts, the contributions become part of a larger social and cultural tradition that evolves and respects the past, present and future.

Questions at the root of this action include:
What is the fabric of place? How is that fabric manifested? What are the tangible patterns of a landscape, city, neighborhood, square or site? How is an intangible fabric manifested in the physical environment? How does the analysis of a city relate to the scale of a room or to a chair?

1   Saarinen, Eliel, "The Maturing Modern", *Time Magazine* 68, 1 (July 2, 1956): 54.

2   Zumthor, Peter, *Thinking Architecture*, trans. Maureen Oberli-Turner (essays 1988-1996), trans. Catherine Schelbert (essays 1998-2004). Basel: Birkhäuser: 17.

3   Peterson, Steve, "Urban Design Tactics", *Architectural Design* 49, 3-4 (1979): 76-81.

Orienting Oneself

The main issue here is using landmarks in a city to help orient oneself both physically and psychologically within a fabric, both in terms of a particular place and movement from place to place. First, the landmarks help us fix ourselves in relation to a known location. We can see the landmark from various points and thus know where we are in the world. When there are two or more landmarks we can have a sense of movement through triangulation. Essentially, we sense movement when the multiple towers, in foreground and background, move in relationship of one another. Landmarks are often prominent objects, such as towers or larger buildings, but they can also be edges, streets or natural elements. For example, Paris' River Seine or Manhattan's hierarchical street grid help orient us in those cities.

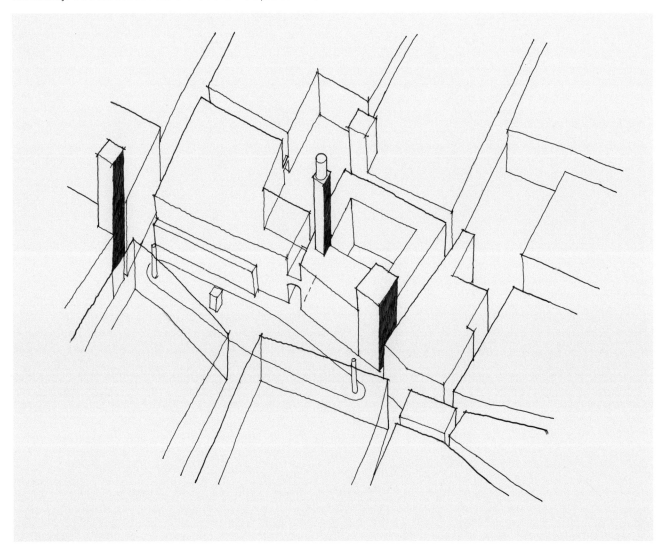

Plan oblique showing the three towers

View from the south

Piazza delle Erbe
Verona, Italy

What elements in a city, campus or neighborhood provide orientation?
What makes the difference of two elements as compared to one element?
What is the nature of these elements in respect to the context?

238

The diagram of Verona's Piazza delle Erbe, which treats all the surrounding buildings as unshaded masses with only the towers shaded on one side, shows how the towers on the square and the free-standing elements within are landmarks at two scales. For those within the square, the free-standing elements, including the colonna del Mercato and the colonna di San Marco, act as a datum within the space. The two towers at either end of the square define the square's boundaries and demarcate entry and exit. On a much greater scale is the diagram of Borneo Sporenburg. Here the diagrams that show the overall plan and the highlighted object-buildings reveal how the designers interspersed large-scale housing blocks to help give some sense of orientation in the low-scale row houses.

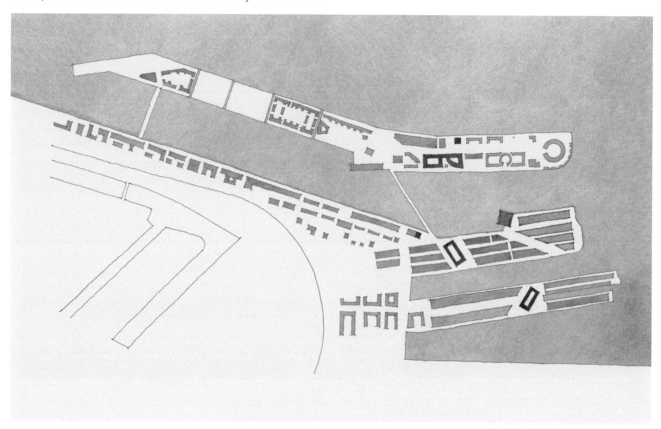

Plan of the redevelopment area

Diagram showing landmarks

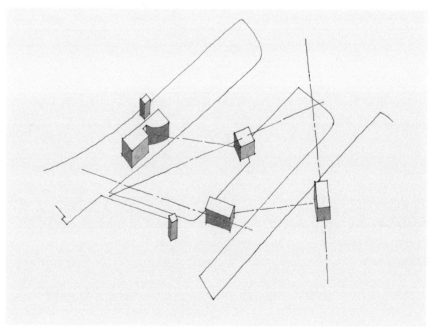

Borneo Sporenburg
Amsterdam, The Netherlands, 1998
West 8

Discovering Lynch's Elements

In his book *The Image of the City*, Kevin Lynch describes five elements of a city that help develop an impression of place and, most importantly, help locate us in that place. Lynch's *Edges*, *Paths*, *Districts*, *Nodes* and *Landmarks* are, at one level, physical and identifiable elements in a city.[1] At the same time, however, they are conceptual elements whose role in making mental maps of complex spatial situations is part of a larger social and cultural construct. And just as they relate both to a larger society and to individuals, the elements also scale in that they can be found not only in cities but also in gardens, buildings and rooms. Though these are distinct elements, they can also overlap or they can share qualities: a node can be a landmark and a path can be an edge. This mutability not only allows for multiple readings but also for more complex spatial arrangements.

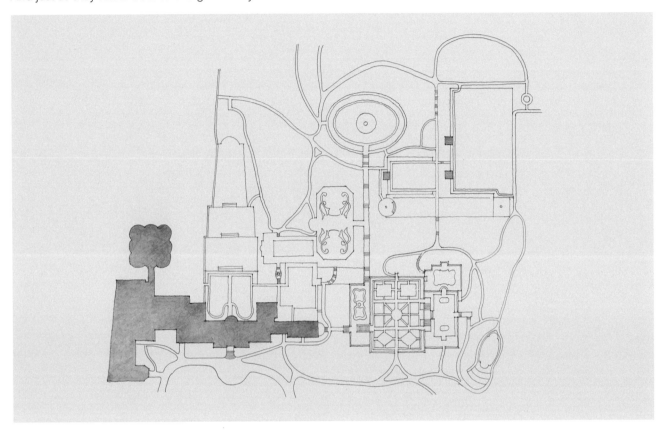

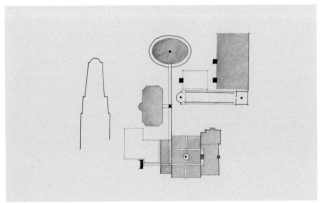

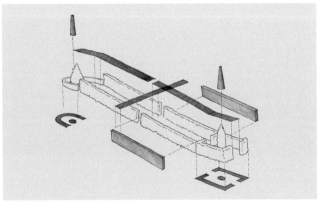

Plan of the garden

Diagram of the garden showing Lynch's elements

Exploded isometric diagram of one portion with Lynch's elements

Dumbarton Oaks Gardens
Washington, DC, 1947
Beatrix Farrand

What are the edges, paths, districts, nodes and landmarks in the city, garden, building or room?

How are the elements distinct and ambiguous?

How would an additional element help clarify place?

How do you know you are in one district and not in another?

Are the elements you perceive also perceived by others?

The diagrams of the Dumbarton Oaks Gardens illustrate how the garden is like a city, with combinations and orchestrations of Lynch's elements. Movement through the garden can be mapped and comprehended by moving along paths, along edges, to varied meeting points or nodes and into assorted districts or zones. The exploded axonometric shows how Lynch's elements can be found even in the part of the garden in which shrubs become edges, individual trees become landmarks and planting beds become districts. These elements are also found, albeit in a different manifestation, in Washington, DC, which might be considered a quintessential Lynchian city, deliberately designed to represent a particular image: laid out with specific districts especially around the National Mall, with its white marble landmarks that can be seen throughout the city, paths that connect important civic buildings with nodes along their length and with edges that distinguish the monumental core from the downtown business district.

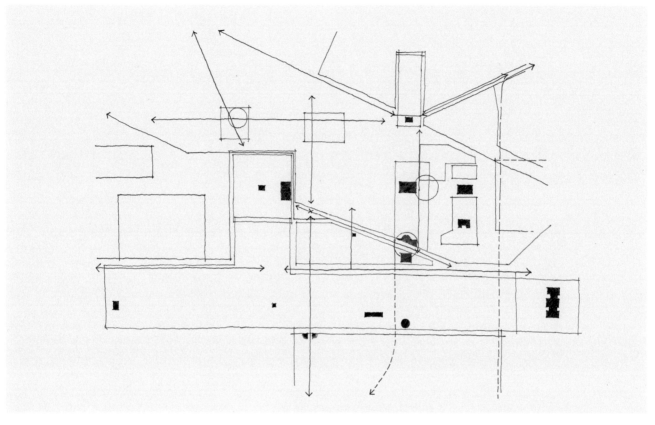

Plan of the city center showing Lynch's elements

Isometric showing elements around the National Mall

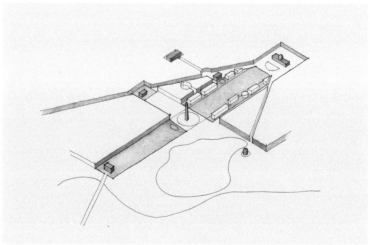

District of Columbia
Washington, DC, 1791
Pierre L'Enfant

1   Lynch, Kevin, *The Image of the City*. Cambridge: MIT Press (1964): 46-90.

Coordinating Object and Fabric

Urban fabric is often a composition of interrelated elements – streets, buildings and plazas merge to form an overall spatial pattern that can be unambiguous or subtle. From more medieval developments emerging from paths and topography to complex street grids that weave in buildings and spaces, a city's form is a layered system that reconciles a fabric of solids and voids and objects and spaces.

The diagram of Bernard Tschumi's Parc de la Villette – based on the diagram that he produced to explain the project – shows the park's fundamental organization as a series of distinct and autonomous layers. These layered elements, in a sense designed separately and then juxtaposed upon one another, form a complex yet unified and identifiable tapestry. Each element or layer contributes to the system to create a unified whole. The diagram of the Muradiye Complex is similar except, in this case, there

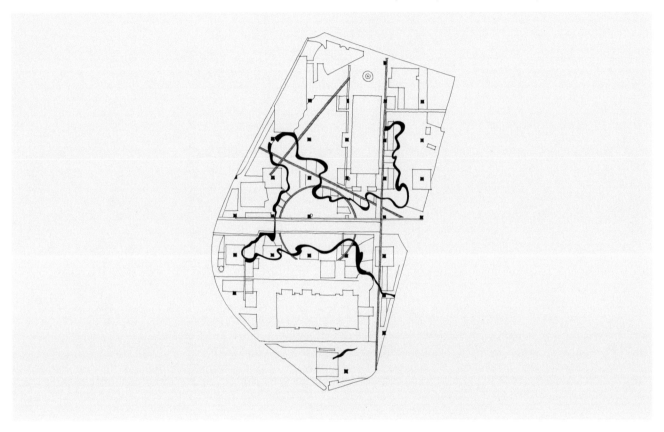

Plan of the park with elements superimposed

Exploded isometric showing individual elements

View of the elevated walkway

Parc de la Villette
Paris, France, 1988
Bernard Tschumi

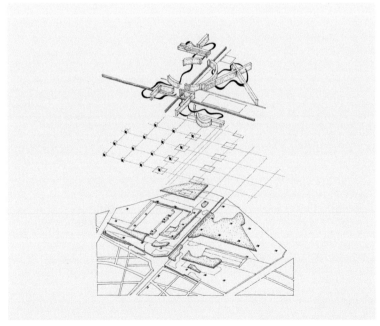

How is the order made complex through varied systems of order?

What are the layers of order on the site?

Can each of these systems be drawn as a separate order?

How are the systems juxtaposed?

are essentially three layers: the free-standing tombs, the trees and the sloping landscape. The tombs are placed within the wooded landscape as objects, yet they become subtly ordered because of the similar form, size, material and orientation within the verdant landscape. The landscape is a foil to the somewhat uniform buildings. If the landscape were flat and without trees, the order would be overt and perhaps banal.

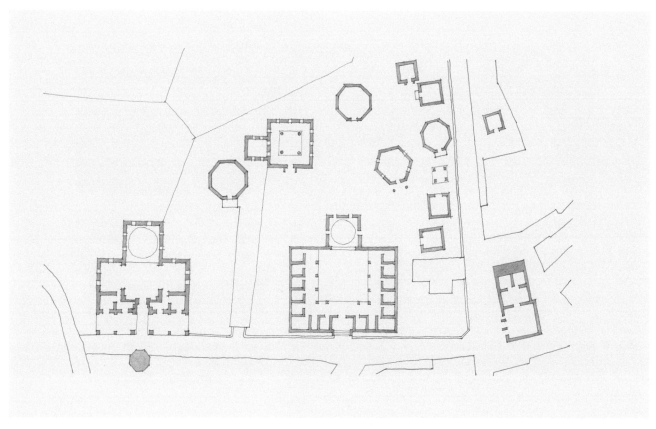

Plan of the complex

Object-building set within a landscape

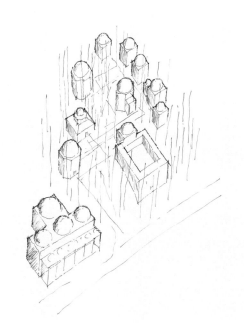

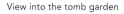
View into the tomb garden

Muradiye Complex
Bursa, Turkey

Resolving Geometries

Conflicting or multiple geometries in a city or a building can be resolved through circular geometries that mitigate change through subtle, often imperceptible axial and directional rotations. These shifts are often indiscernible because of the nature of a curved surface: it is difficult to perceive the center of a curved surface because a curved surface has multiple radii and multiple tangents to which other geometries can intersect and resolve.

The diagram of Vigevano's Piazza Ducale reveals how the concave façade of San Ambrogio resolves the geometries of the piazza and of the church. Although the church's façade is centered on the piazza's longitudinal axis, the church's axis is actually shifted approximately 15 degrees to the north. The curved surface allows an imperceptible shift from the piazza's geometry to that of the nave and is further resolved as the façade continues beyond its interior, so that the church's fourth door is actually a side street.

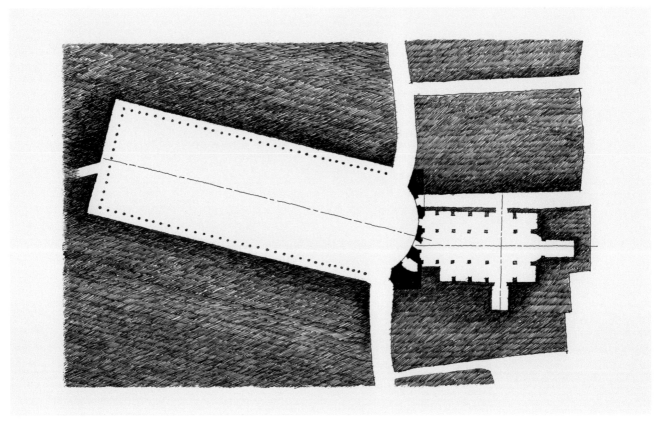

Nolli plan of the piazza and church

Diagram showing shifts

View from the northwest

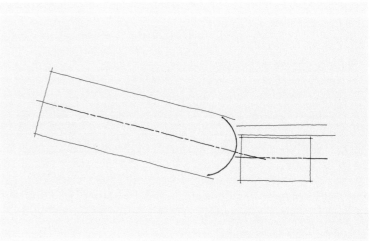

Piazza Ducale
Vigevano, Italy, 1494

How do one or more circular geometries resolve a change in direction?

Is this very perceptible or not at all perceptible?

Can this same subtle shift occur using non-circular geometries?

Similarly, the diagram of the Galleria Umberto I uses only the primary geometric forms and alignments to show how the two geometries resolve with one another. The radial of the center rotunda becomes the radial of the apsidal space facing the opera house. From the opera house, the perceived primary form is the concave surface with two large embedded portals. Behind this concave surface is a colonnade that helps move pedestrians around and into the portal leading to the galleria.

Nolli plan of the galleria

Diagram showing resolution

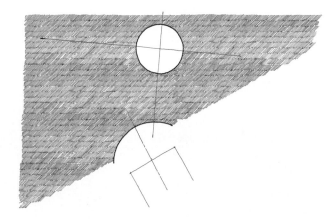

View from the southeast

Galleria Umberto I
Naples, Italy, 1891
Emanuele Rocco

Mediating in Shifts

Axes, alignments, grids and other linear compositional strategies can help organize a garden, urban fabric or urban spaces, yet must adjust to accommodate spatial needs, facilitate movement or resolve site conditions. When moving along axes or on a grid, there is often a need to alter these systems to accommodate a change in direction or to emphasize or de-emphasize particular zones or the path itself. Additionally, axial shifts or shifted alignments may be required for specific site conditions.

The plan diagram of Palais Royal shows how colonnades and intermediary spaces help resolve the varied misaligned axial linear patterns on the site. For example, the diagram shows how the Palais Royal garden's axes terminate into the neutral colonnade screen surrounding the Palais Royal courtyard. The "neutral colonnade" has not one single center but a variety of centers that can accept the varied axes. Likewise, this screen receives, from the opposite direction, the axis from the Place du Palais Royal that aligns

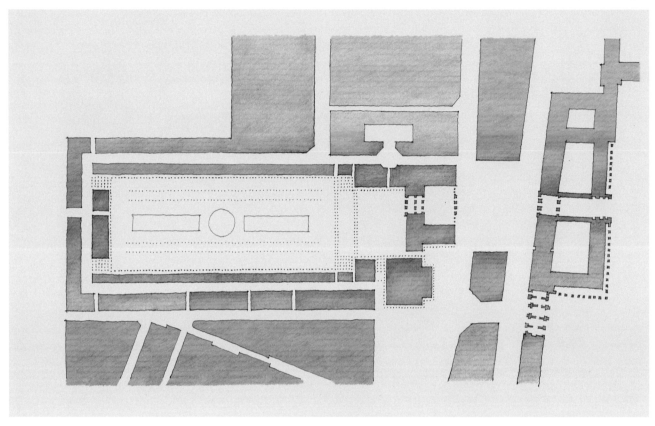

Nolli plan of the garden

Tone and line drawing showing alignments and shifts

View into the colonnades

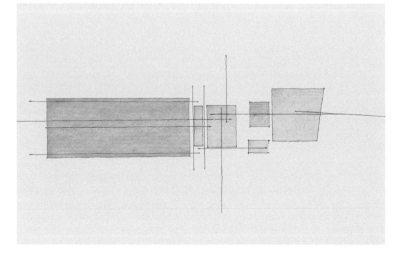

Palais Royal
Paris, France, 1639
Jacques Lemercier

What are alignments on the site?
Do the lines alternate in hierarchy in any way?
How and where are axes shifted or rotated?

with the Louvre gateway – which, incidentally, accommodates yet another slight shift to align from the Louvre courtyard and the Louvre pyramid. Likewise, the diagram of the Deanery Gardens shows axial shifts and alignments at a smaller scale. Here the garden extends from the house through a series of alignments and shifts. More important is the shift in axial hierarchies, as primary axes become secondary and secondary become primary so as to help guide movement through the site.

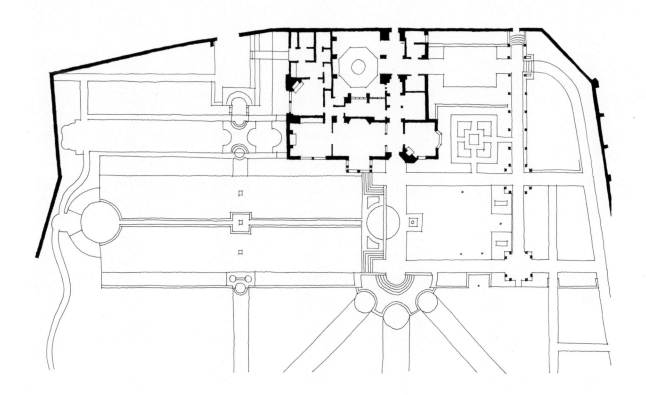

Plan of the house and garden

Line drawing of alignments and shifts

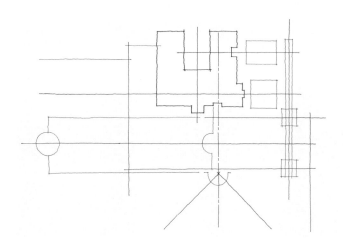

Deanery Gardens
Sonning, England, 1899
Edwin Lutyens

Rotating and Pivoting

While circular forms can resolve multiple geometries with subtle shifts and juxtapositions can articulate conflicts through overlap and simultaneity, a third way to resolve geometries is through pivoting and rotating around a fulcrum or intermediate gasket. As a fulcrum, walls or masses rotate around a vertical element such as a tower or statue. As an intermediate gasket, a third or neutral geometry links two distinct geometries. In both cases, the third element is the adjustable hinge or indefinite glue between distinct forms. In addition to their role as hinges resolving two or more geometries, third elements can also act as landmarks for complex, perhaps even complicated, spaces. Seen from varied points of view, these landmarks offer orientation and stability to those in and even outside the square.

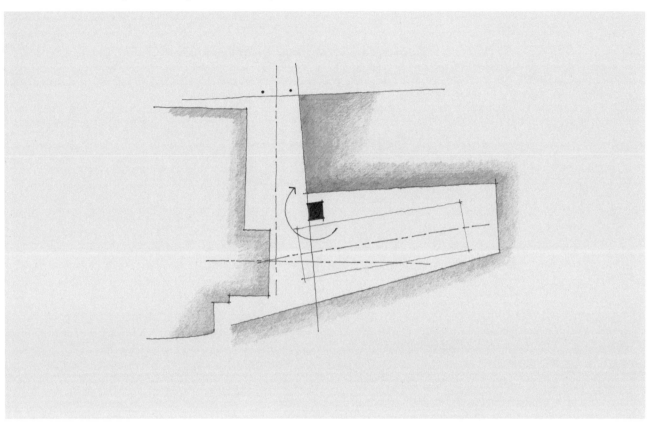

Plan diagram showing rotations

Diagram showing planes and fulcrum

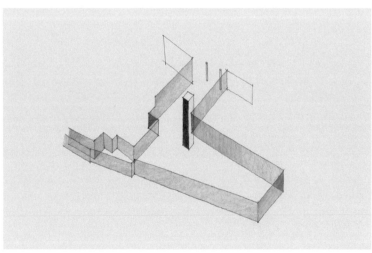

View from the Grande Canal

Piazza San Marco
Venice, Italy

What is the point of rotation in the space?

What element or elements help rotate or guide changes in direction?

What is the relationship of vertical elements to horizontal elements?

What are the geometric relationships in the space?

The diagram of Venice's Piazza San Marco shows how the campanile acts as a fulcrum around which the walls, spaces and even the pedestrians pivot from the larger piazza to the smaller Piazzetta di San Marco. The diagram of Trujillo's Plaza Major shows how the multiple rotations and pivots unite at the central equestrian statue. While the square's west side is quite regular and ordered, this contrasts with the east side, which has contortions that respond to topography but are actually a composition of form.

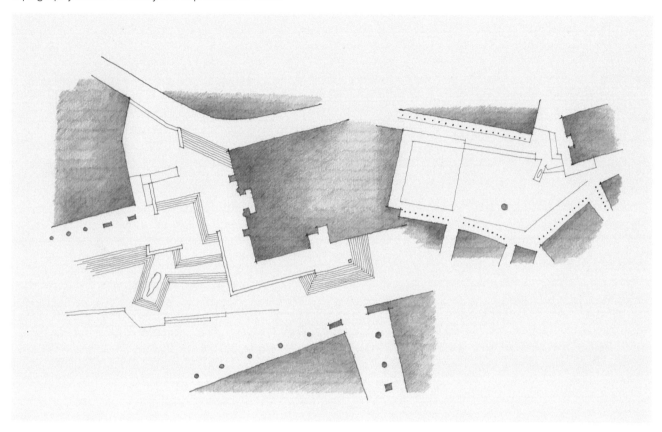

Nolli plan of the plaza

Pivoting and rotating edges of the plaza

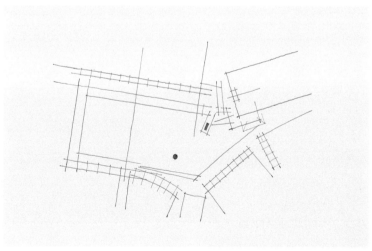

View into the Plaza Major

Plaza Major
Trujillo, Spain

Screening Spaces

Colonnades, arcades, porticoes or lines of trees can enclose space yet, because of their permeability, can be less enclosing than an actual wall and more of an enclosing screen. Visually transparent and translucent, these comb-like screens allow movement back and forth between inside and outside. Additionally, these permeable enclosures, because of their uniformity, can unite disparate elements.

The diagram of St. Peter's in Rome shows how the semicircular colonnade enclosing the piazza, which seems to embrace the faithful, is a series of layers that unify the broad space while screening the odd buildings just outside its perimeter. As a series of layers, the colonnade forms a threshold between inside and outside as well as a linear path along its curving length. The view of the multilayered, concentric rings of columns changes from different vantage points of view. Only at the centerpoints of each circle is it

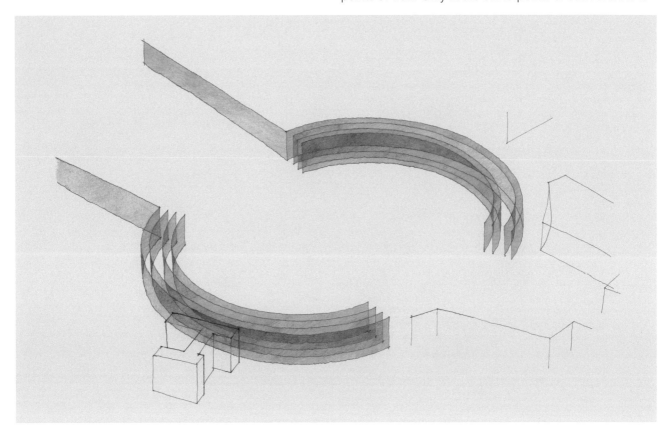

Tones showing the colonnade's layers

View through the colonnade into
the square

St. Peter's Vatican
Holy See (Rome, Italy), 1667
Gian Lorenzo Bernini

How is the perimeter enclosed?
Is there a screen? How is it a screen versus a wall?
What would be the effect if there were no screen?
When is the screen transparent or opaque?

possible to see through all the layers at one time. The diagram of the University of Virginia's colonnade shows how the colonnade links the varied pavilions into a unified container of the lawn. Interlacing through the pavilions' porticoes, this liner provides a covered passageway around the perimeter while containing space.

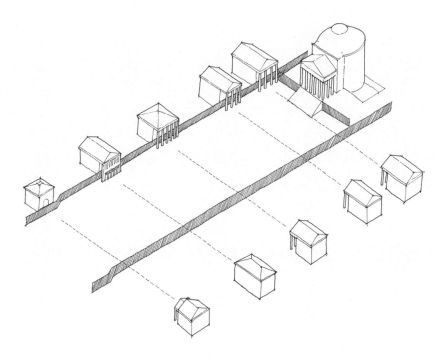

Exploded isometric showing the colonnade as a ribbon

View toward the rotunda

The Academical Village
University of Virginia
Charlottesville, Virginia, 1826
Thomas Jefferson

Lining with Trees

Trees as living, air-processing, long-lived plants that filter sunlight and change with the day and seasons can play a significant, if ineffable, role in defining a space both spatially and experientially. Quantitatively, trees edging a street or public space create a permeable colonnade through which people can see and move; they decrease heat gain, provide shading, absorb stormwater and filter the air. Qualitatively, trees provide a sense of security and scale and have even been attributed with helping to reduce blood pressure. For whatever reason, trees are unique elements that can play multiple roles in defining urban spaces. Incorporating trees as active extensions of a design concept can help imbue architecture with a tree's ineffable qualities and at the same time bring architecture into the landscape. A row of trees can participate in a building's entry or a circle of trees can define an outdoor room.

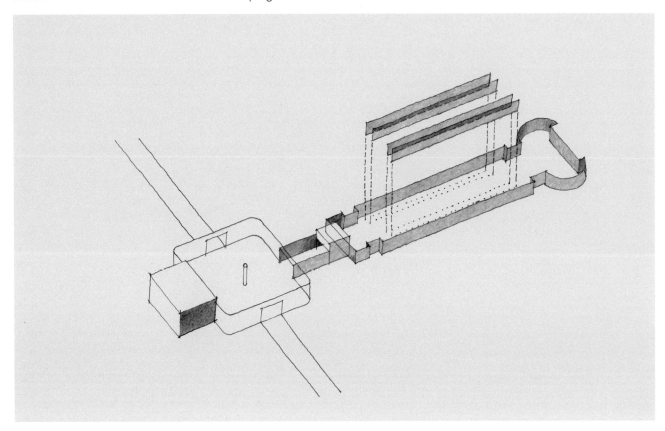

Exploded isometric showing tree liner

View along Place de la Carrière

Place Stanislas, Place de la Carrière and Place d'Alliance
Nancy, France, 1756
Emmanuel Héré

How are trees used to define a space?

How would the space be different if there were no trees?

What is the relationship of order and disorder in the trees?

How do the trees differ from arcades, canopies or other similar enclosures?

Like the diagram of Place des Vosges (cf. p. 255), the exploded isometric diagram of Place de la Carrière shows how the two bosques of pollarded trees are essential elements in the square's design. More than the architecture, the trees make the space. Contrasting the edge of Place de la Carrière, the diagram of Paley Park shows how the trees planted in a checkerboard pattern help create a canopy that encloses a serene, quiet retreat in the city. The second diagram is one in which an element is removed to reveal, perhaps prove, that element's effectiveness. In this case, namely without trees, Paley Park quickly transforms into an inhospitable side lot.

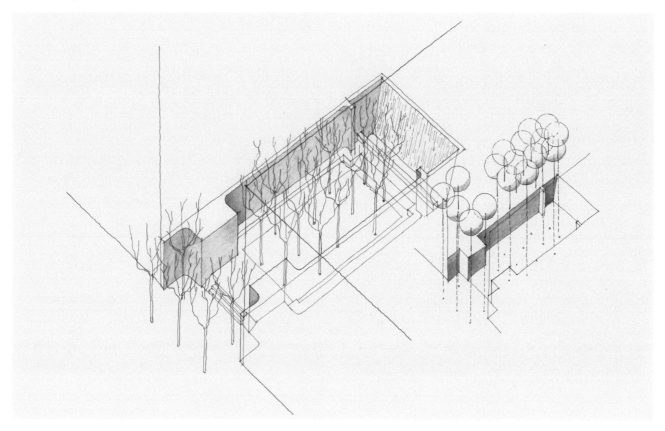

Isometric diagrams showing space defined by trees

View into the park from the street

Paley Park
New York, New York, 1967
Zion and Breene Associates

Layering Space

Urban spaces are sometimes defined by and composed of a series of layers defining particular rooms or zones within a larger space. Building edges, colonnades, trees, low walls, temporary structures, pathways or changes in material can, in turn, define spatial layers or interstitial layers (much like layers of an onion). These interstitial spaces can accommodate different uses and, at the same time, offer scalar gradations from center to edge.

The diagram of Dupont Circle in Washington, DC, shows through differentiation of thin planes how layers in this circular park, which is surrounded by vehicular traffic, shield the traffic and help delineate spaces for varied uses. The outer layer, defined by low bushes, blocks the view of all but the tops of automobiles and defines a concentric pathway; the second layer is a sunbathing and picnicking lawn defined by low bushes and benches; the innermost zone is defined by benches; and the fountain at the center

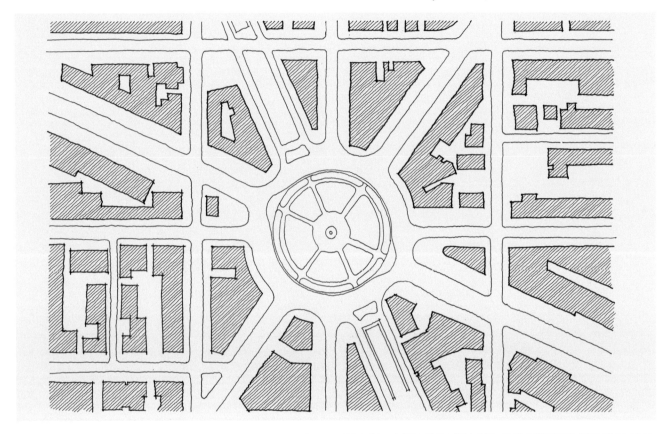

Plan of the circle

Isometric of the park's perceived layers

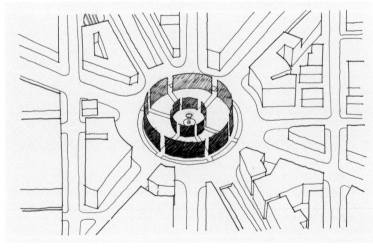

View of Dupont Circle's outer edge

Dupont Circle
Washington, DC, 1791

What are the layers or zones of the space?

How do these layers enclose yet not feel confining? What is the nature of that enclosing layer?

How would the space be different if it were not for the layers?

is a small room most often used as a landmark for *impromptu* and prearranged meetings. The plan and isometric diagrams of Place des Vosges show the multi-layered system created by walkways, arcades and trees that encompass the square. A subtle aspect is that one edge is a through street that allows movement along one layer without disrupting the square's tranquility.

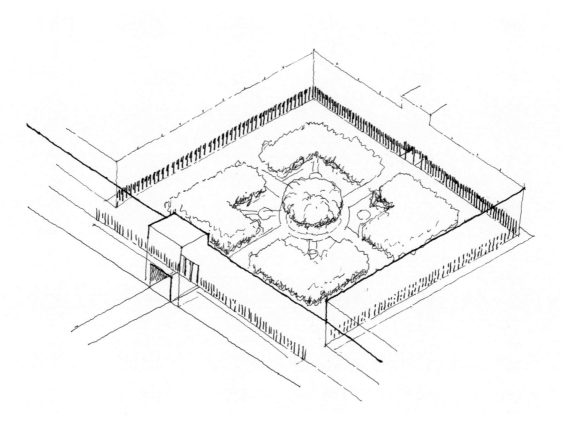

Isometric of the square

Diagram showing the layers and paths

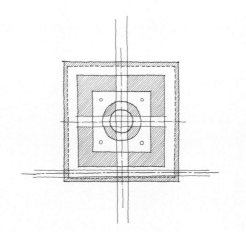

Place des Vosges
Paris, France, 1612

Corresponding Solid and Void

Figure/ground diagrams help clarify the solid-to-void relationship of a city by establishing concisely, perhaps simplistically, that which is building and that which is space in black-and-white. In this way, the figure/ground begins to show how buildings and spaces interlock and intermingle as urban forms. Because we tend to draw using dark materials on lighter materials (ink or pencil on white paper), we tend to draw objects more than voids, a fact which, in turn, tends to favor object-making over void-

making (i.e. it is easier to draw something than it is to draw nothing). A way around this object-over-void tendency is to draw reverse figure/ground diagrams, thereby inverting the traditional designations. This has the benefit of helping us see that a city's voids can be seen and conceived as solids or figural places in the city.

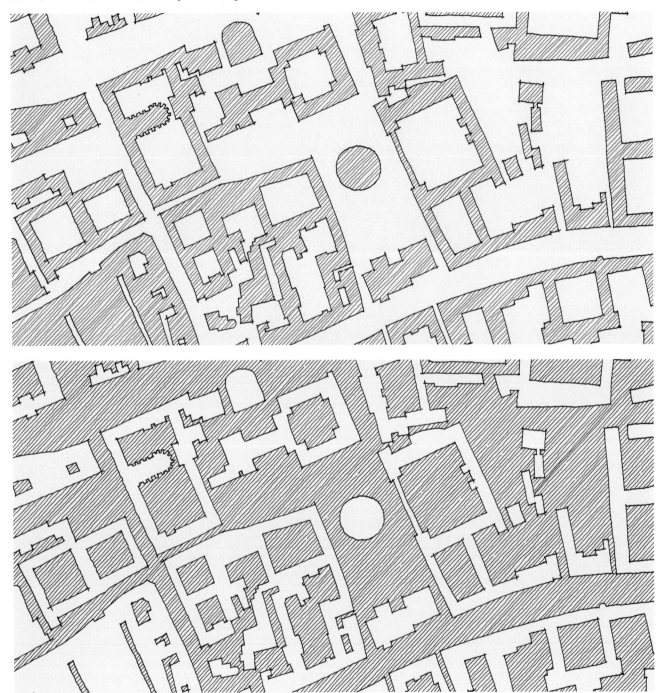

Figure/ground plan of the town and university

Figure/ground reversal of the same area

Oxford, England

How does drawing the void differ from drawing the solid?
How does drawing the void help understand it as a designed object?
How "designed" are the voids in comparison to the solids?
What happens to your thinking or your eyes when you reverse solid and void?

The diagrams show Oxford first in the figure/ground, in which buildings are drawn as *poché* and voids within the city are drawn as white. Conversely, the second diagram is of the voids as solids and solids as voids, which helps illustrate that the voids are or can be actually designed. Another process of drawing both the objects and voids is the diagram of Judiciary Square. Here the buildings are figure/ground objects in the city but related to the figure/ground plan as sketched in an isometric.

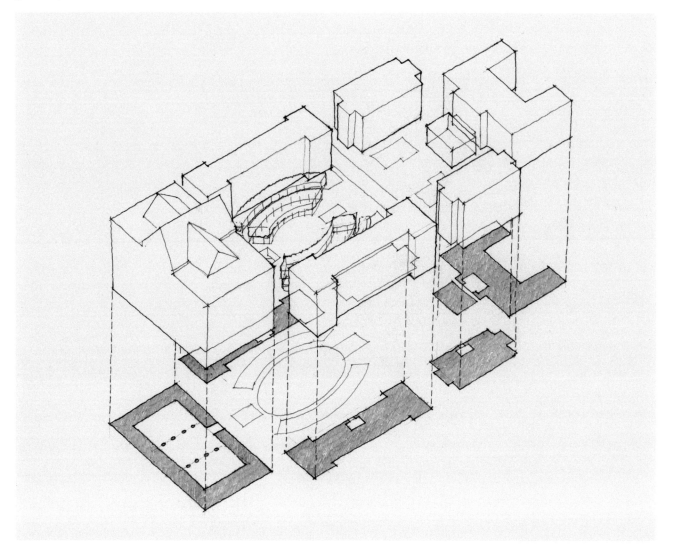

Combined isometric and plan diagrams

View of the square looking south

Judiciary Square
National Law Enforcement Officers Memorial
Washington, DC, 1991
Davis Buckley

Highlighting Space in Fabric

While buildings and the activities within them are essential for a city or other settlement, streets, squares and other public spaces are those civic spaces that allow for social, economic and cultural exchange. As arteries of the city's lifeblood, streets, lanes, alleyways and other paths not only link but also provide opportunities for social interaction. Likewise, public spaces – squares, parks, market places or even a simple widening in the road – allow for social and cultural exchanges. Without streets and public spaces, a city would not be a city. The paths and the spaces of a city – essentially its voids – are designed elements as much as the buildings that form them. Diagramming these designed voids and the sequence in which they occur helps highlight how, as designed objects, their size, sequence, proportion and scale play a vital role in a city.

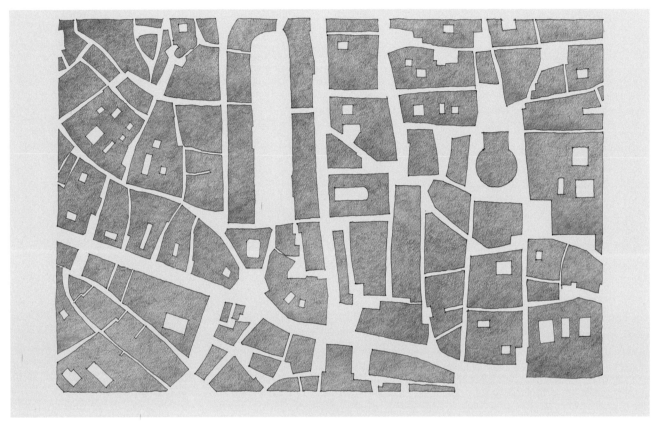

Figure/ground of the historic center of Rome

Diagram showing only streets and squares

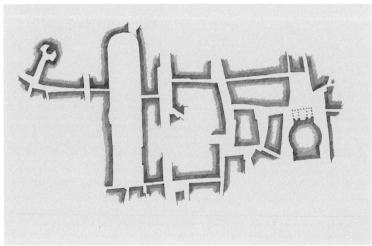

Campo Marzio
Rome, Italy

What are the pathways and spaces along a particular route?

What do you leave in and what do you omit?

What spatial sequence do you discern?

What are the areas of compression and expansion?

The diagrams of Rome's Campo Marzio reveal the streets and spaces within one area of Rome. With a figure/ground drawing as its base, the diagram of one of the east-west paths from Piazza Navona to Piazza della Rotonda shows how paths link a series of smaller and larger public spaces. The diagram eliminates a great deal of information to highlight only the edges of the building masses. Similarly, the diagram of Washington, DC's arts district shows a particular movement from the National Mall north along 8th Street to the National Portrait Gallery and then east to the National Building Museum and the National Law Enforcement Memorial. Like the diagram on Rome, it eliminates general information to help reveal underlying specific patterns.

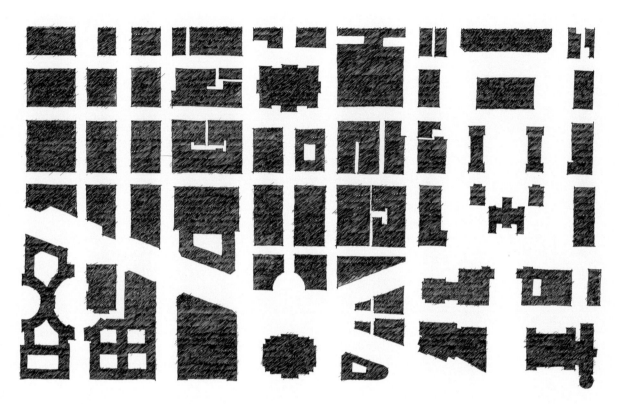

Figure/ground of the 8th Street corridor

Diagram showing only streets and squares

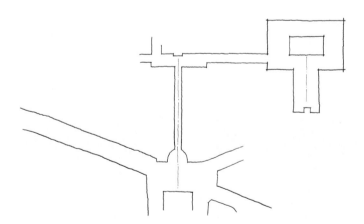

View from the Navy Memorial
to 8th Street

8th Street NW
Washington, DC

Drawing the Nolli

Cousin of the familiar figure/ground plan, Giambattista Nolli's 1748 plan of Rome shows the relationship of urban spaces to buildings – and a bit more. In addition to the figure/ground relationship of buildings to urban space, the Nolli plan expands this relationship by including primary and various secondary public interior voids within a building mass. The result is a plan diagram giving a sense of the link between interior and exterior spaces. This link is especially important when trying to understand a building's interconnected relationship with context and the context's relationship to the building. Likewise, the inclusion of the interior in the figure/ground arrangement helps establish that a solid/void relationship can be more complex than black-and-white. The outdoor and indoor can be "both/and" and the public/private realms can often overlap in architectural frameworks such as porticoes, passages, courtyards or arcades.

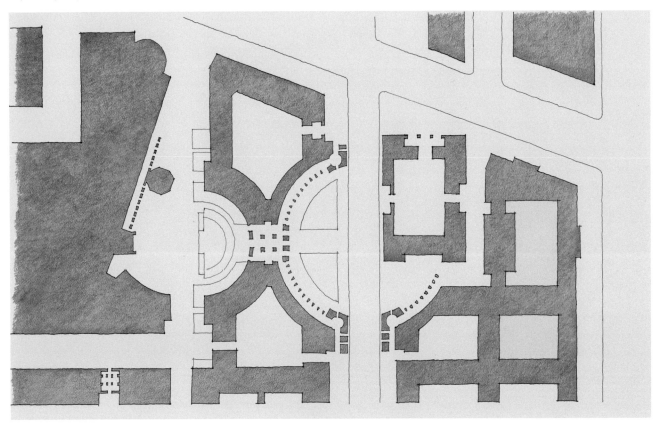

Nolli plan of the Federal Triangle

Diagram showing enclosed exterior spaces and their geometries

Federal Triangle
Washington, DC, 1935
Delano and Aldrich

What is the relationship of interior space to exterior space?

What is "both/and" in the building?

What role do the public spaces have in shaping a building's interior?

In what way is the interior an extension of the exterior spaces?

The Nolli diagram of the Federal Triangle in Washington, DC, helps reveal how public indoor and outdoor spaces are both enclosed and open. The covered passageway and arcade around the semi-circular Grand Plaza, incomplete due to the Old Post Office, allow for the public to engage with and move through the building without actually entering into the more private and secure realm. The diagrams of courtyards at Barcelona's Biblioteca de Catalunya is, first, a plan that shows the spaces from south to north (left to right) through a series of passageways, courtyards, forecourts and out to another street. The isometric shows how this sequence is an even more complex volumetric experience. Vaulted passageways and stairways, arcades and courtyards combine to make a dynamic spatial sequence.

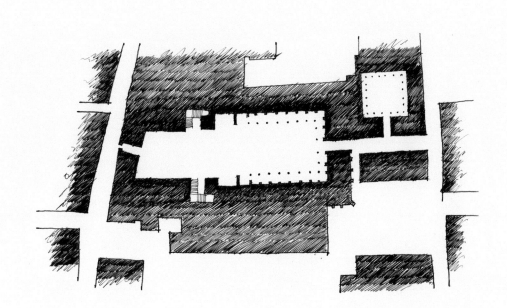

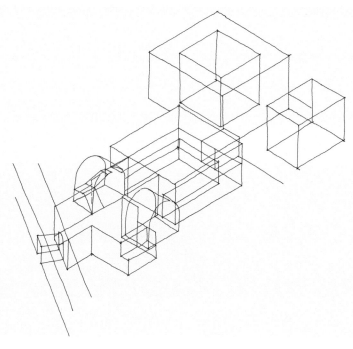

Nolli plan of the public courtyards

Volumetric diagrams of the courtyards

Biblioteca de Catalunya
Barcelona, Spain, 1500

Passing Laterally

Paths in a public space, like those within buildings, are often along its edges. This lateral or asymmetrical arrangement predominates for two reasons. First, shifting the path to one side allows the space, as a room, to remain uninterrupted by traffic passing through it. The square as a large-scale room is a place of rest that remains undisturbed by the traffic of the city. A second reason for this specific path/room organization is that it allows a voyeuristic engagement with the square without an actual or full commitment. Essentially, it offers a choice: you can either look in and pass by or, if you choose, enter the room. As discussed earlier in plan diagrams, lateral movement and the path/room divisions are universal organizational strategies for city fabric, gardens, buildings and small rooms. The need to differentiate where one moves and where one rests remains consistent regardless of size or scale.

Figure/ground of Arras' historic center

Diagram showing paths in relation to squares

Grande Place and Place des Héros
Arras, France

Where are the paths and where are the rooms in the square?

How do the paths bypass the space?

When paths go through the square, what spaces are created for rest?

How does the path change as it touches the square?

The diagram of Arras shows how the city's two squares, the larger Grande Place and smaller Place des Héros, weave together both spatially and architecturally through lateral pathways delineated as broad ribbons. Moving along the squares' edges and under arcades, the pedestrian experiences each square without actually entirely engaging that square's interior. An added, if unintended, spatial experience is the experience of the two spaces along one path: along Grande Place's elongated side and then, without changing direction or paths, along Place des Héros' short side. The diagram of Bologna's Piazza Duomo shows the paths simply as lines with arrows, with rooms or areas of rest delineated as solid "objects" in the city.

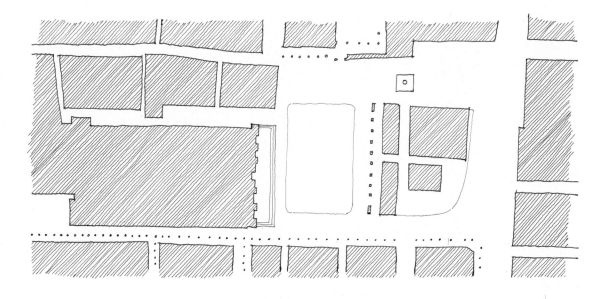

Nolli plan of the piazza

Diagram showing paths and rooms in the square

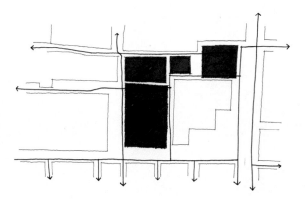

Piazza Duomo
Bologna, Italy

Identifying Building Types

Highlighting building types or uses within an urban fabric helps understand a city as a complex system of interrelated elements. Specifically, diagramming varied building, program or other types highlights particular trends, adjacencies or other relationships. For example, a series of separate diagrams might map the civic buildings in a city: one diagram of schools, another of government buildings, another of museums, etc. Taken as a whole, these separate diagrams help distill an overall underlying pattern of the

civic activities within a city or district and thus allow a quick understanding of how these patterns might influence design studies.

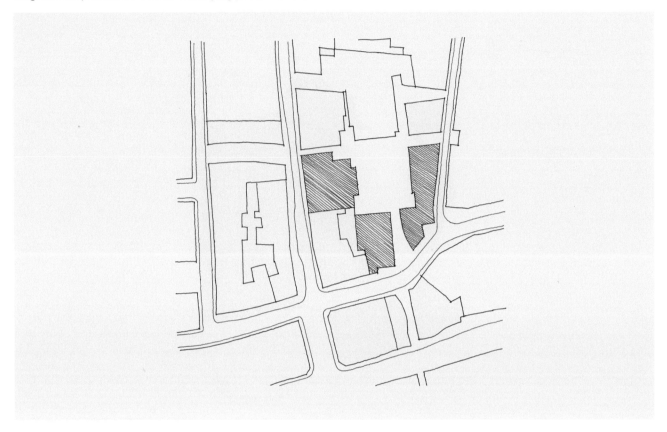

Plan diagram showing composite buildings

Exploded plan oblique showing civic buildings

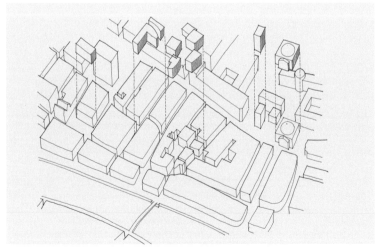

Temple Bar
Dublin, Ireland, 1997
Group 91 Architects

How are different building types distinct or undifferentiated in the urban fabric?
Are there any patterns or rules for distinguishing or diminishing the types?
How do you determine particular types if they are not obvious?

The two diagrams of the Temple Bar neighborhood show how civic buildings are part of the urban fabric. By pulling them out of the fabric, the exploded isometric diagram shows how the civic buildings are part of that fabric. The plan diagram shows how the three buildings yield their identity to public space: buildings deform or contort in order to generate and reinforce urban space. Urban space takes precedence while the more private buildings mutate to insure that primacy. The diagrams of the Campo Marzio neighborhood show, first, the figure/ground plan with all buildings uniformly toned and no particular building type highlighted. The second diagram highlights one particular building type – in this case, churches – and shows their distribution within the fabric.

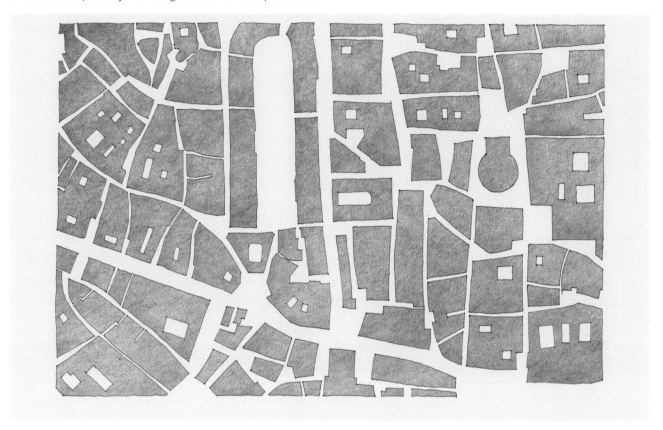

Figure/ground of the historic center of Rome

Diagram highlighting churches only

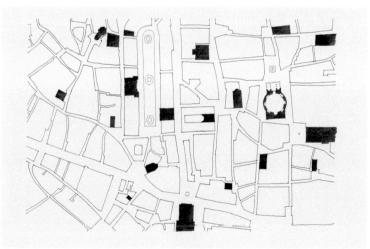

Campo Marzio
Rome, Italy

Emphasizing Types

A systematic study of architecture, urban space or other designed environments is a way to document and discern relationships, commonalities and distinctions over a wider range of samples. While not entirely scientific, a systematic and regular approach helps develop a catalog or library of public spaces, so that their lessons might be understood in the context of other spaces and, more importantly, that observation is comparative rather than consisting of disconnected moments. For example, documenting and diagramming the dimensions of various piazzas might reveal particular spatial patterns common to all squares and thus play a role in the design of new public spaces.

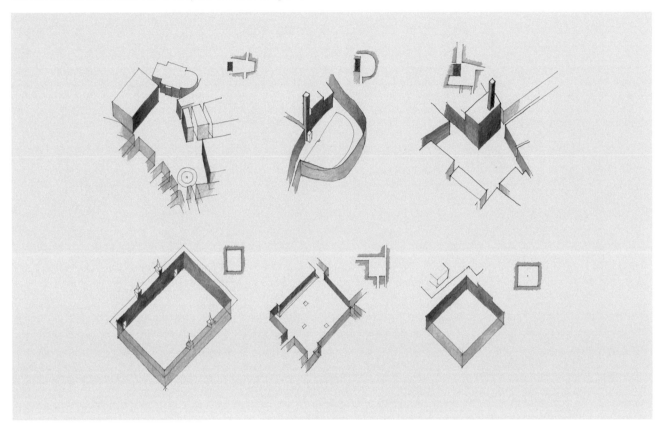

Closed squares and dominated squares

Nuclear squares and ambiguous squares

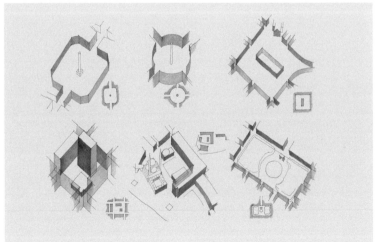

Various Squares

What is the fundamental form of the square?
How are the edges formed?
Where are the paths leading into and through the square?
How do the edges reveal the square?

The diagrams shown here are examples of systematic documentation of squares to help understand proportion, building types, landmarks and configurations. The first set of diagrams, drawn in pencil, are based loosely on types described by Paul Zucker in his book *Town and Square*: closed squares, dominated squares, nuclear squares, ambiguous squares and grouped squares.[1] The fourth set, which documents linear squares, was developed independent of Zucker's five types. The diagrams drawn in ink are similar; however, these include the surrounding context in an attempt to understand in what way the squares are part of a city's urban fabric.

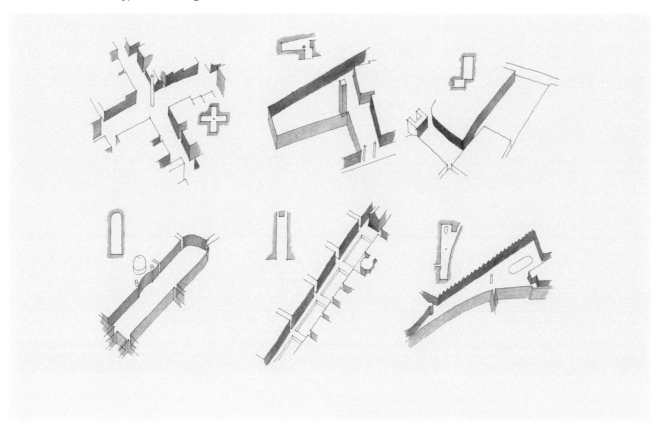

Grouped squares and linear squares

Various squares with framing context

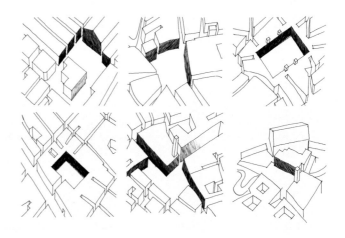

Various Squares

1   Zucker, Paul, *Town and Square: From the Agora to the Village Green*. New York: Columbia University Press (1959): 6-18.

Enclosing Urban Rooms

Careful and systematic study of varied spaces can help develop a sense of how and when particular proportions, wall heights or other dimensions transmit different degrees of enclosure. The two techniques below are just two ways to begin this long-term study.

These comparison diagrams of public spaces, drawn at the same scale, show how spaces with similar dimensions may change substantially as their walls increase and decrease in height. Viewing multiple spaces with this identical lens helps systematize the analytical process and can also begin to reveal trends in those proportions that describe enclosure. Likewise, the diagrammatic sections of several public spaces, all at the same scale, are another way to understand enclosure in a systematic fashion.

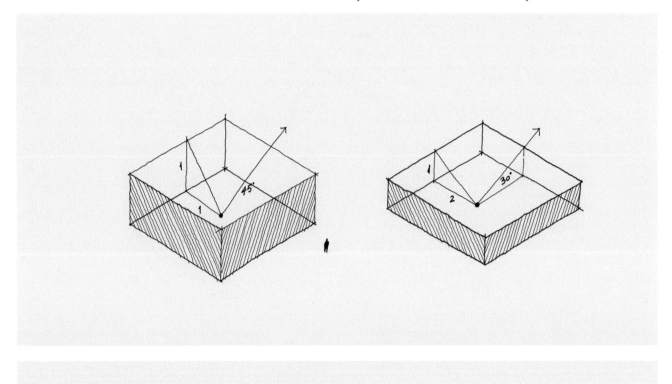

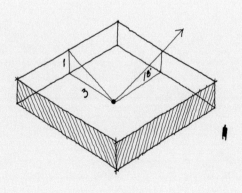
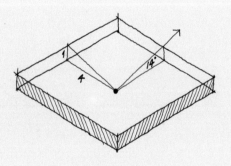

1:1 height to mid-point, 1:2 height to mid-point

1:3 height to mid-point, 1:4 height to mid-point

Proportional Diagrams

What is the sectional proportion of the space?
What is the horizontal dimension in regard to the vertical dimension?
What is the angle from the center of the square to the top of a typical building surrounding the square?
What is the difference in feeling between different squares and does this correlate with proportion and dimension?

Drawn at the same scale, these longitudinal "and/or" cross-sections with a small diagrammatic plan help create a common frame of reference, so that the role of dimension and proportion can be more easily understood at varied sites and cities.

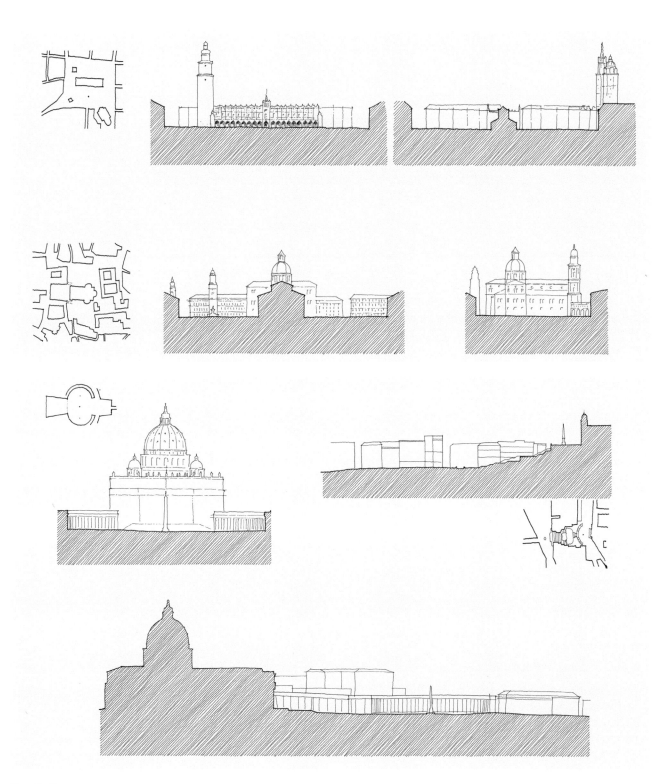

Plaza Sections
Kraków: Rynek Główny
Salzburg: Domplatz, Residenzplatz and Kapitelplatz
Rome: Piazza San Pietro
Rome: Scalinata della Trinità dei Monti

Informing the Street Section

A street's edge, how it is formed, how buildings interact with it and its dimension, are essential in defining the street as a room in the city. Like rooms in buildings, a street room depends greatly on dimension and surface. The proportion of width to height, intermediary elements, the alternation of buildings' surfaces, the activities behind and extension of interior to exterior can play a dramatic role in an urban experience. For instance, there is a great deal of difference between two streets of identical width yet with different building heights, block lengths, or activities within the surrounding buildings. Like the careful and systematic study of squares, the diagrams shown here are some suggested ways to begin a nearly life-long study of street rooms through sections, axonometrics, perspectives and other diagrams.

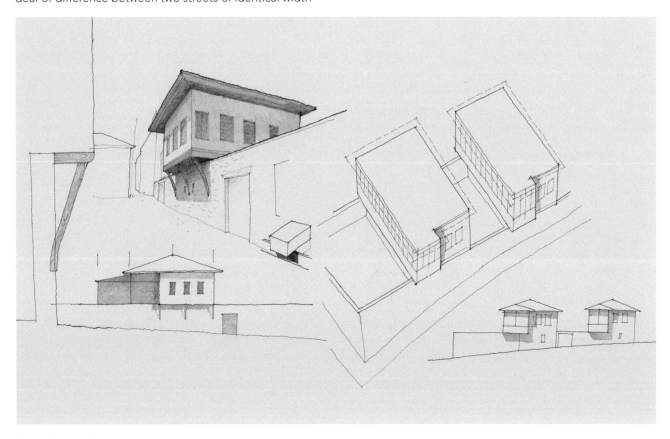

Study of house relationship to street

Street in Birge

Turkish Streets

What is the role of the street edge in making the street?
What is the ratio of width to height?
How does the ground floor activate the street?
What is the role of trees, materials, automobiles, sidewalks, curbs or other elements in shaping the street?

The first set of diagrams is of streets in Birge, Turkey. The overhanging houses provide a sense of enclosure, rhythm and scale to the street. The diagrams are varied and include elevations, axonometric, details and perspectives to understand the nature of the street edge. The second set of diagrams shows a much different method to study street rooms. Here, each street is studied through two lenses: the first and common lens is the street section that shows the ratio of height to width and intervening vertical elements such as trees, arcades or markets. Accompanying this consistent lens are different lenses that offer ways to explore the nature of the street. Each diagram type – isometric, plan, perspective, section axonometric and section perspective – plays a different role and can reveal different aspects of the street room.

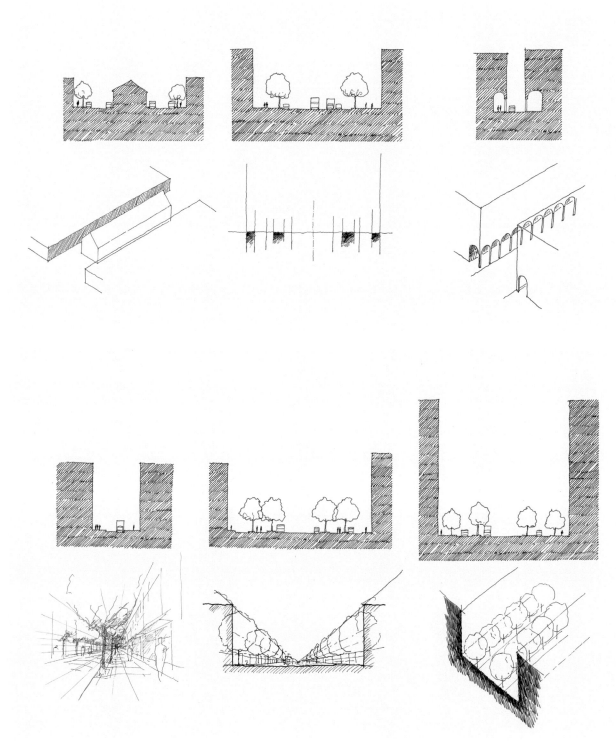

Various Street Section and Diagram Types

Negotiating Stairs and Ramps

Like stairs in a building, stairways and ramps at the urban scale are nearly obligatory opportunities for dynamic spatial experiences. Essentially, ramps and stairs are often necessary and, therefore, opportunities for vertical movement on a site. This is increasingly so for ramps that play an important role in accessibility. Ramps can become integral to a site's spatial layout and, like the grand stairs of the past, become elements that accentuate and celebrate civic presence.

The diagram of the Olympic Sculpture Park explores how the architects conceived the series of ramps, generated from one plane that has been cut and scored. The ramps, which were necessary to get from one side of the site to the other, become active elements in the design. The ramp or ramps gently unfold down the hill, over a roadway and down to the lower street level. The diagram of the ramp and stairway at the Battal Gazi Külliye shows how the stair and ramp are part of a rich spatial experience achieved by

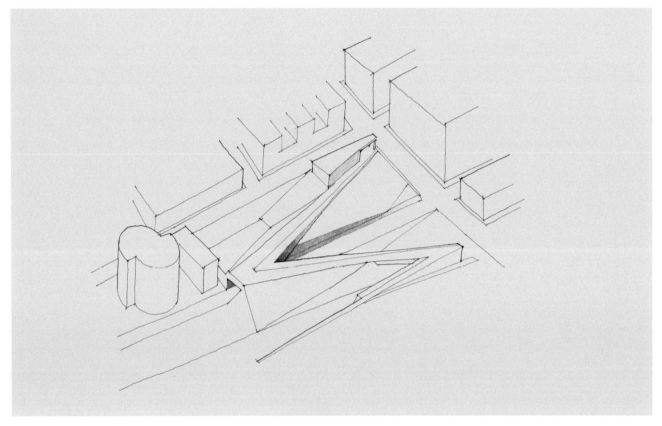

Overall Olympic Sculpture Park ramps and bridges

Diagram of ramp

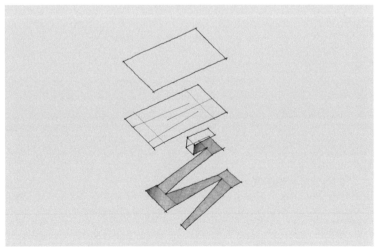

Olympic Sculpture Park
Seattle, Washington, 2007
Weiss/Manfredi

How does the stair or ramp enclosure accentuate the spatial experience?

How does the ramp enliven the spatial sequence?

What happens when the stair or ramp changes direction?

What happens at the points of rest along the ramp or stair?

modulating the steps, ramps, directions, openings and
volumes in the movement from the lower entry to the
upper courtyard. The ramp and stair are held within a
rectilinear volume with an arcade that is open to one side
and, after a turn, open to the opposite side.

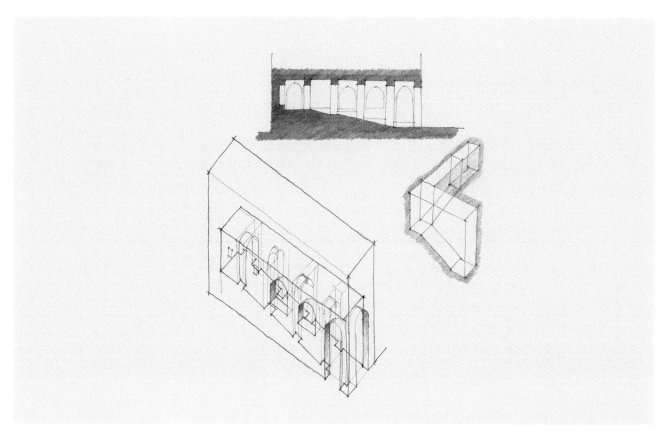

Diagram of enclosed stair and ramp

Plan of the complex

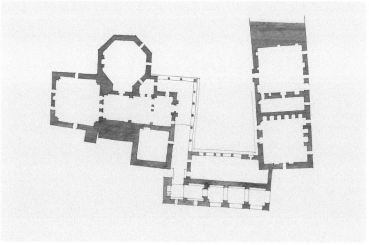

Battal Gazi Külliye
Seyitgazi, Turkey, 1210

273

Strolling through Place

A city, park or square can include a series of critical moments that can be captured through thumbnail perspective sketches. While perspectives might not be considered traditional diagrams, they are included here as a final example of how one might capture and, more importantly, remember a spatial experience quickly and succinctly. While a camera could more easily document these moments, a drawing helps commit them to memory. Using minimal lines with shadows and shade, quick perspective studies such as these mark compression and expansion through portals, arcades, courtyards and plazas. It is important to underscore that these diagrams are less about recording than about contemplating. Walking, standing and sketching a particular sequence for more than an hour offers a kind of reflection not available through a camera lens.

Oxford University
Clockwise from upper left:
From Broad Street through the Bodleian Library courtyard
to Radcliffe Camera
Oxford, England

What are the critical moments along the path?
How does each threshold give a hint to the next threshold?
How is this different from or similar to a photographed sequence?

This particular north-south sequence through Oxford, England, shows the sequence from Broad Street through the old printing house portal, into the Bodleian Library forecourt and concluding at Radcliffe Camera. Each drawing started with a deliberate and repeated definite frame, which helps give some parameter to the sketch that might otherwise extend across the page. Each sketch was done very quickly, mostly with pencil guidelines followed by ink pen to highlight shadows and major lines. These are, in fact, too detailed. More simplified, diagrammatic studies may be appropriate in uncovering the essential lines and forms that shape the spatial sequence.

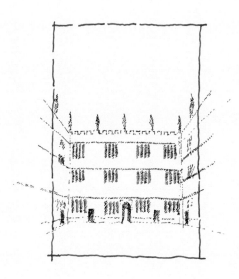

Clockwise from upper left:
Walking from north to south: Broad Street through the
Bodleian Library courtyard to Radcliffe Camera

HOLISTIC ACTS

PART III

HOLISTIC ACTS

It is clearly impossible to fully "know" a building. We can only understand it as a simultaneously manifested group of diverse abstractions, a reduction, a series of fragments, the boundaries and properties of which have a tendency to drift and expand, causing any enumeration of constituent parts to beg for constant revision under the scrutiny of the eye, the testimony of the object, the analysis of active cognition, the reflection of subjective discovery, or to whatever one might subscribe as the source of the need for interpretation.

Douglas Graf[1]

I suppose it is tempting, if the only tool you have is a hammer, to treat everything as if it were a nail.

Abraham Maslow[2]

Drawing One Thing, Many Ways

The following collection of sketches by architects and architecture students illustrate how one place can be drawn in many ways so that, like different lenses used to see varied distances, angles or colors, varied diagrams can help develop a more holisitic understanding of place. These sketches, completed during one visit to each site, reveal how a series of drawings can help a designer explore through intensive scrutiny and succinct execution, mixed with an ease in conveying views simultaneously. Each assemblage emerged from active engagement with place: walking through spaces, pacing off dimensions, peering into locked rooms or around corners and speculating on the obscured. Through this active engagement, the designer acquired a more complete understanding of place that informed her or his design thinking and design process. Accordingly, this collection's overriding intention is to demonstrate how analytical collages can support a holistic design process in which an assembly of varied, interconnected scalar elements can encourage design improvisation.

Like the multiple diagnostic tools physicians use to understand and mend bodily disorders, designers use varied tools to better understand the inherently complex designed environment and, in turn, use these tools in the design process. Tools, in this case, are strategies that help document, analyze and synthesize what one encounters in the world in order to develop comprehension, representation and the thinking process.[3] Intricately linked to analysis and synthesis, sketches, drawing types, diagrams and other representational systems are tools with and through which designers explore and, in turn, shape the designed environment. And like any tool, they influence thinking and production.[4] The more limited the tool box, the more limited one is to see and solve problems. Put more optimistically: the more the tools, the greater potential for extensive exploration. This is even more so for architectural design which must solve more *wicked problems* that may have more than one solution.[5] To help resolve, and perhaps welcome, complex, simultaneous and often conflicting forces into a unified or, at least, intelligible whole, designers generally explore and test options using multiple tools: plan, section and elevation, tangible and digital modeling, collage, painting or any other representation methods. The more tools or views, the more readily can a designer explore possible outcomes. The multiple views and, more importantly, the intellectual approaches are best informed when they correspond with equally complex learning processes and sketch analyses that decode and encode the designed environment. In fact, the more a decoding system matches an encoding system, the more informative the process is overall.[6]

Introducing multiple design tools in analysis can instill a process in which the designer is a *bricoleur*. As described by anthropologist Claude Lévi-Strauss, a *bricoleur* is one who uses a set of tools to solve problems creatively. Lévi-Strauss notes that the *bricoleur* solves problems "with 'what's available', that is, a set, finite at each instance, of tools and materials, heterogeneous to the extreme, because the composition of the set is not related to the current project, or, in any case, to any particular project, but is the contingent result of all the occasions that have occurred to renew or enrich the stock, or to maintain it with the remains of previous constructions or destructions".[7] Developing a *bricolage* design process requires a certain knowledge of multiple tools and, more importantly, a comfort in alternating tools in response to changing situations. One way to inculcate comfort is through draw-collaging in the sketchbook.

By introducing and then juxtaposing diagrams in a relatively unplanned or preconceived fashion, the sketchbook parallels the design as *bricolage*. The hope here is to encourage simultaneity in drawing and thinking, a certain comfort with overlap, and facility to design by beneficent accumulation. In this process, a sketchbook page develops in response to previous moves so that each new response contributes to a unified whole rather than a series of individual, indifferent moves. Composition grows organically so that the page emerges out of yet to be discovered conditions. This accomplishes two objectives. First, it allows students to become increasingly comfortable with working and responding to givens that, most often, they cannot ignore but should engage in and exploit to a greater advantage. Second, encouraging simultaneity and juxtaposition in a sketchbook helps designers become increasingly comfortable when they encounter overlap, conflict, resolution or contrast in the design process.

This, of course, is especially important in developing an approach that responds to and complements what is given: a first drawing prompts and shapes a second, which does the same to the third and so on. As in the surrealist game, the *Exquisite Corpse*, results are often unpredictable, perhaps haphazard, yet they do grow organically and emerge from successive drawings.[8] The larger impact, however, is that each drawing contributes to a greater whole. Contribution is essential. Rather than random, arbitrary or self-referential marks on the page, each subsequent drawing must contribute to a greater, hopefully, more unified whole. One model for this is theatrical improvisation. As an interactive, unplanned exchange, participants develop and contribute to a story line by following agreed rules. One important rule is "yes-and", in which participants agree with one another and, just as importantly, contribute something to the conversation.[9] This develops an ability to see patterns, analyze those patterns and then contribute to the patterns in some beneficial way that, in turn, helps develop abilities to examine and contribute thoughtfully to a given situation.

Conclusion
This book is about a particular way of looking at the designed environment that centers on the benefits of learning, developing and then challenging specific methods or lenses through which to see the world. These lenses are not only the diagrams, but underlying ideas such as developing skills, using specific media, engaging in formal analysis or referring to specific buildings, spaces and architects. Additionally, within the text is, of course, the author's bias about particular rules or guidelines that might help develop analytical thinking – rules that even include the use of plan, section and elevation, anachronistic conventions in an age of parametric modeling. A more seasoned architect or designer will respond to these biases and rules with: "Well, that's not always true", or: "I question that this should be mentioned or diagrammed", or: "Why even sketch at all?" All good questions, but these and other similar comments come from those who have had the luxury of learning these rules or have their own set of rules and know when or how to break them – or, worse, have not fully engaged in sketching as a way of understanding. As Jacques Barzun notes: "The need for rules is a point of difficulty for those who, wrongly equating intellect with intelligence, balk at the mere mention of forms and constraints – fetters, as they think, on the 'free mind' for whose sake they are quick to feel indignant, while they associate everything dull and retrograde with the word 'convention.' Here again the alphabet is suggestive: it is a device of limitless and therefore 'free' application. You can combine its elements in millions of ways to refer to an infinity of things in hundreds of tongues, including the mathematical. But its order and its shapes are rigid. You cannot look up the simplest word in any dictionary, you can not work with books or in a laboratory, you cannot find your friend's telephone number, unless you know the letters in their arbitrary forms and conventional order."[10] Just as James Joyce used the alphabet, Igor Stravinsky used musical notes and Robert Rauschenberg used specific colors. These and other creative thinkers began with fundamentals. Like writers who use an alphabet, composers who use musical notes or artists who use specific paint colors, it is hoped that each individual designer might learn fundamental strategies that will help them develop a unique analytical methodology that, in turn, will inform their design work for the 21st century.

1   Graf, Douglas, "Diagrams", *Perspective*, 22 (1986): 42-71.

2   Maslow, Abraham, *The Psychology of Science: A Reconnaissance*. New York: Harper & Row (1966): 15.

3   Midland, Michael B., "Tools for Knowledge Analysis, Synthesis, and Sharing", *Journal of Science Education and Technology*, 16, 2 (April 2007): 119-153 (120).

4   Maslow, Abraham, *The Psychology of Science: A Reconnaissance*. New York: Harper & Row (1966): 15.

5   Buchanan, Richard, "Wicked Problems in Design Thinking", *Design Issues*, 8, 2 (Spring 1992): 5-21 (14).

6   Larkin, Jill H. and Simon, Herbert, "Why a Diagram is (Sometimes) Worth Ten Thousand Words", *Cognitive Science*, 11 (January-March 1987): 65-99 (70-71).

7   Lévi-Strauss, Claude, *The Savage Mind*. New York: Oxford University Press (1972): 17.

8   Davis, James W., "Visual Dialogue through 'Conversational' Drawings" *Leonardo*, 3, 2 (April 1970): 139-147 (139).

9   Crossman, Mary M., "Improvisation in Action", *Organization Science*, 9, 5 (September-October 1998): 593-599 (596).

10 Barzun, Jacques, *The House of the Intellect*. New York: Harper and Brothers (1959): 6.

Typological Study of Place

This page shows an example of a typological study of a place. A study of Turkish houses and the immediate urban context in Afyon, Turkey, it combines a variety of drawing types including an urban plan, an axonometric of a house's upper level, details, street sections, elevations and house plans. The original used gray watercolor wash but also included some muted colors to underscore specific details or elements in the town. A predominant drawing type are the perspectives of the projecting bays or *cumbas*. The

perspective drawings tend to best represent the dynamic feel from below looking up from the street. This page demonstrates a way in which typology or one focus can be part of a somewhat thorough study of a particular place, element or type. Rather than focus on one building, this study and day spent in the town shows how one type and elemental features can be part of a study.

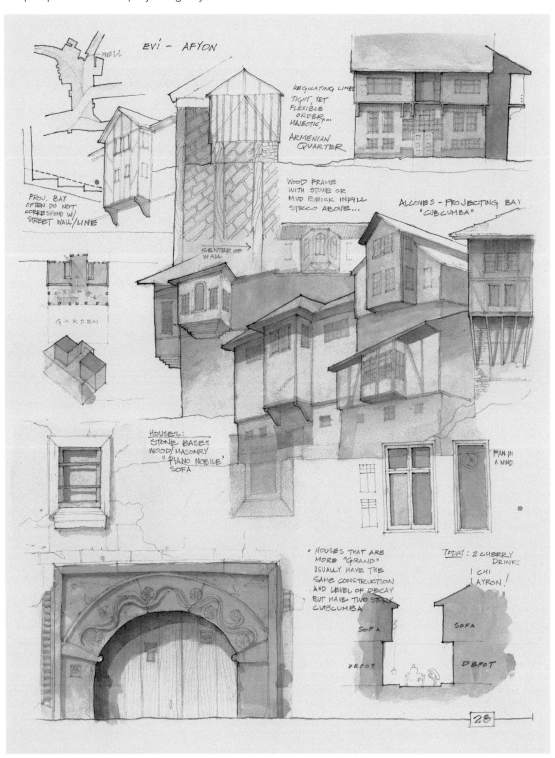

Turkish Houses
Afyon, Turkey
Drawing by Eric J. Jenkins

Discover Artificiality

This page combines nine drawings of one building and its site: perspectives, site sections, detail sections, site axonometric and site plan to help understand a place. The key issue about this drawing is that it was the first visit to the site after years of hearing about the building. The commonly repeated theme is that the villa sits on a hillside when in reality it sits asymmetrically on a plinth within which is carved an entry ramp, which is aligned with a chapel across the small road. The asymmetry helps make each of the nearly identical façades unique in terms of an individual's experience. The idea that the artificial plinth incorporates back-of-house services adds yet another layer to the villa's design and interpretation. The series of drawings attempt to help uncover the villa both as an artifact but also as a design that resolves program layout, site strategies and access of light and air.

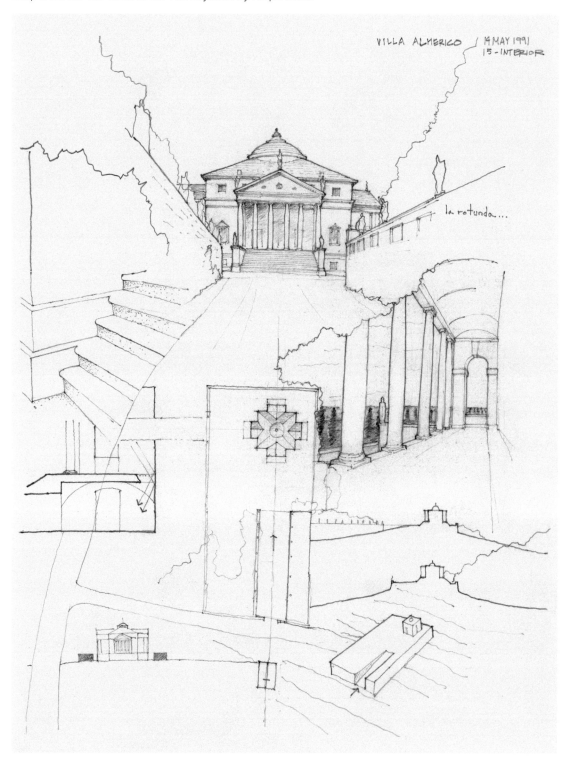

Villa Almerico Capra
Vicenza, Italy, 1570
Andrea Palladio
Drawing by Eric J. Jenkins

Conceptual Memory of Place

Though architect and professor Vyt Gureckas had studied the Salk Institute through published drawings, photographs and descriptions, it was not until he visited and, more importantly, sketched the site that he could say with any confidence that he began to understand the site. The primary intention of this particular page was to study the way in which water emerged, spilled out and terminated through the site by combining plans and views. As an architect and educator, Gureckas notes, "sketching for me is a way to remember a place so that even if I don't look at the sketch again, the place is embedded as an understanding in my mind."[11] More than a literal memory or record, the sketch and the process helped him establish a conceptual memory of place that informed his own design processes. What may have started as a plan of a fountain became the understanding of emergence, flow and conclusion.

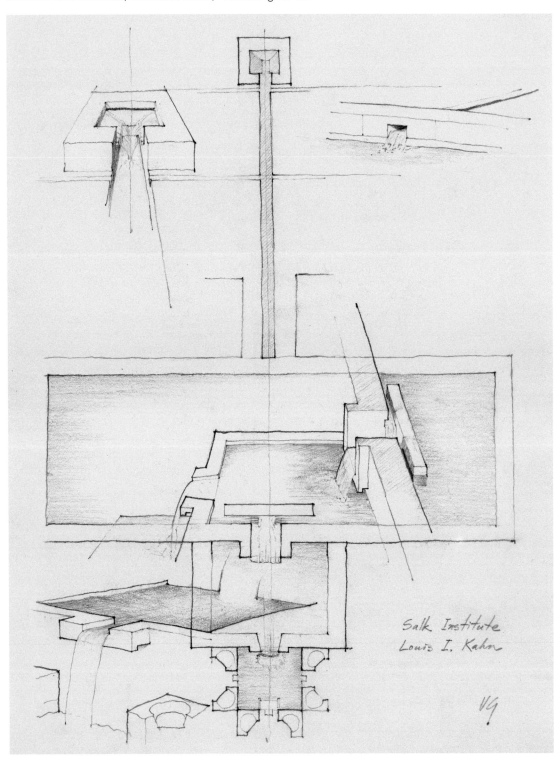

Salk Institute
La Jolla, California 1965
Louis Kahn
Drawing by Vyt Gureckas

11 Gureckas, Vyt, Personal interview, 9 May 2012.

Simply Complex

For Vyt Gureckas, the intention of these two simple sketches was to understand the sequence alongside, up and into the meeting chamber and the ancillary space used for extra seating as well as the geometry of structure. The ancillary space is an aspect he did not fully understand in his studies of the building through published drawings and photographs. Sketching the simple yet complex movement and organization, however, added a new dimension to Gureckas' appreciation of the building. Not only did he

better understand the internal circulation, but he also saw how it connected to the overall landscape and building. Likewise, the structure, which he had also seen many times in photographs, could only be fully studied and appreciated on site. As a composition, the page seems to echo the meeting chamber. The enclosing room with the two wood trusses seems to shelter the chamber.

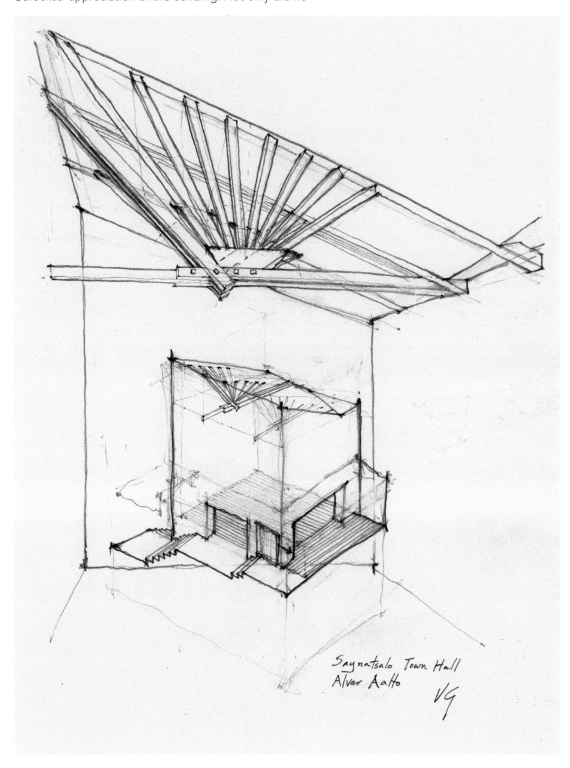

Säynätsalo Town Hall
Säynätsalo, Finland, 1951
Alvar Aalto
Drawing by Vyt Gureckas

Capturing Sense of Place

This sheet combines four drawings: three perspectives and one axonometric diagram. It is about composition and what is implied. The sheet works from top to bottom: first with the perspective looking through the portal into the campo, followed by the general view and lastly the axonometric and the view of the campo's floor pattern and drain – essentially, working down the page and down into the campo. The drawing uses line weights to imply edges and mass. Rather than delineating surfaces and details, it is sufficient to simply outline some buildings and focus on the town hall. The main purpose of the axonometric was to show the semi-circular space with the sloping floor and to suggest the access points through the mass into the square. While the sheet is less analytical, the sequence down, under and into the campo tries to capture a sense of place in the campo, the campanile's and town hall's dominance and the sense of enclosure of this unique square.

Piazza del Campo
Siena, Italy
Drawing by Eric J. Jenkins

A Set of Partial Interpretations

Hawra Esmaeil's study of Piazza Guglielmo and Piazza Vittorio Emmanuele in Monreale, Italy, attempts to understand, first, how the nearly identical, twin squares interlink and, second, why Piazza Vittorio Emanuele is more socially vibrant while Piazza Guglielmo is more subdued. Using plans and sections drawn at the same scale, Esmaeil discovered that factors contributing to social vibrancy included vegetation and urban furniture. Like her other sketching investigations in Europe and the Middle East,

Esmaeil admits that it is difficult for her to remember and grasp a site's entity and that she is "left only with an HB pencil and a sketchbook to establish a set of partial interpretations that register a space's idiosyncrasies".[12] While sketching at the site, she edits and compares the sketched interpretations with the actual place to "create a dialog that amplifies new meanings and interpretations that help me develop speculative and critical design strategies".[13]

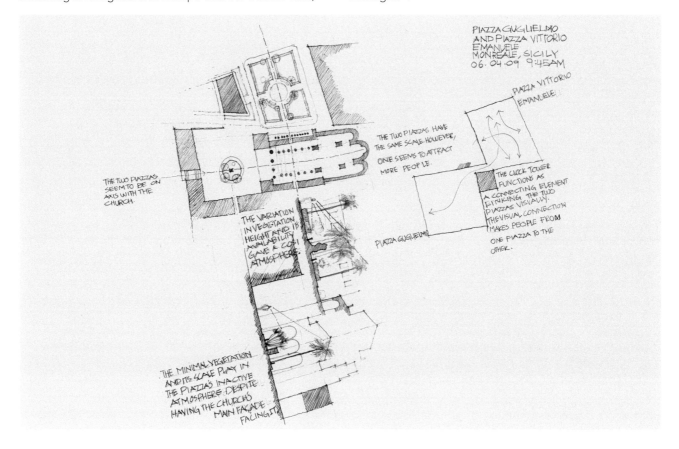

Piazzas Guglielmo and Vittorio Emmanuele
Monreale, Italy
Drawing by Hawra Esmaeil

12 Esmaiel, Hawra, e-mail interview, 5 May 2012.

13 *Ibid.*

Speculate on Systems

This study of Santa Maria Novella by graduate student Christina Cole, speculates on the church's proportional systems and regulating lines in elevation, section, detail and the interior bays. The drawings divide the façade or elevation in two: one half is the elevation with only a ghosted proportional system, while the other half is only the proportional systems or regulating lines. Using varied line types, the diagrams are overlays of systems within systems at varied scales. The study is a careful and considered examination that uses one lens to look at one building and its different parts to compare and contrast the parts to the whole. While the proportional systems drawn here may not have been the actual systems that Alberti consciously or unconsciously employed, the process of making and speculating on possible systems helps develop both an eye and awareness for any systems. Essentially, the search and speculation upon systems cultivates further search and speculation, both at sites and in the design process.

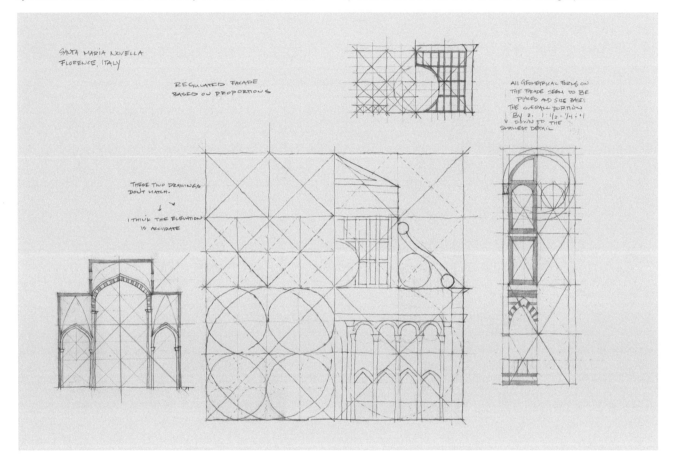

Santa Maria Novella
Florence, Italy, 1470
Leon Battista Alberti
Drawing by Christina Cole

A Meditative Experience

These drawings of Chiesa di San Francesco in Sorrento, Italy, completed by Christina Cole seven years after the Santa Maria Novella sketches, reveal her maturation from student to architect. Here we can start to see how Cole continues her focused investigation yet has expanded from more formal studies to include site and scale. She notes that "sketching has become a meditative experience at a deliberately slow pace".[14] The drawings are more refined and subtle as they capture place by combining a site section that overlaps with a cloister section-perspective that then links into the cloister plan. Her technique has also matured: she limits the toned *poché* as it overlaps with the perspective to further distinguish section and perspective.

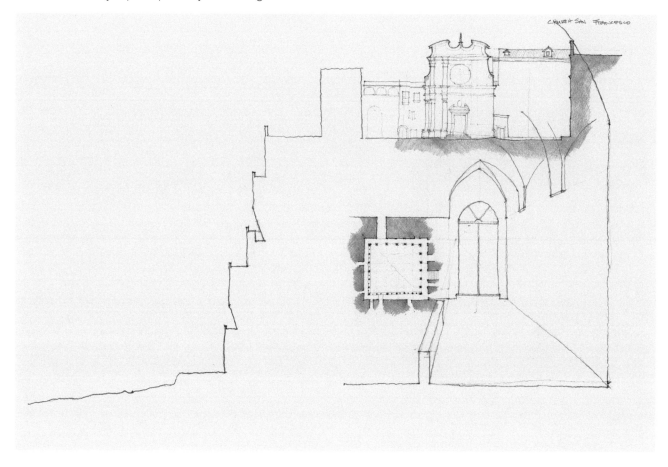

Chiesa di San Francesco
Sorrento, Italy
Drawing by Christina Cole

14 Cole, Christine, e-mail interview, 7 May 2012.

2D to 3D

This page, by graduate student John Lang, is primarily a careful consideration of the Sultan Ahmet Mosque's interior volumes. Lang engages in an exercise of translating two dimensions into three dimensions. This is especially true in the transparent axonometric of the domes and subsidiary spaces. The axonometric, which requires deliberate concentration, is a sketch that, as Lang notes, "forces me to absorb the surroundings. The process of seeing and studying a space and then drawing what is seen and felt reveals a much clearer understanding of a space."[15] Lang prefers to dissect the buildings or spaces "at a variety of scales; from the larger diagrammatic depiction of spatial relationships down to the more intricate detailing of a cornice or arch. By combining these I become part of a space and, later, am able to recall how the space felt when I moved through it."[16]

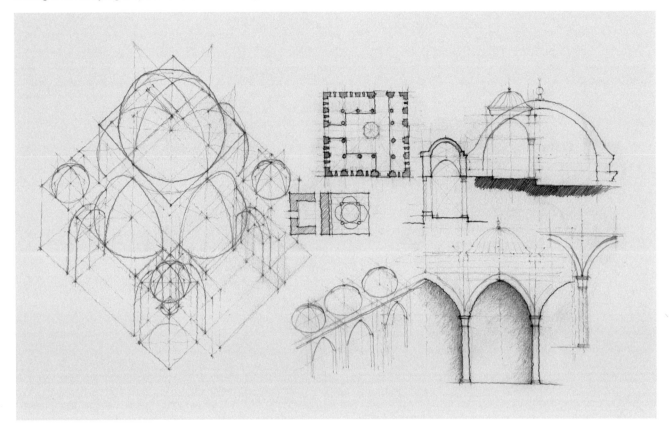

Sultanahmet Camii
Istanbul, Turkey, 1609-17
Mehmet Aga
Drawing by John Lang

15 Lang, John, e-mail interview, 6 May 2012.

16 *Ibid.*

What Makes a Place Unique

Jessica Willard's sketches of the Şehzade mosque in Istanbul, made during the first day in a month-long trip in Turkey, try to capture the many thresholds and layers in Islamic architecture. Through a plan diagram showing floor levels, a large-scale section of the entry portico and a courtyard section Willard discovered how changes in level enhance and articulate a simple diagram or building type. This observation came out of thorough examination. "Sketching", says Willard, "compels me to really look at something, to take the time to verify it from every angle instead of quickly making assumptions."[17] When she sketches she seeks to "extract one or two elements that define a space in order to capture some quality of the place. By examining qualities and quantities such as patterns on the wall, people using the place or even flowers along a path help me understand that which makes a place unique."[18]

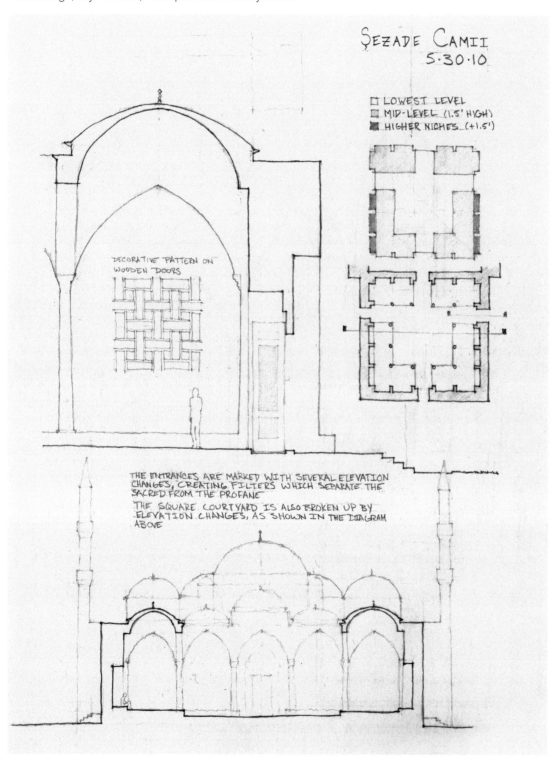

Şehzade Camii
Istanbul, Turkey, 1548
Sinan
Drawing by Jessica Willard

17 Willard, Jessica, e-mail
    interview, 6 May 2012.

18 *Ibid.*

Lines of Thought

Drawn by Paul Yurchak, a junior studying in Barcelona, this page focuses on subtraction and rotations that help introduce light, air and entry into a building mass. This was a breakthrough page for Yurchak. While his field sketches up to this point were quite skillful, he sought verisimilitude. It was only after two months of sketching and when asked to consider housing that Paul fully employed diagrams to explore underlying strategies and, as such, the drawings reveal Paul's newfound intensity to understand place, form and order. Correspondingly, the pen and ink media reinforce a method that accepts and embraces mistakes. More unforgiving than pencil, ink can help develop a student's line craft. While a pencil line can always be erased, unconsciously and consciously, an inked line cannot be easily eliminated: once on the page, the line whether "good or bad" is complete and something we accept and, later, develop.

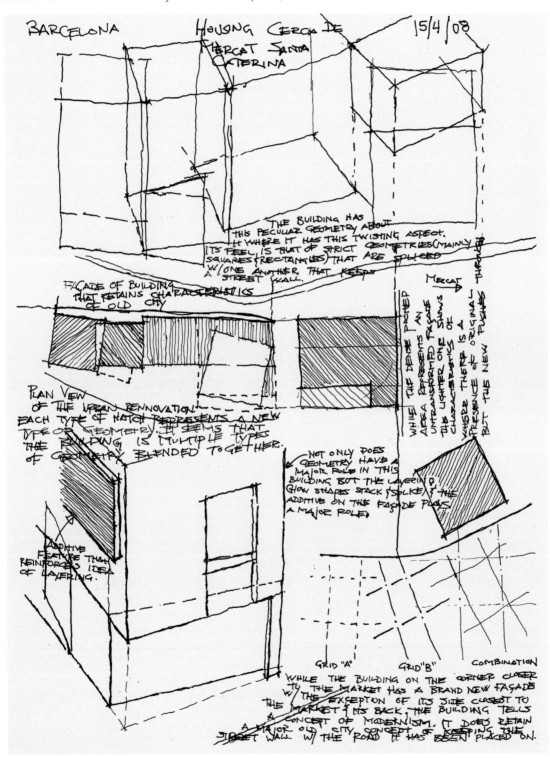

Housing at Santa Caterina Market
Barcelona, Spain, 1999-2003
Bravo and Contepomi
Drawing by Paul Yurchak

Visible Guidelines

For Joshua Humphries, a graduate student studying in Italy, the exhibition armature at the Museo Archeologico Nazionale di Napoli offered a unique opportunity to focus on contemporary design that connects and co-exists with historic fabric at multiple scales. Moreover, his study of connections at the room scale and at the detail scale are part of his conceptual and drawing process. For most of us, underlying guidelines disappear gradually as our sketch develops, but for Humphries, guidelines remain deliberately conspicuous in the completed drawing. He notes that guidelines not only help shape the drawing but also help him "discover relationships and grasp a greater understanding of parts to the whole".[19] The guidelines are both sketching method and conceptual framework that help him perceive and understand scalar shifts. He tends to "gravitate toward the micro, where I focus on connections or details, but this can then through my mind and hand zoom out to the macro".[20]

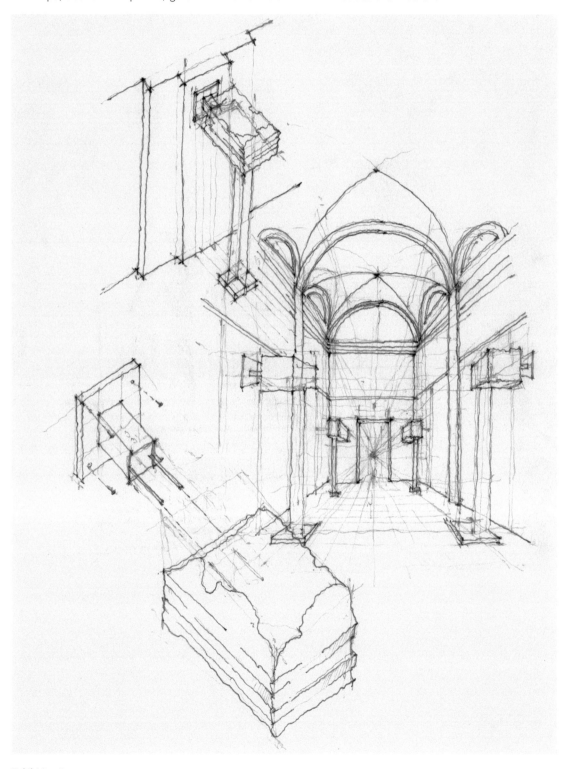

Exhibition Armature
Museo Archeologico Nazionale di Napoli
Drawing by Joshua Humphries

19 Humphries, Joshua, e-mail interview, 1 May 2012.

20 *Ibid.*

The Gem and the Setting

These drawings attempt to understand the octagonal central nave and the way in which it sits within a larger framework and how elements extend from the octagon. As an object, the nave is held gem-like in a setting. This is both a planar issue and a sectional issue: movement from the exterior to the interior is through a series of layered planes but also beneath a series of changing volumes. The offset of the setting to the gem is a subtle shift in plan but perceptible enough to create a kind of dynamic between the gem and the setting. The slight shift creates a different feel on all sides. The octagon is then augmented with alternating arches and half-domes and an elongated altar bay. The drawings are fairly conventional except that the plan oblique attempts to develop the octagon's augmentation and form through shading. The complex shapes drawn in plan oblique were challenging.

Küçükayasofya Camii/Church of Saints Sergius & Bacchus
Istanbul, Turkey, 536 C.E.
Anthemius of Tralles
Drawing by Eric J. Jenkins

In Focus

These sketches of Barcelona's Plaça de Frederic Marès explore the way in which a simple fence can become an important threshold. Located next to the ancient Roman wall in the Barrio Gòtic, the small plaza is closed in the evenings with a security barrier, comprised of a steel pergola through which weave screen-like gates. The tall pergola maintains the street edge yet continues to connect the park to the street even when the gates are closed. The drawing grew from a section that shows the street and the Roman wall and an overlapping plan. This overlap occurred because the plan's focus grew: it became clear rather quickly that the Roman wall was part of the gate's success. The diagrams on the right side show how the pergola is a larger volume through and along which slide the gates and steps.

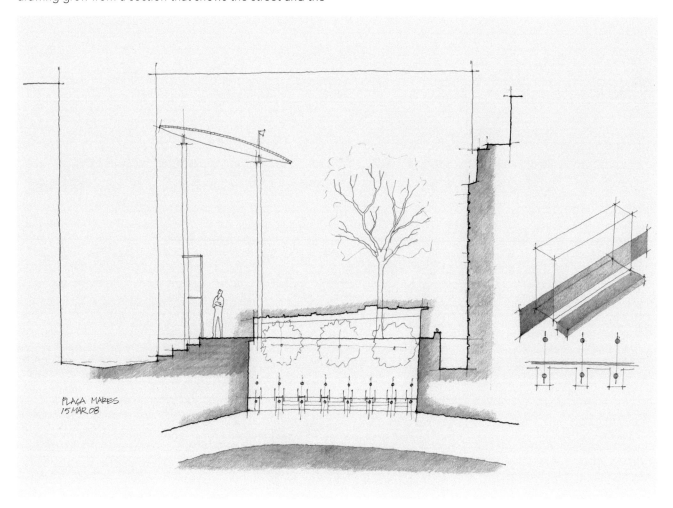

Plaça de Frederic Marès
Barcelona, Spain, 2002
Albert Puigdomènech and Isabel Amador
Drawing by Eric J. Jenkins

Acts of Appreciation

These sketches, drawn by Julio Bermudez on and around the Acropolis from morning to evening (clockwise from the upper left), were part of a remarkable personal and communal aesthetic experience. As a personal aesthetic experience, Bermudez engaged in an intense study to understand the Parthenon's aesthetic allure. Speaking passionately about the drawings and experience, he recalled starting with a simple question: why is this so beautiful? To help answer it, he immersed himself in proportions, harmonies and the connections of temple, landscape and sky. This personal experience transformed unexpectedly into a communal experience as the drawings, which were drawn slowly and carefully over several hours, provoked conversations on the nature of aesthetic pleasure with tourists and Athenians alike. The drawings and the conversations, described by Bermudez as "acts of appreciation"[21], introduced a new level of analytic reflection.

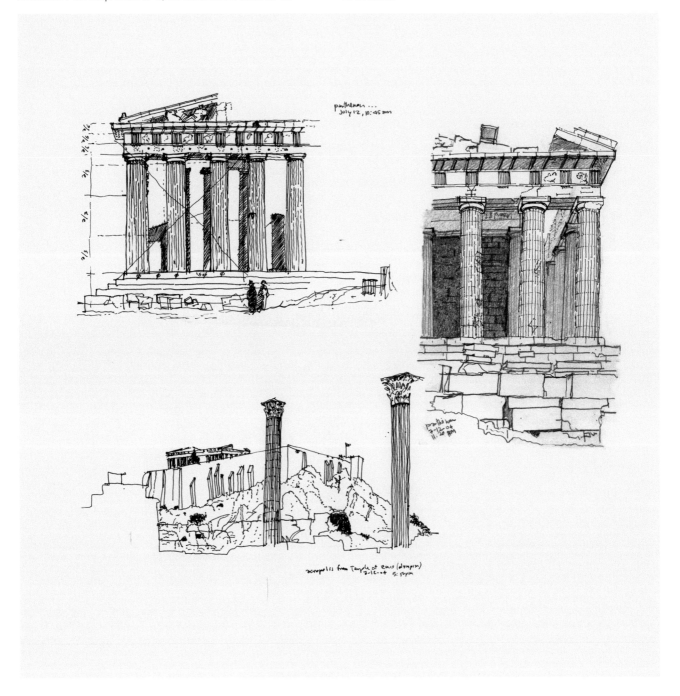

Acropolis
Athens, Greece
Drawing by Julio Bermudez

21 Bermudez, Julio, Personal interview, 9 May 2012.

Self-Awareness in Drawing

These sketches of Casa Malaparte, drawn in pen and ink by undergraduate architecture student Brigid Wright, were part of a life-changing experience. The sun-bleached house perched on sheer cliffs framing dramatic views over the blue sea were at once over-stimulating and difficult to communicate. Wright reflects that, as a result, the site initiated a newly found "focus and level of the self-awareness that I must now have when I draw".[22] Her drawings of the house are unlike any others she drew previously. The page layout and drawings were not predetermined but "uncovered slowly through a process that triggered spatial awareness. Now when I sketch, I select problems and connect parts to a whole to stimulate deeper analyses with my pen. I understand through doing."[23] The drawing media and collage encouraged this reflective journey: she notes that unlike pencil, which can be easily erased, ink "compels me to accept and understand my errors".[24]

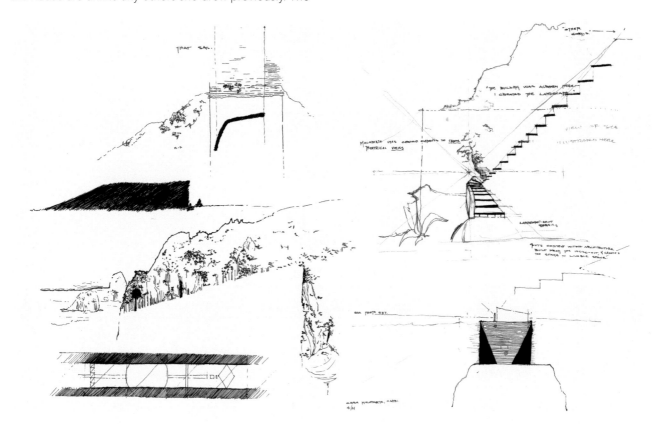

Casa Malaparte
Capri, Italy, 1942
Adalberto Libera
Drawing by Brigid Wright

22 Wright, Brigid, e-mail interview, 4 May 2012.

23 *Ibid.*

24 *Ibid.*

Encounters

Undergraduate student Stephen Riley's exploration of Trajan's Market in Rome focused primarily on the work of Nemesi Studio, whose contemporary insertions meshed sensitively within the archeological site. New access ramps, stairways, doors and windows of steel, wood and glass are distinct not only in material but in their assembly. Riley's highly annotated, multi-scaled drawings reveal an acute attention to material language. Riley notes that this particular *ad hoc* composition and drawing technique

"characterizes the latter half of the semester when I focused on speed" to grasp the essence of a site.[25] Rather than walking the entire site, preconceiving the drawing types and layout and then starting to draw, he thought about a general theme and then moved through the complex, drawing what he encountered along the way. Overlapping diagrams reveal an engaged and curious architect trying to ingest as much of the world as possible.

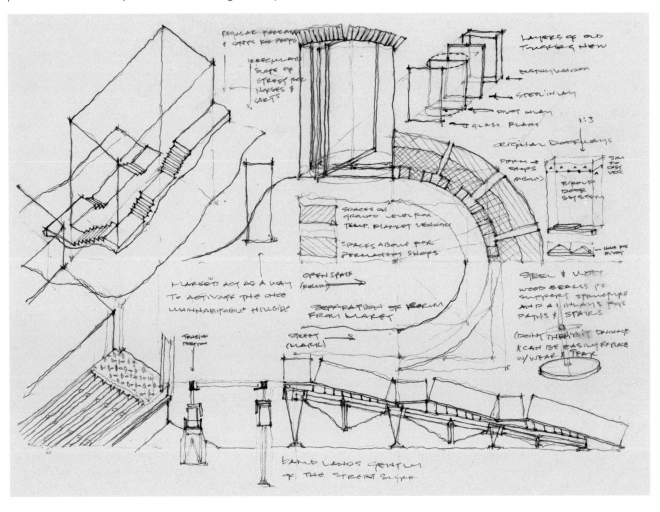

Mercati di Traiano
Museo dei Fori Imperiali
Rome, Italy, 2004
Nemesi Studio
Drawing by Stephen Riley

25 Riley, Stephen, e-mail interview, 7 May 2012.

The Nature of Entry and Threshold

These sketches of the Harem in Istanbul's Topkapi Palace by undergraduate student Christopher Testa explore the nature of entry and threshold. Comprised of partial elevations, plans, site plan and perspective, his sketches document the way in which the floor slope, colonnades, expansion and contraction enhance a spatial sequence. More importantly, these sketches reveal Testa's deliberate attention to his own design education. He explains, "I sketch to discover, to observe and to better understand the subtleties that will make me a better designer."[26] From the larger site to floor patterns, Testa believes that a "sketch is a means of dissecting the intricate parts of a beautifully detailed space. Though a space might be understood through a picture or described by words, there is something about the process of putting pencil to paper that serves to fully understand the broader picture and the details in one composition."[27]

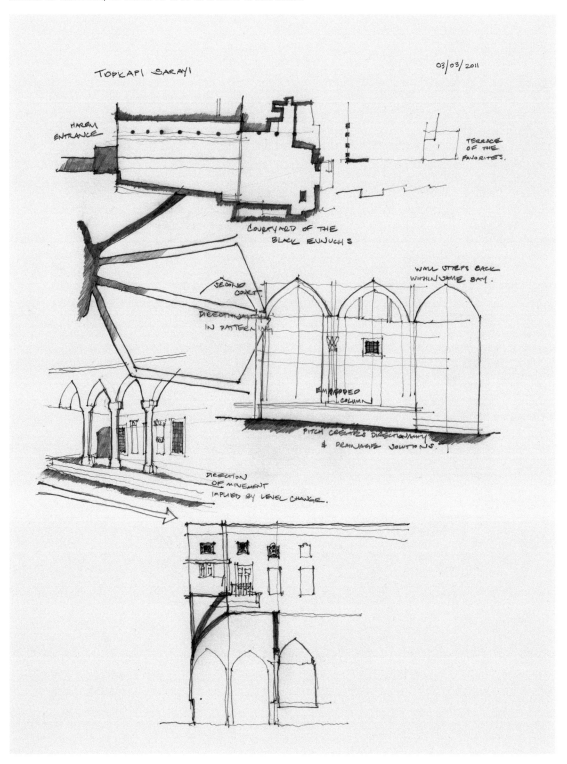

The Harem
Topkapi Palace
Istanbul, Turkey
Drawing by Christopher Testa

26 Testa, Christopher, e-mail interview, 8 May 2012.

27 *Ibid.*

A Holistic Journey

Mark McInturff's journal kept during a walk from Camino to Santiago de Compostela, Spain, records a holistic journey: he mixes architectural and landscape impressions with notes about inns, wine, people, music and conversations. In a sense, it is a sketchbook of total experience of place in which notes and drawings – watercolor, pastel, ink and pencil – reflect a visceral, whole experience and journey of mind and spirit. In these two pages McInturff attempts to capture the way in which the houses that are built of rammed earth are pure masses that merge with the landscape. He does this by blurring the connection between earth and building, by letting the wash and tones overlap with one another: the ground or sky in one drawing becomes the ground or sky of the next.

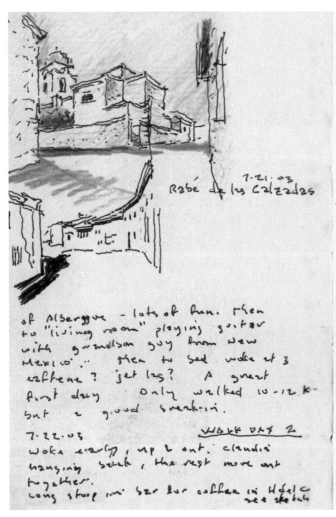

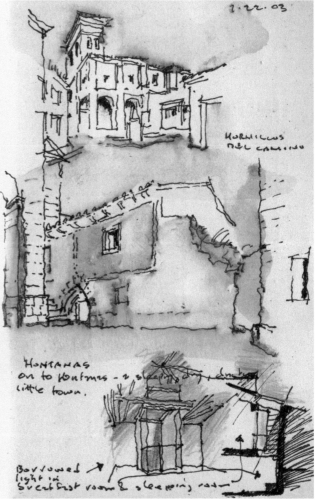

Walk from Camino to Santiago de Compostela,
Rabe de las Calzados and Hontanas
Drawing by Mark McInturff

Conceptual and Perceptual Drawings

McInturff, paraphrasing architect Michael Graves, suggests that there are two types of drawings: conceptual and perceptual. Conceptual are plans, sections and elevations that record dimension, location and situation while perceptual are drawings that try to capture the building as a complete experience. This is best exemplified in his sketches of the Stockholm Public Library in which he tries to understand the building both formally and as an experience. A site plan and plan diagram blend with interior and exterior perspectives drawn in ink and color pencil. The choice of media is no accident. For McInturff there is no set sketching media, but an appropriate media for a particular place or time, adding, "what you draw determines how you draw it".[28] Each landscape, building, town or room has its own media. There are places for watercolor, pen and ink, or pencil and, most recently, digital tablets.

Stockholm Public Library
Stockholm, Sweden, 1926
Erik Gunnar Asplund
Drawing by Mark McInturff

28 McInturff, Mark, Personal interview, 9 May 2012.

APPENDIX

Bibliography

Acton, Mary, *Learning to Look at Paintings*. London: Routledge (1997).

Akin, Ömer and Weinel, Eleanor F., *Representation and Architecture*. Silver Spring: Information Dynamics (1982).

Akin, Ömer, *Psychology of Architectural Design*. London: Pion (1986).

Alexander, Christopher, *Notes on the Synthesis of Form*. Cambridge: Harvard University Press (1964).

Allan, Woody, *Getting Even*. New York: Random House (1966).

Allen, Stan and Agrest, Diana, *Practice Architecture: Technique and Representation*. London: Routledge (2003).

Allen, Stanley, "Projections: Between Drawing and Building", *Architecture and Urbanism*, no. 4 (1992): 40-47.

Anderson, John R., *The Architecture of Cognition*. Cambridge: Harvard University Press (1983).

Anderson, Stanford, "Quasi-Autonomy in Architecture: The Search for an 'In-Between'", *Perspecta* 33 (2002): 30-37.

Anning, A., "A Conversation Around Young Children's Drawing: The Impact of the Beliefs of Significant Others at Home and at School", *International Journal of Art and Design Education* 21 (2002): 197-208.

Archer, L.B., "Design, Innovation and Agility", *Design Studies* 20, no. 6 (1999): 565-571.

Ayer, Fred C., *The Psychology of Drawing, with Special Reference to Laboratory Teaching*. Baltimore: Warwick & York (1916).

Ballesteros, Soledad, *Cognitive Approaches To Human Perception*. Hillsdale: Lawrence Earlbaum (1994).

Bandura, Albert, *Social Learning Theory*. Englewood Cliffs: Prentice Hall (1977).

Barzun, Jacques, *The House of the Intellect*. New York: Harper and Brothers (1959).

Basa, I., "The (In)Secure Position of the Design Jury Towards Computer Generated Presentations", *Design Studies* 26 (2005): 257-270.

Beittel, Kenneth R., *Mind and Context in the Art of Drawing; An Empirical and Speculative Account of the Drawing Process and the Drawing Series and of the Contexts in Which They Occur*. New York: Holt, Rinehart and Winston (1972).

Benedikt, Michael, "Coming to Our Senses: Architecture and the Non-Visual", *Harvard Design Magazine* 26 (2007): 83.

Berger, John, *Selected Essays*. New York: Pantheon Books (2001).

Berger, John, *Ways of Seeing*. London: British Broadcasting Corporation (1972).

Bijl, Aart, *Computer Discipline and Design Practice: Shaping Our Future*. Edinburgh: Edinburgh University Press (1989).

Blackwell, A.F., "Diagrams about Thoughts about Thoughts about Diagrams", in Anderson, M. (ed.), *Reasoning with Diagrammatic Representations II: AAAI 1997 Fall Symposium*. Menlo Park: AAAI Press (1997): 77-84.

Bloomer, Kent C. and Moore, Charles Willard, *Body, Memory and Architecture*. New Haven: Yale University Press (1977).

Boisvert, Raymond D., *John Dewey: Rethinking Our Time*. Albany: State University of New York Press (1998).

Boulding, Kenneth E., *The Image: Knowledge in Life and Society*. Ann Arbor: University of Michigan Press (1956).

Boyer, Ernest L. and Mitgang, Lee D., *Building Community: A New Future for Architecture Education and Practice*. Princeton: The Carnegie Foundation for the Advancement of Teaching (1996).

Bruce, Vicki and Green, Patrick R., *Visual Perception: Physiology, Psychology and Ecology*. London: L. Erlbaum (1985).

Bruner, Jerome S., *On Knowing: Essays for the Left Hand*. Cambridge: Belknap Press of Harvard University Press (1962).

Bryson, Norman and Holly, Michael Ann, *Visual Theory: Painting and Interpretation*. New York: HarperCollins (1991).

Buchanan, Richard, "Wicked Problems in Design Thinking", *Design Issues* 8, no. 2 (Spring 1992): 5-21.

Buttimer, Anne and Seamon, David, *The Human Experience of Space and Place*. New York: St. Martin's Press (1980).

Buxton, William, *Sketching User Experiences: Getting the Design Right and the Right Design*. Amsterdam: Elsevier/Morgan Kaufmann (2007).

Campbell, James, *Understanding John Dewey: Nature and Cooperative Intelligence*. Chicago: Open Court (1995).

Carini, Patricia F., *The Art of Seeing and the Visibility of the Person*. Grand Forks: University of North Dakota (1979).

Casakin, H. and Goldschmidt, G., "Expertise and the Use of Visual Analogy: Implications for Design Education," *Design Studies* 20, no. 2 (1999): 153-175.

Chase, William G. and Simon, Herbert A., "The Mind's Eye In Chess," in Chase, William G. (ed.), *Visual Information Processing*. New York: Academic Press (1972): 215-281.

Ching, Frank, *Architecture: Form, Space and Order*. New York: Van Nostrand Reinhold (1979).

Ching, Frank, *Design Drawing*. New York: Wiley (1998).

Coleman, J., "Differences between Experiential and Classroom Learning", *Experiential Learning* (1976): 49-61.

Collier, Graham, *Form, Space and Vision; Discovering Design Through Drawing*. Englewood Cliffs: Prentice-Hall (1963).

Connell, Paul H., *Report on Architectural Education and Environmental Studies in the United States and Canada*. Durban: University of Natal (1958).

Coutts, G. and Dougall, P., "Drawing in Perspective: Scottish Art and Design Teachers Discuss Drawing", *International Journal of Art and Design Education* 24, no. 2 (2005): 138-48.

Cox, M.V., *The Pictorial World of the Child*. Cambridge: Cambridge University Press (2005).

Cox, S., "Intention and Meaning in Young Children's Drawing", *International Journal of Art and Design Education* 24 (2005): 115-125.

Crossman, Mary M., "Improvisation in Action", *Organization Science* 9, no. 5 (September-October 1998): 593-599.

Crowe, Norman and Laseau, Paul, *Visual Notes for Architects and Designers*. New York: Van Nostrand Reinhold (1984).

Cuff, Dana, "Teaching and Learning Design Drawing", *Journal of Architectural Education* 33, no. 3 (Spring 1980): 5-9, 32.

Czaja, Michael, *Freehand Drawing: Language of Design*. Walnut Creek: Gambol Press (1975).

Dantzic, Cynthia Maris, *Drawing Dimensions: A Comprehensive Introduction*. Upper Saddle River: Prentice Hall (1999).

Davis, James W., "Visual Dialogue through 'Conversational' Drawings", *Leonardo* 3, 2 (April 1970): 139-147.

Delgado, Yanes Magali and Domínguez, Ernest Redondo, *Freehand Drawing for Architects and Interior Designers*. New York: W.W. Norton & Co. (2005).

Dewey, John and McDermott, John J., *The Philosophy of John Dewey*. New York: Putnam & Sons (1973).

Dewey, John, *How We Think*. Boston: D.C. Heath & Co. (1933).

Dewey, John, Hickman, Larry A. and Alexander, Thomas M., *The Essential Dewey*. Bloomington: Indiana University Press (1998).

DiLeo, Joseph, *Young Children and Their Drawings*. New York: Brunner/Masel (1970).

Do, Ellen Yi-luen and Gross, Mark D., "Thinking with Diagrams in Architectural Design", *Artificial Intelligence Review* 15 (2001): 135-149.

Do, Ellen Yi-Luen, Gross, Mark and Zimring, Craig, "Drawing and Design Intentions", in *4th International Design Thinking Research Symposium*. Cambridge: Massachusetts Institute of Technology (1999).

Downing, Frances, *Remembrance and the Design of Place*. College Station: Texas A&M University Press (2000).

Driscoll, Marcy Perkins, *Psychology of Learning for Instruction*. Boston: Allyn and Bacon (1994).

Dulley, J.S. and Permaul, J.S., "Participation in and Benefits from Experiential Education", *Educational Record* 65 (1984): 18-31.

Eastman, Charles M., *On the Analysis of Intuitive Design Processes*. Pittsburgh: Carnegie-Mellon University (1968).

Eastman, Charles M., McCracken, W. Michael and Newstetter, Wendy C., *Design Knowing and Learning Cognition in Design Education*. Amsterdam: Elsevier Science B.V. (2001).

Edwards, Betty, *Drawing on the Right Side of the Brain: A Course in Enhancing Creativity and Artistic Confidence*. Los Angeles: J.P. Tarcher (1979).

Eggleston, John, *Teaching and Learning Design and Technology: A Guide to Recent Research and Its Applications*. London: Continuum, 2000.

Eisenman, Peter, "Autonomy and the Will to the Critical", *Assemblage* 41 (2000): 91.

Eisenman, Peter, *The Formal Basis of Modern Architecture*. Baden: Lars Müller (2006).

Eliade, Mircea, *The Sacred and the Profane: the Nature of Religion*, trans. Willard R. Trask. New York: Harcourt, Brace (1959).

Emmer, Michele, *The Visual Mind: Art and Mathematics*. Cambridge: MIT Press (1993).

Fish, J. and Scrivener, S.A.R., "Amplifying the Mind's Eye: Sketching and Visual Cognition", *Leonardo* 23, no. 1, (1990): 117-126.

Flannery, K.A. and Watson, M.W., "Perceived Competence in Drawing During Middle Childhood Years", *Visual Arts Research* 17(1991): 66-71.

Ford, Edward, "The Inconvenient Friend: On Inaccuracy, Exactitude, Drawing and Photography", *Harvard Design Magazine* (Fall 1998): 12-21.

Forster, Brenda and Prinz, Andrew K., "Travel-Study as Learning in Sociology," *Teaching Sociology* 16, no. 1 (1988): 67-73.

Fraser, Iain and Henmi, Rod, *Envisioning Architecture: An Analysis of Drawing*. New York: Van Nostrand Reinhold (1994).

Freeman, Norman H. and Cox, M.V., *Visual Order: The Nature and Development of Pictorial Representation*. Cambridge: Cambridge University Press (1985).

Garcia, Mark, *The Diagrams of Architecture*. Chichester: Wiley-Blackwell (2010).

Gardner, Howard, *Artful Scribbles: The Significance of Children's Drawings*. New York: Basic Books (1980).

Gardner, Howard, *Five Minds for the Future*. Boston: Harvard Business School Press (2006).

Gardner, Howard, *Frames of Mind: The Theory of Multiple Intelligences*. New York: Basic Books (1983).

Gardner, Howard, *The Disciplined Mind: What All Students Should Understand*. New York: Simon & Schuster (1999).

Garrett, Lillian, *Visual Design: A Problem-Solving Approach*. New York: Reinhold Pub. Corp. (1967).

Gibran, Khalil, *The Prophet*. New York: Alfred A. Knopf (1966): 60.

Glassick, Charles E., Huber, Mary Taylor, Maeroff, Gene I. and Boyer, Ernest L., *Scholarship Assessed: Evaluation of the Professoriate*. San Francisco: Jossey-Bass (1997).

Goel, Vinod, "Ill-Structured Representations for Ill-Structured Problems", *Proceedings of the Fourteenth Annual Conference of the Cognitive Science Society*. Hillsdale: Lawrence Erlbaum Associates (1992): 844-849.

Goel, Vinod, *Sketches of Thought*. Cambridge: MIT Press (1995).

Goldschmidt, Gabriela, "On Visual Design Thinking: The Vis Kids of Architecture", *Design Studies* 15 (1994): 158-174.

Goldschmidt, Gabriela, "Serial Sketching: Visual Problem Solving in Designing", *Cybernetics and Systems: An International Journal* 23 (1992): 191-219.

Goldschmidt, Gabriela, "The Dialectics of Sketching", *Creativity Research Journal* 4, no. 2 (1991): 123-143.

Goldstein, Nathan, *The Art of Responsive Drawing*. Englewood Cliffs: Prentice-Hall (1973).

Golledge, Reginald G., Gale, Nathan, Pellegrino, James W. and Doherty, Sally, "Spatial Knowledge Acquisition by Children: Route Learning and Relational Distances," *Annals of the Association of American Geographers* 82, no. 2 (1992): 223-244.

Golledge, Reginald G., Dougherty, Valerie and Bell, Scott, "Acquiring Spatial Knowledge: Survey Versus Route-Based Knowledge In Unfamiliar Environments", *Annals of the Association of American Geographers* 85, no. 1 (1995): 134-158.

Goodman, Nelson, *Languages of Thought: An Approach To A Theory of Symbols*. Indianapolis: Hackett Publishing Company, Inc. (1968, 1976)..

Gorton, William A., *Karl Popper and the Social Sciences*. Albany: State University of New York Press (2006).

Graf, Douglas, "Diagrams", *Perspecta* 22 (1986): 42-71.

Graves, Michael, "The Necessity of Drawing: Tangible Speculation", *Architectural Design* 47 (1977): 384-394.

Gray, Susan (ed.), *Architects on Architects*. New York: McGraw-Hill (2002).

Groat, Linda N. and Wang, David, *Architectural Research Methods*. New York: Wiley (2002).

Gussow, Sue Ferguson, *Architects Draw*. New York: Princeton Architectural Press (2008).

Hamilton, Edith and Cairns, Huntington (eds.), *The Collected Dialogues of Plato*. Princeton: Princeton University Press (1961).

Hammer, Emanuel F., *Advances in Projective Drawing Interpretation*. Springfield: C. C. Thomas (1997).

Hammock, Claude Stuart, *The Manual Arts for Elementary Schools: Drawing, Design, Construction*. Boston: D. C. Heath & Co. (1909).

Hannah, Gail Greet, *Elements of Design: Rowena Reed Kostellow and the Structure of Visual Relationships*. New York: Princeton Architectural Press (2002).

Harris, Dale B., *Children's Drawings as Measures of Intellectual Maturity: A Revision and Extension of the Good Enough Draw-a-man Test*. New York: Harcourt, Brace and World (1963).

Hays, K. Michael, "Critical Architecture: Between Culture and Form", *Perspecta* 21 (1984): 15-29.

Heidegger, Martin, *Poetry, Language, Thought*, trans. Albert Hofstadter. New York: Harper & Row (1971).

Heller, Morton A., *Touch, Representation and Blindness*. Oxford: Oxford University Press (2000).

Hennessey, J. and Verstijnen, I., "Sketching and Creative Discovery", *Design Studies* 19 (1998): 519-546.

Hertzberger, Herman, *Lessons for Students in Architecture*. Rotterdam: 010 Publishers (1991).

Hinds, George A., "Sketching, Memory and Architecture", *Threshold: Journal of The School Of Architecture*, University of Illinois at Chicago 3 (Autumn 1985): 52-59.

Hubbard, William, "A System of Formal Analysis for Architectural Composition", *Thresholds* 3 (1976): 4-193.

Isaac, Alan Reginald George, *Approach to Architectural Design*. Toronto: University of Toronto Press (1971).

Jeannerod, Marc, *The Cognitive Neuroscience of Action*. Oxford: Blackwell (1997).

Joedicke, Jürgen, *Raum und Form in der Architektur*. Stuttgart: Karl Krämer (1985).

Johnson, Paul-Alan, *The Theory of Architecture: Concepts, Themes & Practices*. New York: Van Nostrand Reinhold (1994).

John-Steiner, Vera, *Notebooks of the Mind: Explorations of Thinking*. New York: Oxford University Press (1997).

Jolley, Richard P., *Children and Pictures: Drawing and Understanding*. Chichester: Wiley-Blackwell (2010).

Kavakli, M. and Scrivener, S., "Structure in Idea Sketching Behavior", *Design Studies* 19 (1998): 485-517.

Kellogg, Rhoda, *Analyzing Children's Art*. Palo Alto: National Press Books (1969).

Kipnis, Jeffrey, "Drawing A Conclusion", *Perspecta* 22 (1986): 94-99.

Kolb, David A., *Experiential Learning: Experience as the Source of Learning and Development*. Englewood Cliffs: Prentice-Hall (1984).

Kuehne, Hugo Franz, *Academic Training in Architecture*. Austin: The University of Texas (1911).

Laneyrie-Dagen, Nadeije, *How to Read Paintings*. Edinburgh: Chambers (2004).

Lange-Küttner, Christiane and Thomas, Glyn V. (ed.), *Drawing and Looking: Theoretical Approaches To Pictorial Representation In Children*. New York: Harvester Wheatsheaf (1995).

Lange-Küttner, Christiane and Vinter, Annie, *Drawing and the Non-Verbal Mind: A Life-Span Perspective*. Cambridge: Cambridge University Press (2008).

Laning, Edward, *The Act of Drawing*. New York: McGraw-Hill (1971).

Lao Tzu, *Tao te Ching*, trans. D. C. Lau. Baltimore: Penguin Books (1963).

Larkin, Jill H. and Simon, Herbert A., "Why a Diagram Is (Sometimes) Worth Ten Thousand Words", *Cognitive Science* 11, no. 1 (1987): 65-99.

Laseau, Paul, *Architectural Drawing: Options for Design*. New York: Design Press (1991).

Laseau, Paul, *Graphic Thinking for Architects and Designers*. New York: Van Nostrand Reinhold (1980).

Lawson, Bryan, *How Designers Think*. London: Butterworth Architecture (²1990).

Lawson, Bryan, *What Designers Know*. Boston: Elsevier/Architectural Press (2004).

Le Corbusier, *Creation is a Patient Search*, trans. James Palmes. New York: Praeger (1960).

Le Corbusier, *Towards an Architecture*, trans. John Goodman. Los Angeles: Getty Research Institute (2007).

Lesgold, Alan M., *Cognitive Psychology and Instruction*. New York: Plenum Press (1978).

Leupen, Bernard, Grafe, Christoph, Körnig, Nicola and Lampe, Marc, *Design and Analysis*. New York: Van Nostrand Reinhold (1997).

Lévi-Strauss, Claude, *The Savage Mind*. New York: Oxford University Press (1972).

Lloyd, P., Lawson, B. and Scott, P., "Can Concurrent Verbalization Reveal Design Cognition?", *Design Studies* 16, no. 2 (April 1995): 237-259.

Logan, R., "Bridging the Traditional and Non-Traditional: A Model for Higher Education", *Liberal Education* 69 (1983): 233-243.

Logie, Robert H., *Visuo-Spatial Working Memory*. Hillsdale: L. Erlbaum Associates (1995).

Loomis, Andrew, *Successful Drawing*. New York: Viking Press (1951).

Lynch, Kevin, *The Image of the City*. Cambridge: MIT Press (1964).

Mackinder, Margaret and Marvin, Heather, *Design Decision Making in Architectural Practice*. York: University of York Institute of Advanced Architectural Studies (1982).

Malpas, Jeff, *Place and Experience: A Philosophical Topography*. Cambridge: Cambridge University Press (1999).

Marble, S. and Smiley, D., *Architecture and Body*. New York: Rizzoli (1988).

Maslow, Abraham, *The Psychology of Science: A Reconnaissance*. New York: Harper & Row (1966).

Matthews, Eric, *Merleau-Ponty: A Guide for the Perplexed*. London: Continuum International Pub. Group (2006).

Mauduit, Caroline, *An Architect in Italy*. New York: C. N. Potter (1988).

McClure, Harlan Ewart, *The Study of Architectural Design*. Minneapolis: Burgess (1949).

McGown, A. and Green, G., "Visible Ideas: Information Patterns of Conceptual Sketch Activity", *Design Studies* 19 (1998): 431-453.

McInturff, Mark, "Recent Works." Lecture at The Catholic University of America, Washington, DC, September 10, 2009.

Merleau-Ponty, Maurice and Fisher, Alden L., *The Essential Writings of Merleau-Ponty*. New York: Harcourt, Brace & World (1969).

Merleau-Ponty, Maurice and Lefort, Claude, *The Visible and the Invisible; followed by Working Notes*. Evanston: Northwestern University Press (1968).

Merleau-Ponty, Maurice, *Phenomenology of Perception*, trans. Colin Smith. London, New York: Routledge (1994).

Midland, Michael B., "Tools for Knowledge Analysis, Synthesis, and Sharing", *Journal of Science Education and Technology* 16, no. 2 (April 2007): 119-153.

Mitchell, C. Thomas, *Redefining Designing: From Form to Experience*. New York: Van Nostrand Reinhold (1993).

Moneo, Rafael, "On Typology", *Oppositions* 13 (Summer 1978): 22-45.

Moon, Jennifer, *Reflection and Learning in Professional Development*. London: Kogan Press (1999).

Moore, Charles, Allen, Gerald and Lyndon, Donlyn, *The Place of Houses*. New York: Holt, Rinehart and Winston (1974).

Mugerauer, Robert, *Interpreting Environments: Tradition, Deconstruction, Hermeneutics*. Austin: University of Texas Press (1995).

Nesbitt, Kate (ed.), *Theorizing A New Agenda for Architecture*. New York: Princeton Architectural Press (1996).

Nevins, Deborah and Stern, Robert A. M., *The Architect's Eye: American Architectural Drawings From 1799-1978*. New York: Pantheon Books (1979).

Niem Tu Huynh, Hall, G. Brent, Doherty, Sean and Smith, Wayne W., "Interpreting Urban Space Through Cognitive Map Sketching and Sequence Analysis", *Canadian Geographer* 52 (Summer 2008): 222.

Norberg-Schulz, Christian, *Genius Loci: Towards a Phenomenology of Architecture*. New York: Rizzoli (1980).

Norberg-Schulz, Christian, *The Concept of Dwelling: On the Way to Figurative Architecture*. Milan: Electa (1985).

Oechslin, Werner, "From Piranesi to Libeskind: Explaining by Drawing", *Daidalos* no.1 (September 1981): 15-35.

Oechslin, Werner, "Geometry and Line: The Vitruvian 'Science' of Architectural Drawing", *Daidalos* no.1 (September 1981): 20-35.

Oliver, Robert S., *The Complete Sketch*. New York: Van Nostrand Reinhold (1989).

Osman, Michael, Ruedig, Adam, Seidel, Matthew and Tilney, Lisa, "Editors' Statement", *Perspecta* 33 (2002): 7.

Pallasmaa, Juhani, "An Architecture of the Seven Senses", *Architecture and Urbanism* (July 1994): 27-37.

Pallasmaa, Juhani, "Hapticity and Time", *Architectural Review*, no. 1239 (May 2000): 78-84.

Pallasmaa, Juhani, "The Geometry of Feeling: A Look at the Phenomenology of Architecture", *Skala: Nordic Journal of Architecture and Art* 4 (June 1986): 22-25.

Pallasmaa, Juhani, *The Eyes of the Skin: Architecture and the Senses*. Chichester: Wiley-Academy (2005).

Panofsky, Erwin, *Meaning in the Visual Arts: Papers In and On Art History*. Garden City: Doubleday (1955).

Parkin, Alan J., *Memory: Phenomena, Experiment and Theory*. Oxford: Blackwell (1993).

Paterson, Robert, *Abstract Concepts of Drawing*. New York: Van Nostrand Reinhold (1983).

Patton, Michael Quinn, *Qualitative Evaluation and Research Methods*. Newbury Park: Sage Publications (1990).

Pearce, Martin and Toy, Maggie, *Educating Architects*. London: Academy Editions (1995).

Pérez-Gómez, Alberto, "Architecture as Drawing", *Journal of Architectural Education* 36, no. 2 (Winter 1982): 2-7.

Pérez-Gómez, Alberto, *Architecture and the Crisis of Modern Science*. Cambridge: MIT Press (1983).

Peterson, John M. and Lansky, Leonard M., "Success in Architecture: Handedness and/or Visual Thinking?", *Perceptual and Motor Skills* 50 (1980): 1139-1143.

Peterson, Steve, "Urban Design Tactics", *Architectural Design* 49, 3-4 (1979): 76-81.

Piaget, Jean and Inhelder, Bärbel, *The Child's Conception of Space*. London: Routledge & K. Paul (1956).

Piaget, Jean and Inhelder, Bärbel, *The Psychology of the Child*. New York: Basic Books (1969).

Piotrowski, Andrzej and Robinson, Julia W., *The Discipline of Architecture*. Minneapolis: University of Minnesota Press (2000).

Podro, Michael, *The Critical Historians of Art*. New Haven: Yale University Press (1982).

Polanyi, Michael, *The Tacit Dimension*. Garden City: Doubleday (1966).

Preziosi, Donald, *The Semiotics of the Built Environment: An Introduction to Architectonic Analysis*. Bloomington: Indiana University Press (1979).

Quayle, Moura, *Ideabook for Teaching Design*. Berkeley: Department of Landscape Architecture, University of California, Berkeley (1983).

Rasmussen, Steen Eiler, *Experiencing Architecture*. Cambridge: MIT Press (1962).

Rawson, Philip S., *Seeing Through Drawing*. London: British Broadcasting Corporation (1979).

Reed, Edward, *The Necessity of Experience*. New Haven: Yale University Press (1996).

Reichlin, Bruno, "Reflections: Interrelations Beween Concept, Representation and Built Architecture", *Daidalos* no. 1 (September 1981): 60-73.

Righini, Paul, *Thinking Architecturally: An Introduction to the Creation of Form and Place*. Cape Town: University of Cape Town Press (2000).

Rose, Sarah E., Jolley, Richard and Burkitt, Esther, "A Review of Children's, Teachers' and Parents' Influences on Children's Drawing Experience", *International Journal of Art & Design Education* 25, no. 3 (2006): 341-349.

Rosensteil, A. K. and Gardner, Howard, "The Effect of Critical Comparison upon Children's Drawings", *Studies in Art Education* 19, no. 1 (1977): 36-44.

Roth, Susan King, "An Investigation in the Cognitive Factors Involved in the Drawing Process", *Journal of Visual Literacy* 11, no. 2 (1992): 57-76.

Rowe, Peter, *Design Thinking*. Cambridge: MIT Press, 1987.

Saarinen, Eliel (quoted by Eero Saarinen), "The Maturing Modern", *Time Magazine* 68 (July 2, 1956): 1, 54.

Sachse, Pierre, Hacker, Winfried and Leinert, Sven, "External Thought—Does Sketching Assist Problem Analysis?", *Applied Cognitive Psychology* 18 (2004): 415-425.

Sanoff, Henry, *Visual Research Methods in Design*. New York: Van Nostrand Reinhold (1991).

Schön, Donald A., *Educating the Reflective Practitioner: Toward a New Design for Teaching and Learning in the Professions*. San Francisco: Jossey-Bass (1987).

Schön, Donald A., *The Reflective Practitioner: How Professionals Think in Action*. New York: Basic Books (1983).

Schumacher, Thomas L., *About Face: On the Architecture of Façades, Classic and Modern*. Unpublished manuscript, University of Maryland, College Park (2009).

Scott Brown, Denise, "On Formal Analysis as Design Research", *Journal of Architectural Education* 32 (1979): 8-11.

Seamon, David and Mugerauer, Robert, *Dwelling, Place and Environment: Towards a Phenomenology of Person and World*. Dordrecht: M. Nijhoff (1985).

Seamon, David, *Dwelling, Seeing and Designing: Toward a Phenomenological Ecology*. Albany: State University of New York Press (1993).

Simpson, Ian, *Drawing: Seeing and Observation*. New York: Van Nostrand Reinhold (1973).

Smith, Kendra Schank, "Architectural Sketches and The Power Of Caricature", *Journal of Architectural Education* 44, no. 1 (1990): 49-58.

Smith, Kendra Schank, *Architects' Sketches: Dialogue and Design*. Amsterdam: Architectural Press/Elsevier (2008).

Smithies, K.W. and Tompkins, Steve, *Principles of Design in Architecture*. New York: Van Nostrand Reinhold (1981).

Snodgrass, Adrian and Coyne, Richard D., *Interpretation in Architecture: Design as a Way of Thinking*. London: Routledge (2006).

Spiegelberg, Herbert and Schuhmann, Karl, *The Phenomenological Movement: A Historical Introduction*. The Hague: M. Nijhoff (1982).

Spiller, Jürg (ed.), *Paul Klee Notebooks: The Thinking Eye*, trans. Ralph Manheim. New York: Wittenborn (1961).

Stamps, Arthur Earl, *Psychology and the Aesthetics of the Built Environment*. Boston: Kluwer Academic (2000).

Steenbergen, Clemens, et al., (eds.), *Architectural Design and Composition*. Bussum: THOTH Publishers (2002).

Steinhart, Peter, *The Undressed Art: Why We Draw*. New York: Alfred A. Knopf (2004).

Suwa, M. and Tversky, B., "What Do Architects and Students Perceive in Their Design Sketches?", *Design Studies* 18, no. 4 (1997): 385-403.

Suwa, M. and Tversky, B., "What Architects See In Their Sketches: A Protocol Analysis", Paper presented at Artificial Intelligence in Design 1996, Stanford University, June 24-27, 1996.

Thiel, P., "A Sequence Experience Notation for Architectural and Urban Space", *Town Planning Review* 32 (April 1961): 33-52.

Thiis-Evensen, Thomas, *Archetypes in Architecture*. Oslo: Norwegian University Press (1987).

Thomas, Glyn V. and Lange-Küttner, Christiane (eds.), *Drawing and Looking*. New York: Harvester Wheatsheaf (1995).

Thompson, C., "Drawing Together: Peer Influence in Preschool-Kindergarten Art Classes", *Visual Arts Research* 25 (1999): 61-68.

Treib, Marc (ed.), *Drawing/Thinking: Confronting an Electronic Age*. Oxford: Routledge (2008).

Turner, Judith, *Judith Turner Photographs Five Architects*. London: Academy Editions (1980).

Turner, Mark, *The Artful Mind: Cognitive Science and the Riddle of Human Creativity*. Oxford: Oxford University Press (2006).

Tversky, B. and Suwa, M., "What do Architects and Students Perceive in Their Design Sketches," *Design Studies* 18 (1997): 385-403.

Tversky, B., "What do sketches say about thinking?" in Stahovic, T., Landay, J. and Davis, R. (eds.), *Proceedings of AAAI Spring Symposium on Sketch Understanding*. Menlo Park: AAAI Press (2002).

Tversky, Barbara, Suwa, Masaki, Agrawala, Maneesh, Heiser, Julie, Stolte, Chris, Hanrahan, Pat, Doantam Phan, Jeff and Klingner, Marie, "Sketches for Design and Design of Sketches", in Lindemann, Udo (ed.), *Human Behavior in Design: Individuals, Teams, Tools*. Berlin: Springer (2003).

Unwin, Simon, *Analysing Architecture*. London/New York: Routledge (²2003).

Usher, R., "Beyond the Anecdotal: Adult Learning and the Use of Experience", *Studies in the Education of Adults* 17 (1985): 59-74.

Uttal, William R., *On Seeing Forms*. Hillsdale: L. Erlbaum Associates (1988).

Van Sommers, Peter, *Drawing and Cognition: Descriptive and Experimental Studies of Graphic Production Processes*. Cambridge: Cambridge University Press (1984).

Venturi, Robert, *Complexity and Contradiction in Architecture*. New York: Museum of Modern Art (1966).

Verstijnen, I. and Tversky, B., "Sketching and Creative Discovery", *Design Studies* 19 (1998): 519-546.

Vesely, Dalibor, *Architecture in the Age of Divided Representation: The Question of Creativity in the Shadow of Production*. Cambridge: MIT Press (2004).

Vidler, Anthony, "The Ledoux Effect: Emil Kaufmann and the Claims of Kantian Autonomy", *Perspecta* 33 (2002): 16-29.

Vidler, Anthony, *The Architectural Uncanny: Essays in the Modern Unhomely*. Cambridge: MIT Press (1992).

Vidler, Anthony, *Histories of the Immediate Present: Inventing Architectural Modernism*. Cambridge: MIT Press (2008).

Warren, Karen, Sakofs, Mitchell S. and Hunt, Jasper S., *The Theory of Experiential Education*. Dubuque: Kendall/Hunt (1995).

Wathen-Dunn, Weiant, *Models for the Perception of Speech and Visual Form*. Proceedings of a Symposium. Cambridge: MIT Press (1967).

Westbrook, Robert B., *John Dewey and American Democracy*. Ithaca: Cornell University Press (1991).

White, Morton Gabriel, *The Origin of Dewey's Instrumentalism*. New York: Columbia University Press (1943).

Whiteman, John, "Criticism, Representation and Experience In Contemporary Architecture: Architecture and Drawing in an Age Of Criticism", *Harvard Architecture Review* 6 (1987): 136-147.

Willats, John, *Making Sense of Children's Drawings*. Mahwah: L. Erlbaum Associates (2005).

Williams, Heather C., *Drawing as a Sacred Activity: Simple Steps to Explore Your Feelings and Heal Your Consciousness*. Novato: New World Library (2002).

Wilson, Frank R., *The Hand: How Its Use Shapes the Brain, Language and Human Culture*. New York: Pantheon Books (1998).

Wright, Frank Lloyd, "In the Cause of Architecture: The Logic of the Plan", *Architectural Record* 63 (January 1928): 49-57.

Zucker, Paul, *Town and Square: From the Agora to the Village Green*. New York: Columbia University Press (1959).

Zumthor, Peter, *Thinking Architecture*, trans. Maureen Oberli-Turner (essays 1988-1996) and Catherine Schelbert (essays 1998-2004), Basel: Birkhäuser (²2006).

Zusne, Leonard, *Visual Perception of Form*. New York: Academic Press (1970).

Photo Credits

On the Author

Eric J. Jenkins is an architect and an Associate Professor at The Catholic University of America's School of Architecture and Planning in Washington, DC, where he teaches design, analytical sketching and research methodologies. He directs the school's Master of Architecture Urban Practice Studio and served as the Associate Dean of Undergraduate Studies.

Eric taught at Virginia Tech's Washington-Alexandria Architecture Consortium, Florida A&M University, Çukurova University in Adana, Turkey, and the University of Maryland. He has lectured for the Smithsonian Associates Program and conducted drawing workshops at the National Building Museum. He has organized architectural tours of Washington, DC, for Corcoran Gallery of Art and the District of Columbia Preservation League as well as university travel programs in North America, Europe, the Middle East and Asia.

He is the recipient of several teaching and design awards. In 1996, the University of Maryland honored him with a Certificate of Teaching Excellence and in 2006 The Catholic University of America honored him with the James E. Dornan Memorial Undergraduate Educator of the Year award.

Eric is the author of *To Scale: One Hundred Urban Plans* (Routledge, 2008) and has presented and published his research in several journals including *Centropa* and MIT's *Thresholds*.

A former board member of the District of Columbia chapter of the American Institute of Architects, his work has earned several design awards, including a Capitol Hill loft, which was published in *Remodeling* and seen on HGTV's "Building Character", and an Inform design award in 2002. He developed the schematic design for a prototypical prefabricated house with the firm Studio 27 Architecture, which earned a 2007 Design Excellence Award from the Virginia Society of the AIA.

He earned a Bachelor of Science in Architecture and a Master of Architecture from the University of Maryland and a Master of Design Studies from Harvard University's Graduate School of Design.

Acknowledgements

This book grew from the support, contributions and encouragement of colleagues, students, friends, family and even strangers. My colleagues, mentors and friends have been extremely supportive and patient, especially Jennifer and Martin Butler, Christine Cole, Gregory K. Hunt, Mark Jarzombek, Roger K. Lewis, Mark McInturff, Andreas Müller, Ismet Odabasi, Thomas L. Schumacher and R. Lindley Vann. I am also grateful for the support of The Catholic University of America and especially James F. Brennan, Randall Ott and Ann Cederna. My sincere appreciation to research assistants Lindsey Dickes, Ryan Horton, John Lang and Matthew Vargas. Thanks to the many students, past and present, who continue to inspire me. Special thanks to William Bechhoefer for providing the initial opportunity and framework for sketching, looking and thinking. Finally, eternal gratitude to my wife Adrienne T. Jenkins for her patience and encouragement.

Index of Buildings and Building Types

Subject Index

Index of Locations

Index of Persons

Index of Media